OPERATIONAL RESEARCH:
techniques and examples

OPERATIONAL RESEARCH:
techniques and examples

Edited by
G. H. Mitchell
Operational Research Executive
National Coal Board

The English Universities Press Ltd

ISBN 0 340 12441 5 Boards

First Printed 1972

The English Universities Press Ltd
St Paul's House Warwick Lane London EC4P 4AH

Set in 10/11 pt. Monotype Times New Roman printed by letterpress, and bound in Great Britain at The Pitman Press, Bath

Preface

This book has its origins almost fifteen years ago when the Operational Research Executive (then called the Field Investigation Group) in the National Coal Board set up study groups. Each study group was assigned the task of keeping itself and the Executive up-to-date in the development of some O.R. technique or of technical advance in some O.R. problem area. Each study group kept the rest of the Executive informed by writing up the current knowledge and keeping the write-up under continuous review, updating it as seemed desirable. As new techniques or problem areas developed new study groups were set up.

The write-ups are used in the Executive's own training programme (now mounted jointly with Brunel University as a Master's Course), and, from time to time, are drawn together to form a textbook. This book is the current drawing together of some of the write-ups and follows almost ten years after the first publication of a similar book (1).

The material available to me in producing a book for publication was far too much to fit into the present book. I therefore decided to restrict myself to those topics which have come to be particularly associated with O.R. and to exclude anything on those topics which, while they form an essential part of the O.R. man's technical armoury, are common to many problem-solving disciplines. Thus there is no treatment of computing, statistics, economics or the behavioural sciences, although such topics figure large in the rounded training of an O.R. man. Nor is there any significant reference to the practicalities of carrying out O.R.: the identification of problems, the choices concerned with the approach to the problem, and the all important task of causing change, receive scant attention. These are also topics which one would hope to see figuring large in any training for O.R.

Even limiting myself in this way imposed a number of problems about what to include and with what emphasis. Broadly I have tried to mention most things which are important either because they are techniques in common use or because they provide insight into the problem in hand. Where I have still been in doubt I have given preference to computable methods or to methods where no simple exposition is readily available.

I have tried to stick at a mathematical level which should, in some cases with a little persistence, be within the reach of anyone with "A" level mathematics, certainly if he has pursued further study in a subject which makes use of mathematics. Where more advanced mathematics is used I have tried to be discursive enough to keep the "A" level man with it. In some cases, some elementary knowledge of probability theory and just occasionally of statistical methods is assumed. This scarcely goes beyond the level of the many excellent introductory books available (2). Some knowledge of computing is assumed in the chapter on simulation but scarcely elsewhere. No one with a minimal experience of a high-level computer language should find any difficulty. Others may find some preliminary reading (3) desirable for an understanding of the simulation chapter.

It would be impossible for me to acknowledge everyone who has contributed to this book. Nevertheless I have drawn heavily on the material of a few people and, in the hope that those not mentioned will forgive me, I should like to mention particularly M. G. Simpson (Chapter 3), A. S. Harding (Chapter 4), T. Dobson (Chapter 5), F. J. Toft (Chapter 6), H. Boothroyd (Chapters 6 and 8), J. G. Fergusson (Chapter 9) and L. M. Jones and C. M. Price (Chapter 10). I should perhaps add, however, that I have sometimes been a ruthless editor, in parts of some chapters to the point of total rewriting, so I take full responsibility for any errors or omissions.

It would be remiss of me not to mention also B. H. P. Rivett, B. T. Houlden and R. C. Tomlinson, successive heads of the O.R. Executive, each of whom has encouraged the pursuit of technical knowledge in the Executive. Finally I must thank Miss B. P. Noad who, as well as having done much skilful typing, has also helped assemble the diverse material on which I have drawn.

References

1. Houlden, B. T. (Ed.) *Some Techniques of Operational Research*. The English Universities Press 1962.
2. Mood, A. M. and Graybill, F. A. *Introduction to Theory of Statistics*. McGraw-Hill 1963.
3. Hollingdale, S. H. and Tootill, G. C. *Electronic Computers*. Penguin Books 1965.

Contents

1 Introduction

Operational research is concerned with the application of the scientific method to management problems. Among other things the scientific method implies building a model of some sort of the system under study. Some writers (1) take as their standpoint that operational research is model building or, to be more pertinent, useful model building. The model may be of any kind and of any complexity. It will be useful if its behaviour analogues the real system sufficiently well to enable the behaviour of the real system to be predicted and understood to the point that the real system can be changed in some way that is desirable. It will be even more useful if determining its behaviour (or putting it another way, experimenting on it) is much cheaper than experimenting on the real system.

A particularly powerful type of model is a mathematical model, that is one which relates the performance of the system to its measurable characteristics through mathematical formulae. In principle such a model can be manipulated so as to get the best performance by choosing those values of the measurable characteristics which are at our disposal which maximize the relevant measure of performance. In practice it is not always possible to model a system with such precision as to make this step altogether useful. What can usually be done however is to build a model which sheds some light on the way to improve the system's performance or at least gives some insight into the sort of policy which should be adopted to ensure improvement.

There are a great many mathematical methods that might be used in building these models and analysing their behaviour. We shall be concerned in this book with a few which have become particularly associated with operational research. Firstly there are those methods which are useful because they are capable of modelling so many real situations. Into this category come linear and dynamic programming, network theory and simulation which are all useful beyond dispute in the everyday sense of enabling certain things to be done more efficiently by their application. Decision theory and the theory of games also come into this category. Although it can be argued that their practical usefulness is comparatively slight there is little doubt that application of either can be useful in ordering one's thoughts about very general classes of problems.

Secondly there are those methods which have grown up about specific problem areas, so to speak: queuing theory, stock control theory and replacement and renewal theory fall into this category. These methods are purpose built to tackle narrowly defined classes of problems and the problems themselves are more general than the methods. Other problem areas have given rise to such special methods and could easily have led to more chapters, but the ones covered are among the commoner ones and are certainly among the ones for which methods have been most highly developed.

Methods of the first type, because of their generality, can be developed in a highly abstract way. On the whole the reader will find that they are given a rather more abstract treatment in this book than the second type of method. Generally, however, the treatment here is intended to be practical to the extent that only useful methods are given much space and that emphasis is laid on the efficient use of methods rather than on, for example, mathematical rigour or over careful attention to a strictly logical development.

The ordering of chapters is to some extent arbitrary and the chapters are very largely independent of one another so that they can be read separately. However some attention has been given to avoiding forward referencing. Thus the chapter on decision theory and the theory of games (which it could be argued is so general that it should come first) is placed so that use can be made of linear programming which is introduced in an earlier chapter. Whether the student will want to read the book from start to finish seems doubtful. He will probably be best advised to intersperse his reading from three or four chapters at a time.

Each chapter is followed by a bibliography which includes suggestions for further reading as well as papers and books directly referred to in the chapter. Most of the references given should be readily obtainable through a good library. Exercises also follow each chapter. There are three types. Firstly there are those which are exercises directly on the material of the chapter and secondly those which extend or amplify the material of the chapter: answers to these first two types are given. Thirdly there are exercises which pose questions designed to illuminate the practicalities of the techniques described in the chapter. Answers for these are given where appropriate but the questions are often ones which have no absolute answer; the reader, wherever possible helped by discussions with other interested students, must provide his own answers.

Before leaving this introductory chapter it would be well to repeat that this book is mainly about the mathematical methods of model building and analysis. Carrying out successful operational research includes being good at model building and analysis of some sort, but the converse is not true. Some of the many concomitants to successful operational research are discussed in reference (2) which gives many illustrative cases.

References

1. Churchman, C. W., Ackoff, R. L. and Arnoff, E. L. *Introduction to Operations Research.* John Wiley & Sons Inc. 1957.
2. Tomlinson, R. C. (Ed.) *O.R. Comes of Age: A review of the work of the O.R. Branch of the National Coal Board.* 1948–1969. Tavistock Publications Limited 1971.

2 Linear programming and its extensions

Introduction

Many business problems are concerned with trying to find the best allocation of resources in circumstances where the resources have limited availability and where some combinations of resource allocation are impossible. For example we might be seeking to allocate markets and capital to the several factories which make up our firm. There are limits to the size of the markets for each of the six products we make; each factory has different capacities for each of the three stages which are common to the manufacture of the six products; each product absorbs different amounts of capacity at each factory; the selling prices for each product are different and, because we pay the cost of transport to the customers, in effect vary from factory to factory; and costs at the factories can be changed by capital expenditure.

The methods of mathematical programming have been designed to help solve such problems. A mathematical model is developed in terms of variables (let us call them x_1, x_2, x_3, . . .) which represent the levels of the various activities going on in the situation. In the example outlined above x_1 might represent the quantity of product 1 made at factory 1 which is sent to market 1 in the first quarter of the time period for which we are seeking to plan the allocation of resources. The profit, or more generally the criterion by which we shall compare alternative allocations, is expressed as a function of x_1, x_2, x_3, ... We denote this function by

$$Z = Z(x_1, x_2, x_3, \ldots)$$

The various restrictions, or constraints as they are often called, are then formulated. In our example one such constraint is that the amounts of the products produced at factory 1 must, in combination, be such that the capacity for carrying out the first stage of manufacture at factory 1 is not exceeded. The typical constraint will take the form

$$f(x_1, x_2, x_3, \ldots) \leqslant A$$

or perhaps

$$g(x_1, x_2, x_3, \ldots) = B$$

or perhaps

$$h(x_1, x_2, x_3, \ldots) \geqslant C$$

The mathematical programming problem is then: find the values of x_1, x_2, x_3, . . . which maximize $Z(x_1, x_2, x_3, \ldots)$ and which also satisfy all the constraints. (It may be that no combination of x_1, x_2, x_3, . . . satisfies the constraints, so in that respect one should perhaps state the problem as: check that there are values of $x_1, x_2, x_3, \ldots$ which satisfy the constraints and, if so, choose those which maximize Z. This is more than an academic point: in very complex allocation problems it might be extremely valuable simply to find an allocation that works.) We note that the x's as defined in our example problem are all non-negative. They may take the value zero or any positive value but we cannot make -10 units of product 1 at factory 1 to send to market 1 in quarter 1. Thus among the constraints are $x_1 \geqslant 0$, $x_2 \geqslant 0$, $x_3 \geqslant 0$ and so on.

Classical mathematical methods are not a great deal of help in solving maximization problems of this type. It is true that the inequality constraints in the problem can always be converted into equality constraints by introducing new variables (for example

$$f(x_1, x_2, x_3, \ldots) \leqslant A$$

can be written as

$$f(x_1, x_2, x_3, \ldots) + y = A$$

where y is a new non-negative variable which happens not to enter into the expression for Z); and it is therefore tempting to think that the method of Lagrange multipliers might be used to solve the problem. But this founders on the non-negativity constraints, and although some insight into the problem can be obtained by using Lagrange multipliers no computationally useful results can be found.

An important class of mathematical problems is those in which Z, the objective function as it is called, and all the constraints are linear functions of the x's and the x's may take only non-negative values. The problem of maximizing Z in such circumstances is called linear programming. Thus the problem:

$$\text{maximize } Z = 1 \cdot 07 x_1 + 1 \cdot 09 x_2$$

for $x_1 \geqslant 0$, $x_2 \geqslant 0$ subject to $x_1 \leqslant 250$, $x_1 + x_2 \leqslant 400$, $0 \cdot 4 x_1 + 0 \cdot 7 x_2 \leqslant 200$ is an example of a linear programming problem (and one which we shall solve later). Z and all the constraints are linear in x_1 and x_2, that is they do not involve any terms other than constant multiples of each variable added or subtracted one from another.

A good many allocation problems can be put into the linear programming form and we shall give a number of examples as the chapter develops. In particular constraints are very often linear, as they would almost certainly be in the example we have been discussing. The objective function is less likely to be linear. In our example for instance the prices we are able to command in the market may fall off the more we sell, or costs may be reduced in a non-linear fashion as the capital invested in a factory increases. However, it is frequently the case that the objective function is linear, or sufficiently well approximated by a linear function, over the range of values of the x's of interest to us.

In this chapter we shall therefore devote most of our attention to linear

programming, the more so as it is the most highly developed form of mathematical programming from the point of view of practical computation. We
shall however touch briefly upon various extensions of linear programming,
some of which allow non-linearities to be taken into account. Our aim will be
to discuss the mathematical basis of the various methods without rigour but
to a degree which will help the reader to know what is going on inside the
computer which he will almost certainly use (and is recommended to use) for
all but the most trivial problems. Very little attention is given to the statement
of precise mechanical rules for solving linear programming problems by hand
for just the reason that one would expect no one these days to solve his
problems in this way. We also try to give some flavour of the range of possible
application of the techniques introduced and, by example, an indication of
how problems can be formulated.

Finally in these introductory remarks we note that dynamic programming,
which is a potentially very powerful form of mathematical programming, is
dealt with in the ensuing chapter.

The general linear programming problem

The general linear programming problem can be written as follows (the a's
and b's being known constants):

Maximize Z for non-negative $x_1, x_2, \ldots, x_n$ subject to

$$\left.\begin{array}{c} Z + a_{01}x_1 + a_{02}x_2 + \ldots + a_{0n}x_n = b_0 \\ a_{11}x_1 + a_{12}x_2 + \ldots + a_{1n}x_n = b_1 \\ \ldots \qquad \ldots \qquad \ldots \\ a_{m1}x_1 + a_{m2}x_2 + \ldots + a_{mn}x_n = b_m \end{array}\right\} \qquad (2.1)$$

We note that this formulation includes a minimization problem (since minimize Z is just the same thing as maximize $(-Z)$). It also includes the case of
inequality constraints since inequality constraints can always be made into
equality constraints by the introduction of new non-negative variables which
do not enter Z, the objective function. This is best illustrated by example.
Suppose we have a constraint

$$a_{01}x_1 + a_{02}x_2 \geqslant b_0$$

We can introduce a new variable, say x_3, defined by

$$x_3 = b_0 - a_{01}x_1 + a_{02}x_2$$

which, for the constraint to be satisfied, must be non-negative. The constraint
can then be written

$$a_{01}x_1 + a_{02}x_2 - x_3 = b_0$$

Likewise the constraint

$$a_{11}x_1 + a_{12}x_2 \leqslant b_1$$

can be written as

$$a_{11}x_1 + a_{12}x_2 + x_4 = b_1$$

where x_4 is a new non-negative variable. x_3 and x_4, as used here, are called slack variables because they take up the slack in the inequalities.

We assume that $m + 1$, the number of equations, is not more than $n + 1$, the number of variables (counting Z as a variable), for if not the equations do not generally have a solution. In these circumstances we can solve the equations for any $m + 1$ of the variables in terms of the other $n - m$ variables, in just the normal way that one solves any set of simultaneous linear equations by adding and subtracting multiples of the equations one from another. (This assertion assumes that the equations have at least one solution. It would not be true, for example, of the equations

$$x + y + Z = 2, \qquad x + 2y = 3 \qquad \text{and} \qquad 2x + 3y + Z = 6$$

To be precise the assertion is true only if (i) the equations have at least one solution and (ii) the equations are linearly independent (which we can ensure by eliminating sufficient equations if the original set were linearly dependent). Even then we may not be able to solve the equations for literally any $m + 1$ variables, but we can solve them for at least one set of $m + 1$ variables. However we shall not concern ourselves too much with the mathematical niceties and be content to pursue the argument as an illustrative one). For example if the equations are

$$\left. \begin{aligned} Z + 10x_1 + 3x_2 + 2x_3 &= 5 \\ 6x_1 + 3x_2 + 4x_3 &= 8 \\ 2x_1 + 2x_2 + x_3 &= 4 \end{aligned} \right\} \qquad (2.2)$$

we could solve these equations for Z, x_1 and x_2 to give

$$\left. \begin{aligned} Z &= -\frac{17}{3} + \frac{16}{3}x_3 \\ x_1 &= \frac{2}{3} - \frac{5}{6}x_3 \\ x_2 &= \frac{4}{3} + \frac{1}{3}x_3 \end{aligned} \right\} \qquad (2.3)$$

Obviously the set of equations resulting from this operation is identical with the original set: we have merely re-written them. So the problem: Maximize Z for non-negative x_1, x_2, x_3 subject to equations (2.2), and the problem: Maximize Z for non-negative x_1, x_2, x_3 subject to equations (2.3), are one and the same problem.

Thus we can generate a great many versions of the same problem by solving equations (2.1) for various combinations of $m + 1$ variables from the $n + 1$ variables that go to make up the problem.

We now note that there is one particular form of a linear programming problem which is trivially easy to solve. Consider the problem of maximizing Z for non-negative $x_1, x_2, \ldots, x_n$ subject to

$$
\left.
\begin{aligned}
Z &= b'_0 - (a'_{0,m+1}x_{m+1} + a'_{0,m+2}x_{m+2} + \ldots + a'_{0,n}x_n) \\
x_1 &= b'_1 - (a'_{1,m+1}x_{m+1} + a'_{1,m+2}x_{m+2} + \ldots + a'_{1,n}x_n) \\
&\;\;\cdots \qquad\qquad \cdots \qquad\qquad\qquad \cdots \qquad\qquad\qquad \cdots \\
x_m &= b'_m - (a'_{m,m+1}x_{m+1} + a'_{m,m+2}x_{m+2} + \ldots + a'_{m,n}x_n)
\end{aligned}
\right\} \quad (2.4)
$$

where $a'_{0,m+1}, a'_{0,m+2}, \ldots, a'_{0,n}, b'_1, b'_2, \ldots, b'_m$ are all positive.

We are at liberty to give $x_{m+1}, x_{m+2}, \ldots, x_n$ any non-negative values (the other variables $Z, x_1, \ldots, x_m$ then being determined) which give non-negative values to $x_1, \ldots, x_m$. But to maximize Z we must give $x_{m+1}, \ldots, x_n$ each the value zero because to give any of them a positive value can only reduce the value of Z below $b'_{0,1}$: for example if we give x_{m+1} the value $+1$ the effect is to substract $a_{0,m+1}$, which is positive, from the value of Z obtained by putting x_{m+1} equal to zero. Moreover $x_1, \ldots, x_m$ take positive values if $x_{m+1}, \ldots, x_n$ are each given the value zero because $b'_1, \ldots, b'_m$ are all positive.

Thus if we can solve equations (2.1) for Z and m other variables to obtain a solution of the type indicated by equations (2.4), we have solved the problem. The solution is

$$Z = b'_0, \; x_1 = b'_1, \; x_2 = b'_2, \ldots, x_m = b'_m, \; x_{m+1} = x_{m+2} = \ldots = x_n = 0$$

(Of course, it will not usually be the $x_1, x_2, \ldots, x_m$ of the original equations which are non-zero, but some other set m of the original variables, namely that set for which the original equations can be put into the form of equations (2.4).)

The simplex method, which we introduce in the next section, is simply a fairly efficient way of finding the m variables which, if the equations (2.1) are solved in terms of them, give a solution of the form (2.4).

Before going on to the simplex method we will clear up one or two odds and ends. Firstly, if $a'_{0,m+1}, a'_{0,m+2}, \ldots, a'_{0,n}, b'_1, b'_2, \ldots, b'_m$ are non-negative, rather than positive (that is, some of them may be zero) the above argument still holds. It is true that if, for example, $a_{0,m+1} = 0$, then x_{m+1} can take a non-zero value without reducing Z compared with putting $x_{m+1} = 0$. However, there is nothing to be gained by doing this in terms of increasing Z and there is the possibility that giving x_{m+1} a positive value might lead one of $x_1, \ldots, x_m$ to take a negative value. What we could do is to give x_{m+1} any value up to the lowest value of x_{m+1} which makes one of $x_1, \ldots, x_m$ zero. This amounts to saying that there is an infinity of possible solutions to the problem corresponding to the range of values that x_{m+1} may take, at each of which Z has the same value. This might be of some practical importance as there may be some reason outside the problem as formulated to prefer one of these solutions to another, but the point is of no theoretical importance.

Secondly, we may not be able to find a solution of the type (2.4). There may be two reasons for this: we cannot find a solution in which all of b'_1, b'_2, . . ., b'_m are non-negative, or we cannot find a solution in which all of $a'_{0,m+1}$, $a'_{0,m+2}$, . . ., $a'_{0,m}$ are also non-negative.

If we cannot find a solution in which all of b'_1, b'_2, . . ., b'_m are non-negative then we cannot find any solution of the original equations (2.1) in which x_1, x_2, . . ., x_n are all non-negative. This is not difficult to see and is left as an exercise to the reader. It is not uncommon in practice to find that the equations as originally formulated do not have a solution for non-negative x's. This is because when formulating the equations, particularly if there are a large number of them, it is sometimes difficult to avoid asking for mutually contradictory inequalities to be fulfilled. One would therefore have to isolate which inequalities were causing the difficulty and reformulate the problem.

If we cannot find a solution in which all of $a'_{0,m+1}$, $a'_{0,m+2}$ . . ., $a'_{0,m}$ are also non-negative, Z can be made as large as we please. This again is not difficult to see and is left as an exercise for the reader. If this were to happen in practice the most likely explanation would not be that Z really could be made as large as we please but that an error, which would have to be found, had been made in formulating the problem.

Finally in this section we introduce some terminology. If we solve equations (2.1) for Z, x_1, x_2, . . ., x_m we are said to have put them in canonical form with respect to Z, x_1, x_2, . . ., x_m; Z, x_1, x_2, . . ., x_m are said to be basic variables or to be in the basis; the other x variables are said to be non-basic. Any solution of the equations in which all the x's are non-negative is said to be a feasible solution; if there is no such solution we shall say the equations are inconsistent. A basic solution to the equations is obtained by putting $n - m$ of the variables equal to zero. If Z is in the basis and a basic solution is found in which the non-zero x's are non-negative the solution is said to be a basic feasible solution. The equations written out are often referred to as the tableau.

We have thus shown in this section that Z is maximized by a solution of the equations which is a basic feasible solution.

The basic solutions of equations (2.2) are

$$Z = -\frac{17}{3}, x_1 = \frac{2}{3}, \quad x_2 = \frac{4}{3}, \quad x_3 = 0 \tag{2.5}$$

$$Z = -\frac{65}{3}, x_1 = -\frac{8}{3}, \quad x_2 = 0, \quad x_3 = -4 \tag{2.6}$$

$$Z = -\frac{7}{5}, \quad x_1 = 0, \quad x_2 = \frac{8}{5}, \quad x_3 = \frac{4}{5} \tag{2.7}$$

$$Z = 0, \quad x_1 = -\frac{7}{32}, x_2 = \frac{27}{16}, x_3 = \frac{17}{16} \tag{2.8}$$

(2.5) and (2.7) are basic feasible solutions. The reader might care to check that

$$Z = -\frac{7}{5} - \frac{32}{5} x_1$$
$$x_2 = \frac{8}{5} - \frac{2}{5} x_1 \qquad\qquad (2.9)$$
$$x_3 = \frac{4}{5} - \frac{6}{5} x_1$$

is a solution of equations (2.2).

The simplex method

In the simplex method (which was introduced by Dantzig (see for example reference 1)) we first find a solution of the equations (2.1) which gives us a basic feasible solution. We see whether this is the optimum solution by checking whether the coefficients of the x's in the expression for Z are all positive. If not, we move to a new basis by taking one variable out of the basis and putting a non-basic variable into the basis in its place. We choose the variable to put into the basis to be one which will give an increased value of Z at the new basic solution; we choose the variable to take out of the basis as the one which will ensure that the new basic solution is a basic feasible solution.

The process is best explained by an example, which we will first formulate. The problem is how much coal should be washed and how much unwashed in a given situation. When the coal in question is washed, different proportions of different sizes are produced than when it is unwashed:

	Washed	Unwashed
Large	0·1	0·3
Graded	0·5	—
Unwashed smalls	0·4	0·7
Profit/tonne (£'s)	1·07	1·09

The capacity of the colliery supplying the coal is 400 tonnes/hour and that of the washery 250 tonnes/hour. Only 200 tonnes/hour of unwashed smalls can be sold. How much coal should be produced, how much washed and how much unwashed in order to obtain maximum profit? Let x_1 tonnes be washed and x_2 tonnes be sold untreated. Then the washery capacity can be expressed as

$$x_1 \leqslant 250 \qquad\qquad (2.10)$$

and the overall availability as

$$x_1 + x_2 \leqslant 400 \qquad\qquad (2.11)$$

and the maximum of untreated smalls as

$$0.4x_1 + 0.7x_2 \leqslant 200 \tag{2.12}$$

Also we cannot have negative tonnages, so

$$x_1 \geqslant 0 : x_2 \geqslant 0 \tag{2.13}$$

and   the profit $= 1.07x_1 + 1.09x_2$ $\tag{2.14}$

The problem is now a linear programming one of maximizing the function (2.14) subject to the constraints (2.10), (2.11), (2.12) and (2.13). This can be formulated as:

Maximize Z for non-negative x_1, x_2, x_3, x_4, x_5 subject to

$$
\begin{aligned}
Z - 1.07x_1 - 1.09x_2 \qquad\qquad\qquad &= 0 \\
x_1 \qquad\quad + x_3 \qquad\qquad &= 250 \\
x_1 + x_2 \qquad + x_4 \qquad &= 400 \\
0.4x_1 + 0.7x_2 \qquad\qquad + x_5 &= 200
\end{aligned}
\tag{2.15}
$$

An immediately obvious basis is Z, x_3, x_4, x_5. This happens to give a basic feasible solution ($Z = 0$, $x_3 = 250$, $x_4 = 400$, $x_5 = 200$), not optimal as the coefficients of x_1 and x_2 in the expression for Z (namely $Z = 0 - (-1.07x_1 - 1.09x_2)$) are negative. Let us introduce x_2 in the basis, since we can expect to find a basic feasible solution with x_2 in the basis which has a higher value than 0 for Z. This is because every unit by which we can increase x_2 increases Z by 1.09 units. (Note that we have chosen the non-basic variable with the most negative coefficient to bring into the basis. This is conventional and also a good working rule. It is not necessary for solving the problem but it is necessary to pick a non-basic variable with a negative coefficient if we want to guarantee reaching the optimum value of Z.)

In bringing x_2 into the basis we are intent upon increasing its value. However we notice that if we increase x_2 beyond 400 it will make x_4 negative; worse still, if we increase it beyond $200/0.7$ it will make x_5 negative. In the interests of retaining feasibility therefore we should take x_5 out of the basis. Let us therefore re-solve equations (2.15) for Z, x_2, x_3 and x_4. This is very easily done. We have only to multiply the fourth equation by $1.09/0.7$ and add it to the first; to multiply it by $1/0.7$ and subtract it from the third; and to divide by 0.7.

The result of doing this is

$$
\begin{aligned}
Z - 0.45x_1 + 1.56x_5 &= 311.4 \\
x_3 + x_1 \qquad\qquad &= 250.0 \\
x_4 + 0.43x_1 - 1.43x_5 &= 114.3 \\
x_2 + 0.57x_1 + 1.43x_5 &= 285.7
\end{aligned}
\tag{2.16}
$$

In the usual terminology we have now performed one iteration of the simplex method. Our current basis is Z, x_3, x_4, x_2 and our current value of the objective function is 311.4. The current solution in full is $Z = 311.4$, $x_3 = 250.0$, $x_4 = 114.3$ and $x_2 = 285.7$ and $x_5 = 0$. The coefficients of the non-basic variables in the expression for Z are called the reduced costs. They represent the gain in the value of Z (or loss if negative) to be obtained by introducing one further unit of the relevant non-basic variable.

This solution is not optimal since the coefficient of x_1 is negative. Let us therefore introduce x_1 into the basis. What variable should leave the basis? As x_1 increases from zero it forces x_3 down to zero when it reaches 250, x_4 when it reaches $114 \cdot 3/0 \cdot 43 = 265 \cdot 8$ and x_2 when it reaches $285 \cdot 7/0 \cdot 57 = 501 \cdot 2$. The best we can do therefore is to move to a basic feasible solution in which $x_1 = 250$, that is we take x_3 out of the basis. This we do by adding $0 \cdot 45$ times the second of equations (2.16) to the first and so on to give us:

$$\left.\begin{array}{l} Z + 0 \cdot 45x_3 + 1 \cdot 56x_5 = 423 \cdot 9 \\ x_1 + x_3 \qquad\qquad = 250 \cdot 0 \\ x_4 - 0 \cdot 43x_3 - 1 \cdot 43x_5 = \quad 6 \cdot 8 \\ x_2 - 0 \cdot 57x_3 + 1 \cdot 43x_5 = 143 \cdot 2 \end{array}\right\} \qquad (2.17)$$

All the reduced costs are now positive and the maximization of Z subject to these equations is trivial: Z is maximized when $x_3 = x_5 = 0$ and $Z = 423 \cdot 9$, $x_1 = 250 \cdot 0$, $x_4 = 6 \cdot 8$ and $x_2 = 143 \cdot 2$.

Let us formalize the simplex method for the general case by describing algebraically what we have done to perform one iteration. Suppose our current solution represents a feasible but non-optimal basis as follows:

$$\left.\begin{array}{l} Z = b''_0 - (a''_{0,m+1}x_{m+1} + a''_{0,m+2}x_{m+2} + \ldots + a''_{0n}x_n) \\ x_1 = b''_1 - (a''_{1,m+1}x_{m+1} + a''_{1,m+2}x_{m+2} + \ldots + a''_{1n}x_n) \\ \qquad\qquad\qquad \cdots \\ x_m = b''_m - (a''_{m,m+1}x_{m+1} + a''_{m,m+2}x_{m+2} + \ldots + a''_{mn}x_n) \end{array}\right\} \qquad (2.18)$$

We perform an iteration by the following steps:

(i) Select a negative $a''_{0,j}$ $(j = m+1, m+2, \ldots, n)$. Usually we select the most negative $a''_{0,j}$. Although this is not strictly necessary it is quite good practice. This selects the variable to enter the basis, x_j say.

(ii) Calculate $b''_1/a''_{1,j}, b''_2/a''_{2,j}, \ldots, b''_m/a''_{m,j}$ for all i for which $a''_{i,j} > 0$ $(i = 1, 2, \ldots, m)$ and find the smallest of these, say $b''_i/a''_{i,j}$. (In the event of a tie—that is the smallest is one of two or more of the numbers—select any one of the equal smallest.) This tells us the maximum value to which x_j can be increased without losing feasibility. If x_j is given this value, x_i (or more generally the basic variable in the ith equation) becomes zero and is the variable to enter the basis. (If none of $a''_{i,j} > 0$ we can increase x_j indefinitely and the solution is unbounded.)

(iii) We now solve the equations for $Z, x_1, x_2, \ldots, x_{i-1}, x_j, x_{i+1}, \ldots, x_m$ by dividing the ith equation through by $a''_{i,j}$ to give

$$x_j = \frac{b''_i}{a''_{i,j}} - \left(\frac{a''_{i,m+1}}{a''_{i,j}}x_{m+1} + \ldots + \frac{1}{a''_{i,j}}x_i + \ldots + \frac{a''_{i,n}}{a''_{i,j}}x_n\right)$$

$$(2.19)$$

Equation (2.19) is then multiplied in turn by $a''_{0,j}$, $a''_{1,j}$, . . ., $a''_{i-1,j}$, $a''_{i+1,j}$, . . ., $a''_{m,j}$ and added to each of equations (2.18) except the ith in turn. This completes the iteration.

There is one possible snag with the simplex method. In equations (2.18) it is possible that one or more of b''_0, b''_1, . . ., b''_m may be zero. The current solution is then said to be degenerate. Generally this does not matter but there is a risk in such a case that the simplex method will get stuck and start to cycle round the same path that has already been taken. Such cycling very rarely occurs in practice; if it does do so it can be resolved by giving those of b''_0, b''_1, . . ., b''_m which have a zero value a small positive value which is subsequently removed from the equations.

Discussion of the final tableau

When we have the equations in the form typified by equations (2.17) (that is, all the reduced costs are positive and the solution with the non-basic variables put equal to zero is a feasible one) we are said to have the final tableau. The final tableau tells us what the maximum value of Z is and what the related values of the x-variables are. In the case of equations (2.17) we note that the non-basic variables, which take the value zero at the optimum situation, are two of the slack variables implying that two constrained resources are fully used. In this case the two resources are the washery—we are using it up to capacity—and the market for unwashed smalls—we are selling as much as we can. The other slack variable, x_4, is not zero, showing that we should not fully utilize our production capacity.

How much would we gain if we had an extra tonne per hour of washery capacity? The answer is 0·45, because then we could make $x_3 = -1$ in equations (2.17) without losing feasibility in the true variables, as opposed to the slack variables, of the problem; in other words, the value per unit of increased capacity is the reduced cost of the relevant slack variable in the final tableau. (Alternatively we might argue that the process of going from the original equations (2.15) to the final tableau (2.17) involves only the addition and subtraction of multiples of the original equations. In particular the expression for Z in equations (2.17) is the original expression for Z plus some multiple of each of the other equations. Since a slack variable has unit coefficient in the original equations its coefficient in the final equation for Z is the multiplier for the corresponding equation. Thus our final equation for Z is, in terms of equations (2.15), (the first equation) $+0·45$ (the second equation) $+1·56$ (the fourth equation). It follows that the optimum value for Z is $0·45 \times 250 + 1·56 \times 200$. If 250 is increased to 251, the optimum value of Z is increased by 0·45. More generally the optimum value for Z is

$$b_0 + \lambda_1 b_1 + \lambda_2 b_2 + \ldots + \lambda_m b_m \quad \text{and} \quad \frac{\partial Z}{\partial b_i} = \lambda_i$$

where λ_i is the shadow price on the ith row in the final tableau. The λ's are often referred to as the simplex multipliers.) This is of considerable practical importance: it tells us up to how much per tonne/hour it is worth paying in order to increase the washery capacity. More generally the reduced costs of the slack variables in the final tableau give us some indication of how much it is worth paying to alleviate a constraint. These reduced costs are known as the shadow prices on the constraints. Note that the shadow price on the production constraint is zero: there is no value attached to increasing a capacity which is not fully utilized. The ratio of shadow price to cost per unit of constraint alleviation for those constraints which can be alleviated by capital expenditure is a useful index by which to guide capital investment.

The shadow prices do not tell us the whole story, however, because there comes a stop to the gain from increasing the washery capacity, since if we increase it sufficiently far it no longer remains a critical constraint. We return to this point later in the chapter. It is sufficient at this stage to say that the shadow price represents the marginal gain per unit increase in washery capacity.

As it happens there are no non-slack variables which are non-basic in the solution to our problem. If there were the reduced costs attached to those in the final tableau would represent the increase in the profit (or the decrease in the cost) per unit associated with them necessary to make it worthwhile giving them a non-zero value.

Finding a first feasible solution

The simplex method iterates from one feasible basic solution to another. In the example we worked through we were rather fortunate in being able to spot a feasible basis very easily. This was because every equation had one variable in it which did not appear in any other equation, and these variables had coefficients whose signs were such that the equations could be solved for them with positive constant terms.

Unfortunately it is not always as easy as this to find an initial feasible basis. Suppose in the example discussed above that instead of a maximum production of 400 tonnes/hour the constraint was that exactly 350 tonnes/hour must be sold. Instead of equation (2.10) one would therefore have

$$x_1 + x_2 = 350 \tag{2.20}$$

Suppose also there was a requirement that at least 50 tonnes/hour of large coal (washed or unwashed) must be supplied. A new equation

$$0 \cdot 1 x_1 + 0 \cdot 3 x_2 - x_6 = 50 \tag{2.21}$$

would have to be introduced. The revised problem is thus:

Maximize Z for non-negative x_1, x_2, x_3, x_5, x_6 subject to

$$\begin{aligned}
Z - 1{\cdot}07x_1 - 1{\cdot}09x_2 &\qquad\qquad\qquad\qquad = 0 \\
x_1 &\qquad + x_3 \qquad\qquad\quad = 250 \\
x_1 + \quad x_2 &\qquad\qquad\qquad\qquad = 350 \\
0{\cdot}4x_1 + 0{\cdot}7x_2 &\qquad + x_5 \qquad\quad = 200 \\
0{\cdot}1x_1 + 0{\cdot}3x_2 &\qquad\qquad\quad - x_6 = 50
\end{aligned} \tag{2.22}$$

There is now no obvious initial feasible basis because of the absence in the third and fifth of equations (2.22) of a suitable variable in terms of which to solve the equations (x_6 being unsuitable because

$$x_6 = -50 + 0{\cdot}1x_1 + 0{\cdot}3x_2$$

the minus sign preventing feasibility).

We can get round this problem simply by inventing non-negative variables w_1 and w_2 say which are called artificial variables and introducing them to the third and fifth equations thus:

$$\begin{aligned}
x_1 + \quad x_2 \qquad + w_1 \qquad\quad &= 350 \\
0{\cdot}1x_1 + 0{\cdot}3x_2 - x_6 \qquad + w_2 &= 50
\end{aligned} \tag{2.23}$$

Z, x_3, w_1, x_5 and w_2 now give a first feasible basis. However in any true solution of equations (2.22) w_1 and w_2 must both be zero. To find a basic feasible solution for which this is the case we therefore first maximize

$$W = -(w_1 + w_2)$$

using the ordinary simplex method: this is often called the first phase of the two-phase simplex method. (Of course, the maximum value of W is zero if equations (2.22) have a feasible solution. If the maximum value of W is less than zero, equations (2.22) have no feasible solution.) $w_1 + w_2$ is often called the sum of the infeasibilities. When we have equations (2.23) in the final form from the first phase we shall have a basic feasible solution for the original problem. We can then simply forget about w_1 and w_2 and proceed to the solution of the original problem by the usual simplex method: this is referred to as the second phase.

To illustrate the point, let us obtain a basic feasible solution for the original problem by maximizing W for non-negative x_1, x_2, x_3, x_5, x_6, w_1, w_2 subject to

$$\begin{aligned}
W &\qquad\qquad\qquad\qquad\quad + w_1 + w_2 = 0 \\
x_1 &\qquad + x_3 \qquad\qquad\qquad\quad = 250 \\
x_1 + \quad x_2 &\qquad\qquad\quad + w_1 \qquad\quad = 350 \\
0{\cdot}4x_1 + 0{\cdot}7x_2 &\quad + x_5 \qquad\qquad\qquad = 200 \\
0{\cdot}1x_1 + 0{\cdot}3x_2 &\qquad\quad - x_6 \qquad + w_2 = 50
\end{aligned} \tag{2.24}$$

The first basis is W, x_3, w_1, x_5, w_2 and we must first express W in terms of the non-basic variables, that is

$$W - 1{\cdot}1x_1 - 0{\cdot}4x_2 + x_6 = -400 \tag{2.25}$$

Following the rules of the simplex method, we bring x_1 into the basis and remove x_3 from it. Performing this iteration leads to the equations:

$$
\begin{array}{l}
W \quad\quad - 0 \cdot 4x_2 + 1 \cdot 1x_3 \quad\quad + x_6 \quad\quad\quad = -125 \\
x_1 \quad\quad\quad + \quad x_3 \quad\quad\quad\quad\quad\quad = 250 \\
\quad\quad x_2 - \quad x_3 \quad\quad\quad + w_1 \quad\quad = 100 \\
\quad 0 \cdot 7x_2 - 0 \cdot 4x_3 + x_5 \quad\quad\quad\quad = 100 \\
\quad 0 \cdot 3x_2 - 0 \cdot 1x_3 \quad\quad - x_6 \quad\quad + w_2 = 25
\end{array} \right\} (2.26)
$$

The next iteration brings x_2 into the basis and removes w_2, and the following one brings in x_6 and removes w_2. Performing these iterations in turn leaves the following equations:

$$
\begin{array}{l}
W \quad\quad\quad\quad\quad\quad\quad + \quad w_1 + \quad w_2 = \quad 0 \\
x_1 \quad\quad + \quad x_3 \quad\quad\quad\quad\quad\quad\quad = 250 \\
\quad\quad - 0 \cdot 2x_3 \quad + x_6 \quad\quad\quad + 0 \cdot 3w_2 = \quad 5 \\
\quad + 0 \cdot 3x_3 + x_5 \quad\quad + 0 \cdot 7w_1 \quad\quad = \quad 30 \\
x_2 - \quad x_3 \quad\quad\quad\quad + \quad w_1 \quad\quad = 100
\end{array} \right\} (2.27)
$$

We have now maximized W and can drop w_1 and w_2 from the equations. What remains, together with the equation

$$Z - 1 \cdot 07x_1^2 - 1 \cdot 09x_2 = 0$$

is equivalent to the original problem. We need only express Z in terms of the current non-basic variables (that is, $Z - 0 \cdot 02x_3 = 376 \cdot 5$) to put down the original problem in a form for which an initial feasible base is immediately obvious, thus:

Maximize Z for non-negative x_1, x_2, x_3, x_4, x_6 subject to

$$
\begin{array}{l}
Z \quad\quad - 0 \cdot 02x_3 = 376 \cdot 5 \\
x_1 + \quad x_3 = 250 \\
x_6 - \quad 0 \cdot 2x_3 = \quad 5 \\
x_5 + \quad 0 \cdot 3x_3 = \quad 30 \\
x_2 - \quad x_3 = 100
\end{array} \right\} (2.28)
$$

One iteration is sufficient to complete the problem. x_3 is brought into the basis and x_5 removed from it to give

$$
\begin{array}{l}
Z \quad\quad + 3 \cdot 33x_5 = 378 \cdot 5 \\
x_1 - \quad 3 \cdot 33x_5 = 150 \\
x_6 + \quad 0 \cdot 67x_5 = \quad 25 \\
x_3 + \quad 3 \cdot 33x_5 = 100 \\
x_2 + \quad 3 \cdot 33x_5 = 200
\end{array} \right\} (2.29)
$$

There is an alternative way of finding an initial feasible basis which is formally the same as maximizing W but which is computationally quicker in most cases. In this method artificial variables are entered only in genuine equality rows. Thus the constraints of (2.22) would be written as

$$
\begin{array}{l}
x_1 \quad\quad + x_3 \quad\quad\quad\quad = 250 \\
x_1 + \quad x_2 \quad\quad\quad + w_1 = 350 \\
0 \cdot 4x_1 + 0 \cdot 7x_2 \quad + x_5 \quad\quad = 200 \\
0 \cdot 1x_1 + 0 \cdot 3x_2 \quad\quad - x_6 \quad\quad = \quad 50
\end{array} \right\} (2.30)
$$

where w_1 is the only artificial variable. We now proceed to maximize

$$W = -w_1 + x_6$$

or, more generally, $W = -$ the sum of the artificial variables which are in the current basis $+$ the sum of any slacks which are in the basis and which take a negative value in the current basic solution. The ordinary simplex method is used to maximize W starting from an initial basis of W, x_3, w_1, x_5 and x_6. The fact that this is infeasible need not worry us; provided we do not allow any new variables to enter the basis with negative values we shall eventually reach a feasible basis if one exists. The reason this approach is usually quicker than the previous one is that time is not wasted keeping artificial variables feasible unnecessarily.

Finally in this section we note that there might be some point in retaining the artificial variables which, like w_1, have been introduced into equality constraints, in the problem until the final tableau is reached. This is because their reduced costs in the final tableau are the shadow prices on the equalities.

Graphical representation

The problem formulated by equations (2.15) is essentially a two dimensional problem in that we can pose it as find non-negative values of any two of the x's (let us say, x_1 and x_2) which maximize Z and for which equations (2.15) are satisfied for non-negative x_3, x_4 and x_5. This is because given any two of the x variables the values of Z and the other x's are determined by solving equations (2.15). In general if there are $m + 1$ equations and $n + 1$ variables (including Z) the problem is one in $n-m$ dimensions.

The two dimensional problem can be solved graphically and we do so in what follows. The graphical solution will perhaps help the reader to get some feel for what is happening in the simplex method not only in two dimensions but also in the larger number of dimensions of the typical problem.

In equations (2.15) put Z, x_3, x_4, $x_5 = 0$ and draw the resulting lines, as shown in Figure 2.1 opposite.

The first point we notice is that any point for which x_3, x_4 and x_5 are all non-negative must lie inside the region $OABC$ or on its boundaries. This is because, for example, the line $x_5 = 10$ (that is $0 \cdot 4 \, x_1 + 0 \cdot 72 \, x_2$) lies below the line $x_5 = 0$. Conversely any point lying in the region $OABC$ defines a solution to equations (2.15) for which x_1, x_2, x_3, x_4 and x_5 are non-negative. Note that the line $x_4 = 0$ plays no part in determining the region $OABC$: it is not a critical constraint. Note also that there is a region of solution points, showing that the original problem is feasible. If there were a constraint

$$x_1 + x_2 \geqslant 400$$

the problem would have been inconsistent.

Suppose now we draw the line $Z = Z_0$ where Z_0 is a positive number. It is a line parallel to the line $Z = 0$. As Z_0 increases this line moves rightwards. Our problem is therefore, putting it rather crudely: what is the furthest we can displace the line $Z = 0$ to the right, keeping it parallel to itself, but still making sure that at least one point of it remains in the region $OABC$. The answer is obviously to keep moving until B is reached. This is shown by the dotted line which is $Z = 423.9$. At the point B $x_1 = 250$, $x_2 = 143.2$ by solving

$$x_1 + x_2 = 400 \quad \text{and} \quad 0.4x_1 + 0.7x_2 = 200$$

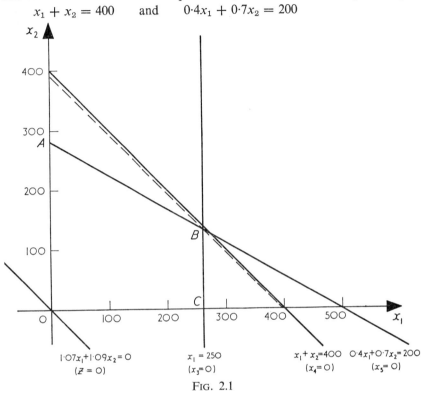

FIG. 2.1

Also $x_3 = x_5 = 0$ either by substitution or simply by noting that these equations define B. Finally $x_4 = 6.8$ by substitution. This is just the solution we reached before.

What did the simplex method do? It started with Z, x_3, x_4 and x_5 in the basis and evaluated Z for

$$x_1 = x_2 = 0$$

Graphically we looked at point O. Then x_2 was brought into the basis and x_5 removed from it. Then Z was evaluated at

$$x_1 = x_5 = 0$$

which is the point A. Finally we reached point B by taking x_3 from the basis and bring in x_1 and evaluating Z at

$$x_3 = x_5 = 0$$

We moved in fact from a vertex to a neighbouring vertex at each iteration: each basic feasible solution corresponds to a vertex of $OABC$ and vice versa.

The graphical method makes it obvious that the optimum solution lies at a vertex, that is at a basic feasible solution. However if the line $Z = 0$ had been parallel to one of the lines defining B the solution would not have been unique. Thus if the first of equations (2.15) were replaced by

$$Z - 0\cdot4x_1 - 0\cdot7x_2 = 0$$

any point on the line AB maximizes Z. The reader might care to check what happens in following the simplex method in this case. He will find that an optimum solution is reached after one iteration but that the reduced cost of one of the non-basic variables (actually x_1) is zero. In our previous discussion of this situation we said this showed x_1 can be increased until its value forces a basic variable to zero. The reader will see that increasing x_1, consistent with the equations, traces out the line AB and any point on this line maximizes Z. When B is reached x_1 cannot be further increased as feasibility is lost.

It is left as an exercise to the reader to put graphical interpretations on degeneracy and on the shadow prices.

The revised simplex method

Most computer codes for linear programming use the simplex method but organize the calculations in a rather different way from that indicated in the manual example worked above. They generally use instead some form of the revised simplex method, which was also introduced by Dantzig. It is easiest to introduce the revised simplex method by discussing critically the ordinary simplex method.

In performing an iteration using the simplex method (assuming we have a feasible base) we examine the equations to decide whether the current basis is optimal and, if not, which variable to bring into the basis and which to remove. To do this we make use of the coefficients of the non-basic variables in the equation for Z to find a negative one. Say the coefficient of x_i is negative. We now use the coefficients of x_i in all the equations together with the current values of the constant terms on the right hand sides of these equations to decide which variable to remove from the basis. All the other coefficients, which we have so laboriously calculated, are not used at all. It is natural to wonder whether there is not some more efficient way of calculating the coefficients we need when we need them. This is what the revised simplex method provides, at least in the form it is used in computer codes. At each iteration only those coefficients we actually need are calculated from the coefficients in the initial formulation of the problem.

The revised simplex method works in the following way. Suppose at an iteration x_j is the variable to enter the basis and the basic variable in the ith equation the one to leave. Let a_{pq} be the coefficient of x_q in the pth equation before the iteration is performed, and a'_{pq} the coefficient afterwards. Then

$$
\left.
\begin{aligned}
a'_{iq} &= \frac{a_{iq}}{a_{ij}} \\
\text{and} \quad a'_{pq} &= a_{pq} - a_{pj}a'_{iq} \\
\text{for} \quad p &\neq i
\end{aligned}
\right\}
\tag{2.31}
$$

Also, of course, if x_q is in the current basis and figures only in the rth equation,

$$a_{pq} = a'_{pq} = 0$$

if $p \neq r$ and

$$a_{rq} = a'_{rq} = 1$$

Thus we need only bother with equations (2.31) if x_q is not basic unless it is the variable to be removed from the basis. We also notice that if the constant terms in the equations are denoted by $a_{p,n+1}$, equations (2.31) apply to them also.

Thus if we want to calculate the a'''s we can do so from the a's together with a knowledge of i and the coefficients a_{iq} ($q = 0, 1, \ldots, m$). Moreover they in turn can be calculated from the coefficients in the equations before the previous iteration from a knowledge of which variable entered the basis in the previous iteration and its coefficients in the then equations. Pursuing this argument back through all the iterations we see that provided we keep a record of which variable entered the basis at each iteration and its coefficients in order in the equations at that iteration, we can calculate any a_{pq} we require by using equations (2.31) successively, starting from the original coefficients. In particular we can calculate those coefficients we need to perform the iteration and since they include the ones we need to perform the calculations of equations (2.31), they are the only ones we need bother to calculate. However, we also use the constant terms on the right-hand sides of the equations at every iteration so they might as well be kept up-dated also.

To continue the argument it is desirable to use matrix algebra. Let the equations using the ordinary simplex method after r iterations be

$$\mathbf{A}_r \begin{bmatrix} Z \\ x_1 \\ x_2 \\ \cdot \\ \cdot \\ \cdot \\ x_n \\ -1 \end{bmatrix} = 0 \tag{2.32}$$

$\mathbf{A}_0$ of course being the original matrix. Let $\mathbf{P}$ be an $(m + 1) \times (m + 1)$ matrix whose elements are all zero except the diagonal elements and the elements of its ith column. (For convenience we shall number the rows and columns of $\mathbf{P}$ from 0 to m, so the column on the right of the matrix is the 0th column, the next the 1st and so on.) The diagonal elements are all 1 except the diagonal element in its ith row. The element in the ith column and the ith row is $1/a_{ij}$, and in the ith column and the pth row ($p \neq i$) $- a_{pj}/a_{ij}$. The equations show that

$$\mathbf{A}_r = \mathbf{P}_r \mathbf{A}_{r-1} = \ldots = \mathbf{P}_r \mathbf{P}_{r-1} \ldots \mathbf{P}_1 \mathbf{A}_0 \tag{2.33}$$

In a computer the $\mathbf{P}$'s are stored very economically since one need identify only which column is not a unit column (that is, column i) and what its m

elements are. Also the matrix multiplication, as the reader will convince himself, is very easy because of the simple form taken by the **P**'s.

Let us define

$$\mathbf{Q}_r = \mathbf{P}_r\mathbf{P}_{r-1} \ldots \mathbf{P}_1$$

so that

$$\mathbf{Q}_r\mathbf{A}_0 \begin{bmatrix} Z \\ x_1 \\ x_2 \\ \cdot \\ \cdot \\ \cdot \\ x_n \\ -1 \end{bmatrix} = 0 \qquad (2.34)$$

are the equations after the rth iteration. $\mathbf{Q}_r$ is called the current inverse matrix being the inverse of the matrix that pre-multiplies the current basic variables in the original equations. Let $Q_{0,j}^{(r)}$ be the jth element of the top row of $\mathbf{Q}_r$. Then we see that the current reduced cost of variable x_i is

$$Q_{0,1}^{(r)}a_{1,j} + Q_{0,2}^{(r)}a_{2,i} + \ldots + Q_{0,m}^{(r)}a_{m,i}$$

where a_{ji} is the coefficient of variable i in the jth of the original equations. Thus the reduced costs are easily found if $Q_0^{(r)}$, $Q_0^{(r)}$, . . ., $Q_{0n}^{(r)}$ are known. But these in turn are easily found by forming the product.

$$[1, 0, 0, \ldots, 0]\mathbf{P}_r\mathbf{P}_{r-1} \ldots \mathbf{P}_0 \qquad (2.35)$$

and this is the way the reduced costs are usually calculated in a computer code. If x_i happened to be a slack variable in the jth row of the original equations $a_{ji} = 0$ unless $k = j$ and $a_{ji} = 1$. The reduced cost of such an x_i would therefore be $Q_{0,j}^{(r)}$. In the final tableau, therefore, $Q_{0,j}$ represents the shadow price on row j: $Q_{0,j}$ is often called the current jth simplex multiplier.

We are now almost in a position to work through an example to indicate how the revised simplex method works but first we must decide how we are going to go about getting a first feasible basis. Most computer codes use the second of the methods introduced earlier. Artificial variables are introduced into any of the original equation which were equalities. A further variable, say w, and another equation

$$w + \Sigma A - \Sigma x = 0$$

are introduced, where A is any artificial variable which is currently non-zero and x is any basic variable which currently takes a negative value. Putting this another way we can redefine an objective function w at every iteration by

$$w - (c_1x_1 + c_2x_2 + \ldots + c_mx_m) = 0$$

where x_j = the variable in the jth ($j > 0$) row of the current basis, and
$c_j = -1$ if x_j is an artificial variable,
  $= +1$ if x_j is not an artificial variable and the current $b_j < 0$,
  $= 0$ otherwise.

Now in terms of the current non-basic variables, a typical basic variable is given by

$$x_j + \sum_{\substack{k=1,\ldots,m \\ l \text{ summed} \\ \text{over non-basic} \\ \text{variables}}} [Q_{j,k}^{(r)} a_{k,l} x_l - Q_{j,k}^{(r)} a_{k,n+1}] = 0$$

and so the current expression for w in terms of the non-basic variables is

$$w + \sum_{j,k,l} c_j Q_{j,k}^{(r)} a_{k,l} x_l = \sum_{j,k} c_j Q_{j,k}^{(r)} a_{k,n+1}$$

These coefficients of x_l are the numbers we must scan to find the most negative and so which variable to make basic. But this is no different from our earlier task except that $Q_{0k}^{(r)}$ is replaced by

$$\sum_{j=1}^{m} c_j Q_{j,k}^{(r)}$$

Thus to find the reduced costs for the variables we form

$$\mathbf{c}^{(r)} \mathbf{P}_r \mathbf{P}_{r-1} \ldots \mathbf{P}_0$$

($\mathbf{c}^{(r)}$ being the value at the rth iteration of the row vector $(0, c_1, c_2, \ldots c_m)$), and multiply it into each vector of the coefficients of the non-basic variables.

Note that $\mathbf{c}^{(r)}$ changes with each iteration until feasibility is achieved. In practice a lot of time is spent in the first stage when $\mathbf{c}^{(r)}$ is changing and when, therefore, there is no point in trying to keep the top row, a_{0j}, up to date.

Let us now work through an example to illustrate the revised simplex method. The problem is maximize $3x_1 + 2x_2 + x_3 + 10$ for $x_1, x_2, x_3 \geqslant 0$ and

$$\left. \begin{array}{l} x_1 + x_2 + x_3 \leqslant 10 \\ 2x_1 - x_2 \qquad \geqslant 2 \\ \qquad 2x_2 + x_3 = 7 \end{array} \right\} \tag{2.36}$$

We introduce Z as the objective function, x_4 and x_5 as slack variables and x_6 as an artificial variable and the problem is rewritten maximize Z for x_1, $x_2, x_3, x_4, x_5 \geqslant 0$, $x_6 = 0$ and

$$\left. \begin{array}{l} Z - 3x_1 - 2x_2 - x_3 \qquad\qquad = 10 \\ x_1 + x_2 + x_3 + x_4 \qquad\quad = 10 \\ -2x_1 + x_2 \qquad\quad + x_5 \qquad = -2 \\ 2x_2 + x_3 \qquad\qquad + x_6 = 7 \end{array} \right\} \tag{2.37}$$

The solution method is given iteration by iteration. The full working for just one iteration, the third, is given. The variables are numbered 0 to 6, the equations 0 to 3. (Note the $\mathbf{A}$ is the matrix of the coefficients going to make up equations (2.37). The column of $\mathbf{A}$ corresponding to the variable selected to enter the basis at an iteration is usually called the pivot column; the row of **A** corresponding to the equation which contains the variable selected to leave the basis is called the pivot row; and the element common to them is called the pivot element. The process of calculating the reduced costs of the non-basic variables is sometimes called pricing the columns. One also finds the reduced costs sometimes called the column prices.)

Iteration	1	2	3	4
Current basis	4, 5, 6	4, 1, 6	4, 1, 2	5, 1, 2
Current constant terms	10, 10, −2, 7	13, 9, 1, 7	$\frac{101}{4}, \frac{15}{4}, \frac{11}{4}, \frac{7}{2}$	$\frac{73}{2}, \frac{15}{2}, \frac{13}{2}, \frac{7}{2}$
Current c	0, 0, 1, −1	0, 0, 0, −1	1, 0, 0, 0	1, 0, 0, 0
Current simplex multipliers	0, 0, 1, −1	0, 0, 0, −1	$1, 0, -\frac{3}{2}, \frac{7}{4}$	$1, 3, 0, -\frac{1}{2}$
Reduced costs	−2, −1, −1	−2, −1, 0	$\frac{3}{4}, -\frac{3}{2}$	$\frac{3}{2}, 3$
Variable to enter basis	1	2	5	
Coefficients of this variable	−3, 1, −2, 0	$-\frac{7}{2}, \frac{3}{2}, -\frac{1}{2}, 2$	$-\frac{3}{2}, \frac{1}{2}, -\frac{1}{2}, 0$	
Equation from which current basic variable is to be removed	2	3	1	
P matrix	$\frac{3}{2}, \frac{1}{2}, \frac{1}{2}, 0$	$\frac{7}{4}, -\frac{3}{4}, \frac{1}{4}, \frac{1}{2}$	3, 2, 1, 0	
Comments	(a)	(b) (c)	(d)	(e)

(a) Z is implicitly in the basis.

(b) Note that the reduced costs refer to variables 2, 3 and 5, that is the variables not in the basis in order.

(c) We are now apparently feasible in that the constant terms are all positive, but we are not genuinely so since x_6, the artificial variable, is still in the basis. We choose c to force x_6 to zero.

(d) We are now genuinely feasible and can drop x_6 if we wish to.

(e) The optimum has been reached. It is $Z = \frac{73}{2}$ when $x_1 = \frac{13}{2}$, $x_2 = \frac{7}{2}$, $x_3 = x_4 = 0$, $x_5 = \frac{15}{2}$.

The full working for iteration 3 follows:

The new constant terms are $\mathbf{P}_2$ times the old constant ones, that is

$$\begin{pmatrix} 1 & 0 & 0 & \frac{7}{4} \\ 0 & 1 & 0 & -\frac{3}{4} \\ 0 & 0 & 1 & \frac{1}{4} \\ 0 & 0 & 0 & \frac{1}{2} \end{pmatrix} \begin{pmatrix} 13 \\ 9 \\ 1 \\ 7 \end{pmatrix} = \begin{pmatrix} 13 + \frac{49}{4} \\ 9 - \frac{21}{4} \\ 1 + \frac{7}{4} \\ \frac{7}{2} \end{pmatrix} = \begin{pmatrix} \frac{101}{4} \\ \frac{15}{4} \\ \frac{11}{4} \\ \frac{7}{2} \end{pmatrix}$$

The simple form of the **P**'s allows such calculations to be performed more quickly than by full matrix multiplication.

The current simplex multipliers are

$$(1 \quad 0 \quad 0 \quad 0)\mathbf{P}_2\mathbf{P}_1$$

$$= (1 \quad 0 \quad 0 \quad 0)\begin{pmatrix} 1 & 0 & 0 & \frac{7}{4} \\ 0 & 1 & 0 & -\frac{3}{4} \\ 0 & 0 & 1 & \frac{1}{4} \\ 0 & 0 & 0 & \frac{1}{2} \end{pmatrix}\begin{pmatrix} 1 & 0 & -\frac{3}{2} & 0 \\ 0 & 1 & \frac{1}{2} & 0 \\ 0 & 0 & -\frac{1}{2} & 0 \\ 0 & 0 & 0 & 1 \end{pmatrix}$$

$$= (1 \quad 0 \quad 0 \quad \tfrac{7}{4})\begin{pmatrix} 1 & 0 & -\frac{3}{2} & 0 \\ 0 & 1 & \frac{1}{2} & 0 \\ 0 & 0 & -\frac{1}{2} & 0 \\ 0 & 0 & 0 & 1 \end{pmatrix}$$

$$= (1, \quad 0, -\tfrac{3}{2}, \quad \tfrac{7}{4})$$

Again, these are actually calculated more quickly than by full matrix multiplication.

The reduced costs for variables 3 and 5, the non-basic ones, are worked out using the simplex multipliers. Column 3, referring to the original formulation, is

$$\begin{pmatrix} -1 \\ 1 \\ 0 \\ 1 \end{pmatrix} \text{ so it prices out at}$$

$$(1, 0, -\tfrac{3}{2}, \tfrac{7}{2})\begin{pmatrix} -1 \\ 1 \\ 0 \\ 1 \end{pmatrix} = -1 + \tfrac{7}{4} = \tfrac{3}{4}$$

Column 5 prices out at

$$(1, 0, -\tfrac{3}{2}, \tfrac{7}{4})\begin{pmatrix} 0 \\ 0 \\ 1 \\ 0 \end{pmatrix} = -\tfrac{3}{2}$$

The pivot column is the 5th (it is the only one with a negative reduced cost) and its elements are determined by

$$\mathbf{P}_2\mathbf{P}_1\begin{pmatrix} 0 \\ 0 \\ 1 \\ 0 \end{pmatrix}$$

that is

$$\begin{pmatrix} 1 & 0 & 0 & \frac{7}{4} \\ 0 & 1 & 0 & -\frac{3}{4} \\ 0 & 0 & 1 & \frac{1}{4} \\ 0 & 0 & 0 & \frac{1}{2} \end{pmatrix} \begin{pmatrix} 1 & 0 & -\frac{3}{2} & 0 \\ 0 & 1 & \frac{1}{2} & 0 \\ 0 & 0 & -\frac{1}{2} & 0 \\ 0 & 0 & 0 & 1 \end{pmatrix} \begin{pmatrix} 0 \\ 0 \\ 1 \\ 0 \end{pmatrix}$$

$$= \begin{pmatrix} 1 & 0 & 0 & \frac{7}{4} \\ 0 & 1 & 0 & -\frac{3}{4} \\ 0 & 0 & 1 & \frac{1}{4} \\ 0 & 0 & 0 & \frac{1}{2} \end{pmatrix} \begin{pmatrix} -\frac{3}{2} \\ \frac{1}{2} \\ -\frac{1}{2} \\ 0 \end{pmatrix} = \begin{pmatrix} -\frac{3}{2} \\ \frac{1}{2} \\ -\frac{1}{2} \\ 0 \end{pmatrix}$$

Again, the simple form of the **P**'s allows quick processing. We calculate

$$\frac{101/4}{-3/2}, \frac{15/4}{1/2}, \frac{11/4}{1/2}, \frac{1/2}{0}$$

and take the smallest positive one to find the pivot row. Obviously it is the 2nd, that is row 1 (remembering that the rows are numbered 0, 1, 2, 3). Finally the elements of P_3 are summarized by its 2nd row, row 1, and are

$$\frac{-(-3/2)}{1/2}, \frac{1/1}{2}, \frac{-(-1/2)}{1/2}, \frac{-0/1}{2}$$

that is the element of the pivot row divided by minus the pivot element—the one common to pivot row and column—except that the pivot element does not divide itself but is inverted.

The reader will find it instructive to work this example by the ordinary simplex method. He might also care to solve the earlier examples using the revised simplex method.

Some computational points

The working of a small example by the revised simplex method obscures its main advantages over the ordinary simplex methods, indeed it tends to make the revised method look far more complicated. The reasons the revised simplex is much to be preferred are actually not theoretical ones so much as practical ones. They stem from the fact that all the calculations are performed on the coefficients in the original equations. In a computer this gives considerable advantages in storing data (the **P**'s are much easier and less costly of space to store than would be the task of storing the updated coefficients at each iteration). Moreover, and this is perhaps the main advantage, the original coefficients often include a great many zeros; it is not uncommon to find 95% of the coefficients zero in large scale practical applications. Unfortunately the ordinary simplex method tends to introduce progressively more non-zero coefficients with each iteration, increasing both the storage space required and the arithmetic since the computer can be programmed to ignore zero coefficients.

There are a number of dodges, some of which are included in most computer packages, to cut computing time even further. Most of these are rather specialized points and we will not go into them, but an example might help to give the feel of things.

So far we have assumed all the reduced costs are updated at each iteration but this is rather time-consuming. In fact, we can often save some computing time by updating until we come to the first negative reduced cost and use this to define the variable to be made basic at this iteration. Alternatively we might stop at the first a_{oi} which is less than -1, or some other number. Some computer codes save time by selecting several negative reduced costs and doing a small ordinary simplex on the corresponding variables.

One or two other points seem to be worth mentioning as they may help to clarify the reasons for a number of practical points which are often quoted. For example, it should now be clear why the number of non-zero coefficients in the original equations is important, and why the number of constraints is more important than the number of variables. Empirical evidence suggests in fact that the time taken to solve a linear programming problem is roughly proportional to m^3.

One can also see how it is that we can easily add more variables to an already solved problem. Let $\mathbf{Q}$ be the final inverse so that

$$\mathbf{QA_0} \begin{bmatrix} Z \\ x_1 \\ \cdot \\ \cdot \\ \cdot \\ x_n \\ -1 \end{bmatrix} = 0$$

gives the solution to the problem.

Suppose we introduce some new variable x_{n+1}, pre-multiplied by $\mathbf{B_0}$, into the original equations. Then

$$\mathbf{Q[A_0 B_0]} \begin{bmatrix} Z \\ \cdot \\ \cdot \\ \cdot \\ x_n \\ -1 \\ x_{n+1} \end{bmatrix} = 0$$

will not in general now define an optimal basis but it will define a feasible basis from which we can start a new set of iterations. Thus we avoid having to start again with all the time that would involve.

This last point is fairly closely related to the important practical device of declaring an initial feasible basis to start the simplex form. If one can name m variables which one can say will yield a feasible basis it will usually pay to start calculations from this basis, thereby avoiding the first stage of the simplex method altogether. There is no need to be certain that the declared basis will be feasible, although it will help if it is not too badly infeasible. Such a basis might be, say, present policy or perhaps the basis found in an earlier problem which has now been slightly modified.

Computer packages are geared to invert immediately to any declared basis. This they do by inverting the relevant matrix by exactly similar methods to those described above (that is by generating elementary matrices of the **P**-type) but with an important difference: we can invert the matrix in whatever manner suits us—we need not bother with feasibility on the way. A much more efficient inversion can often be obtained than would result from following the steps of the simplex method.

In just the same way some packages occasionally re-invert the matrix. Perhaps the number of **P**'s being stored gets excessive. The current basis is known to be feasible. We therefore re-invert to it as efficiently as possible, almost certainly finishing up with many fewer **P**'s than before.

Duality

Consider the following problem, which we shall call the primal:

Maximize Z for non-negative $x_1, x_2, \ldots, x_{n+m}$ subject to

$$
\left.
\begin{aligned}
Z + c_1 x_1 + \ldots + c_n x_n &= (bc) \\
a_{1,1} x_1 + \ldots + a_{1,n} x_n + x_{n+1} &= b_1 \\
\cdots \qquad\qquad \cdots \qquad\qquad & \\
a_{m,1} x_1 + \ldots + a_{m,n} x_n \qquad\quad + x_{n+m} &= b_m
\end{aligned}
\right\} \quad (2.38)
$$

$x_{n+1}, x_{n+2}, \ldots, x_{n+m}$ being slack variables. (The reader should convince himself that this formulation is a completely general one. Note that any of the b's can be negative and that an equality constraint, for example

$$x_1 + x_2 = 10$$

can always be replaced by two equalities involving slack variables x_s and and x_{s+1} thus: $x_1 + x_2 + x_s = 10$, $-x_1 - x_2 + x_{s+1} = -10$.)

To this problem there corresponds what is called its dual problem, namely:

Maximize U for non-negative $y_1, y_2, \ldots, y_{n+m}$ subject to

$$
\left.
\begin{aligned}
U + b_1 y_1 + \ldots + b_m y_m &= -(bc) \\
- a_{1,1} y_1 - \ldots - a_{m,1} y_m + y_{m+1} &= +c_1 \\
\cdots \qquad\qquad \cdots \qquad\qquad & \\
- a_{1,n} y_1 - \ldots - a_{m,n} y_m \qquad + y_{n+m} &= +c_n
\end{aligned}
\right\} \quad (2.39)
$$

Note the way the dual is set up and particularly the signs of the various coefficients. Note too that the dual of the dual is the primal.

Suppose we were to rewrite equations (2.38), by solving them in terms of Z and a different m of the x's. This rewritten problem would also have a dual. We leave the reader to satisfy himself that the dual of the rewritten problem is in fact the dual problem rewritten. Now suppose equations (2.38) were the final tableau for the primal problem, so that $c_1, c_2, \ldots, c_n, b_1, b_2, \ldots, b_m$ were all non-negative. Then equations (2.39) would be the final tableau of the dual problem. It follows, then, that $\max Z = -\max U = (bc)$ if equations (2.38) and (2.39) are the final tableaux. Moreover the values of the y's which maximize U are the reduced costs and shadow prices in the primal and vice versa. Thus if we can solve the dual we have solved the primal. This fact might be useful if, for example, the number of rows in the primal is much greater than the number of non-slack variables, for the dual will then have fewer rows than the primal and will be quicker to solve. In extreme cases the number of rows in the primal might exceed the maximum number of rows that can be handled by the available computer which in turn exceeds the number of rows in the dual; in this case the problem can be solved only by solving the dual.

We note in passing that if the primal is infeasible the dual is unbounded and if the primal is bounded the dual is infeasible. This follows because the primal is infeasible if no rewriting of its equations gives non-negative values to $b_1, b_2, \ldots, b_m$ which is just the condition that the dual should be unbounded. Similar remarks apply to the other results.

The dual problem has a certain economic significance. Suppose we have n resources of which resource i is a typical one and m products of which product j is a typical one. Let b_i be the availability of resource i, a_{ij} the units of i required to make one unit of product j, $-c_j$ the profit from producing one unit of j, and x_j the number of units or j produced.

The primal problem is, therefore, one of deciding how to maximize profit of a production plant with limited availability of resources. The fact that the c's are fixed implies that one is selling the products j in a market where "pure competition" exists, that is many production plants make the products j and no single plant is capable of influencing the selling price, and that the marginal costs of production are independent of the level of production.

In the dual problem the meaning of the a's, b's and c's is unchanged. However it is necessary to put a meaning to the y's. Since the dimensions of the a's are [units of i/unit of j] and of the c's are [£/unit of j], the y's must have dimensions [£/unit of i]. It is therefore possible to interpret the y's as values on the resources and $(-U)$ will be the total value attached to all the available resources.

The dual problem can then be interpreted as how to minimize the total value placed on resources, whilst ensuring that values are allotted to the individual resources in such a way that the total value of resources used to make any product j is at least as great as the profit to be obtained from producing j.

One should note that the y's are not the actual costs of the resources, they are values that can be attached to the resources when they have given availabilities for the particular production plant in question. The values of the non-slack y's in the final tableau are, of course, the shadow prices discussed earlier. The reader will therefore readily convince himself that they represent opportunity costs, that is the cost in loss of profit, from not fully utilizing an available scarce resource. The values of any slack y's in the final tableau are the reduced costs of non-slacks in the final tableau in the primal. They also represent opportunity costs but in a different sense: the profit forgone by making an unprofitable product.

This interpretation of the dual has special application in economic theory where it is used in connection with Leontief and similar models of the economy.

Two alternative methods to the simplex method have been proposed for solving the standard linear programming problem, both of which are based on the dual.

The dual simplex algorithm (2) eliminates the need for artificial variables. It starts with a basic solution which satisfies the conditions for optimality in the ordinary simplex tableau (that is all reduced costs are non-negative) but which is not necessarily feasible. Such a solution is said to be dual feasible; the dual to the solution is feasible but not optimal. From this solution it works toward feasibility (keeping the optimality conditions satisfied at each stage) by replacing the variables in the solution one at a time as in the original simplex technique. The criteria for choosing the variables are based on considerations from the dual problem; we keep the dual feasible and work towards its optimality and the primal's feasibility.

The primal-dual method (3) still requires the use of artificial variables in the primal. It is designed so that the process of reducing the artificial variables to zero is accompanied by a positive movement towards optimality so that by the time the last of the artificial variables has been removed the solution is optimal. Again the criterion used for choosing the variables to replace the artificial variables is based on considerations from the dual problem.

Neither of these methods is much used in practice because of the computational superiority of the revised simplex method, although the basic ideas of the dual simplex method are used in some mixed integer methods (see below).

Transportation problems

Transportation problems are a class of linear programming problems whose symmetry makes them suitable for solution by simpler and more compact methods than the simplex method. They were first studied and solved by Hitchcock (4) before more general linear programming problems.

Consider the following problem. A product is available in known quantities at each of m sources. Specified amounts are required at each of n sinks and the cost of supplying a unit of product from each source to each sink is known. The problem is to determine the pattern of distribution from sources to sinks which minimizes the total cost.

Suppose that the amount available at the ith source is a_i $(i = 1, \ldots, m)$ and the amount required at each sink is b_j $(j = 1, \ldots, n)$. The cost of supplying one unit from source i to sink j is c_{ij}. The problem is to find those x_{ij} (the quantity flowing from source i to sink j) which minimize the total cost.

We assume that

$$a_1 + a_2 + \ldots + a_m = b_1 + b_2 + \ldots + b_n$$

that is the same total amount is available at the sources as is required at the sinks. The problem is a linear programming problem:

Maximize Z for non-negative values of $x_{11}, x_{12}, \ldots, x_{mn}$ subject to

$$Z + c_{11}x_{11} + \ldots + c_{1n}x_{1n} + \ldots + c_{m1}x_{m1} + \ldots + c_{mn}x_{mn} = 0$$

$$
\left.
\begin{array}{l}
x_{11} + \ldots + x_{1n} = a_1 \\
\qquad \cdots \qquad\qquad \cdots \\
\qquad\qquad\qquad\qquad x_{m1} + \ldots + x_{mn} = a_m \\
x_{11} \qquad\quad + x_{21} \qquad + \ldots + x_{m1} = b_1 \\
\qquad \cdots \qquad\qquad \cdots \\
x_{1n} \qquad\quad + x_{2n} \qquad + \ldots + x_{mn} = b_n
\end{array}
\right\}
$$

$$(2.40)$$

The equations, apart from the first, reflect the fact that each source/sink can only supply/receive exactly as much as is available/required.

Note that all coefficients of the variables are either 0 or 1 and that each variable appears with a non-zero coefficient in only two constraints.

Note that this notation (which is standard for transportation problems) is slightly different from that we have used in the discussion so far. It should become apparent why this notation is used when we get onto formulating the problem in the transportation tableau. Also note that we are using words (such as source, sink and flow) which apparently have some meaning in a physical sense. These words are the standard jargon in which the transportation problem is discussed, but the formulation can be used for a wider range of problems.

Before we discuss how to solve the transportation problem, we shall state some results which are useful in examining it.

A feasible solution exists because a feasible (although non-basic) solution can be constructed by writing

$$x_{ij} = \frac{a_i b_j}{A}$$

where $A = a_1 + a_2 + \ldots + a_m$
$\qquad\quad = b_1 + b_2 + \ldots + b_n$

Moreover all feasible solutions are finite. This follows immediately from equations (2.40) because no x_{ij} can be negative and therefore no x_{ij} can be greater than a_i or b_j.

A basic feasible solution contains at most $m + n - 1$ variables in solution, not counting Z. This is perhaps surprising as there are $(m + n + 1)$ constraints and therefore one might expect $(m + n)$ of the x's in a basic feasible solution. However, one constraint is redundant. One can demonstrate this by adding together the first m of equations (2.40) and subtracting the next $n - 1$ equations. We are left with the $(m + n)$th equation. So only $m + n - 1$ of the x's can be in a basis. Note that, $m + n - 1 < mn$ for all values of m and

n greater than 1 (when the problem is trivial). This means that there are several basic feasible solutions, so that we need to search for the optimum.

We also note that every basic feasible solution has integral values, provided that all a_i, b_j are integers. A basic feasible solution has $(m + n)$ variables at most in solution. Select any $(m + n - 1)$ variables in the simplex tableau and set all others to zero. One variable is immediately determined and all the others can be derived by addition or subtraction. Since all the a_i and b_j values are integer, then so are all of the x_{ij} values in this basic feasible solution.

We could, of course, solve the problem using the simplex method. However, the symmetry of equations (2.40) leads one to suspect that a simpler method might be found and indeed there are several simpler methods. We illustrate one such but first briefly consider the theory upon which it is based.

Suppose we put equations (2.40) into canonical form with respect to Z and $m + n - 1$ of the x's of which x_{ij} is one. In order to do this we shall need to have subtracted from the last of equations (2.40) either a multiple of the ith of equations (2.40), or a multiple of the $(m + j)$th or some combination of the two since they are the only equations which contain x_{ij}. Suppose, in fact, we subtracted $U_i x$ the ith equation and $V_j x$ the jth equation. Then $U_i + V_j$ must equal c_{ij}. Now there must be at least one basic variable in every one of equations (2.40). Thus there are numbers $U_1, U_2, \ldots, U_m, V_1, V_2, \ldots, V_n$ corresponding to the $(m + n)$ equations and they are linked by $m + n - 1$ equations of the form $U_i + V_j = C_{ij}$ if x_{ij} is one of the $m + n - 1$ x's in the basis.

These equations can be readily solved for the U's and V's by giving one of them an arbitrary value and inferring the rest by addition and subtraction. Moreover, if x_{rs} is not a basic variable, its reduced cost is $C_{rs} - U_r - V_s$. Thus if we can find a basic feasible solution of equations (2.40) (and in practice we can easily do so, as will be seen presently) we can readily find the reduced costs of the non-basic variables and thus decide whether we have an optimal solution or, if not, which variable to bring into the basis. Finally in these brief remarks on the theory of the transportation technique, we note that as long as we identify the basic variables there is little point in not retaining the equations in their original form throughout the solution of the problem; for when we have reached an optimal solution it will be easy enough to put the non-basic variables equal to zero and solve the equations for the basic variables (only addition and subtraction will be involved); and the decision about how large the variable to enter the basis can be made without losing feasibility should be fairly easily made by examining the equations owing to their straightforward form. To solve the problem manually it is convenient to keep the equations in tabular form as at the top of page 31.

The method of solution will be illustrated by the following simple example:

There are three collieries which can supply coal. Colliery 1 can supply 6 tonnes, Colliery 2 10 tonnes and Colliery 3 15 tonnes (total supply being 31 tonnes). There are three consumers. Consumer 1 requires 14 tonnes, Consumer 2 12 tonnes and Consumer 3 5 tonnes (total requirements being 31 tonnes).

Sinks

	1	2	$\cdots$		n	Total
1	x_{11} c_{11}	x_{12} c_{12}	$\cdots$		x_{1n} c_{1n}	a_1
2	x_{21} c_{21}	x_{22} c_{22}	$\cdots$		x_{2n} c_{2n}	a_2
Sources . . .	. . .	. . .	. . .		. . .	. . .
m	x_{m1} c_{m1}	x_{m2} c_{m2}	$\cdots$	x_{mj} c_{mj}	x_{mn} c_{mn}	a_m
Total	b_1	b_2	$\cdots$	b_j	b_n	A

The costs for transporting 1 tonne of coal from each colliery to each consumer (in £'s) are given in the following table:

Consumers (Sinks)

		1	2	3
Collieries (Sources)	1	6	8	4
	2	4	3	9
	3	1	2	6

If x_{ij} represents the amount of coal flow from colliery i (source i) to consumer j (sink j), it is clear that the problem of minimizing the total transport cost can be formulated as a transportation problem; $m = n = 3$, $a_1 = 6$, $a_2 = 10$, $a_2 = 15$, etc. We set up a table as at the top of page 32.

We must now find a first basic feasible solution to the problem. One systematic method of obtaining such a solution is known as the North West Corner rule. A start is made by allocating as much as possible to the route in the top left-hand corner (i.e. $x_{11} = \min(a_1, b_1)$). In the example $x_{11} = a_1 = 6$. The next stage is to consider x_{12} and x_{21} and allocate to whichever of these is available the maximum possible. In the example because $x_{11} = a_1$, $x_{12} = 0$ and $x_{21} = \min(a_2, b_1 - a_1)$. x_{22} is then considered and the maximum possible allocated to it. This process continues in a similar fashion until all the coal has been allocated. The result of this procedure is shown in the second table on page 32, zero values of x_{ij} being omitted.

Sinks

		1	2	3	Total
Sources	1	x_{11} 6	x_{12} 8	x_{13} 4	6
	2	x_{21} 4	x_{22} 9	x_{23} 3	10
	3	x_{31} 1	x_{32} 2	x_{33} 6	15
	Total	14	12	5	31

Sinks

		1	2	3	Total
Sources	1	6 6	8	4	6
	2	8 4	2 9	3	10
	3	1	10 2	5 6	15
	Total	14	12	5	31

Total cost of allocation

$$= 6 \times 6 + 8 \times 4 + 2 \times 9 + 10 \times 2 + 5 \times 6$$
$$= £136$$

We now determine the U's and V's. A convenient way of doing so is to imagine that the cost of transporting is made up of two part costs, a cost of despatch and a cost of reception. It is assumed that one of the costs of despatch is zero, say at source 1; then, according to the cost in cell 1, 1 (i.e. 6) the cost of reception at sink 1 must be 6. The cost in cell 2, 1 is 4 and thus the cost of despatch from source 2 is -2. This procedure is followed for cells in which there is an allocation so that all three costs of sending and the three costs of receiving are found. They are entered in the next table opposite.

The unused cells, corresponding to the non-basic variables, can now be considered. Where the sum of the receiving and sending costs for any un-used cell exceeds the true cost which is marked within the cell, there is a saving in cost to be made by using this so far unused cell. The variable corresponding to it has a negative reduced cost.

Next, goods are transferred into the unused cell which will give the largest saving; this is cell 1, 3 for which the reduced cost is $15 + 0 - 4 = 11$. Putting it another way, we bring $x_{1,3}$ into the basis. Suppose we give it a value θ. Then to maintain the row and column totals at their right values $x_{1,1}$ must be reduced to $6 - \theta$ and $x_{3,3}$ to $5 - \theta$; the new value of $x_{1,1}$ in turn implies that $x_{2,1}$ must be increased to $8 + \theta$; the new value of $x_{3,1}$ implies that $x_{3,2}$ must be increased to $10 + \theta$; and finally $x_{2,2}$ must be reduced to $2 - \theta$. This is shown in the next table. Now to retain feasibility, θ cannot exceed 2 otherwise $x_{2,2}$ will become negative. The new basic feasible solution would therefore be shown in the table if θ were given the value 2.

		a	b	c	Total
		6	11	15	
1	0	$6 - \theta$		$+\theta$ $\boxed{11}$ 4	6
2	-2	$8 + \theta$ 4	$2 - \theta$ 9	3	10
3	-9	1	$10 + \theta$ 2	$5 - \theta$ 6	15
Total		14	12	5	31

$\boxed{11}$ indicates sum of part costs exceeds actual cost by £11, i.e. total cost can be reduced by £11 $\times \theta$ (if a quantity θ is sent by route Ac). $\theta = 2$ tonnes. Total cost = £114.

Successive steps are carried out until all the real costs in the cells either equal or exceed the sum of the part costs for sending and receiving. When this state is reached the optimum solution has been achieved. Two steps are necessary to reach the optimum which is shown in the first table on page 34.

As an alternative to the north-west corner rule, the first non-degenerate basic feasible solution can be constructed by starting the allocation at the cell with the lowest cost and continuing to the cell with the next lowest cost, etc. A lower cost first solution is generally obtained by this rule than by the north-west corner rule. This is illustrated in the second table on page 34.

If at any stage of the computation the allocation uses less than $m + n - 1$ routes the problem is degenerate. With, for example, only $m + n - 2$ routes in use it is not possible to compute all the part costs. The difficulty is over-come by increasing the requirements of each customer by a very small quantity x and the production of any colliery by nx. There will always be $(m + n - 1)$ routes in use if the problem is worked with these slight adjustments. When the final answer has been obtained the x's are ignored. This is exactly analogous to degeneracy in the equivalent simplex problem.

		a	b	c	Total
		6	7	4	
1	0	1 (6)	(8)	5 (4)	6
2	-2	10 (4)	(9)	(3)	10
3	-5	3 (1)	12 (2)	(6)	15
Total		14	12	5	31

No further improvement possible. Minimum cost £93.

		a	b	c	Total
A		(6)	6 (8)	(4)	6
B		(4)	5 (9)	5 (3)	10
C		14 (1)	1 (2)	(6)	15
Total		14	12	5	31

Step 1. Basic feasible solution by commencing the allocation at the cell with the lowest cost and continuing the next lowest cost cell, etc. Total cost = £124.

Two simple devices for extending the range of problems which can be tackled as transportation problems are worth mentioning.

If the total that can be sent exceeds the total that is required then we can introduce a dummy sink which requires the difference. The transport costs to this sink are all zero. Similarly if the total requirement is greater we can introduce a dummy source. These devices are simply adding appropriate slack variables.

The situation can also arise in which one or more routes are not allowable, perhaps because of some physical constraint (the lorries from colliery 1 cannot be unloaded at consumer 3, for example). In this case one simply puts a very high cost on such routes to prevent the relevant variable entering the solution.

If a problem can be formulated as a transportation problem it should be solved as such. The transportation technique is quicker than the simplex and it also requires less computer storage, indeed on any given computer a much larger transportation problem can be solved than an ordinary linear programming problem.

Many problems which are not self-evidently transportation problems can nevertheless be formulated as such. One example is the problem of planning production to meet a known but varying daily demand. The product can be made in ordinary time at a unit cost c_1, say, but there is a limit, C_1 say, on the quantity of production; c_2 and C_2 are corresponding figures for overtime. A cost c_3 per unit per day is associated with holding the product in stock. Daily demands are $d_1, d_2, \ldots, d_n$. This can be set up as a transportation problem. The sources are ordinary time production on day 1, day 2, $\ldots$, day n and overtime production on day 1, day 2, $\ldots$, day n; the sinks are demands on day 1, day 2, $\ldots$, day n. The availabilities are severally C_1, C_2 and the requirements $d_1, d_2, \ldots, d_n$. The costs are $c_1 + c_3(i - j)$ from ordinary production on day j to demand on day i and $c_2 + c_3(i - j)$ from overtime production as long as $i \geqslant j$. If $i < j$ the costs are made prohibitively large.

A second example is the ordinary transportation problem complicated by there being alternative methods (say road and rail) of transport with different costs and moreover capacity restrictions on some or all methods at some or all sinks and sources. This may be formulated as a transportation problem by introducing for each true source artificial sinks, one for each method of transport and each requiring the capacity for the relevant method at that source. These artificial sinks are also sources in the tableau. Likewise artificial sources are introduced at each true sink and they in turn are also sinks in the tableau. We assign zero costs to a true source supplying its artificial sinks and to a true sink being supplied by its artificial sources. All other flows are inhibited by assigning them very high costs except flows between the artificial sinks treated as sources and the artificial sources treated as sinks which are assigned the original costs.

Post-optimality analysis and parametric programming

One is frequently interested in practical linear programming in the way changes in either the coefficients of the objective function or in the constant terms in each constraint affect the optimal solution. Some general idea can be obtained by using the techniques of post-optimality analysis.

To take a simple example suppose we want to maximize Z where

$$
\begin{aligned}
Z - 6x_1 - 2x_2 - 3x_3 &= 4 \\
x_1 + x_2 + x_3 + x_4 &= 7 \\
- x_2 + 6x_3 + x_5 &= 5 \\
x_1 - 2x_2 + 3x_3 + x_6 &= 14
\end{aligned} \right\} \tag{2.41}
$$

The optimal solution is

$$
\begin{aligned}
Z + 4x_2 + 3x_3 + 6x_4 &= 46 \\
x_1 + x_2 + x_3 + x_4 &= 7 \\
- x_2 + 6x_3 + x_5 &= 5 \\
- 3x_2 + 2x_3 - x_4 + x_6 &= 7
\end{aligned} \right\} \tag{2.42}
$$

The shadow prices or simplex multipliers on the rows are 6, 0, 0 (the co-efficients of the slack variables in the final expression for Z). This tells us that if we increased the right hand sides in the original equations from 7, 5, 14 to $7 + a$, $5 + b$, $14 + c$ (where a, b and c are small) the optimal value of the objective function would be increased to $46 + 6a + 0b + 0c$. We can go a bit further than this. The constant terms in the final tableau would be $7 + a$, $5 + b$, $7 + c - a$. The reader might care to check this and to satisfy himself that it is easy for these figures to be generated in a computer code. We can now ask: by how much can a, b and c vary independently before the optimal policy changes? (The word policy is used to mean which variables are in the basis, as opposed to the word solution which is taken to mean the values these variables have at the optimum.) The policy would change if variation in a, b or c led to one of the constants becoming negative; changes in the constant terms can affect feasibility but not optimality. In this case a can vary between -7 and $+7$, b from -5 upwards and c from -7 upwards. We can also say which variables would need to enter the basis if any limit were slightly exceeded. In the case of $a = +7$, x_2 would enter the basis, x_2 being the choice because it has a negative coefficient and the least ratio, among those variables in that row which have negative coefficients, of reduced cost to minus the coefficient. The case $a = -7$ is rather special because the problem is then infeasible; no x_1, x_2, x_3's satisfy the revised constraints.

Similarly we can examine the effect of changes in the coefficients of the objective function. Indeed this is just the dual problem to the above. Note here that the changes have no effect on feasibility but can affect optimality. Putting it another way, dual feasibility is lost. The processes described above are often referred to as carrying out a post-optimality analysis.

Parametric programming is a simple extension of these ideas. It is simply ordinary linear programming in which either one or more of the constant terms in the original equations or one or more of the coefficients in the objective function are allowed to vary between fixed limits. The maximum value of the objective function is determined over the range of variation.

A practical example is that one of the restrictions might be how much capital is available. We want to know how maximum profit varies as capital availability varies, perhaps to see at what level of capital investment the marginal return on capital reaches some value of interest. Another example might be that in our objective function the costs are actually met in different currencies. We suspect one of these currencies may be revalued by up to 15%. We wish to know how any revaluation in this range affects our optimum policy and our profits.

In the first case, call it case (a), we simply formulate our capital availability constraint with a right hand side $b + y$ where b is the lowest capital availability and y the range of variation. If several right hand sides interest us simultaneously the formulation is $b + yb^1$ where b and b^1 are vectors. Note we allow only one variable, y. The right hand sides must vary in step.

In the second case, case (b), we wish to vary some terms in the objective function, which is

$$\sum_{i=1}^{n} c_i x_2$$

say. We work instead with an objective function

$$\sum_{i=1}^{n} (c_i + y c_i^1) x_i$$

with c_i^1 defined to suit our purpose.

In both cases suppose we have an optimal solution to the problem with $y = 0$.

In case (a) the value of y has no effect on optimality (that is to say, the current basis remains an optimal basis—the actual values taken by the variables in the optimal basis do, of course, change), but, as y increases from 0, we might lose feasibility. Now the coefficient of y in the final right-hand sides is easily determined, particularly using the revised simplex method in which case one simply multiplies the final inverse into b^1. What we then do is to find the smallest value of y which would cause one of the final constant terms to go negative. We then pivot on that row, the pivot column being selected as indicated above, and then increase y again till the next infeasibility arises. Between successive values of y which cause infeasibility, the optimum value of the objective function is linear.

In case (b) as y increases there is no loss of feasibility but optimality might be lost. y is increased until a reduced cost becomes negative, this defines the pivot column and the simplex method proceeds in the ordinary way. An example might help to clarify the approach of parametric programming on the objective function.

Let us suppose we have the problem defined by equations (2.41) but wish to maximize, for $0 \leqslant v \leqslant 10$,

$$\begin{aligned} z(v) &= 6x_1 + 2x_2 + 3x_3 + v(x_1 + 2x_3) + 4 \\ &= (6 + v)x_1 + 2x_2 + (3 + 2v)x_3 + 4 \end{aligned} \qquad (2.43)$$

It is helpful to define x_0 and x_{-1} by

$$\left. \begin{aligned} x_0 \ - 6x_1 - 2x_2 - 3x_3 &= 4 \\ x_{-1} - \ x_1 \qquad\quad - 2x_3 &= 0 \end{aligned} \right\} \qquad (2.44)$$

(x_0 is the normal objective function. x_{-1}, which must never enter the basis, defines an extra row in the problem and is there so that we can keep its coefficients updated as necessary). The full initial problem is thus

$$
\left.
\begin{aligned}
x_0 \quad - 6x_1 - 2x_2 - 3x_3 \qquad\qquad &= 4 \\
x_{-1} - \quad x_1 \qquad\; - 2x_3 \qquad\qquad &= 0 \\
x_1 + \; x_2 + \; x_3 + x_4 \qquad\qquad &= 7 \\
- \; x_2 + 6x_3 \qquad + x_5 \qquad &= 5 \\
- 2x_2 + 3x_3 \qquad\qquad + x_6 &= 14
\end{aligned}
\right\} \quad (2.45)
$$

and, for $v = 0$, the final tableau is

$$
\left.
\begin{aligned}
x_0 \qquad\quad + 4x_2 + 3x_3 + 6x_4 \qquad\qquad &= 46 \\
x_{-1} \qquad + \; x_2 - \; x_3 + \; x_4 \qquad\qquad &= 7 \\
x_1 + \; x_2 + \; x_3 + \; x_4 \qquad\qquad &= 7 \\
- \; x_2 + 6x_3 \qquad + x_5 \qquad &= 5 \\
- 3x_2 + 2x_3 - \; x_4 \qquad + x_6 &= 7
\end{aligned}
\right\} \quad (2.46)
$$

Now

$$Z = x_0 + vx_{-1} = 46 - [(4 + v)x_2 + (3 - v)x_3 + (6 + v)x_4]$$

This solution is optimal until $v = 3$. Put $v = 3 + w$ and our Z row becomes

$$Z + (7 + w)x_2 - wx_3 + (9 + w)x_4 = 67 + 7w$$

We must now put x_3 into the basis, choosing which variable to remove from the basis in the usual way. In this case it is x_5, giving a new tableau:

$$
\left.
\begin{aligned}
Z \qquad + \left(7 + \frac{5}{6}w\right)x_2 \qquad + (9 + w)x_4 + \frac{w}{6}x_5 \qquad &= 67 + \frac{5}{6}w \\
x_1 + \frac{7}{6}x_2 \qquad\qquad + x_4 \qquad \frac{1}{6}x_5 \qquad &= \frac{37}{6} \\
- \frac{1}{6}x_2 + x_3 \qquad\qquad + \frac{1}{6}x_5 \qquad &= \frac{5}{6} \\
- \frac{3}{8}x_2 \qquad\qquad + x_4 \qquad \frac{1}{3}x_5 + x_6 &= \frac{16}{3}
\end{aligned}
\right\}
$$

$$(2.47)$$

No matter how big we make w this solution will remain optimal. The way $Z(v)$ varies with v is shown in Figure 2.2.

This is, of course, rather a trivial example. In practice with a large problem a parametric programming exercise might involve several 10's of iterations.

Parametric programming both on the objective function and on the right hand side are standard features of any good computer code.

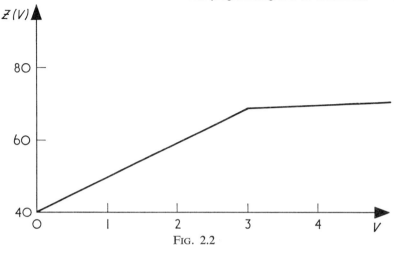

FIG. 2.2

Decomposition

The decomposition method (5) is suitable for solving linear programming problems in which the original tableau has this schematic form:

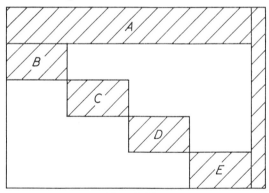

FIG. 2.2A

where the non-shaded areas include only zero coefficients. (The shaded column on the right represents non-zero right hand sides.) Such tableaux arise very frequently in large scale applications. The rectangles B, C, D and E might, for example, be linear programming models for four factories which go to make up a single firm; the rectangle A then might represent the constraints for the firm as a whole on certain resources (typically capital available or total markets, etc.). Another possibility is that B, C, D and E might be linear programming models for the four quarters of a year for one factory while A represents the constraints linking the quarters (for example, that stock at the end of one quarter is starting stock for the next).

Rather than solve the whole problem in one go it is tempting to think one might be able to solve each of the smaller problems corresponding to the factories and somehow to combine these to provide a solution for the whole. The decomposition method makes use of this idea. It makes use of one new mathematical idea which is perhaps best illustrated in practical terms first.

Let us think of a concrete practical example. Suppose you are at the firm's headquarters and you have to produce the optimum plan for the whole firm. There is just one restriction for the firm as a whole, namely on capital available, otherwise the individual factories can plan to attain their own optima. There is a linear programming expert at each factory and you ask the man for factory B to produce for you several (to make it specific say three) feasible plans which use different quantities of capital Q_1, Q_2 and Q_3, say. Then, and this is the important point, you can be sure that he can produce a feasible plan which uses a quantity of capital $y_1 Q_1 + y_2 Q_2 + y_3 Q_3$ for any set of non-negative numbers y_1, y_2 and y_3 which are such that

$$y_1 + y_2 + y_3 = 1$$

Moreover, if his plans showed profits P_1, P_2 and P_3 this plan would show a profit $y_1 P_1 + y_2 P_2 + y_3 P_3$. This is not too difficult to see. If the factory B expert has formulated his problem in the manner of equations (2.1) what we are saying is that if

$$(Z = P_1, \; x_1 = Q_1, \; x_2 = R_{12}, \ldots, \; x_n = R_{1n}),$$
$$(Z = P_2, \; x_1 = Q_2, \; n_2 = R_{22}, \ldots, \; x_n = R_{2n})$$

and

$$(Z = P_3, \; x_1 = Q_3, \; x_2 = R_{32}, \ldots, \; x_n = R_{3n})$$

each satisfies the equations, so does

$$(Z = y_1 P_1 + y_2 P_2 + y_3 P_3, \; x_1 = y_1 Q_1 + y_2 Q_2 + y_3 Q_3,$$
$$x_2 = y_1 R_{12} + y_2 R_{22} + y_3 R_{32}, \ldots, \; x_n = y_1 R_{1n} + y_2 R_{2n} + y_3 R_{3n}).$$

The reader will easily check this.

This is useful because it means that you at the central headquarters of the firm, given the factories submit a few plans, have only to choose the weights you will give to each to solve your problem. This is just a linear programming problem for you.

The decomposition method is not quite as simple as that because we have to ask two further questions: how does the man at factory B know which of the infinity of feasible plans for his factory to submit to us?; and how do we know when we have got enough?

One gets round these questions by calling systematically for plans one at a time at each stage asking the factory experts to put an artificial price (which is different from stage to stage) on the resources which are constrained for the problem as a whole: this can be thought of as an attempt to ration by price. At each stage the artificial price put on the constrained resources is the shadow price on that row in your problem at headquarters. This is sensible because the shadow price represents the opportunity cost of using that resource. One stops when a stage is reached at which none of the factory experts has a new proposal to make.

Consider a simple example which should clarify things and will also allow us to introduce some terminology.

Suppose we wish to maximize Z where

$$
\begin{array}{llr}
\text{Row 0} & Z - 15x_1 - 2x_2 - x_3 + 14x_4 & = 3 \\
1 & x_1 + x_2 + x_3 + x_4 + x_5 & = 10 \\
2 & 3x_1 + x_2 \qquad\qquad\qquad + x_6 & = 36 \\
3 & 7x_3 - x_4 \qquad\qquad + x_7 & = 9
\end{array}
$$

$$(2.48)$$

(Rows 0 and 1 are called the common rows. Row 2 represents constraint on factory B, say, and $x_1 + x_2$ is the call on the scarce resource governed by row 1 by factory B. Similarly row 3 is a constraint on factory C and $x_3 + x_4$ its call on the scarce resource.)

We now define two sub-problems, one for factory B and one for factory C. These are:

B Maximize Z_1 for non-negative x_1, x_2 subject to

$$
\left. \begin{array}{l}
z_1 - 15x_1 - 2x_2 + p(x_1 + x_2) = 0 \\
3x_1 + x_2 + x_6 = 36
\end{array} \right\}
$$

$$(2.49)$$

C Maximize Z_2 for non-negative x_3, x_4 subject to

$$
\left. \begin{array}{l}
z_2 - x_3 + 14x_4 + p(x_3 + x_4) = 0 \\
7x_3 - x_4 + x_7 = 9
\end{array} \right\}
$$

$$(2.50)$$

At any stage p is the price we are going to put on the scarce resource.

To make a start let us solve these problems for $p = 0$ and $p = 100$. This gives two proposals, as they are called, from each factory. For factory B the two solutions $z_1 = 180$, $x_1 = 12$, $x_2 = x_6 = 0$ and $z_1 = x_1 = x_2 = 0$, $x_6 = 36$; for factory C they are $z_2 = x_3 = \frac{9}{7}$, $x_4 = x_7 = 0$ and $z_2 = x_3 = x_4 = 0$, $x_7 = 9$.

These proposals are put up to headquarters and they can construct a master problem, as it is called:

Maximize Z for non-negative y_1, y_2, u_1, u_2 subject to

$$
\left. \begin{array}{llr}
\text{Row 0} & Z - 180y_1 - 0y_2 + \frac{9}{7}u_1 - 0u_2 & = 3 \\
1 & 12y_1 + 0y_2 + \frac{9}{7}u_1 + 0u_2 + x_5 & = 10 \\
2 & y_1 + y_2 & = 1 \\
3 & u_1 + u_2 & = 1
\end{array} \right\}
$$

$$(2.51)$$

In this master problem row 0 expresses the value of the objective function as a linear combination of the two proposals made from each factory and row 1 says how much of the scarce resource this combination of plans would use. Rows 2 and 3, usually called the convexity rows, simply restrict the linear combinations to feasible ones.

The solution to this master problem is $x_0 = 150$, $y_1 = \frac{5}{6}$, $y_2 = \frac{1}{6}$, $u_1 = 0$, $u_2 = 1$ and it puts a shadow price of 15 on row 1.

We must now invite fresh proposals from the factories based on the current shadow price of 15. This means solving

B Maximize Z_1 for non-negative x_1, x_2 subject to

$$\left. \begin{array}{l} z_1 - 15x_1 - 2x_2 + 15(x_1 + x_2) = z_1 + 13x_2 = 0 \\ 3x_1 + x_2 + x_6 = 36 \end{array} \right\} \qquad (2.52)$$

The solution is $z_1 = x_1 + x_2 = 0$, $x_6 = 36$.

C Maximize Z_2 for non-negative x_1, x_2 subject to

$$\left. \begin{array}{l} z_2 - x_3 + 14x_4 + 15(x_3 + x_4) = Z_2 + 14x_3 + 29x_4 = 0 \\ 7x_3 - x_4 + x_7 = 9 \end{array} \right\}$$

$$(2.53)$$

The solution is $z_2 = x_3 = x_4 = 0$, $x_7 = 9$.

This introduces no new proposals and the problem is solved. We can thus allocate $12y_1 + 0y_2 = 10$ of the scarce resource to factory B and none of it to factory C and be sure that if they optimize their own affairs the total firm optimum will be reached. This, of course, is an absurdly simple problem and the reader should satisfy himself that he could formulate the new master problem if a new proposal had been introduced. He might also care to check the solution by solving the problem in the ordinary way.

Suppose the original problem had $m_1 + 1$ common rows (including the objective function row) and m_2, m_3, . . ., m_k rows in the sub-problems. In computational terms the decomposition method substitutes one problem with $m_1 + m_2 + m_3 + \ldots + m_k + 1$ rows by a master problem with $2m_1 + 1$ rows and $k - 1$ sub-problems with $m_i + 1$ rows ($i = 2$, . . ., k). There is the need to solve each several times but each solution after the first at least starts from a feasible base. Just whether the decomposition method is any quicker than the more direct method depends on cases, but one point worth making is that the time taken to reach the optimum solution increases rapidly with the number of common rows.

A big appeal of the decomposition method is, of course, that it might at least provide a feasible way of handling problems otherwise too big to be dealt with.

Stochastic programming

It is very common in formulating linear programming problems to find that many of the "constant" terms are random variables. (The phrase constant term is used here not merely to mean the right hand sides of the original equations but all the coefficients in the initial tableau. Note that parametric programming is restricted to variations in the right hand side and the coefficients in the objective function.) For example, market sizes cannot usually be predicted accurately, blending problems are often concerned with products in which the proportion of a constituent substance varies, and so on. To some extent post-optimality analysis and parametric programming can contribute to the study of such problems, but generally speaking each problem has to be treated on its merits. Beale gives a number of illustrative examples (6).

It is probably worth mentioning some of the more important difficulties. One obvious point is that one has to decide what one is doing: for example what is one trying to maximize (expected values?), what view is one to take of breaking a constraint through chance phenomena?

There are other more technical questions. If some or all of the coefficients in the initial tableau are random variables and we have to nominate a solution before any of the actual values of the coefficients have manifested themselves we cannot even be sure our proposal will be feasible let alone optimal. Even to find the probability that the solution will be feasible is quite tricky. We might be able to specify a solution for which each of the constraints is satisfied with a high probability (chance constrained programming (7)) but this is likely to lead to very conservative policies.

If, however, we do not have to nominate a solution until all the actual values of the coefficients are known then the only problem is to predict the distribution of optimal values into the future. Here again quite large scale computation might be involved.

When some part of the solution has to be specified before any actual coefficients are known and other parts as they become known we are in the field of sequential stochastic programming. (An example problem is production planning through time. Initial plans have to be made in ignorance of stocks at the end of the first time period, these being generated by the effect of random demand. However what one actually does in the second time period can be decided, in the event, with a definite knowledge of the stocks.) Problems in this sort of field can be attacked using dynamic programming but again the computational load can be a big one.

Sensibly used, linear programming can undoubtedly be useful in situations of high variability. At least considerable insight into the situation can usually be obtained. But there is no doubt that the full power of linear programming is lost where variability abounds.

Separable programming

A great many mathematical programming problems cannot be realistically formulated as ordinary linear programs: costs are not always linear with throughput, production does not always increase linearly with manpower, and so on. Quadratic programming (6) may be helpful but is much less general of application than separable programming (8), which we shall discuss. Separable programming is a simple idea which is nevertheless a very powerful way of handling non-linearities in either the objective function or the constraints or both. What separable programming suggests is that the non-linear functions in the problem, should each be approximated by a series of lines, thus:

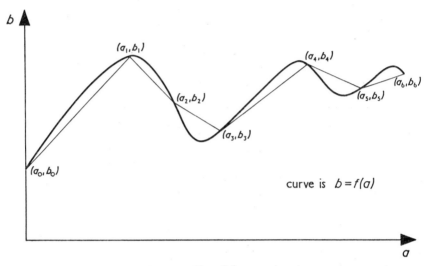

FIG. 2.3

If the end-points of the straight lines are at $(a_0, b_0 = f(a_0)) (a_1, b_1) \ldots (a_k, b_k)$ we simply introduce $(k + 1)$ new variables $y_0, y_1, \ldots, y_k$ and new constraints

$$
\left.
\begin{aligned}
y_0 + \quad y_1 + \ldots + y_k &= 1 \\
a_0 y_0 + a_1 y_1 + \ldots + a_k t_k &= x \\
b_0 y_0 + b_1 y_1 + \ldots + b_k y_k &= f(x)
\end{aligned}
\right\}
\qquad (2.54)
$$

In order for the y's to define a point on our approximate curve all must be zero except at most two neighbouring ones.

We can now introduce the y's as variables into the ordinary linear programming problem but with the following proviso: if two y's are in the current basis no further y is eligible to enter it and if one y is in the current basis only either, but not both, of its neighbours may enter.

An apparent drawback to separable programming is that the non-linear functions must be functions of a single argument, but in fact this can easily be got round. For example $f(x_1 x_2) = x_1 x_2$ can be formulated as the difference of two functions of newly defined variables $x_3 = x_1 + x_2$ and $x_4 = x_1 - x_2$ by noting that

$$
\frac{x_3^2}{4} - \frac{x_4^2}{4} = x_1 x_2
$$

A more fundamental objection is that separable programming might lead to a local optimum if the non-linear functions introduce non-convexity, but in this case any optimization technique runs the same risk.

Separable programming is implemented in most good computer codes. There is no serious limit to the number of non-linear functions that can be introduced. Most packages also include the facility to pinpoint an optimum pretty closely by imposing a finer grid on the original (probably coarse) grid used. Thus one might start off by approximating a curve by 3, 4 or 5 straight lines (it would be good practice to keep this number fairly low to avoid very long running times). Having found that the optimum solution corresponds to a point between points A and B on this curve one might wish to look rather more closely at the curve between these points by approximating it by a further 3 or 4 lines.

One final point to note is that one must, in using separable programming, define the range of the variable. This does not usually present serious difficulty.

As an example of separable programming consider the following problem:

Maximize Z for non-negative x_1, x_2, x_3, x_4, x_5 subject to

$$\left.\begin{array}{llll}
Z - x_1 - x_1^2 - 9x_2 & & & = 3 \\
x_1 & + x_2 + x_3 & & = 8 \\
-x_1 & + x_2^2 & + x_4 & = 4 \\
-x_1 & + x_2 & + x_5 & = 4
\end{array}\right\} \quad (2.55)$$

We have two non-linear functions x_1^2 and x_2^2. From the second row it is clear that the maximum range of both x_1 and x_2 is from 0 to 8. Let us represent x_1^2 and x_2^2 each by two straight lines joining the points (0, 0), (4, 16) and (8, 64). (Given that we are going to use two straight lines we could probably choose a better two, but no matter.)

We must now introduce six new variables in two sets y_1, y_2 and y_3 and y_4, y_5 and y_6, and new constraints

$$\left.\begin{array}{lll}
y_1 + & y_2 + y_3 = 1 \\
x_1 - & 4y_2 - 8y_3 & = 0 \\
x_1^2 - & 16y_2 - 64y_3 & = 0 \\
y_4 + & y_5 + y_6 = 1 \\
x_2 - & 4y_5 - 8y_6 & = 0 \\
x_2^2 - & 16y_5 - 64y_6 & = 0
\end{array}\right\} \quad (2.56)$$

The problem can now be formulated in two ways:

Maximize Z for non-negative x's and y's when no more than two adjacent y's in either set are non-zero subject to either both equations (2.55) and (2.56) (in this case, to preserve linearity one would write x_1^2 as x_6 and x_2^2 as x_7), or equations (2.55) after equations (2.56) have been substituted into them.

The second is preferable for manual work so we write the constraints as:

$$
\begin{array}{llll}
Z & - 20y_2 - 72y_3 & - 36y_5 - 72y_6 & = 3 \\
 & 4y_2 + 8y_3 & + 4y_5 + 8y_6 + x_3 & = 8 \\
 & - 4y_2 - 8y_3 & + 16y_5 + 64y_6 \qquad + x_4 & = 4 \\
 & - 4y_2 - 8y_3 & + 4y_5 + 8y_6 \qquad\qquad + x_5 & = 4 \\
 & y_1 + y_2 + y_3 & & = 1 \\
 & & y_4 + y_5 + y_6 & = 1
\end{array}
$$

$$(2.57)$$

x_0, x_3, x_4, x_5, y_1 and y_4 form a natural initial basis. Only y_2 and y_5 are eligible to enter the basis and we bring y_5 in. The variable to be removed from the basis is x_4. (We give only the top row of subsequent tableaux: the reader is invited to fill out the full tableaux.)

The new tableau includes

$$Z - 29y_2 - 90y_3 + 72y_6 + \tfrac{9}{4}x_4 = 12 \qquad (2.58)$$

Next we bring y_2 into the basis, y_1 being the variable to remove. The new tableau includes

$$Z + 29y_1 - 61y_3 + 72y_6 + \tfrac{9}{4}x_4 = 41 \qquad (2.59)$$

Now that y_1 has left the basis y_3 is eligible to enter, the variable to leave being x_3. The new tableau includes

$$Z - 32y_1 - 25\tfrac{3}{5}y_6 + \tfrac{61}{5}x_3 - \tfrac{4}{5}x_4 = 65\tfrac{2}{5} \qquad (2.60)$$

Neither y_1 nor y_6 is eligible to enter the basis but x_4, being a normal variable, is. Either y_2 or y_5 could leave the basis. Let us choose y_5. The new tableau has a top row of

$$x_0 - 32y_1 + 16y_5 + 32y_6 + 3x_3 = 75 \qquad (2.70)$$

and we have therefore reached an optimal solution even though the reduced cost of y_1 is negative, since y_1 is not eligible to enter the basis. At the optimum the non-zero variables are $y_3 = 1$, $x_4 = 12$, $x_5 = 12$, $y_4 = 1$. In terms of x_1 and x_2 the solution is $x_1 = 8$, $x_2 - 0$.

As it happens this solution is an exact solution to the original problem defined by equations (2.55). This is because the solution in terms of the y's has only 0's and 1's in it. But generally this will not be so as the solution will not always lie at an end point of one of the lines but somewhere in the middle of one where, again in general, the true constraint will not be satisfied. For example, the solution in the last but one iteration corresponded to $x_1 = \tfrac{26}{5}$, $x_2 = \tfrac{12}{5}$, $x_3 = 0$, $x_4 = 0$, $x_5 = \tfrac{36}{5}$ and one can easily see that this does not exactly satisfy the original constraints. This is why one might, having got an optimum solution, examine the region of this solution by a finer separable programming exercise.

The example gives a hint as to why separable programming can give rise to long running times. In the nature of the method one can spend a lot of time creeping round a curve (for example, consider a y variable set $y_1, y_2, \ldots, y_6$

where y_5 and y_6 are in the final basis and y_1 in the initial one). The worst excesses of this are avoidable, and would have been in our example, by not accepting any y's in the initial basis—it was only coincidental that we were able to put them in in the example—and starting with artificial variables on rows like $y_1 + y_2 + y_3 = 1$.

Integer and mixed integer programming

A very important extension to linear programming, which is frequently called for by practical considerations, is the straight linear programming problem in which some or all of the variables are restricted to take integer (whole number) values.

To begin with there are many situations in which some or all of the variables are integer by their very nature. For example, one variable might be the number of loading bays at a warehouse or the number of men to be deployed to a certain activity. (Because integers slow down a program one must be a little careful here. If one is talking in terms of hundreds or thousands of men, one would not bother to restrict the number of men to integer values.)

The importance of integer variables is not, however, limited to such cases; indeed these are probably the least important applications. Of much more importance is the fact that one can formulate many non-linearities by judicious use of integers. Moreover many problems which are not self-evidently linear programming problems at all can be formulated as integer or mixed-integer linear programming problems (in integer programming all variables are forced to be integers; in mixed-integer programming only some, which are specified, are). Let us consider some example formulations.

Almost any combinatorial problem can be put into the form of an integer linear programming problem. A simple example is the assignment problem. N men are available to work on N machines. A_{ij} is the output if man i works on machine j. How should the men be assigned to machines? The problem is:

Maximize Z for non-negative integers x_{ij} subject to

$$
\left.
\begin{aligned}
Z - \sum_{\substack{i=1,\ldots,N \\ j=1,\ldots,N}} x_{ij}A_{ij} &= 0 \\
\sum_{i=1,\ldots,N} x_{ij} &= 1 \quad \text{for all } j \\
\sum_{j=1,\ldots,N} x_{ij} &= 1 \quad \text{for all } i
\end{aligned}
\right\}
\qquad (2.80)
$$

In this example the variables are either zero or one. Problems of this form (zero-one problems) have received a good deal of special treatment. The assignment problem is a rather special case which has received individual treatment.

Note that many other "practical" constraints can be added to the above problem. Suppose man 5 and man 6 must not work on adjacent machines.

This introduces constraints $x_{50} + x_{61} \leqslant 1$, $x_{60} + x_{51} \leqslant 1$, . . ., $x_{5j} + x_{6j+1} \leqslant 1$ and so on.

Another "classic" combinatorial problem is the knapsack problem. A set of articles numbered $1, . . ., n$ is available. The ith has weight w_i and value V_i. A man has a knapsack capable of holding total weight W. Which combination of articles should he carry to maximize the value? A zero-one programming formulation is:

Maximize V for zero-one x_i subject to

$$\left.\begin{aligned} V - \sum_{i=1}^{n} v_i x_i &= 0 \\ \sum_{i=1}^{n} w_i x_i &\leqslant W \end{aligned}\right\} \tag{2.81}$$

The problem of fixed costs is easily formulated using integer variables. Suppose the capacity of a factory is P, and x_1 denotes the production from it. Costs are 0 if $x_1 = 0$, $C + ax_1$ if $x_1 \geqslant 0$ and $\leqslant P$ (that is, there is a fixed cost C which is incurred only if some production is undertaken). This can be formulated by introducing an integer variable x_2 and a new variable x_3 to represent cost together with the following constraints:

$$\left.\begin{aligned} x_3 &= Cx_2 + ax_1 \\ x_1 &\leqslant Px_2 \\ x_2 &\leqslant 1 \end{aligned}\right\} \tag{2.82}$$

More generally we can formulate any non-linearity by mixed-integer formulation by methods analogous to separable programming.

A linear programming problem covering several, say n, time periods might include the possibility of a capital investment which increases the capacity of a factory from Q to R. This can be formulated by introducing integer variables $x_1, . . ., x_n$ and, if production at the factory is denoted by $y_1, . . ., y_n$, the following are the constraints

$$\left.\begin{aligned} x_1 + x_2 + . . . + x_n &\leqslant 1 \\ y_1 &\leqslant Q + Rx_1 \\ y_2 &\leqslant Q + R(x_1 + x_2) \\ . . . \quad &\quad . . . \\ y_n &\leqslant Q + R(x_1 + x_2 + . . . + x_n) \end{aligned}\right\} \tag{2.83}$$

and the cost of the capital investment is represented in the cost function by $C_1 x_1 + C_2 x_2 + . . . + C_n x_n$, where C_i is the cost of making the investment in period i.

These are just a few examples of how integer and mixed-integer formulations might arise. What about their solution? Algorithms exist which guarantee finding optimal solutions. Unfortunately computer running times can be exceedingly long and one frequently has to stop before the optimal solution has been reached. Some skill is usually called for in deciding what it is reasonable to stop. A good deal of attention has been given to computer efficiency and the development of useful stopping rules. Note that the solution to the problem in which all variables are allowed to take non-integer values provides an upper bound for the integer or mixed-integer problem. Thus one can make statements, using this upper bound, like: the current solution, while not optimal, is at most 2% from the best and therefore good enough. This might be a useful basis for a stopping rule. (We recall in passing that integer transportation problems present no difficulties: the solution using the ordinary method comes out in integer form.)

The method most commonly used in mixed-integer programming is the branch and bound method (9). Suppose the problem is formulated in terms of variables $x_1, x_2, \ldots, x_r$ which may take any non-negative value and $y_1, y_2, \ldots, y_s$ which may take any non-negative integer values.

In the branch and bound approach we first solve this problem treating the y's as continuous variables. If this solution happens to give the y's integer values the problem is solved. If not we branch on one of the non-integral y's. If its value in the final solution is $y_k = n + f$ where n is an integer and f a fraction we solve two problems, the original problem augmented by on the one hand the constraint $y_k \leqslant n$, on the other by $y_k \geqslant n + 1$. We then branch on one of these problems and so on until we have a feasible solution (that is, a solution which is feasible in the ordinary sense and in which all the y's are integers). Denote the value of the objective function at this solution by X. We now return and start to branch on another y and so on. However if at any stage we have a non-feasible problem for which the value of the objective function is less than X, there is no point in branching on it any further because any new constraint we introduce can only reduce the value of the objective function (or at most leave it unchanged).

We go on in this way replacing X by any higher value of a feasible objective function as it arises until there are no more useful branching options, when we stop.

As an example of the branch and bound method consider this problem:

Maximize Z for non-negative integers x_1, x_2, x_3 subject to

$$\left.\begin{aligned}
Z - 7x_1 - 3x_2 - 4x_3 &= 0 \\
5x_1 + x_2 \phantom{{}+ 3x_3} &\leqslant 21 \\
7x_2 + 3x_3 &\leqslant 29
\end{aligned}\right\} \qquad (2.84)$$

We first solve the problem ignoring the integer requirements. Slack variables x_4 and x_5 are introduced and the optimum solution is $Z = 68\frac{1}{15}$, $x_1 = 4\frac{1}{5}$, $x_2 = 0$, $x_3 = 9\frac{2}{3}$. We branch on x_1 to give two new problems: the original problem with $x_1 \leqslant 4$ added and the original problem with $x_1 \geqslant 5$ added. The first of these has an optimal solution $Z = 66\frac{2}{3}$, $x_1 = 4$, $x_2 = 0$, $x_3 = 9\frac{2}{3}$. Now branch on x_3 introducing a new constraint $x_3 \leqslant 9$. This problem has the solution $Z = 64\frac{6}{7}$ with $x_1 = 4$, $x_2 = \frac{2}{7}$ and $x_3 = 9$. Branching again we introduce $x_2 \leqslant 0$ which has an optimal solution $Z = 64$, $x_1 = 4$, $x_2 = 0$ and $x_3 = 9$. This is our first fully feasible solution.

Return now to the first branch and solve the original problem with $x_1 \geqslant 5$ added. The problem does not have a feasible solution so we move on to the next unexplored branch which is the original problem with $x_1 \leqslant 4$ and

$x_3 \geqslant 10$ added. Again this has no feasible solution. The next unexplored branch is the original problem with $x_1 \leqslant 4$, $x_3 \leqslant 0$ and $x_2 \geqslant 1$ added. This has an optimal solution $Z = 60\frac{1}{3}$ at $x_1 = 4$, $x_2 = 1$ and $x_3 = 7\frac{1}{3}$. Because $60\frac{1}{3}$ is less than 64 there is no point in exploring this branch any further (even though x_3 is not an integer, since to constrain it again would at best leave Z at its present value—this is the point of the method).

There are now no unexplored branches left and the optimal solution is $Z = 64$ at $x_1 = 4$, $x_2 = 0$, $x_3 = 9$.

This example shows how branch and bound methods can take a long time: they involve solving many ordinary linear programming problems on the way to the solution. However one does not have to solve each fresh problem from scratch. Advantage can usually be taken of the final tableau of the previous problem to derive a solution to the current problem fairly quickly. The reader might care to consider whether we have branched very efficiently in this example. Much attention has been given to branching strategy.

It seems worth mentioning one other integer programming method, the cutting plane method. In this approach we again solve the problem ignoring the need for integers. If the solution is non-integral we introduce a new constraint which cuts off the solution point (that is makes the present solution point infeasible in the new problem) but does not cut off any genuinely feasible point. The method can be illustrated on the previous example. It works only when the coefficients and right-hand sides in the original tableau are all, or can all be made, integers. This ensures that the slack variables also take integer values.

The final tableau in the original problem of the previous example was

$$\left. \begin{array}{l} Z + 7\frac{11}{15}x_2 + 1\frac{2}{5}x_4 + 1\frac{1}{3}x_5 = 68\frac{1}{5} \\ x_1 + \frac{1}{5}x_2 + \frac{1}{5}x_4 \qquad\qquad = 4\frac{1}{5} \\ x_3 + 2\frac{1}{3}x_2 + \frac{1}{3}x_5 = 9\frac{2}{3} \end{array} \right\} \qquad (2.85)$$

Now consider a new variable s_1 say defined by

$$\tfrac{1}{5}x_2 + \tfrac{1}{5}x_4 = \tfrac{1}{5} + s_1$$

(that is, using the fractional parts of the x_1 row. The fractional part of, say, $+2\frac{1}{4}$ is $\frac{1}{4}$, the integral part 2; however the fractional part of $-2\frac{1}{4}$ is $\frac{3}{4}$ and the integral part -3). At any genuinely feasible point s_1 must be an integer because x_1, x_2 and x_4 would be integers so therefore would $x_1 - 4$ (or, more generally, $x_1 + N_2x_2 + N_4x_4 - 4$ where N_2 and N_4 are the integral parts of the coefficients of x_2 and x_4). Moreover s_1 is certainly at least $-\frac{1}{5}$ by definition (x_2 and x_4 being non-negative). Therefore s must be non-negative.

We thus introduce a new constraint to our problem namely s_1 0 which cuts off the current solution but does not cut off any genuine solution. Put another way, we introduce a new constraint

$$x_2 + x_4 - 5x_6 = 1$$

where x_6 is an integer slack variable. (Alternatively we could have derived a new constraint

$$x_2 + x_5 - 3x_6 = 2$$

by constructing the new equation from the third row of the final tableau.)

We proceed step by step introducing new constraints derived from the fractional parts of one row of the current basis. The procedure terminates but it can be a long-winded one. The method we have outlined above is due to Gomery (10). It was the first successful method proposed for integer programming, but it is not the most efficient of its type, nor have we necessarily used it very efficiently (we could have chosen many other constraints to introduce). A more efficient method is described in Martin (11).

Beale and Tomlin (13) have pointed out that many integer programming formulations and also indeed separable programming formulations can be cast in less general terms than using integers. They introduce ordered sets of variables and constraints of two forms (i) only one variable in a given set may be non-zero and (ii) two adjacent variables may be non-zero. Form (ii) covers separable programming while form (i) covers, for example, the problems defined by equations (2.80) and (2.82) above. In (2.82) for example (x_1, x_2, . . ., x_n, x_{n+1}), x_{n+1} being a slack variable, is the appropriate ordered set. They have developed a branch and bound method for handling problems which can be formulated in this way more efficiently than by direct application of the branch and bound method described above.

Linear programming in practice

In the introduction to this chapter we described a fairly complicated planning problem in which we implied linear programming might be a suitable aid. Many organizations are now using linear programming as a routine for such problems. The exercises at the end of the chapter illustrate some possible application areas. Quite large numbers of variables and constraints (typically some hundreds) can be involved particularly if the formulation is extensive not only in its coverage of the firms activities but also through time. Such large problems present a number of practical difficulties which we shall discuss only very briefly.

Firstly there are sometimes problems of deciding how to formulate the problem so as to minimize computing expenditure or even, if the number of constraints is very large, so as to reduce the problem to a size manageable by the computer. There is usually some choice in formulation, for example the natural formulation often contains a number of redundant equations which serve only to define one variable (say a factory's total production) in terms of other variables (the production item by item), so that other constraints which involve the one variable can in turn be more easily formulated. Often the balance to be struck in deciding between formulations is between putting more zeros into the initial matrix and increasing the number of constraints. These and other such points are well treated by Beale (6).

Secondly there are problems concerned with the vast implied data collection, the preliminary processing of the data to produce the required coefficients and the assembly of the initial matrix. Computer programs, usually called matrix generators, are often used to transform the raw data into the initial matrix.

Finally the computer output from such large problems often needs transforming into a readily understood form. The untransformed output—typically the values of the variables at the optimum and their reduced costs and hence the shadow prices—might be best assembled into some statement of plan of the kind used in the organization's budgetary processes, say. Computer programs for doing this are also often used and they are usually referred to as report writers.

References

1. Dantzig, G. B. *Linear Programming and Extensions.* Princeton University Press 1963.
2. Lemke, C. E. The Dual Method of Solving the Linear Programming Problem. *Nav. Res. Log. Quart.* **1.1** pp. 48–54 1954.
3. Dantzig, G. B., Ford, L. R. and Fulkerson, D. R. in Kuhn & Tucker (Eds) *Linear Inequalities and Related Systems.* Princeton University Press 1956. A Primal-Dual Algorithm for Linear Programming.
4. Hitchcock, F. L. The Distribution of a Product from Several Sources to Numerous Localities. *J. Math. Phys.* **20** 1941.
5. Dantzig, G. B. and Wolfe, P. Decomposition Principle for Linear Programming. *Opns. Res.* **8.2** 1960.
6. Beale, E. M. L. *Mathematical Programming in Practice.* Sir Isaac Pitman & Sons Ltd 1968.
7. Charnes, A. and Cooper, W. W. Chance Constrained Programming. *Man. Sc.* **6.1** 1959.
8. Miller, C. E. The Simplex Method for Local Separable Programming. Chapter in ref. 12.
9. Land, A. H. and Doig, A. G. An Automatic Method of Solving Discrete Programming Problems. *Econometric* **28** 1960.
10. Gomory, R. E. An Algorithm for Integer Solutions Linear Programs. Chapter in ref. 12.
11. Martin, G. T. An Accelerated Euclidean Algorithm for Integer Linear Programming. Chapter in ref. 12.
12. Graves, R. L. and Wolfe, P. (Eds.) *Recent Advances in Mathematical Programming.* McGraw-Hill Book Co. Inc 1963.
13. Beale, E. M. L. and Tomlin, J. A. Special Facilities in a General Mathematical Programming System Using Ordered Sets of Variables. Paper in Lawrence, J. R. (Ed.) *OR69.* Tavistock Publications 1970.

Further reading

References 1, 6 and 12 above.
Gass, S. I. *Linear Programming*. McGraw-Hill Book Co. Inc. 1958.
Hadley, G. C. *Linear Programming*. Addison-Wesley Publishing Co. Inc. 1962.
Vajda, S. *Mathematical Programming*. Addison-Wesley Publishing Co. Inc. 1961.
Vajda, S. *Readings in Mathematical Programming*. Sir Isaac Pitman & Sons Ltd 1962.
Garvin, W. *Introduction to Linear Programming*. McGraw-Hill Book Co. Inc. 1960.
Simmonard, M. *Linear Programming*. Prentice Hall 1966.
Chung, Au-min. *Linear Programming*. C. E. Merrill (Ohio) 1963.
Abadie, J. (Ed.) *Nonlinear Programming*. North Holland 1967.
Beale, E. M. L. (Ed.) *Applications of Mathematical Programming Techniques*. The English Universities Press 1970.

Examples for solution

1. Collieries *A*, *B*, *C* and *D* produce 950, 300, 1,350 and 450 tonnes/week of steam coal respectively. Consumers *E*, *F*, *G*, *H* and *J* require 250, 1,000, 700, 650 and 450 tonnes/week of steam coal respectively. The cost of coal transport from each colliery to each consumer is given below, in pence per ton.

Colliery	Consumer					
	E	*F*	*G*	*H*	*J*	
A	23	27	32	30	43	950
B	15	15	20	16	35	300
C	14	19	25	21	37	1350
D	35	44	47	45	60	450
	250	1000	700	650	450	3050

Find the steam coal allocation which gives the minimum transport cost.

2. In question 1 the collieries' production in 1 week alters to 1,150, 650, 1,000 and 250 tonnes respectively. Find the new minimum cost allocation.

3. A factory manufactures five synthetic fuels, Godite, Halite, Meadite, Stevite and Willite. In the manufacture, coals from five seams, Top Len, Upper Mike, Yard Frank, Brian Main and High Pat are used. There is a restricted supply of the first four of these coals. The coals are mixed in different proportions according to which fuel is made. The pit head price of the coals, the manufacturing costs, and the selling prices are all given, in pence per tonne.

Coal	Proportion of coals in fuels (%)					Tons of coal available	Pit head price (p/tonne)
	G	H	M	S	W		
Top Len	10	10	20	20	30	130	350
Upper Mike	20	10	30	30	20	250	375
Yard Frank	40	40	20	10	40	240	400
Brian Main	30	40	30	30	10	295	425
High Pat	—	—	—	10	—	Unlimited	300
Selling price of fuel p/tonne	542·5	537·5	475·0	495·0	542·5		

The manufacturing cost is 25p per tonne for each fuel. How much of each fuel has to be made in order to maximize profit?

4. A refinery makes 3 grades of petrol (A, B, C) from 3 crude oils (d, e, f). Crude f can be used in any grade but the others must satisfy the following specifications:

Grade	Specification	Selling price (p/l.)
A	Not less than 50% crude d. Not more than 25% crude e.	8·0
B	Not less than 25% crude d. Not more than 50% crude e.	6·5
C	No specifications.	5·5

There are capacity limitations on the amounts of the three crude elements that can be used:

Crude	Capacity (000 l.)	Price (p/l.)
d	500	9·5
e	500	5·5
f	300	6·5

It is required to produce the maximum profit.

5. A manufacturer produces paper in a roll 205 cm wide. His orders on one day are for:

700 m of 55 cm width,
1,000 m of 70 cm width,
700 m of 80 cm width.

The customer will accept these orders in a number of lengths of the required width. The manufacturer can therefore combine his orders and cut them together. He wants to minimize the area of scrap which results from the cutting process. How does he?

6. A caterer has to supply napkins to his customers. He can forecast the number of customers he will receive on each of seven days and wants to supply each with a clean napkin at minimum cost. There are three alternatives, either

(1) he can buy new napkins at 15p each, or
(2) have his dirty napkins laundered quickly, taking 2 days and costing 10p each, or
(3) have them laundered slowly, taking 4 days at a cost of 5p each.

He starts the period with a stock of 50 clean napkins and on the seven days requires 25, 25, 30, 30, 15, 20, 25 respectively. He also wants to have a stock of 50 clean napkins at the end of the period. What should his policy be?

7. Two collieries A and B can supply two washeries 1 and 2 either by rail or by road. The cheapest allocation of coal to routes is required.

The transport costs are given in the table, and the daily capacities of routes, and the tonnages available and required are given below that.

Transport Costs (£/tonne)

Washery		1		2	
Colliery		Road	Rail	Road	Rail
A	Road	0·4		0·6	
A	Rail		0·7		0·8
B	Road	0·3		0·7	
B	Rail		0·8		0·6

Colliery A Road   1,100 tonnes
Rail   2,000 tonnes
Total available = 2,400 tonnes

3

Colliery B	Road	700 tonnes
	Rail	1,000 tonnes
	Total available =	1,500 tonnes
Washery 1	Road	600 tonnes
	Rail	500 tonnes
	Total required =	900 tonnes
Washery 2	Road	2,000 tonnes
	Rail	2,000 tonnes
	Total required =	3,000 tonnes

8. What meaning attaches to the shadow prices in each of questions 3, 4 and 5. What ranges of capacities in question 4 do not disturb the optimal solution? Examine how the maximum profit varies as the price of crude d increases over the range 95 to 100.

9. How could you handle the case where one variable is not constrained to be non-negative in an otherwise standard linear programming problem?

10. Formulate the following problem as a mixed integer programming problem.

A certain manufacturer supplies three customers A, B and C located at three different sites. He has two manufacturing plants A' and B' which are next door to A and B respectively. Transport costs are in £ per unit:

	A	B	C
A'	0	2	3
B'	2	0	3

Availabilities at A' and B' are 1,000 and 2,000 units per year respectively and requirements are 500 at A, 1,500 at B and 1,000 at C. Demand is expected to rise once and for all by 10% at each of A, B and C. Production capacity can be increased at A and B in steps of 100 units per year at a cost of £1,000 per year fixed plus £1 per unit variable. A new plant could be built at C again in steps of 100 at a cost of £3,000 per year fixed plus £1 per unit variable. Variable production costs at the present plants are £1 per unit. The manufacturer's profit is £7 per unit less transport costs which he pays himself.

Where if at all should he increase production capacity?

11. It is required to maximize a convex function of non-negative variables subject to linear constraints. The function is approximated by a series of straight lines as for separable programming. Is it necessary to use separable programming to solve the problem?

12. What is the dual problem of the following primal: Maximize $6x + 3y + 7z$ for non-negative x, y, z subject to

$$x + y + z \geqslant 1$$
$$3x - 4y + z \leqslant 0$$
$$6x + 2y - 7z = 1$$

13. Drawing from your own experience suggest applications of the techniques described in this chapter. How many of the assumptions made either explicitly or implicitly, in using the techniques would certainly be satisfied? Would you accept the results of the application of the technique if you were the executive decision maker?

3   Dynamic programming

Introduction

Consider the problem of a wheat farmer who must decide what proportion of his harvest to sell each year and what proportion to sow for his next year's harvest. He wishes to maximize his total income over a number of years, assuming he must sell all his harvest at the end of this period, and that income is not proportional to the amount sold. The decision to sell a certain amount of wheat in one year determines the amount of wheat available for sale in the following year. Thus, to decide how much to sell in the first year, the farmer must determine his selling policy for all the years in the period.

The farmer's problem belongs to a class of problems involving multi-stage decision processes since he must make a sequence of decisions in which a decision at one stage of the process determines the possible decisions that can be made at the next stage. Other examples of such problems are bidding in bridge, investment programmes, and stock control. Dynamic programming is a technique designed to deal with this class of problems and it ensures that the decisions are made in such a way as to optimize a pre-defined objective function, e.g. to maximize the farmer's income.

In this chapter a simple example introduces the basic principles, which are then more fully stated. The farmer's problem is examined to explain the approach more comprehensively. The nature and scope of dynamic programming are then explored prior to considering more complex problems and practical applications of the technique. The basic ideas of dynamic programming are due to Bellman [1] and the development in this chapter draws heavily on his work.

The motorist example

A motorist wants to minimize the distance he has to travel from town A to town F, between which there is no direct route. His map shows that the villages en route conveniently fall into groups, which are portrayed in Table 3.1.

TABLE 3.1

$$
\begin{array}{ccccc}
 & B_1 & & E_1 & \\
A - & B_2 - C_1 - D_1 - & E_2 - F \\
 & B_3 \quad C_2 \quad D_2 \quad E_3 & \\
 & B_4 & &
\end{array}
$$

| Stage | 1 | 2 | 3 | 4 | 5 |

Each column represents a group of villages and from each village in any group it is only possible to drive to any of the villages in the next group. Any such move is a stage of the problem and the decision-making process thus consists of five stages. The state of the process at the beginning of any particular stage is defined by the village the motorist is in. The decision of which route to take at each stage transforms the state of the process into a new state at the next village. The distances between villages are given in Table 3.2.

TABLE 3.2

$AB_1 = 4$	$B_1C_1 = 5$	$C_1D_1 = 5$	$D_1E_1 = 6$	$E_1F = 4$
$AB_2 = 6$	$B_1C_2 = 7$	$C_1D_2 = 3$	$D_1E_2 = 8$	$E_2F = 2$
$AB_3 = 7$	$B_2C_1 = 6$	$C_2D_1 = 4$	$D_1E_3 = 5$	$E_3F = 3$
$AB_4 = 6$	$B_2C_2 = 8$	$C_2D_2 = 6$	$D_2E_1 = 5$	
	$B_3C_1 = 6$		$D_2E_2 = 5$	
	$B_3C_2 = 3$		$D_2E_3 = 6$	
	$B_4C_1 = 4$			
	$B_4C_2 = 4$			

There are 48 possible five-stage routes from A to F. The motorist wishes to choose the shortest route, i.e. the optimal policy. He can, of course, calculate the distance for all 48 routes and choose the lowest. A more sophisticated approach is to reduce the number of possibilities that must be considered at any one time by dealing with each stage separately.

To solve the problem we work backwards through Table 3.2 and determine the shortest route to F from each village, considering the groups in turn. Starting with group E, we find $\overline{E_kF}$ (a bar signifying the shortest distance to F) from each of the villages k in E. (N.B. $\overline{E_kF} = E_kF$.) We then consider group D. If the motorist were at village D_1, for example, the shortest distance to F would be the least of $D_1E_1 + \overline{E_1F}$, $D_1E_2 + \overline{E_2F}$, $D_1E_3 + \overline{E_3F}$ so we can write

$$\overline{D_1F} = \min_{i=1,2,3} [D_1E_i + \overline{E_iF}]$$

We find that $i = 3$ gives the minimum value (for $i = 1$ the distance is 10, for $i = 2$ the distance is also 10, but for $i = 3$ the distance is only 8). Thus the shortest distance from D_1 to F is 8 kilometres via E_3, which we denote as

$$\overline{D_1F} = 8[E_3]$$

Having calculated $\overline{D_1F}$ and $\overline{D_2F}$ we proceed to group C. To determine the shortest distance to F from, say, C_1, i.e. $\overline{C_1F}$, involves only choosing the minimum of $C_1D_1 + \overline{D_1F}$ and $C_1D_2 + \overline{D_2F}$, so we can write

$$\overline{GF} = \min_{i=1,2} [C_1D_i + \overline{D_i}]$$

Proceeding in this manner we find the shortest distances to F for all villages, as shown in Table 3.3.

Working back through Table 3.3, it is seen that the shortest route from A to F is

$$A - B_1 - C_1 - D_2 - E_2 - F = 19 \text{ kilometres}$$

TABLE 3.3

$\overline{E_1F} = 4$	$\overline{D_1F} = 8 \ [E_3]$	$\overline{C_1F} = 10 \ [D_2]$	$\overline{B_1F} = 15 \ [C_1]$	$AF = 19 \ [B_1]$
$\overline{E_2F} = 2$	$\overline{D_2F} = 7 \ [E_2]$	$\overline{C_2F} = 12 \ [D_1]$	$\overline{B_2F} = 16 \ [C_1]$	
$\overline{E_3F} = 0{\cdot}33$			$\overline{B_3F} = 15 \ [C_2]$	
			$\overline{B_4F} = 14 \ [C_1]$	

This method not only gives the solution more quickly than by calculating the distance for all 48 routes, it also gives an insight into the structure of the problem and a range of further possible solutions. For example, if the motorist decides that the scenery at B_3 is more important than conserving time and money, the results already obtained tell him the optimal route, i.e. $\overline{B_3F}$.

Fundamentals of dynamic programming

From the motorist example it can be seen that at each stage of the solution the range of all possible optimal policies is obtained for use at the next stage. However, the determination of these optimal policies depends only on the state at the beginning of the stage (the optimal routes and mileages from the villages of the present group to F) and the stage parameters (the mileages connecting the present group to the next group).

It is because the optimal policy for a given stage depends only on the present state of the process that the dynamic programming approach is possible. This property enables us to deduce equations which in turn enable us to formulate and solve a problem. (In some cases we may need to exercise care in deciding exactly how to describe the present state of the process so that this property holds, but generally it will be obvious enough.)

General Procedure. Let us now see how dynamic programming is applied to a general N-stage decision process. We define the initial state of the process to be s_0. Any set of policies

$$d_1, d_2, \ldots, d_j, \ldots, d_N \tag{3.1}$$

where $d_j \varepsilon D_j$, the set of admissible policies at the jth stage, will successively transform the initial state into the states

$$s_1, s_2, \ldots, s_j, \ldots, s_N \tag{3.2}$$

Note that by such a transformation for any stage j

$$s_j = s_j(d_j, s_{j-1}) \tag{3.3}$$

and

$$D_j = D_j(s_{j-1}) \tag{3.4}$$

That is, the state at the jth stage depends on the state at the $(j-1)$th stage and the policy applied then; and the set of admissible policies, that is the policies which can be applied, depends on the state of the process.

The policies d_j are chosen to optimize

$$\sum_{j=1}^{N} r_j$$

where r_j is the return from stage j. (If the process is time-dependent, i.e. an N-unit time period is involved, it might be desirable to define r_j as the return in stage j discounted back to stage 1, since all decisions are actually made at the beginning of the period. Thus the motorist determines his route for the whole journey while still at town A.) The optimal d_j are chosen in the following manner:

First consider the final state s_N; for each possible level of s_{N-1} the particular $d_N \varepsilon D_N$ which optimizes r_N is chosen. Next consider s_{N-1}; for each possible level of s_{N-2} the optimal d_{N-1} is chosen such that $r_{N-1} + r_N$ is optimized. This is comparatively easy to do because we know the value of r_{N-1} corresponding to any d_{N-1} and any level of s_{N-2}, we know the corresponding level of s_{N-1} and the consequent optimal value of r_{N-1}. We continue to consider the states $s_{N-2}, \ldots, s_j, \ldots, s_1, s_0$, at each stage choosing the d_j to optimize $r_j + (r_{j+1} + \ldots + r_N)$ for each level of s_{j-1}. Since the initial state s_0 is not considered until the last, the fullest possible range of s_j must be considered at each stage, as we do not know which d_j and s_j will be included in the optimal policy. When we do reach s_0, which is given, the optimal d_j and s_j are easily determined from (3.3) and (3.4) by working forwards from $j = 1, \ldots, N$. (The above procedure should be compared with that for solving the motorist problem.)

Functional Equations. A functional equation is a mathematical means of writing the possible policies for each stage and of deciding which policy to choose. We define $f_i(s_j)$ to be the return for an N-stage process starting in state s_j and using an optimal policy, where $j = 0, 1, 2, \ldots, N-1$, $i = N - j$. Then, if $r(d_j, s_{j-1})$ is the return from using policy d_j on state s_{j-1}, we have, for the 1-stage process starting in state s_{N-1}, the functional equation

$$f_1(s_{N-1}) = \max_{d_N} r(d_N, s_{N-1}) \tag{3.5}$$

We now obtain an equation for $f_2(s_{N-2})$ in terms of $f_1(s_{N-1})$. For this 2-stage process the total return will be the return from the first stage plus that from the second stage. Whatever the policy d_{N-1} chosen, d_N must be optimal for the remaining stage, from the principles stated above. The functional equation for the second stage is therefore

$$f_2(s_{N-2}) = \max_{d_{N-1}} [r(d_{N-1}, s_{N-2}) + f_1(s'_{N-1})] \tag{3.6}$$

where s'_{N-1} is the state resulting from policy d_{N-1} on state s_{N-2}.

In general, starting in state s_j at stage $j + 1$,

$$f_{N-j}(s_j) = \max_{d_{j+1}} [r(d_{j+1}, s_j) + f_{N-j-1}(s'_{j+1})] \tag{3.7}$$

where $j = 0, 1, \ldots, N - 1$. The notation for the functional equation is conventionally shortened so that (3.7) would be written

$$f_i(S) = \max_d \, [r(d) + f_{i-1}(S')] \qquad (3.8)$$

When we reach the final equation for the initial state, i.e. $f_N(S_0)$, it is possible to determine the optimal d_1. This gives the optimal s_1, which in turn determines the optimal d_2, and so on, until finally we have the optimal $d_1, d_2, \ldots, d_N$ and $s_1, s_2, \ldots, s_N$.

As an example, consider the second stage of the motorist problem. The functional equation for the route B_1F is

$$\overline{B_1F} = \min \, (B_1C_1 + \overline{C_1F}, \; B_1C_2 + \overline{C_2F}) \qquad (3.9)$$

In this example

$$f_4(B_1) = B_1F$$

the two decisions are d_1 to go to C_1 and d_2 to go to C_2, and the state s_1 is B_1. So, writing

$$r(d_1) = B_1C_1$$
$$r(d_2) = B_1C_2$$

we have

$$f_4(B_1) = \min_{k=1,2} \, [r(d_k) + f_3(C_k)] \qquad (3.10)$$

which may be compared with equation (3.8). Both $\overline{B_1F}$ and $\overline{B_2F}$, i.e. $f_4(B_1)$ and $f_4(B_2)$ must be calculated, since we do not know at this stage which of them will appear in the optimal solution.

The farmer problem

We may now use the formulation developed in the previous section to solve the problem posed in the introduction. Suppose that the farmer wishes to sell all of his harvest in the Nth year and he has x_1 tonnes of wheat at the beginning of the N-year period. He may sow $x_1 - y_1$ and sell y_1 of these x_1 tonnes $(0 \leqslant y_1 \leqslant x_1)$. The $x_1 - y_1$ tonnes will yield

$$a(x_1 - y_1) = x_2$$

at the next harvest $(a > 1)$ and the y_1 tonnes sell for $p(y_1)$. The notation

$$x_{j+1} = a(x_j - y_j)$$

is adopted for convenience. It could as easily be

$$x_{j+1} = a(x_j - y_{j+1})$$

as in the previous section. In order to maximize his income over N years the farmer must determine the y_j, $j = 1, 2, \ldots, N$, that maximize

$$P = \sum_{j=1}^{N} p(y_j)$$

Let $f_i(x_j)$ be the total income obtainable when starting with x_j tonnes and adopting an optimal policy of selling and sowing over $N - j$ years, $i = N - j$. All the wheat harvested in year N will be sold, so that

$$f_0(x_N) = p(x_N) = p(y_N) \tag{3.11}$$

In year $N - 1$ he will have x_{N-1} tonnes to sow or sell and his total income for the last 2 years would be $p(y_{N-1}) + f_0[a(x_{N-1} - y_{N-1})]$, where

$$a(x_{N-1} - y_{N-1}) = x_N \tag{3.12}$$

To maximize this income the value of y must be determined. Therefore the functional equation for this stage is

$$f_1(x) = \max_{0 \leqslant y \leqslant x} [p(y) + f_0(a[x - y])] \tag{3.13}$$

The general functional equation is thus as follows:

$$f_i(x) = \max_{0 \leqslant y \leqslant x} [p(y) + f_{i-1}(a[x - y])] \tag{3.14}$$

Putting $i = 1$ we have equation (3.13); $i = N - 1, \ldots, 2$ gives the functional equations for the other stages.

The solution of the equations in order completely solves the problem. In solving the N-year problem for a particular value of x_1 we have also solved the problem for any period of less than N years and for any value of the initial state less than x_1. These two properties of the solution are typical of dynamic programming.

The methods which can be used to solve the set of N functional equations depend essentially on the form of the function $p(y)$. If, for example,

$$p(y) = K\sqrt{y}$$

the equations can be solved analytically, but for most practical problems $p(y)$ will not be of such a convenient form and numerical or graphical methods might be more useful. If the function $p(y)$ and the coefficient a were different in different years, the structure of the equations and the method of obtaining a solution would be unchanged.

Let us consider how the problem would be approached by classical methods. In any year j the farmer sells y_j tonnes and sows $(x_j - y_j)$ tonnes which yield

$$a(x_j - y_j) = x_{j+1} \text{ tonnes}$$

at the next harvest. We thus have the series of equations:

$$
\left.
\begin{aligned}
x_2 &= a(x_1 - y_1) \\
x_3 &= a(x_2 - y_2) \\
&\;\;\vdots \\
x_{j+1} &= a(x_j - y_j) \\
&\;\;\vdots \\
x_{N-1} &= a(x_{N-2} - y_{N-2}) \\
x_N &= a(x_{N-1} - y_{N-1})
\end{aligned}
\right\}
\tag{3.15}
$$

Clearly also

$$
y_N = x_N \tag{3.16}
$$

The total income over the period is

$$
P = p(y_1) + \ldots + p(y_N) \tag{3.17}
$$

and we have to maximize P subject to the constraints

$$
\left.
\begin{aligned}
x_j &\geqslant 0 \\
y_j &\geqslant 0
\end{aligned}
\right\}
\tag{3.18}
$$

for all j

and the equations (3.15) and (3.16). After a little algebra these constraints reduce to

$$
a^{N-1}x_1 = y_N + ay_{N-1} + \ldots + a^{N-1}y_1 \tag{3.19}
$$

and

$$
y_j \geqslant 0 \quad \text{for all } j
$$

It can be shown that for $p(y)$ linear or concave upwards, the solution is trivial, since the farmer would obviously sell nothing until the last year. If $p(y)$ is of any other form, P is extremely difficult to maximize by classical methods. Dynamic programming can solve the problem for any form of $p(y)$.

Types of multi-stage decision process

In both the examples discussed above it was possible to formulate the problem as a sequence of decisions which were dependent, i.e. a decision made at any stage has an effect on decisions later in the process. Three properties of such processes can now be identified:

(a) The outcome of a decision may be deterministic or stochastic. In the deterministic case, given the state of the process, the outcome of a decision at any stage is uniquely determined and known. In a stochastic process there is a set of possible outcomes given by a known probability distribution. Both the motorist and farmer problems were of the deterministic type. In real life all decisions have stochastic outcomes since the future cannot be perfectly predicted, but many processes can be regarded as deterministic for convenience (especially if the variances of the probability distributions are small).

For a stochastic process the functional equations are formulated as follows: If

$f_i(x)$ = the optimal expected return from an N-stage process starting in state x,

$P(r)$ = probability density function of return r using policy y on state x,

$Q(x')$ = probability density function of the state x' using policy y on state x,

then

$$f_i(x) = \max_y \left(\int_r rP(r)dr + \int_{x'} f_{i-1}(x')Q(x')dx' \right) \tag{3.20}$$

One can think in this context of y representing a control policy to be applied to the process.

(b) The number of decisions it is possible to make at any stage may be finite or infinite. The motorist had a finite (and quite small) number of villages of the next group to which he could travel from any one village. The farmer, however, could split his wheat in an infinite number of proportions at each stage, i.e. continuously varying the proportion sold between 0 and 1.

(c) The total number of stages in the process may be finite or infinite, and known or unknown (i.e. to be determined as part of the solution). The motorist, the formulation of the procedure, and the farmer all had a known and finite number of stages.

None of the differences in properties, except that of an infinite number of stages, affects the method of approach to the problem. In many problems the stages are defined by time (e.g. the farmer problem) but this is not always the case (e.g. the motorist problem).

General discussion

Dynamic programming can be used to solve any problem which can be formulated as a multi-stage decision process. Many problems in which the decision process is not immediately obvious can be re-formulated as multi-stage decision problems. Some of the fields of applicability are purchasing, scheduling, stock control, replacement, "buy" or "make" type problems, and allocation problems with non-linear objective functions.

Whenever dimensionality is a formidable obstacle dynamic programming may be able to help. The farmer problem showed how a problem virtually insoluble in classical terms can be feasibly solved. Dynamic programming reduces problems of many dimensions to a series of one dimensional problems.

The functional equations describe the decision process exactly, and thus give considerable insight into the structure of the solution. The final solution is embedded in a set of solutions automatically obtained at the same time, so that variations in the numbers of stages and the initial state are easily treated by the one set of calculations. Computation may be saved by this technique (e.g. the motorist problem) although often the quantity of computation is an obstacle to the use of dynamic programming. For example any linear programming problem can be tackled by dynamic programming but the former method is usually computationally simpler.

A useful feature of dynamic programming is the dual relationship between the objective function and the policy function. There are always two parallel functions in the solution of a problem by dynamic programming. When we optimize a function, at the same time we determine the policy that optimizes it. In the farmer problem the general functional equation is

$$f_i(x) = \max_{0 \leqslant y \leqslant x} [p(y) + f_{i-1}(a[x-y])] \tag{3.21}$$

If $y = \bar{y}$ for the optimum value of $f_i(x)$ then both f_i and $\bar{y}$ are functions of x.

$\bar{y} = \bar{y}(x)$ is the policy function
$f_i = f_i(x)$ is the objective function.

Finally in this section we describe briefly how infinite stage processes can be handled (if N is large we might want to consider the infinite stage process as an approximation). Consider the farmer problem, and let $N \to \infty$. In this case we now have a single equation instead of (3.21)

$$f(x) = \max_{0 \leqslant y \leqslant x} [p(y) + f(a[x-y])] \tag{3.22}$$

with a single allocation function $y = y(x)$ determined by the equation. It is by no means obvious that $f(x)$ exists for all forms of $p(y)$, although it is expected that $f(x)$ would exist in practical cases. Existence and uniqueness theorems can be established for equations like (3.22). It is sufficient to state here that solutions do exist for a wide range of such equations and that, when a solution does exist, it may be obtained by solving the corresponding equation for an N-stage problem and using the result that $f_N(x) \to f(x)$ as $N \to \infty$, as one would expect.

Example and applications

We conclude this chapter by working through an illustrative example problem and by going on to note a few other industrial and commercial applications of dynamic programming.

A Purchasing Problem. Suppose a buyer has to purchase a certain type of equipment in a range of sizes, which we will assume is continuous. A size greater than or equal to that required may be supplied and incurs no extra cost in use. The buyer can obtain bulk discounts by buying large quantities of a few sizes. Given the demand for each size and the discount rates, how many and what sizes should be purchased in order to minimize total purchasing costs?

Let

$d(s)$ = the total number of items of size $\leqslant s$ required.
$p(n, s)$ = the cost of n items of size s.
$c_i(s)$ = the minimum cost of buying all the $d(s)$ items using up to i distinct sizes.
s = the size of the largest item needed.

We assume that $(1/n)p(n, s)$ increases as s increases and decreases as n increases.

The problem then, is to balance the discounts against the cost of buying larger items than required. There will be a value, N, of i for which

$$c_N(s) \leqslant c_{N+j}(s), j = 1, \ldots, \infty$$

i.e. there is no advantage in buying more than N distinct sizes. Both N and $c_N(s)$ have to be determined.

If we buy only one size to satisfy the demand for sizes $\leqslant s$ then all

$$c_1(s) = p[d(s), s] \tag{3.26}$$

Suppose we allow two sizes to be bought. If these sizes are s and s', then

$$c_2(s) = \min_{s' \leqslant s} (p[d(s) - d(s'), s] + c_1(s')) \tag{3.27}$$

If $c_2(s) < c_1(s)$ it is worthwhile to buy two sizes rather than one.

In general, if we buy i sizes to satisfy the demand for all items $\leqslant s$, then the largest size must be s, and if the largest size other than s is s', then

$$c_i(s) = \min_{s'} (p[d(s) - d(s'), s] + c_{i-1}(s')) \tag{3.28}$$

We calculate whether $c_i(s) < c_{i-1}(s)$ for each value of i until $c_{i+1}(s) = c_i(s)$ at $N = i$. At this point we stop the process as the optimum number of distinct sizes has then been found.

As an example, let

$$d(s) = s$$
$$p(n, s) = s(n + k)$$
$$s = 20k$$

Then we have, if buying only one size,

$$n = d(s) = s$$

so that

$$c_1(s) = s(s + k) \tag{3.29}$$

and, in general

$$c_i(s) = \min_{s'} [s(s - s' + k) + c_{i-1}(s')] \qquad (3.30)$$

Using this equation the reader may verify, by induction, that

$$c_i(s) = \frac{i+1}{2i} s(s + ik) - \frac{i(i^2 - 1)}{24} k^2 \qquad (3.31)$$

and that this solution is given by

$$s' = \frac{(i - 1)}{i} (s - \tfrac{1}{2}ik) \qquad (3.32)$$

For exactly i sizes to be needed to satisfy the demand for all items $\leqslant s$ in an optimal manner,

$$\tfrac{1}{2}i(i - 1)k \leqslant s \leqslant \tfrac{1}{2}i(i + 1)k \qquad (3.33)$$

a result which can also be verified by induction.

From (3.33), and since $s = 20k$, we need six distinct sizes. The largest size is s. The next is, from (3.32) with $i = 6$,

$$s' = 5\left(\frac{20}{6} k - \frac{1}{2}k\right) = \frac{17}{24} s \qquad (3.34)$$

Repeatedly using (3.32), we see that we should standardize on sizes s, $\frac{17}{24}s$, $\frac{7}{15}s$, $\frac{11}{40}s$, $\frac{2}{15}s$, $\frac{1}{24}s$.

The above example may be classified as having deterministic outcomes, an infinite number of possible decisions, a finite but unknown number of stages, and an artificially created multi-stage decision process.

Other Practical Applications

(a) A chemical factory (4) is usually composed of interconnected process units, each a stage in the transformation of raw materials into a finished product—e.g. a stream of reactants passing from a mixer to a pre-heater, a reactor, a cooler, and an extraction column with operating variables and state variables at each stage. With the objective of maximizing the difference between the increase in the value of the stream due to the process and the cost of the process, a multi-stage decision process can be defined and delineated.

(b) Optimal satellite trajectory (5). Dynamic programming has been used to calculate the thrust control and fuel consumption policies that are required to put a satellite into orbit at a specified altitude and maximum horizontal velocity.

(c) Manganese problems (5). A problem analagous to the "make or buy" type is that of whether to import or produce domestically. This has been studied for manganese. With domestic production involving a build-up of capacity, and with a stochastic political situation internationally, manganese should be obtained at minimum expected total cost.

(d) Transportation (1). Given a number of sources, with resources x_i, and a number of destinations with demands y_j, it is required that the x_i must satisfy the y_j at minimum transport cost and

$$\sum_i x_i = \sum_j y_j$$

The transportation method solves this easily if linear transport costs can be assumed, but dynamic programming will solve the problem for non-linear or stochastic costs.

(e) Scheduling (6). If there are a number of different items to be processed on a number of machines of different type, which must be used in a fixed order, and if the process times for each item on each machine is known, in what order should the items be processed to minimize total processing time?

(f) Allocation of resources (1). For a complex of industrial processes (collieries, washeries, mining machinery factories, transport facilities, coking plants) all employed in the production of coke, we can allocate resources, such as money, men, equipment, to produce, wash or transport coal, or make coke, or sink collieries, build washeries, factories, railways, or coke plants. What allocation policy maximizes the tonnage of coke produced in a given period?

(g) Stock control (7). A reservoir collects water during high river flow for use during low flow to generate electricity. Future river flow is unknown, steam plants are available to supplement the electricity supply when water is not available, and the supply of some customers may be interrupted. How should the present versus future use of water be balanced against the uncertain future flow to minimize the expected cost of supplemented energy?

(h) Replacement (2), (3). In rubber tyre manufacture a machine simultaneously moulds a tyre onto each of two "bladders". If a bladder fails while producing a tyre, that tyre must be scrapped and the bladder replaced, which means stripping down the machine. While the machine is stripped the second bladder can be replaced relatively cheaply. The chance of failure increases with the age of a bladder (i.e. the number of tyres already produced on it). It is required to find a policy for bladder replacement which minimizes the cost of producing N tyres.

(i) Networks (1). A map has N district locations numbered $i = 1, 2, \ldots, N$ and a matrix $T = (t_{ij})$ tells the time to travel from i to j. Starting in the first location we wish to pursue a route which minimizes the total time required to travel to the Nth point, using any of the other locations. If f_i = time required to go from i to N, $i = 1, 2, \ldots, N - 1$, then

$$f_i = \min_j (t_{ij} + f_j)$$

(j) Equipment resetting (8), (9). A piece of equipment is producing goods and the proportion of goods produced which are defective increases in a known statistical manner because the setting of the equipment departs through time from its original value. When should it be reset?

(k) Siting pylons (10). An overhead electric power transmission line has to be got from *A* to *B* using pylons. There are numerous physical constraints which must be satisfied. How, within these constraints, can construction costs be minimized?

References

1. Bellman, R. *Dynamic Programming*. Princeton University Press 1957.
2. Sasieni, M. W. A Markov Chain Process in Industrial Replacement. *Opnl. Res. Quart.* **7.4** pp. 148–155 1956.
3. Dreyfus, S. E. A Note on an Industrial Replacement Process. *Opnl. Res. Quart.* **8.4** pp, 190–193 1957.
4. Aris, R. *The Optimal Design of Chemical Reactors: A Study in Dynamic Programming*. Academic Press 1961.
5. Dreyfus, S. Dynamic Programming. *Progress in Operations Research*, Vol. 1. (Ed. Ackoff, R. L.) John Wiley & Sons Inc. 1961.
6. Bellman, R. and Gross, O. Some Combinatorial Problems Arising in the Theory of Multi-Stage Processes. *J. Soc. Indust. Appl. Math.* **2.3** pp. 175–183.
7. Little, J. D. C. The Use of Storage Water in a Hydroelectric System. *Opnl. Res.* **3.2** pp. 187–197 1955.
8. Hall, R. I. and Eilon, S. Controlling Production Processes which are subject to Linear Trends. *Opnl. Res. Quart.* **14.3** pp. 279–289 1963.
9. White, D. J. Dynamic Programming and Equipment Resetting Decision Rules. *Opnl. Res. Quart.* **15.2** pp. 133–137 1964.
10. Ranyard, J. C. and Wren, A. The Optimum Arrangement of Towers in an Electrical Power Transmission Line. *Computer Journal* **10.2** pp. 1957–1962 1967.

Further reading

Reference 1 above.
White, D. J. *Dynamic Programming*. Oliver & Boyd 1969.
Hadley, G. *Non-linear and Dynamic Programming*. Addison-Wesley Publishing Co. Inc. 1964.
Bellman, R. E. and Dreyfus, S. E. *Applied Dynamic Programming*. Princeton University Press 1962.
Howard, R. A. *Dynamic Programming & Markov Processes*. J. Wiley & Sons 1960.

Examples for solution

1. A barge whose maximum capacity is 100 tonnes is loaded with three different kinds of package. The weight and value of each kind of package is as follows:

Package	Weight (tonnes)	Value (£)
1	29	38
2	22	27
3	16	19

How many packages of each kind should be loaded to carry as valuable a cargo as possible? Show that this problem can be solved by computing three functions, of which the first is

$$f_1(W) = V_1[W/w_1]$$

and the general equation is

$$f_i(W) = \max_{0 \leqslant n \leqslant [W/w_i]} (nV_i + f_{i-1}(W - nw_i)) \quad \text{for} \quad i > 1$$

where W = total weight of a cargo,
  V_i = value of ith package,
  w_i = weight of ith package,
  n = number of packages of kind i,
and $[x]$ = largest integer $\leqslant x$.

2. We have 32 sacks of coal, all the same weight except one which is heavier, and a balance. Show that the weighing procedure which minimizes the maximum number of weighings required to locate the odd sack can be determined by repeated use of the equation

$$H_i = \min_s [\max (H_{i-2s}, H_s)] + 1$$

and hence calculate H_{32}.

What is the maximum number of sacks that can be handled in a total of 5 weighings?

3. A colliery is working four faces and has three machines of two different types, A and B, available. Any face not worked by machine would be hand-filled. Determine the largest possible daily output from the colliery from the following table of outputs.

Method of working	Face				Machines available
	1	2	3	4	
Hand-filling	200	220	180	250	
Machine A	250	260	240	270	1
Machine B	260	290	260	330	2

Hint for formulation: let $f_i(a, b)$ = maximum output from the first i faces with a machines of type A and b machines of type B available.

4. Consider the following stock control situation. The stock level, x, of one item is reviewed at fixed, equally spaced intervals and the level made up to a new chosen level, y. Over an N-interval period a policy consists of a set of levels $(y_1, y_2, \ldots, y_N)$ to which the stock is made up. Suppose that the stock is at level x at the beginning of the first interval. The cost of ordering one item is k and the cost of a stock-out of one item is c. Orders are assumed to be filled immediately and one demand is made in each interval. The size of this demand is determined by a probability distribution; $p(s)$ is the probability that the demand in a period will be s.

The problem is to determine the policy which minimizes the expected total cost of ordering plus stock-outs. Formulate this as a dynamic programming problem.

5. We are buying lorries. For a typical lorry the cumulative undiscounted cost up to a time t after purchase is $P + Qe^{2at} - Q$ where P is the purchase price and Q is a random variable. Assume we are going to go on replacing lorries indefinitely and that £1 spent at time t from now has a present value £e^{-at}. Show that the best scrapping rule is:

$$\text{Scrap when } t = \frac{1}{2a} \log \left(\frac{C}{2Q}\right)$$

where $C = 2\{E\sqrt{2Q}\}^2 + P - 2EQ + 2E\sqrt{2Q}\sqrt{(E\sqrt{2Q})^2 + P - 2EQ}$.

For the special case $P = 50$, $Q = 2$ with probability half and 8 otherwise, show that $C = 100$.

Show that the cost of adopting the best policy which assumes all lorries equal exceeds the cost of the policy you have developed by about 5% in present value terms.

6. Show how to formulate the general linear programming problem as a problem in dynamic programming.

Use dynamic programming to maximize $6x + 2y + 3z$ subject to $x, y, z \geqslant 0$, $2x + 3y + z \leqslant 10$, $x + 7y + 2z \leqslant 18$.

Would there be any virtue in using a dynamic programming based method for solving the linear programming problem in preference to the usual simplex method?

7. Solve the farmer problem described in the chapter when $p(y) = \sqrt{y}$. Consider the case when the number of stages is very large by letting N tend to infinity. Does the solution to the infinite stage problem make sense? Are any deficiencies in the model implied? Consider a modified problem in which a unit return 1 period hence is worth only $\alpha(<1)$ now. Comment on the new solution.

Finally, examine the problem when a is a random variable which is A with probability q and O with probability $1 - q$.

4   Decision theory and theory of games

Introduction

The general decision situation is this: faced with an imperfectly known state of nature, we have to choose one of a set of alternative decisions. The degree of preference we attach to the various possible decisions depends on the true state of nature that exists when the decision becomes effective. The term "state of nature" is used here to mean those factors, outside our control, which are relevant to the outcome of the decision we have to take.

Before making a final decision, certain exploratory studies may be made. These studies will be designed to provide information on the true state of nature in order to improve our final decision, and may be carried out in a number of stages, the results of each stage suggesting the form of the subsequent studies. The decisions defining the studies we are to make are known as experimental decisions, and the alternative final decisions are known as terminal decisions.

The set of all possible terminal decisions, together with all possible experimental decisions associated with each stage of a decision situation defines the total decision space. A rule that tells us which experimental decision to take first, which are succeeding stages and, depending on the outcome of each of these, which terminal decision to take is known as a decision rule or decision function. A random element may be introduced so that depending on the outcome of a particular stage, the next decision is to be chosen at random from some subset of possible decisions. Different religious beliefs which provide their adherents with principles to guide their actions are an example of different decision rules. Which is the best rule to adopt will depend on the true state of nature.

Adoption of a particular decision rule leads to two types of cost: the cost of the experimentation and the loss from making an incorrect terminal decision. With each rule we associate a risk function, the sum of these two costs. The value of the risk function will depend on the rule adopted and on the true state of nature. The problem of decision theory is the selection of optimum decision rules.

The behaviour of a decision rule may be judged by the values that the associated risk function takes for the various values of the state of nature. If we can find a decision rule that is best for all possible values of the state of nature, the decision problem is solved. In general we shall find that one decision rule will be best for certain values of the state of nature, but inferior to other rules for values outside this range. The number of decision rules that have to be considered may be reduced in two ways:

(a) By looking for admissible decision rules. An admissible rule is best for at least one possible value of the state of nature.

(b) By looking for a complete class of decision rules. For any rule not in the complete class we can find a rule in the class that is better for all possible values of the state of nature. In general the complete class is the class of all admissible decision rules.

To decide between the various admissible decision rules a criterion is required. Several criteria have been suggested and these are discussed later.

The above general development is due primarily to Wald (1). Examples of a sequential decision procedure are found in quality control but in other fields some more or less arbitrary simplification is usually made, either to make a decision without experimentation, or to decide in advance which variables are to be observed: the usual non-sequential case found in statistics.

The degree of preference to be attached to a particular decision for a specific value of the state of nature may be measured either in absolute terms—utility is the usual word—or relative to the merits of the other possible decisions in the same conditions—known as loss or regret. Both utility and regret are discussed below.

Later in the chapter we go on to consider a particular type of decision in which the states of nature in the above description are replaced by states taken up by some opponent who is acting in his own interests which are presumably not our interests also. As we shall see it is sometimes useful to think of nature as an opponent of this type: if we are unsure about the probabilities of the states of nature there might be something to be said for assuming that nature acts as an opponent in the sense that we assume nature arranges itself in the way most inconvenient to ourselves. Competitive situations of this type have given rise to the theory of games.

Example application of decision theory

A simple example will help to illustrate the above description of the general decision theory problem. Similar examples will be found in reference 2.

A depot for the distribution of smokeless fuel is to be established. There are two possible sites, one in town *A*, the other near town *B*. Whichever site is adopted the customer will pay the same price for his fuel, so it is not thought that the location of the depot will influence the potential market to any extent. The state of nature is considered to have three possible values: either more than 60% of future demand will be from town *A*, or more than 60% from town *B*, or the future demand will be divided approximately equally between them. Calculations of the transport costs from the supplying plants to each of the possible depots, and from the depots to each of the two towns, enable us to set up the following matrix showing the utility associated with each decision for each possible value of the state of nature. (In this example we can assume that utility is measured by the present value of all profits ensuing from the decision.) The alternative decisions are a_1 and a_2. The possible values of the state of nature are s_1, s_2 and s_3.

Utility

	s_1 (bulk of sales to town *A*)	s_2 (sales equally divided)	s_3 (bulk of sales in town *B*)
a_1 (site in town *A*)	100 (very good)	40	0 (very bad)
a_2 (site in town *B*)	10 (bad)	60	80 (good)

The above utility matrix shows the value to us of the various possible outcomes. We can convert it to a regret matrix. For each possible value of the state of nature, the entries in the regret matrix show the amount by which the decision chosen falls short of the best possible decision. s_1, s_2 and s_3 are mutually exclusive and have unit total probability.

Regret

	s_1	s_2	s_3
a_1	0 (very good)	20	80 (bad)
a_2	90 (very bad)	0 (very good)	0 (very good)

Thus if s_1 is the true state of nature we shall have zero regret if we adopt a_1. If we adopt a_2 the value of the outcome will be $(100 - 10) = 90$ units worse, so that our regret will be 90 units. Note that regret is measured in the opposite sense to utility. For the rest of this example we shall use the regret matrix.

A sample survey is designed and a questionnaire sent to householders in each town. It is decided to classify the results of the survey as favourable to town *A* if more than 70% of positive replies are from town *A*, as favourable to town *B* if more than 70% are from town *B*, and otherwise as indicating no definite difference. The result of the survey may not represent the true state of nature. The following matrix indicates the probability of obtaining each of the possible results of the survey, for the three possible values of the state of nature. The possible results of the survey are labelled z_1, z_2 and z_3.

	s_1	s_2	s_3
z_1 (favourable to town A)	0·6	0·3	0·2
z_2 (not decisive)	0·3	0·5	0·3
z_3 (favourable to town B)	0·1	0·2	0·5

Deciding to make the above survey constitutes our experimental decision. We have excluded the possibility of further experiment. There are two possible terminal decisions, a_1 and a_2.

All the possible decision rules can be represented in a convenient form by using ordered suffices to denote the decision to be taken when observation z_i is made. The rules are represented by r_{kmn}, where $k, m, n = 1$ or 2, and mean that decision a_k is taken if z_1 is observed, decision a_m if z_2 is observed and decision a_n if z_3 is observed. There are a total of eight possible rules. We compute the possible values of the risk function. For example, r_{122}:

if the true state is s_1, the regret is

$$0·6 \times 0 + 0·3 \times 90 + 0·1 \times 90 = 36$$

if the true state is s_2, the regret is

$$0·3 \times 20 + 0·5 \times 0 + 0·2 \times 0 = 6$$

if the true state is s_3, the regret is

$$0·2 \times 80 + 0·3 \times 0 + 0·5 \times 0 = 16$$

The argument is that if the true value of the state of nature is s_1, we have a 0·6 chance of observing z_1 which under this rule will lead us to adopt a_1 with associated regret (for s_1) of zero. We have a 0·3 chance of observing z_2 which will lead us to adopt a_2 with associated regret of 90 units, etc.

The cost of experiment has been fixed in advance in this example and does not depend on the decision rule adopted. This cost may therefore be ignored whilst we are evaluating the decision rules so that here risk and loss (regret) are equivalent.

The possible values of the risk function for each decision rule can be tabulated:

	s_1	s_2	s_3
r_{111}	0	20	80
r_{112}	9	16	40
r_{121}	27	10	56
r_{122}	36	6	16
r_{211}	54	14	64
r_{212}	63	10	24
r_{221}	81	4	40
r_{222}	90	0	0

The rules of r_{211} and r_{212} are inadmissible since each is inferior to r_{122}. The six remaining form a complete class. The first, r_{111}, is best when s_1 is the true value of the state of nature and the last, r_{222}, is the best for s_2 or s_3, but the worst for s_1. The others are intermediate and some criterion is required to judge between them.

If we can obtain some idea of the relative probabilities of s_1, s_2 and s_3 that is independent of our sample survey, we can select the decision rule which minimizes the expected risk. For instance if we consider (before the survey) s_1 to be as likely as s_2 and s_3 together, and s_2 rather more likely than s_3, we might attach prior probabilities 0·5 to s_1, 0·3 to s_2 and 0·2 to s_3. The expected risk for r_{111} is then:

$$0.5 \times 0 + 0.3 \times 20 + 0.2 \times 80 = 22$$

Working out the expected risk for each rule we obtain the following:

for r_{111} the expected risk is 22·0
for r_{112} the expected risk is 17·3
for r_{121} the expected risk is 27·7
for r_{122} the expected risk is 23·0
for r_{221} the expected risk is 49·7
for r_{222} the expected risk is 45·0

and rule r_{112} with expected risk 17·3 is seen to minimize the expected risk. A rule selected in this way by using prior probabilities is known as a Bayes' strategy. Had we used the utility matrix and worked throughout with utilities instead of risks we should have obtained the same optimum strategy. This is a property of Bayes' strategies and is not true for some of the criteria discussed below.

We can calculate if the sample survey is expected to be worthwhile. In its absence we should merely select the a_i which minimizes the risk. Under a_1 the risk is:

$$0.5 \times 0 + 0.3 \times 20 + 0.2 \times 80 = 22$$

and under a_2 the risk is:

$$0.5 \times 90 + 0.3 \times 0 + 0.2 \times 0 = 45$$

so that the best rule is a_1 with expected risk 22. Comparing this with the minimum expected risk after the sample survey of 17·3, we see that the expected value of the survey is $(22 - 17.3) = 4.7$ units.

Expected value of perfect information

It would be worth paying out up to 4·7 units to have the survey undertaken. However it is not an awfully good survey in that if the true state of nature is s_1 the survey is only 60% likely to indicate so. How much would it be worth to get a survey carried out which measured the true state of nature with certainty? The answer is clearly anything up to 22 units, since if the survey is that good we can be sure, for example, that if its outcome is favourable to town A, s_1 is the true state of nature and we choose decision a_1 in the sure knowledge that our regret will be zero. Thus our expected regret represents how much we are willing to pay to undertake such a survey. Just as importantly it represents the maximum amount we are willing to pay to get information of any kind. Since even perfect information can save only 22 units of regret, there is no point in conducting any experiment which costs more.

The expected regret is often referred to as the expected value of perfect information.

Let us check the assertion made above that for a Bayes' strategy maximizing utility minimizes regret by calculating the expected utility with and without a perfect survey. Without a perfect survey, and recalling that we are assigning probabilities 0·5, 0·3 and 0·2 to states s_1, s_2 and s_3 respectively, we see that the expected utility of a_1 is 62 and of a_2 39. (These figures should be compared with the corresponding regrets of 22 and 45; the difference between the two decisions is the same.) We therefore choose a_1 in the absence of the survey to maximize our expected utility. Our perfect survey will give us the information that a specific one of the states of nature is certain to occur. The probability that it will tell us s_1 is certain to occur in 0·5, that s_2 is certain 0·3 and that s_3 is certain 0·2. If it tells us s_1 is certain to occur we shall take decision a_1 to obtain a utility of 100; if s_2, a_2 to obtain a utility of 60; and if s_3, a_2 to obtain a utility of 80. Our expected utility is thus

$$0.5 \times 100 + 0.3 \times 60 + 0.2 \times 80 = 84$$

so there is a gain in utility of 22 units if a perfect survey is undertaken which is consistent with the figure previously calculated for the reduction in regret.

Decision trees

A convenient way to analyse decisions where probabilities can be assigned to the states of nature is by the use of decision trees. This is particularly the case if lengthy sequences of decisions, possibly taken as a consequence of an interwoven sequence of experiments, is necessary. We shall use the same example to illustrate the use of decision trees although the reader should bear in mind that this example is a comparatively simple one.

In considering the smokeless fuel depot problem we might initially make one of three decisions; a_1, a_2 and a_3, where a_3 is the decision to undertake the survey. We draw up a figure starting from a point called a decision node, which we shall represent by a square, with three lines leaving it representing these three decisions, thus:

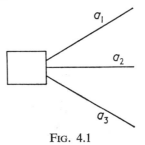

FIG. 4.1

There is an outcome of taking each decision which depends on which of the three possible states of nature occur. Chance dictates which state actually does occur. We represent these possible outcomes by lines emanating from a so-called chance node, which we shall represent by a circle, thus:

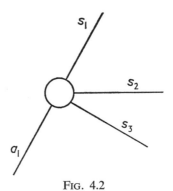

FIG. 4.2

We continue with choice nodes and chance nodes alternating until we reach the end of the tree when no more decisions need to be taken. The full tree is drawn up thus:

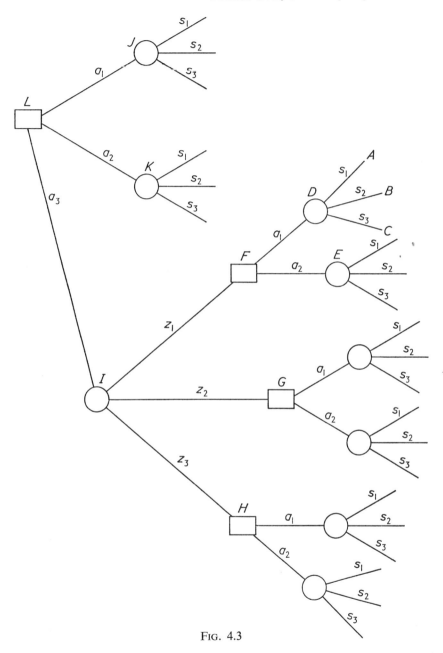

FIG. 4.3

It will be seen that there are 24 possible outcomes according to the way we decide and the states nature actually takes up. Let us now suppose that undertaking the survey reduces any subsequent utilities by 4 units. What would be the utility if point A in the diagram were reached as a consequence of our taking decision a_3, the survey giving result Z_1, our taking decision a_1 and finally nature taking state s_1? It would be 96, 100 from the utility matrix less 4 for the cost of the survey. We can similarly fill in utilities for all the end points. Those for B and C, for example, are 36 and −4.

We now ask: what is the expected utility for point D? That is, what is our expected utility given that we have undertaken the survey, its result is Z_1 and we have taken decision a_1? The answer is

$$p_1 96 + p_2 36 + p_3(-4)$$

where p_i is the probability that nature will take up state s_i given that the survey result was Z_1. It is not immediately obvious what the value of p_i is, but it can be inferred from the table of probabilities of Z_i for the different s's and the prior probabilities of the s's, in this way: the probability that Z_1 is the result of the survey is

$$0{\cdot}6 \times 0{\cdot}5 + 0{\cdot}3 \times 0{\cdot}3 + 0{\cdot}2 \times 0{\cdot}2 = 0{\cdot}43$$

being the probability that Z_1 results when s_1 is the true state of nature times the probability that s_1 is the true state of nature plus corresponding terms for s_2 and s_3. Thus 43 times out of 100 we would expect to get the result z_1. Moreover in 30 of these 43 times the true state of nature would be s_1, in 9 times s_2 and in 4 times s_3. Thus $p_1 = \frac{30}{43}$, $p_2 = \frac{9}{43}$ and $s_3 = \frac{4}{43}$, and the expected utility for point D is $\frac{3188}{43}$.

In a like manner we can find the expected utilities at the other chance nodes one node in from the end nodes. That for point E, for example, is $\frac{986}{43}$.

We now ask what value attaches to point F which is a decision node. The answer is $\frac{3188}{43}$ because if we were at point F—that is we had undertaken the survey with result Z_1—we should be at liberty to choose which of points D and E to make for. We would clearly opt for D which has the higher expected utility.

Expected utilities can be attached to G and H in just the same way as to F; then to I in the same way in relation to F, G and H as for D in relation to A, B and C; then to J and K; and finally to L in relation to I, J and K just as for F in relation to D and E. The reader might care to work through this process. He will find that a_3 is the preferred initial decision; a_1 is the preferred decision if and when either of points F and G is reached; and a_2 if and when point H is reached. The decision tree approach has therefore led to the same conclusions as the previous approach. The reader will be able to convince himself that in effect the same calculations have been done. He will also probably have noticed that we have used what is essentially a dynamic programming approach: if not it would be a useful exercise for him to convince himself that we have.

Decision trees are often to be preferred to the approach of evaluating the risk associated with each decision rule. Less arithmetic is needed and it is easily organized. The best decision rules emerge naturally from it. Note the data requirements: the utility associated with each of the end points and the probabilities of the chance events given that the chance node from which they emanate has been reached, the conditional probabilities as they are called. In deciding what utility to attach to an end point we must be clear exactly what reaching that end point implies so that we can put a value on it. We shall probably be able to put a cash value on the point once it has been reached (perhaps the present value of future cash flows) but we must not overlook the cash cost of reaching it. It is often convenient to put cash flows on each line in the decision tree (including the lines leading to the end points where the flow is the cash value of having reached that end point) and to calculate the cash position at each end point by summing the cash flows along the path of the decision tree leading to it. The cash position at the end point could then be transformed into utility (see below).

To summarize, in using a decision tree we set up a network of choice and chance nodes as described above; to each line emanating from a chance node we assign conditional probabilities; and to each terminal point we assign a utility. The tree is worked through backwards assigning utilities to all nodes. The utility of a chance node is the weighted sum of the utilities of the decision nodes which follow it, the weightings being the probabilities. The utility of a decision node is the maximum utility of the chance nodes which follow it, which also indicates which decision we should take at that node.

Decision criteria

In the absence of any prior beliefs about the relative probabilities of the s_i we cannot compute expected risk or expected regret or expected utility: some other criterion for deciding between the decision rules must be adopted. A number of such criteria have been developed primarily by writers on game theory (3), and are not entirely appropriate for games against nature into which category the above example falls. The reader will see when we discuss games that we consider that our opponent attempts always to maximize his gain at our expense. This seems unduly pessimistic when the opponent is nature. Furthermore the proposed criteria assume complete ignorance of the relative probabilities of our opponent's strategies, which is in most cases unrealistic for games against nature. This is in contrast to the Bayes' strategy used above where we assume we know these probabilities. There are certain other objections to the matrix representation of the decision problem which will be outlined later.

However even when the probabilities are known we might prefer a criterion other than expected something. Our decisions are either in situations which recur many times, such as whether to take an umbrella, or in situations which are, in general, relatively infrequent, such as buying a house or marrying. In the former it is reasonable to minimize the expected loss, whereas in the latter we may be concerned with avoiding some calamitous possibility which has a very limited probability (4).

We shall state each of a number of criteria, apply it to the above example and indicate the comments that have been made about it. The nomenclature we shall adopt is that the outcome of decision i in face of the jth possible value of the state of nature has expected utility U_{ij}.

Minimax. The criterion tells us to adopt the decision which maximizes the least possible utility:

$$\max_i \min_j [U_{ij}]$$

Going back to the utility matrix of the example above, values (j) of the state of nature decisions (i)

	s_1	s_2	s_3
a_1	100	40	0
a_2	10	60	80

we see that the minimum utility for a_1 is zero and for a_2 is 10. Thus a_2 maximizes the least possible utility. A competitive situation has a solution only when the game has a saddlepoint, which is not the case here. This is explained fully later in the chapter.

Minimax corresponds to maximizing one's security level, or being completely pessimistic about the possible outcome of any situation. It is hardly to be recommended for stockjobbers. The size of possible gains is ignored. Consider for example:

	s_1	s_2
a_1	0	10
a_2	1	1

and

	s_1	s_2
a_1	0	1,000
a_2	1	1

In each case minimax recommends a_2.

Where alternative decisions have equal utilities in one situation but one, say a_1, is preferred to a_2 is another situation, then it seems reasonable that a_1

should still be preferred to a_2 in a third situation which is a (probability) mixture of the first two. This is not the case with minimax for:

	s_1	s_2
a_1	0	−9
a_2	−992	0

here a_1 is preferred,

	s_3	s_4
a_1	1,000	0
a_2	1,000	0

here a_1 and a_2 are equivalent,

	$s_1 + s_3$	$s_2 + s_4$
a_1	1,000	−9
a_2	8	0

but here a_2 is preferred.

Minimax Regret. Formally this is equivalent to minimax where instead of the utility matrix we use the regret matrix. The elements in the regret matrix are defined by:

$$r_{ij} = \max_r U_{rj} - U_{ij}$$

We select the decision for which:

$$\min_i \max_j [r_{ij}]$$

The min and max are interchanged compared with the previous criterion because regret measures loss, in the opposite sense to utility.

In our example, using the regret matrix:

	s_1	s_2	s_3
a_1	0	20	80
a_2	90	0	0

we see that a_1 with a possible regret of 80 units, minimizes the maximum regret. In this example the two criteria described so far give different results.

Hurwicz (5). This criterion attempts an averaging procedure. For each possible decision we take a weighted average of the best and worst possible outcomes for that decision, and select the decision whose average is greatest: select a_i to maximize

$$H(a_i) = k \max_j U_{ij} + (1 - k) \min_j U_{ij}$$

where k, known as the optimism–pessimism index, lies between 0 and 1. Its precise value depends on the decision maker and is found by asking for what value of X, a_1 and a_2 represent equally attractive decisions in:

	s_1	s_2
a_1	0	1
a_2	X	X

The value of k is $1 - X$. Where $k = 0$ the criterion is equivalent to the minimax criterion.

Suppose we take $k = \frac{2}{3}$ in our example. Then

$$H(a_1) = 66\frac{2}{3}$$

and

$$H(a_2) = 56\frac{2}{3}$$

so that a_1 is selected. In fact a_1 will be preferred when k lies between 1 and $\frac{1}{3}$, and a_2 otherwise.

Two objections have been raised. It does not seem entirely reasonable that a_1 and a_2 should be equivalent (under this criterion) where:

	s_1	s_2	$s_3 \ldots s_n$
a_1	0	1	$1 \ldots 1$
a_2	1	0	$0 \ldots 0$

A third decision which is a (probability) mixture of two others, both of which have the same Hurwicz average, may have a different average itself. Thus for:

	s_1	s_2	s_3
a_1	0	1	0
a_2	1	0	0
a_3	$\frac{1}{2}$	$\frac{1}{2}$	0

where a_1 and a_2 have the same average, and a_3 is a mixture of a_1 and a_2, we see that

$$H(a_1) = H(a_2) = 2H(a_3)$$

Does this seem reasonable to you?

Bernoulli (Insufficient Reason). This criterion assumes that all n possible values of the state of nature are equally likely and selects the a_i which maximizes the mean utility: select i to maximize

$$\sum_j \frac{U_{ij}}{n}$$

In our example the mean utility of a_1 is $46\frac{2}{3}$ and of a_2 is 50 so we should select a_2.

The selection of the optimum decision under this criterion is sensitive to the precise way in which we define the possible decisions. Thus two possible partitions for a member of an O.R. Group might be:

(a) change job/do not change job
(b) take holy orders/become a self-employed consultant/do not change job

where the two relevant values of the state of nature are considered to be:

promotion in the Group within 3 months/no promotion

Fitting utilities to the possible outcomes:

	promotion	no promotion
change	0	1
stay	10	−5
holy orders	10	−4
consultant	−10	6
stay	10	−5

we see that for the first matrix it is best to stay, and for the second matrix it is best to enter holy orders, i.e. to change. The same objection will apply to others of the criteria.

Partial Ignorance. In practice we often have some inkling of the relative probabilities of the values of the state of nature and thus fall between criteria assuming complete ignorance, and a Bayes' strategy which requires numerical values for the probabilities. No totally satisfactory solution has been put forward, although we shall see later that the theory of games offers a partial solution. The interested reader might also care to consult references 5 and 6.

A fundamentally different approach which in principle avoids this difficulty is due to Savage (7), (8). He has built up a theory based on the notion of subjective probability. What matters is not some objective prior probability— which we cannot determine—but rather the probability we attach in our own mind to each possible value of the state of nature. We thereby make the best decision of which we are capable. The subjective probability is assessed by simple questions. For example to assess the subjective probability of values s_1, s_2 and s_3, we consider hypothetical acts a_1 and a_2 to give us this situation:

	s_1	s_2	s_3
a_1	100	0	0
a_2	Y	Y	Y

Then we ask:

(a) For what value of Y are we indifferent between a_1 and a_2? Say it is Y_0.
(b) For what probability p are we indifferent between on the one hand receiving Y_0 and on the other a gamble in which we receive 100 with probability p, and zero with probability $(1 - p)$? Say it is p_0.

For our answers to (a) and (b) to be consistent we must attach probability p_0 to s_1. A similar procedure will enable us to determine the probabilities we attach to s_2 and s_3. It is not certain that the three probabilities we obtain will be consistent. Savage (7) discusses an interesting example which he claims has enabled him to become more rational, but before describing this an outline will be given of utility theory as employed in decision making.

Utility theory

Our first evaluation of alternative decisions will be in financial terms. The monetary scale is not entirely satisfactory because the desirability of a certain sum of money may depend on the resources we have at the start. If I have to choose between two jobs, one at £1,200 p.a., and the other at £1,500, the extra £300 will have considerably more weight than in choosing between two others at say £4,200 and £4,500 (even apart from tax considerations). This is expressed in the question: why does a poor man walk in the rain while the rich man takes a cab? There are two problems here: the non-linear form of one person's preference scale, and secondly the incompatibility of rankings between different people. Similar problems may be found within and between sections of large organizations and numbers of experiments have been done to explain the apparent rationality of a person's choices (9).

What we need is some measure which genuinely reflects the decision maker's preferences and we call this measure utility. The decision maker will always choose the decision which has the highest utility to him.

If the decision is quantifiable with certainity in cash terms, it will be sufficient to have a utility function which converts cash to utility. However,

generally, the decision maker will have, in effect, a choice between gambles
and it will be more useful to define utilities in terms of gambles: the decision
maker will take that gamble which has the highest utility to him. (A special
case of a gamble is getting, or losing, a fixed sum with certainty.)

The achievement of Von Neumann and Morgenstern (10), was to show
that by the choice of a suitable utility function, preference can be made linear.
This is expressed by the following theorem: given two gambles f and g and
probabilities p and q, where $p + q = 1$, then there exists a function U such
that U satisfies certain axioms and $U(pf + qg) = pU(f) + qU(g)$ for all
values of p. (By $U(f)$ we mean the value we attach to the gamble f. The
"certain axioms" in question are spelled out in reference 10. They broadly
reflect common sense views of properties a utility function should have. "If
$U(f) > U(g)$ and $U(g) > U(h)$ then $U(f) > U(h)$" is one simple example.
Whether people's behaviour actually satisfies these axioms is a moot point.)

What is being said can be illustrated in this way. Suppose you offer to toss
a coin and give me £100 if it falls heads if I will give you £90 if it falls tails. I
attach a certain utility U_1 to this gamble which might be low if £90 would
bankrupt me. (I might even be willing to pay out say £20 to avoid such a
gamble.) You offer me a second gamble: heads I win £1,000, tails I give you
£90. I attach a utility U_2 to this gamble. U_2 is presumably higher than U_1.
You now offer me a rather more complicated gamble. I am to draw a card
from a randomly shuffled pack. If it is the Ace of Spades you will offer me
gamble 2, if not gamble 1. If I am to be consistent I shall attach a utility
somewhere between U_1 and U_2 to this gamble. If moreover my preference is
linear I shall attach a utility $\frac{51}{52}U_1 + \frac{1}{52}U_2$ to it. The theorem states that a
function of the odds and the stakes exists which defines the utility of the
gambles, in terms of the stakes and odds of each, which is such that the utility
I attach to this gamble, viewed on its own merits, equals $\frac{51}{52}U_1 + \frac{1}{52}U_2$, U_1
and U_2 now being the utility I attach to the first and second gambles using
this utility function; and that the utility function so defined has the common
sense properties one would expect of a utility function.

The reader will be interested to satisfy himself that using this utility
function, the difference between the utilities I attach to a certain £1,000 and
a certain £100 is $2(U_2 - U_1)$.

The point of all this is that, once the correct utilities have been entered, we
need consider only expected values, and the way we have computer expected
utilities and regrets in our earlier examples is justified. We assume that no
decision has infinite utility, although Pascal suggested that the choice of
heaven has. A fuller discussion is to be found in reference 2.

Returning to Savage's example, he argues as follows: suppose we have to
make a choice in each of two independent situations.

Situation 1—choose between

Gamble 1   £1m. with probability 1·00
Gamble 2   £5m. with probability 0·10
           £1m. with probability 0·89
           0   with probability 0·01

and

Situation 2—choose between

Gamble 3   £1m. with probability 0·11
        0   with probability 0·89
Gamble 4   £5m. with probability 0·10
        0   with probability 0·90

He first chose gamble 1 and gamble 4, but in terms of utility this implies:

$$1{\cdot}00U(1) > 0{\cdot}10U(5) + 0{\cdot}89U(1) + 0{\cdot}01U(0)$$
$$0{\cdot}10U(5) + 0{\cdot}90U(0) > 0{\cdot}11U(1) + 0{\cdot}89U(0)$$

from which we see that

$$0{\cdot}11U(1) > 0{\cdot}10U(5) + 0{\cdot}01U(0) > 0{\cdot}11U(1)$$

which is inconsistent. The reader who chose gambles 1 and 3 in the first place may compliment himself on his own rationality.

The need for a utility function arises also when we have to balance quantities measured on different scales. In studying an ambulance service, for example, one might have to try to strike a balance between the cost of the service and the time to answer a call on it.

Matrix representation of the decision problem

Formulation of the decision problem in the matrix form described above requires:

(a) A precise statement of the alternative courses of action.
(b) A partition of the state of nature into disjoint possible values.
(c) Evaluation of the outcome of each course of action for each of the possible values of the state of nature.
(d) Assignment of probabilities to the various values of the state of nature, or the adoption of a suitable criterion in the absence of any knowledge of these probabilities.

It may not be easy to meet these requirements. For example we have seen in the discussion of the Bernoulli criterion that the way we partition the state of nature may affect the choice of decision.

There are also great practical difficulties in assessing the relative probabilities. The computation attached to evaluating the various possible decisions will often be considerable. Nevertheless the attempt to formulate a decision problem in this way will focus our attention on the most important considerations and may disclose areas where further research is required. Experience has shown that even a clear statement of the alternative decisions open to us is sometimes overlooked.

Any computational difficulties can sometimes be avoided because occasionally a practical problem can be approximated by a model which allows the best decision rules to be developed without excessive numerical calculation. Such might be the case if the states of nature are described by a single (possibly vector) parameter, θ say, and the probability density function of θ is known, $f(\theta)$ say; and the utilities associated with a decision d_i and state of nature θ is $U(d, \theta)$. In this case we should choose d to maximize $\int U(d, \theta)f(\theta)d\theta$. In another case the risk function might be $R(d, \theta)$ and we choose d to minimize $\int R(d, \theta)f(\theta)d\theta$. If U, R and F have simple forms it might be possible to perform these operations very simply. (Rather more generally θ might have a prior distribution $f(\theta)$ and we can, by experiments which cost money, derive posterior distributions for θ, $f_2(\theta)$ for example, which pinpoint its likely value more precisely. d then includes the decision to experiment and R includes the cost of experimentation while f depends on d. However the general principles followed are the same as those followed in working numerical examples and the other difficulties are basically the same. See example 2 at the end of the chapter.

Theory of games

Decision theory deals with the choice of the best decision in any situation where full information is lacking. The theory of games, which was developed before decision theory and largely independently of it, arose from the study of a limited part of this field (10). It is concerned particularly with situations in which several independent participants each have to make decisions. Usually there is a conflict of interest between the participants. The development of the theory has been based almost exclusively on the minimax criterion, although in principle any criterion could be adopted.

The situations described here will be subject to the following restrictions:

(a) There are a finite number of participants (interested and disinterested parties).
(b) Each participant has a finite number of possible courses of action.
(c) The participant wishing to apply the theory must know all the courses of action available to the others but must not know which of these will be chosen.
(d) After all have chosen their courses of action their respective gains are finite.
(e) The gain of each participant depends upon the actions of the others as well as himself.
(f) All possible outcomes are calculable.

Situations which have all of these properties are called games. Solutions were first derived for games in which only two parties are involved and in which the losses of one are the gains of the other. Such situations are called zero sum two person games. The restrictions that apply to them are stringent and much recent work has been applied to finding general solutions under weaker restrictions. We shall, however, restrict our attention in the main to zero sum two person games and situations involving one interested party in which the other participants are disinterested forces.

Zero sum, two person games

The terminology often used in the theory of zero sum two person games is given below:

(a) Each interested party is called a player.
(b) A play of the game results when each player has chosen a course of action.
(c) After each play of the game one player pays the other an amount determined by the courses of action chosen.
(d) The decision rule by which a player determines his course of action is called a strategy. (To reach the decision regarding which strategy to use, neither player needs to know the other's strategy.)
(e) A mixed strategy is one where a player decides in advance to use all or some of his available courses of action in some fixed proportion. If a player decides to use only one particular course of action he is said to use a pure strategy.
(f) The value of a game is the average amount per play that one of the players would win in the long run if both players used their best strategies.
(g) A gain matrix is a table showing the amounts received by the player named at the left hand side after all possible plays of the game. The payment is made by the player named at the top of the table.

Setting up the Gain Matrix. For convenience we will call the players A and B. If they have N and M courses of action respectively, there are $N . M$ possible outcomes to every play. A table is constructed in which the columns are identified by B's courses of action and the rows are identified by A's courses of action. At the intersection of each row and column is indicated the amount that A would receive were the corresponding courses of action chosen by A and B.

This is the gain matrix of the game. This game is known as an $N \times M$ game, since A has N possible courses of action and B has M. For example, the table at the top of page 91 represents the gain matrix of a 3×4 game.

This matrix shows that were A to choose his course of action Z, and B to choose his course of action T, then A would be paid an amount k by B and similarly for other cells in the table.

The gains given in the table represent payments by B to A. If we re-draw the table so that B's courses of action identified rows and A's courses of action identified columns and if we also reversed the signs of the gains, the new table would represent the gain matrix for payments by A to B.

		T	U	V	W
		B's courses of action			
A's courses of action	X	a	b	c	d
	Y	e	f	g	h
	Z	k	l	m	n

Gain Matrix of a 3 × 4 game.

If the rules of the game are such that the payments of one player to another depend on chance, the gains shown would be the expected value of the gain in each case. For example, if when B chose course U and A chose Y, a coin was tossed to decide whether B should pay p or q units to A, the figure representing the gain to A in the table would be put equal to $\frac{1}{2}(p + q)$, i.e. its expected value.

If in the course of a series of plays A chooses courses X, Y and Z at random in the proportions $x:y:z$ respectively and B similarly chooses courses T, U, V and W in the proportions $t:u:v:w$ respectively, then A's strategy is written $A(x, y, z)$ and B's strategy is written $B(t, u, v, w)$. These are examples of mixed strategies.

A game is solved when the following has been determined:

(a) The average amount per play that A will win in the long run if A and B each uses his best strategy. This is the value of the game.
(b) The strategy to be used by A to ensure that his average gain per play is at least equal to the value of the game.
(c) The strategy to be used by B to ensure that his average loss per game is no more than the value of the game.

These strategies, (b) and (c), imply that both A and B adopt the minimax criterion.

Saddle Points. Suppose a game has the following gain matrix:

		1	2	3	
		B			
A	1	3	−1	2	−1
	2	−4	−1	13	−4
	3	2	−2	−1	−2
		3	−1	13	

Now player B is trying to minimize A's gain and player A to maximize it.

On studying the matrix, player A will note that by always playing A_1 he cannot lose more than 1, A_2 restricts his losses to 4, and A_3 to 2. Thus although A may be tempted to play A_2 and stand a chance of winning 13, if player B is using B_1 A may lose 4.

Player B notices that by sticking to B_2 throughout he cannot lose no matter what A may do.

Thus in this game each player has a best strategy which entails using the same course of action throughout. The solution to this game is written $A(1, 0, 0)$; $B(0, 1, 0)$. The value of the game to A is -1. Note that if A deviated from his best strategy he will lose 1 or 2, and if B does he will lose 3 or 2; this assumes in each case that the opponent continues to play his best strategy.

When the solution involves each player using only one course of action throughout the game is said to have a saddle point. The saddle point is the point of intersection of the two courses of action and the gain at this point is the value of the game.

A saddle point exists only when the maximum of the row minima equals the minimum of the column maxima. This result enables us to detect a saddle point.

Dominance. Consider the following gain matrix for A, which has no saddle point:

$$B$$

	1	2	3	4
1	2	2	3	4
2	4	3	2	2

A (rows 1, 2)

B's strategy 1 loses him 2 and 4 against A_1 and A_2 respectively, whereas by playing B_2 he loses 2 and 3.

Thus he should ignore strategy 1 since he can always do better by using B_2. B_1 is said to be dominated by B_2. Similarly B_4 is dominated by B_3.

Thus the game reduces to

$$B$$

2	3
3	2

A

The general rules for dominance are:

(a) If all the elements in a column, are greater than or equal to the corresponding elements in another column, then that column is dominated.

(b) Similarly, if all the elements in a row are less than or equal to the corresponding elements in another row, that row is dominated.

Dominated rows or columns may be deleted which reduces the size of the game, and one should always look for dominance when solving a game.

Solution of Zero Sum Two Person Games. If there is no saddle point, both players must mix their courses of action to optimize their returns. Linear programming provides a general method for determining the appropriate strategies. Consider the following game

$$B$$

		1	2	3
	1	6	0	3
A	2	8	-2	3
	3	4	6	5

There is no saddle point and no dominance so no rows or columns can be deleted.

Consider the game from B's point of view. Let the value of the game to A be V. B is trying to minimize V.

Let $B(y_1, y_2, y_3)$ be his optimum strategy. Then, if A pursues his first strategy, the value of the game to A is $6y_1 + 0y_2 + 3y_3$. B wishes to choose y_1, y_2 and y_3 to ensure that this is at most V. Thus B's strategy is subject to the constraint:

$$6y_1 + 0y_2 + 3y_3 \leqslant V$$

Consideration of the value to A of his pursuing his second and third strategies gives two other constraints:

$$8y_1 - 2y_2 + 3y_3 \leqslant V$$
$$4y_1 + 6y_2 + 5y_3 \leqslant V$$

In addition

$$y_1 + y_2 + y_3 = 1$$

by definition. B's problem is thus a linear programming problem. He must maximize Z where

$$
\begin{array}{lll}
Z & & + V = 0 \\
6y_1 & + 3y_3 + y_4 & - V = 0 \\
8y_1 - 2y_2 + 3y_3 & + y_5 & - V = 0 \\
4y_1 + 6y_2 + 5y_3 & + y_6 - V = 0 \\
y_1 + y_2 + y_3 & = 1
\end{array}
$$

y_1, y_2 and y_3 are obviously non-negative and y_4, y_5 and y_6 are non-negative slacks. However V (the value of the game) can be either positive or negative and to ensure that all the variables in the problem are non-negative V is expressed as the difference of two non-negative variables $V = V_1 - V_2$. Thus the full linear programming problem is:

Minimize Z for non-negative $y_1, y_2, y_3, y_4, y_5, y_6, V_1$ and V_2 subject to

$$
\begin{aligned}
Z & & + V_1 - V_2 &= 0 \\
6y_1 \qquad + 3y_3 + y_4 & & - V_1 + V_2 &= 0 \\
8y_1 - 2y_2 + 3y_3 \qquad + y_5 & & - V_1 + V_2 &= 0 \\
4y_1 + 6y_2 + 5y_3 \qquad + y_6 & - V_1 + V_2 &= 0 \\
y_1 + y_2 + y_3 & & &= 1
\end{aligned}
$$

In this example either of two final tableaux arise (this is a case when one of the reduced costs of a non-basic variable in the final tableau is zero):

$$
\begin{aligned}
Z \qquad\qquad + \tfrac{1}{6}y_5 + \tfrac{5}{6}y_6 &= \tfrac{14}{3} \\
y_4 - \tfrac{2}{3}y_5 - \tfrac{1}{3}y_6 &= \tfrac{2}{3} \\
y_1 - y_2 \qquad + \tfrac{1}{6}y_5 - \tfrac{1}{6}y_6 &= \tfrac{1}{3} \\
2y_2 + 1y_3 \qquad - \tfrac{1}{6}y_5 + \tfrac{1}{6}y_6 &= \tfrac{2}{3} \\
- \tfrac{1}{6}y_5 + \tfrac{7}{6}y_6 + V_1 - V_2 &= \tfrac{14}{3} \\[6pt]
Z \qquad\qquad + \tfrac{1}{6}y_5 + \tfrac{5}{6}y_6 &= \tfrac{14}{3} \\
y_4 - \tfrac{2}{3}y_5 - \tfrac{1}{3}y_6 &= \tfrac{2}{3} \\
y_1 \qquad + \tfrac{1}{2}y_3 \qquad \tfrac{1}{12}y_5 - \tfrac{1}{12}y_6 &= \tfrac{2}{3} \\
y_2 + \tfrac{1}{2}y_3 \qquad - \tfrac{1}{12}y_5 + \tfrac{1}{12}y_6 &= \tfrac{1}{3} \\
- \tfrac{1}{6}y_5 + \tfrac{7}{6}y_6 + V_1 - V_2 &= \tfrac{14}{3}
\end{aligned}
$$

From either tableaux we see that the value of the game is $\tfrac{14}{3}$. In the first tableau B's optimum strategy is $(\tfrac{1}{3}, 0, \tfrac{2}{3})$; in the second $(\tfrac{2}{3}, \tfrac{1}{3}, 0)$. He is indifferent between these strategies.

What is A's best strategy. We could formulate A's problem as a linear programming one. If his strategy is (x_1, x_2, z_3) he will want to maximize the value of the game subject to constraints like

$$6x_1 + 8x_2 + 4x_3 \geqslant V$$

(if B pursues his first strategy A wants to ensure his gain is at least V). If the reader goes on to formulate A's problem he will find that it is just the dual of B's problem. Therefore, A's best strategy is given by the reduced costs of the slack variables in the final tableaux, that is $(0, \tfrac{1}{6}, \tfrac{5}{6})$.

An Alternative Method of Solution. The method of solution by linear programming just described is a general method which can be used to solve any zero sum two person game. The special significance of it will be seen when games against nature are discussed in the next section. The following method can be used so long as there are no restrictions on B's courses of action.

Consider the following game:

			B	
		1	2	3
	1	3	−4	2
A	2	1	−3	−7
	3	−2	4	7

This game has no saddle point and no dominance. When the matrix is tested for a saddle point we see that the value must lie between −2 and +3. Therefore if 2 is added to every element in the matrix, the value of the new game will be non-zero and positive. We do this because the method of solution as shown below cannot be used if the value of the game is negative or zero. The new game is thus:

			B	
		1	2	3
	1	5	−2	4
A	2	3	−1	−5
	3	0	6	9

Let B's best strategy be y_1, y_2, y_3. The constraints are:

$$\left.\begin{array}{r} 5y_1 - 2y_2 + 4y_3 \leqslant V \\ 3y_1 - y_2 - 5y_3 \leqslant V \\ 6y_2 + 9y_3 \leqslant V \\ y_1 + y_2 + y_3 = 1 \end{array}\right\} \tag{4.1}$$

Dividing through equations (4.1) by $V(>0)$ and putting $y_i/V = Y_i$ we get:

$$\left.\begin{array}{r} 5Y_1 - 2Y_2 + 4Y_3 \leqslant 1 \\ 3Y_1 - Y_2 - 5Y_3 \leqslant 1 \\ 6Y_2 + 9Y_3 \leqslant 1 \\ Y_1 + Y_2 + Y_3 = \dfrac{1}{V} \end{array}\right\} \tag{4.2}$$

Since B is trying to minimize V, he must maximize $1/V$, so his problem is to maximize $1/V$ for non-negative Y_1, Y_2 and Y_3 subject to equations (4.1) and (4.2).

The final tableau is:

$$\frac{1}{V} + \tfrac{19}{10}Y_3 + \tfrac{1}{5}Y_4 + \tfrac{7}{30}Y_6 = \tfrac{12}{30}$$

$$Y_1 + \tfrac{7}{5}Y_3 + \tfrac{1}{5}Y_4 + \tfrac{1}{15}Y_6 = \tfrac{4}{15}$$

$$Y_5 - \tfrac{77}{10}Y_3 - \tfrac{3}{5}Y_4 + \tfrac{1}{30}Y_6 = \tfrac{11}{30}$$

$$Y_2 + \tfrac{3}{2}Y_3 \qquad - \tfrac{1}{6}Y_6 = \tfrac{1}{6}$$

Y_4, Y_5 and Y_6 being the slack variables. The solution is thus $V = \tfrac{30}{13}$, $y_1 (=VY_1) = \tfrac{8}{13}$, $y_2 = \tfrac{5}{13}$ while A's strategy is $(\tfrac{6}{13}, 0, \tfrac{7}{13})$.

This formulation is simpler to solve than the previous one—there are fewer rows and columns and no need to introduce artificial variables—but care must be taken to ensure that the value of the game is neither zero nor negative before using it.

Games against nature

Games against nature are rather different from a normal zero sum two person game because nature cannot be considered as an interested party. Nature does not know anything about the theory of games; thus we can often arrive at a better result for the player by imposing restrictions on nature's courses of action based upon previous experience. (In the depot siting example discussed earlier, which can be regarded as a game against nature, we assumed that nature's course of action was specified exactly.)

When such restrictions are imposed, saddle points, and dominant columns must be ignored, since nature will not necessarily ignore dominated courses of action; nature is not trying to do her best.

Bearing this in mind, and using all the knowledge at our disposal regarding nature's activities, we can calculate what player A should do in order to maximize his winnings against the worst that nature is able to do. The principles are illustrated by an example solved by linear programming. (More generally we might need some other form of mathematical programming to solve a game against nature.)

A firm making wireless sets discovers that a valve in one of its sets wears too quickly. The firm which supplies the valves recommends that a new type be installed. The new valve costs less than the old one but has not been tested in these sets. The question is, would the changeover be economically worthwhile to the wireless firm?

The wireless firm has three alternative courses of action:

(1) To change over immediately to the new valves.
(2) Test the new valves in some sets and make the change if the trial is successful.
(3) Ignore the suggestion and carry on installing the old valves.

Nature has the following alternative courses of action:

(1) The new valves will appear to be a success from the trial but they will not overcome the problem.
(2) The new valves will appear to be a success from the trials and will overcome the problem.
(3) The trial will indicate that the new valves will be unsuccessful and they will in fact be successful.
(4) The trial will indicate that the new valves will be unsuccessful and they will in fact be unsuccessful.

If the present valves are used, an additional cost of 5 units will be incurred on the manufacture of these sets.

A trial would cost one unit to carry out and the cost of a complete change-over to the new valves would be three units.

If the new valves were used and found to be successful, a reduction of 10 units in the cost of manufacturing the sets would result.

If the trial is unsuccessful the wireless firm will be credited with two units by the valve manufacturers.

The gain matrix for the wireless firm is given below.

Nature

		1	2	3	4
Wireless firm	1	$(-3 - 5)$	$(10 - 3)$	$(10 - 3)$	$(-3 - 5)$
	2	$(-1 - 3 - 5)$	$(10 - 1 - 3)$	$(-1 - 5 + 2)$	$(-1 - 5 + 2)$
	3	(-5)	(-5)	(-5)	(-5)

Nature

		1	2	3	4
Wireless firm	1	-8	7	7	-8
	2	-9	6	-4	-4
	3	-5	-5	-5	-5

Let nature's strategy be written $N(x_1, x_2, x_3, x_4)$. The valve firm tells the wireless firm the following:

(a) There is at least a 10% chance that the new valves will be successful so

$$x_2 + x_3 \geqslant 0{\cdot}1 \quad \text{or} \quad x_1 + x_4 \leqslant 0{\cdot}9$$

(b) If the valves would be unsuccessful, the trial will indicate this with a probability of at least 0·7. So

$$\frac{x_4}{x_1 + x_4} \geqslant 0{\cdot}7 \quad \text{or} \quad 0{\cdot}7x_1 - 0{\cdot}3x_4 \leqslant 0$$

(c) There is at least an 80% chance that if the new valves would be successful the trial will indicate this. So

$$\frac{x_2}{x_2 + x_3} \geqslant 0.8 \quad \text{or} \quad -0.2x_2 + 0.8x_3 \leqslant 0$$

Hence the restrictions on nature are all linear, being:

$$
\begin{aligned}
x_1 \qquad\qquad\qquad + \quad x_4 &\leqslant 0.9 \\
0.7x_1 \qquad\qquad\qquad - 0.3x_4 &\leqslant 0.0 \\
- 0.2x_2 + 0.8x_3 \qquad\quad &\leqslant 0.0 \\
x_1 + \quad x_2 + \quad x_3 + \quad x_4 &= 1
\end{aligned}
$$

The game is now solved from nature's point of view using the restrictions
and the inequations

$$
\begin{aligned}
-8x_1 + 7x_2 + 7x_3 - 8x_4 &\leqslant V \\
-9x_1 + 6x_2 - 4x_3 - 4x_4 &\leqslant V \\
-5x_1 - 5x_2 - 5x_3 - 5x_4 &\leqslant V
\end{aligned}
$$

where V is the value of the game to the wireless firm.

We now proceed as shown before. Let $V = V_1 - V_2$, and insert non-
negative slack variables x_5, x_6, x_7, x_8, x_9 and x_{10} to transform the inequations
into equations. The problem is now:

Maximize Z for non-negative x_1, x_2, . . ., x_{10}, V_1 and V_2 subject to

$$
\begin{aligned}
Z \qquad\qquad\qquad\qquad\qquad\qquad\qquad\qquad\qquad + V_1 - V_2 &= 0 \\
- 8x_1 + 7x_2 + 7x_3 - 8x_4 + x_5 \qquad\qquad\qquad - V_1 + V_2 &= 0 \\
- 9x_1 + 6x_2 - 4x_3 - 4x_4 \quad + x_6 \qquad\qquad - V_1 + V_2 &= 0 \\
- 5x_1 - 5x_2 - 5x_3 - 5x_4 \qquad\qquad + x_7 \qquad - V_1 + V_2 &= 0 \\
x_1 + x_2 + x_3 + x_4 \qquad\qquad\qquad\qquad &= 1 \\
x_1 \qquad\qquad\quad + x_4 \qquad\qquad + x_8 \qquad\qquad &= \tfrac{9}{10} \\
\tfrac{7x_1}{10} \qquad\qquad\quad - \tfrac{3x_4}{10} \qquad\qquad\qquad + x_9 \qquad &= 0 \\
- \tfrac{x_2}{5} + \tfrac{4x_3}{5} \qquad\qquad\qquad\qquad\qquad + x_{10} &= 0
\end{aligned}
$$

This is solved in the usual way.

Nature's best strategy is found to be (0·17, 0·08, 0·02, 0·63) and the firm's
best strategy (0, 1, 0), so the firm should adopt decision (2) and test the new
valves before deciding to instal them. The value of the game to the firm is
−4·55 which is a little better than the cost of the present difficulties. In the
event nature may not do her worst (from the firm's viewpoint) and the firm
might wish it had adopted a different decision. But by choosing decision (2)
the firm has ensured that the worst that can happen is better than the worst
had it decided differently—against decision (1) nature has a feasible strategy
that loses the firm 6·5 and against decision (3) nature always wins 5. The reader
might care to verify these figures.

N-person games

We shall indicate, but only briefly, an approach to games involving more than two interested parties. These games are usually called N-person games.

These games are usually treated as if two coalitions are formed by the N persons involved. The characteristics of such a game are the value of the various games between every possible pair of coalitions.

For 4 players there are 7 possible pairs of coalitions that can form if the players are A, B, C, D the possible coalitions are: A against BCD, B against ACD, C against ABD, D against ABC, AB against CD, AC against BD, and AD against BC.

The value of the game to a coalition of one is considered to be the minimum value that player is prepared to accept.

A solution of such a game is said to be any set of values which are at least equal to the set of values of the game to the coalitions of one. For example, if for the games A v. BCD, B v. ACD, C v. ABD and D v. ABC the values to A, B, C and D respectively are, say, 4, 6, 8 and 5, a solution to the main game would be any set of numbers V_1, V_2, V_3, V_4 where

$$V_1 \geqslant 4$$
$$V_2 \geqslant 6$$
$$V_3 \geqslant 8$$
$$V_4 \geqslant 5$$

The coalitions that are formed determine which strategy should be adopted by each player.

Other types of game situation

Two brief examples of game type situations which are excluded by restricting our attention to zero-sum competitive games follow. They are included mainly to draw the reader's attention to the fact that such situations are excluded, but the ingenious reader will find them interesting to speculate on.

Example of an Infinite Game. Consider a game represented by the following matrix:

		Player B								
		1	2	3	4	5	.	.	.	.	.
	1	0	−1	−1	−1	−1	.	.	.	.	.
	2	1	0	−1	−1	−1	.	.	.	.	.
	3	1	1	0	−1	−1	.	.	.	.	.
Player A	4	1	1	1	0	−1	.	.	.	.	.
	.	.	.	.	.	.	.	.	.	.	.
	.	.	.	.	.	.	.	.	.	.	.

Any finite termination has value zero but the general game is limited by practical considerations of the time taken to define one's decision.

Example of a Non-competitive Game. Two rustlers were arrested after taking part in the same robbery. The Sheriff presented them with the following formulation of their predicament. The payoffs are in months' imprisonment for each man, prisoner 1 first:

| | | Prisoner 2 | |
		Not Confess	Confess
Prisoner 1	Not Confess	1, 1	10, $\frac{1}{4}$
	Confess	$\frac{1}{4}$, 10	8, 8

Reference (12) discusses this and similar types of situation.

The value of the theory of games

Much the same criticisms can be levelled against the theory of games as against decision theory (see page 88), the more so as the theory is well developed only for the minimax criterion which implies more conservative policies than many firms would wish to pursue. The assumption that both players are equally skilful and equally well informed also tends towards conservative policies: one often hopes to be in a better position than one's competitors as far as, say, market research information goes.

Likewise a similar defence for the theory of games as for decision theory can be made. It provides a logical orderly way of looking at competitive situations and it provides guidance and ideas about the type of policy which may be most appropriate. Reference (11) gives a spirited defence of game theory.

References

1. Wald, A. *Statistical Decision Functions*. John Wiley & Sons Inc. 1950.
2. Chernoff, H. and Moses, L. E. *Elementary Decision Theory*. John Wiley & Sons Inc. 1959.
3. Thrall, R. M., Coombs, C. H. and David, R. L. *Decision Processes*. John Wiley & Sons Inc. 1954.
4. Barnard, G. A. Sampling Inspection and Statistical Decisions. *J.R. Statist. Soc.* B. **16.2** pp. 151–165 1954.
5. Hurwicz, W. N. *Econometrica* **19** pp. 343–344 1951.

6. Hodges, J. L. Jnr. and Lehmann, E. L. The Use of Previous Experience in Reaching Statistical Decisions. *Ann. Math. Stat.* **23** pp. 396–407 1952.
7. Savage, L. J. *Foundations of Statistics.* John Wiley & Sons Inc. 1954.
8. Savage L. J. *et al. The Foundations of Statistical Inference.* Methuen & Co. Ltd 1962.
9. Ackoff, R. L. *Progress in Operations Research.* Volume 1. John Wiley & Sons Inc. 1961. (See Chapter 2.)
10. Von Neumann, L. and Morgenstern, O. *The Theory of Games and Economic Behaviour.* Princeton University Press 1947.
11. Morgenstern, O. Game Theory: A New Paradigm of Social Science. Paper in Zwicky, F. and Wilson, A. G. (Editors). *New Methods of Thought and Procedure.* Springer 1967.
12. Howard, N. The Theory of Meta-Games and the Mathematics of Meta-Games. *General Systems* **11** pp. 167–200 1966.

Further reading

References 1 to 12 above.

Luce, R. D. and Raiffa, H. *Games and Decisions.* John Wiley & Sons Inc. 1957.

Blackwell, D. and Girshick, M. A. *Theory of Games and Statistical Decisions.* John Wiley & Sons Inc. 1954.

Raiffa, H. and Schlaifer, R. *Applied Statistical Decision Theory.* Harvard University Press 1961.

White, D. J. *Decision Theory.* Allen & Unwin 1970.

Adelson, R. M. and Norman, J. M. Operational Research and Decision-making; followed by a critique by Croston, J. D. and Gregory, G. *Opl. Res. Qtly.* **20.4** pp. 399–420 1969.

Williams, J. D. *The Complete Strategist, Being a Primer to the Theory of Games.* McGraw-Hill Book Co. Inc. 1954.

McKinsey, L. C. C. *Introduction to the Theory of Games.* Rand Corporation 1952.

Vajda, S. *The Theory of Games and Linear Programming.* Methuen & Co. Ltd 1956.

Shubick, M. The Uses of Game Theory in Management Science. *Management Science* **2.1** pp. 40–54 1955.

Beresford, R. S. and Peston, M. H. A Mixed Strategy in Action. *Opns. Res. Quart.* **6.4** pp. 173–175 1955.

Examples for solution

1. What do you understand by rational behaviour? Does it make sense to talk about the rational behaviour of an organization? In what ways do the rules for rational behaviour in an organization differ from those for an individual?

2. Future demand for an expensive item is expected to be Poisson but the mean, which depends on the economic climate, is unknown. Analysis of records suggests the exponential distribution fits the unknown mean θ. Obtain the optimum decision

function where there are two possible decisions, d_1 and d_2 with the following utilities:

for d_1, utility $= C_1\theta^{k_1}$ $(k_1 > 0)$
for d_2, utility $= C_2\theta^{k_2}$ $(0 > k_2 > -1)$

A small sample survey forecasts a demand of zero. Which decision should we adopt? Examine the special case where $k_1 = \frac{1}{2} = -k_2$ and $C_1 = 2C_2$.

3. Develop a simple model describing the insurance of goods on board a ship from the standpoint of shipper and insurer. Take the probability of loss as 1 in 10 and make Bernoulli's assumption that utility is proportional to the logarithm of assets. Assume that the assets of the shipper and insurer are £100,000 and £50m respectively and that the cargo is worth £10,000. Fix a reasonable premium.

4. Do you think unit trust managers are making use, either consciously or not, of decision theory or game theory? Do you think the board of a company which seeks to diversify is doing so? If not, why not?

5. (a) Two players A and B play the following game: A holds a bag containing three counters, one worth 1 unit, one worth 3 units and one worth 6. A takes a counter from the bag and before it is exposed, B guesses what it is. If he, B, is right he takes the counter, if he is wrong he gives A a counter of equal value to the draw.

   (i) Is this a fair game?
   (ii) What are A and B's best strategies?
   (iii) What is the value of the game to A?

   (b) After a run of losing A now decides to alter the rules thus: If B is wrong he pays A the sum of the draw and guess. If B is right A pays B twice the value of the draw.

   (i) Should B continue playing?
   (ii) If he does, what are the optimum strategies?

   (c) B decides he will not play this game, and says he will play so long as A pays him n times the counter drawn each time B guesses correctly. What value of n will make the game fair to B? Assume that each player has all strategies active.

6. In the game of two fingered Morra, each player extends one or two fingers and also guesses how many his opponent will show. If both are right or both are wrong, there is no payment, if only one player guesses correctly, he is paid the sum equivalent to the total number of figures shown.

   Write down the pay-off matrix and find the best strategy for each player.

7. A colliery intends to drive a 2,000 m horizontal tunnel through inclined strata. There are four kinds of powder that may be used and it is required to determine the powder buying policy which minimizes the maximum expected powder cost.

   Certain information is at hand concerning the strata through which we must drive. There are 5 kinds of strata, A, B, C, D, E, likely to be encountered.

> No more than 10% will be of type A
> No more than 20% will be of type B
> No more than 20% will be of type C
> No more than 60% will be of type D

The powder cost of drivage per metre is known for each type of strata and for each powder. These costs are given in the gain matrix below.

Strata		A	B	C	D	E
	1	−2	−3	−4	−5	−6
Powder	2	−2	−2	−3	−5	−6
	3	−4	−6	−6	−3	−1
	4	−3	−3	−3	−6	−5

(All the gains are negative since they represent payments by the colliery.)

8. A man wishes to dispose of a piece of land. He wishes to maximize the expected amount of money he gets subject only to selling within 6 months.
There are three ways in which he can effect the sale:
  (i) by immediate private sale at any time for 100 units;
  (ii) by auction; or
  (iii) through an agent.
If he sells by auction he will receive the money 2 months hence. The auctioneer thinks there is a 25% chance he will get 130 units, a 50% chance he will get 120 units and a 25% chance he will get 110 units. The auctioneer's fee will be 10 units. The man can put a reserve price on the land but will still have to pay the auctioneer's fee. He can put the land up for auction only once.
The agent is sure he can sell the land in 6 months if a price of 110 units is asked. In fact he estimates the probabilities of sale as follows:

			Month			
Price	1	2	3	4	5	6
140	0·0	0·1	0·1	0·1	0·2	0·2
130	0·1	0·1	0·1	0·1	0·2	0·2
120	0·1	0·1	0·1	0·2	0·2	0·2
110	0·1	0·1	0·2	0·2	0·2	0·2

The agent's fee will also be 10 units whether he sells the land or not. However the agent will refuse to sell the land if it has previously been put up for auction. He also insists that once he has announced a price it should not be changed, but accepts that the land can be withdrawn from offer through him at any time.
What should the man do? (Ignore the possibility of investing money.)

9. An oil company is planning to exploit a certain area of land. The profits from different quantities of oil found and the probabilities of finding them are:

Quantity	Profit	Probability
5	25	0·1
4	14	0·2
3	6	0·3
2	0	0·2
1	−5	0·1
0	−10	0·1

How much would the company be prepared to pay for a survey which would say with certainty whether there was oil there or not? And how much would a survey be worth that would predict with certainty how much oil was there?

5 Networks

Introduction

A network can be thought of as a set of n cities (nodes) every two of which may or may not be connected by a road (link). The distance from city i to city j is d_{ij}. The set of distances is not necessarily symmetrical (that is, d_{ij} and d_{ji} are not necessarily equal). Every city is directly connected by a single link to at least one other city. For the sake of uniformity we can treat the case of two cities being not directly connected as though they were so connected with distance equal to infinity ($d_{ij} = \infty$).

The "distance" can be generalized to mean cost, time or capacity. All these quantities will be assumed to be non-negative. A route or path (ij) will be defined as a connected set of links which can be traversed to get from one stated node (i) to another (j).

A number of problems can be considered in connection with routes through such a network. Examples are:

(a) Find the path joining two nodes such that the sum of the link values along the path is a minimum (the shortest route problem). An extension of this is the travelling salesman problem in which the route required must pass through every node once and return to the starting point.
(b) The longest route problem is similar to (a) with "maximum" substituted for "minimum", but additional restrictions must be imposed if the result is to be meaningful (for example, loops must be excluded, otherwise the sum is unbounded).
(c) Find the kth best route, or the k best routes between two nodes.
(d) Find the maximum flow capacity between two nodes allowing all routes between the nodes to be used.
(e) Find the single route of maximum flow capacity between two nodes.

Some applications of the methods to be described might be:

(a) Location of, and deliveries from, a warehouse. By finding the shortest routes between each potential warehouse site and the points to which deliveries are to be made, an optimum location of the warehouse can be made. (This would apply when there is a fixed schedule of deliveries to be made.)
(b) Production planning. A part can be made in a number of different ways. One node represents the start, another the completion of the part. Intermediate nodes represent various states of finish. d_{ij} represents the cost of the work necessary to move from state i direct to state j.

(c) Road systems and traffic schedules. This is an obvious application. An instance is in the estimation of the traffic likely to be diverted to a (possible) new road, proceeding on the assumption that traffic between any two points will flow along the shortest route.

(d) Communication networks. This is another obvious example. An instance is routing telephone calls through exchanges.

The applications mentioned above would be concerned with the shortest route case. The kth route might be required in traffic studies if, for instance, it was assumed that traffic will flow along the k shortest routes rather than along the shortest route alone. A possible application of the maximum capacity route problem could be in a communications network in which the nodes represent exchanges (or their equivalent) that can accept only one input at a time from among a number of sources.

Later in the chapter we shall discuss the special case in which the distances represent times and flows along each link are allowed in only one direction. If the links represent activities which go to make a total project and the network represents the logical order in which they must be carried out, then the length of the longest route through the network is the shortest time in which the total project can be accomplished. This is probably the most widespread application of networks and has many names: network planning, network scheduling, critical path methods and so on.

The shortest route problem (1)

The shortest route problem can be stated: Find the path from node i to node j such that the sum of the values of the links traversed is a minimum. It may be required to find all such minimum paths from a given node to all other nodes, or to find the minimum paths between every pair of nodes.

It is a property of the shortest path between two nodes that every sub-route contained in the shortest route is also optimal (cf. dynamic programming). It can be seen that if this were not so, then by substituting an optimal sub-route (k, l, say) for the non-optimal sub-route (k, l) a reduction would be made in the length of the path (i, j). Most methods for solving the shortest route problem make use of this property by building up the optimal route one or more links at a time.

However, the addition of any two (or more) optimal paths will not, in general, give an optimal path; therefore when extending the known optimal path(s), all possible summations of optimal sub-routes must be considered. The methods to be described below differ mainly in the way this process is organized rather than in the principles used. The methods can be divided into two main groups, "labelling" and "matrix" methods. We shall describe one labelling method in detail and one matrix method.

A Labelling Method for the Shortest Route Problem (1), (2), (3), (4). A set of links connecting every node in a network which does not contain any loops is called a tree. It has the property that a path between any two nodes is unique. If one node is taken as an origin and the shortest-routes from the origin to all other nodes are drawn, the result is a tree, or can be reduced to a tree. For if the result was not a tree, then to at least one node (other than the origin) there would be a choice of paths; either one path is longer than the other and therefore must be deleted, or the two paths are equal in length and then one may be deleted, thus reducing the system to a tree.

A labelling method due to Minty consists of building up the shortest route tree one link at a time, working outwards from the origin. Let us suppose that at some stage we have found the shortest routes to r of the nodes, $X_i, i = 1 \ldots r$. Each of the nodes will be labelled with its shortest distance from the origin, $m(X_i)$. To find the next node and link to be added to the tree we list all the links that lead from a labelled node X_i to an unlabelled node, one link away. We call these "adjacent" nodes $Y_j, (j = 1 \ldots k$ say). Let the length of a link from X_i to Y_j be $x_{ij} \geqslant 0$. For each of the links we form the sum of the length of the link and the label at its labelled end.

Each of these sums represents the distance of an unlabelled node from the origin along a route which is at least optimal as far as the last but one node. The node and link for which the sum is smallest are the required additions to the shortest route tree. That is, we select i, j such that $m(X_i) + x_{ij}$ is a minimum.

Let the i, j for this minimum be p and q so that

$$m(X_p) + x_{pq} \leqslant m(X_i) + x_{ij} \qquad \text{for all } i, j \qquad (5.1)$$

(In the case of ties it does not matter which pair is chosen.) The new node is Y_q and the optimal path to Y_q passes through X_p.

To prove this, we note that any other path to Y_q that has not been taken into account in the relation (5.1) must have at least two links between an X_i and Y_q, one of which must be from an X_i to some Y_j (other than Y_q). Therefore, the expression for the distance from the origin to Y_q along such a path must be of the form $m(X_i) + x_{ij} + y$ where $y \geqslant 0$.

From (5.1) it follows that

$$m(X_i) + x_{ij} + y \geqslant m(X_p) + x_{pq} \qquad \text{for } i \neq p, j \neq q$$

Therefore, the path to Y_q through X_p is optimal, and Y_q can now be labelled. The process can be set down formally as:

Step 1. Label origin with "distance" zero. Go to Step 2.
Step 2. Look for links whose tail ends are labelled and whose heads are unlabelled. (Regarding the directed links as though they were arrows.) For each such link form the sum of the label at the tail end and its length. Tick the link for which this sum is a minimum and label the head with this sum. Return to the beginning of Step 2.

This process terminates when (a) the terminal node is labelled, (b) all nodes have been labelled (if the distance of all the nodes from the origin are required) or (c) the minimum of the sums formed in Step 2 is "infinite".

The ticked links will form a shortest route tree.

The method will be illustrated by an example.

The network is shown in Figure 5.1. The origin is taken as *A*, and the terminal node *J*. Between each pair of nodes that are directly connected there

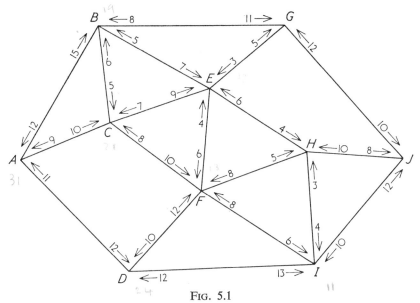

Fig. 5.1

are two one-way links (or directed links) whose lengths in the two directions are not the same (i.e. the problem is asymmetric).

Step 1. Label *A*, zero.

Step 2. (1) The links with a labelled tail and an unlabelled head are those from *A*, i.e. *AB*, *AC* and *AD* and the sums of their label and length are

$$0 + 15 = 15$$
$$0 + 10 = 10$$
$$0 + 12 = 12$$

The smallest of these sums is that for *AC*, therefore link *AC* is ticked and *C* is labelled with value 10. We now return to the beginning of Step 2.

(2) Links to be considered:

AB sum:	$0 + 15 = 15$	
AD	$0 + 12 = 12$	Tick *AD*, label *D*, 12
CB	$10 + 6 = 16$	
CE	$10 + 9 = 19$	
CF	$10 + 10 = 20$	

It can be seen from the above two steps that many of the links considered at each stage are the same (e.g. *AB* and *AD*), and the procedure can be laid out to take advantage of this. Once a node has been labelled all links entering that node can be deleted, and those whose tail ends are at that node (i.e. those which leave that node) can be added to the list of links to be considered.

Working through the network in this way we find that the distance of the terminal node J from the origin is 31. To find the path from A to J we work backwards along the shortest route tree which is indicated by the ticked links. We find that the link into J is HJ, that into H is EH, to E is EC and to C is AC; therefore the required path is $A - C - E - H - J$. (It should be noted that the shortest route tree found is for paths away from A and does not apply to paths to A, since the set of network distances is asymmetrical.)

A disadvantage of the method is that it may involve dealing with a large set of numbers at each stage. D'Esopo (1) has proposed an alternative method which alleviates this to some extent but which usually calls for more iterations. His method deals with one labelled node at a time (call it the master node) and all adjacent nodes are labelled with the sum of the label of the master node and the distance between it and the adjacent node unless the adjacent node is already labelled with a smaller number. The first time a node is labelled it is given an index number and the next master node on the completion of an iteration is the node with the next index number.

A Matrix Method for the Shortest Route Problem (1). Labelling methods generate the shortest route tree and thus the shortest route to all nodes from the origin node. They also generate the shortest routes between other pairs of nodes as an incidental if this pair of nodes happens to lie on a shortest route from the origin. Generally however if we wanted to find the shortest routes between every pair of nodes in a network we should be obliged to carry through many labelling exercises each starting from a different origin. A basically different method using matrices has been developed by Shimbel (5), (7), Pollock and Wiebenson (1). Bellman (6) independently suggested an equivalent method. This method finds the shortest routes between all pairs of nodes. Consequently it could be used to find the shortest route between a specific pair, but labelling methods are generally more efficient for the specific problem. The method is briefly described.

For a network of n nodes, we can define an n by n matrix D^k, whose elements are:

$d_{ii}^k = 0,$
$d_{ij}^k = $ minimum distance from i to j by a path of k or fewer links,
$d_{ij}^k = \infty$ if there is no path of k or fewer links from i to j.

D^1 is, of course, the matrix of the original d_{ij}'s. Again all d_{ij}'s are assumed non-negative.

The elements of D^k can be obtained by a succession of operations of the form:

$$d_{ij}^{k+1} = \min_h (d_{ih}^k + d_{hj}^1) \qquad h = 1, 2 \ldots n$$

or

$$d_{ij}^{k+1} = \min_h (d_{ih}^1 + d_{hj}^k) \qquad h = 1, 2 \ldots n$$

Successive D^k's can be derived in this way until $D^{k+1} = D^k$ or until $k + 1 = n - 1_k$ (since an optimal path cannot have more than $n - 1$ links, d_{ij} being $\geqslant 0$). The element d_{ij} of this last matrix is equal to the length of the minimum path between the nodes i and j (for all ij).

To speed up the calculation k may be doubled at each stage instead of being increased by 1; D^k is used to form D^{2k} rather than D^{k+1} using

$$d_{ij}^{2k} = \min_h (d_{ih}^k + d_{hj}^k) \qquad h = 1 \ldots n$$

and one stops when $D^{2k} = D^k$ or when $2k \geqslant n - 1$ as before.

This doubling of k instead of increasing it by one at each stage can also save space (which may be important if a computer is being used) since the elements of D^{2k} can be put back into D^k as they are derived and there is no need to store D^1.

The final D matrix gives only the optimal path lengths and not the nodes through which they pass. These can be obtained by either of two methods.

Firstly one might keep a record of the optimal paths at each stage by recording the nodes through which each optimal route of k or fewer links passes for every pair of nodes and up-dating this record as necessary. Unfortunately this procedure is very costly of storage space.

Alternatively one can infer the optimal path from the final (say D^{2k}) matrix if one has retained D_1. For example, a procedure to find the optimal path from i to j is:

(i) Determine from D^{2k} the distance of node j from node i.

(ii) Find from D^{2k} the distances of the nodes (h, say), from i, that are connected to j by just one link.

(iii) Find from D^1 the lengths of the links from these nodes h to j (i.e. the links (h, j)).

(iv) Select the node (h) whose distance from i is less than the distance from i to j by exactly the length of (h, j); this is the next to last node on the optimal path (i.e. is such that $d_{ih} + d_{hj} = d_{ij}$).

(v) Repeat this process until we have worked back to i.

The example of Figure 5.1 will be used to illustrate the method. The first step is to write down the D^1 matrix. We number the nodes, in this case in alphabetical order, i.e. $A = 1, B = 2$, etc. All the elements d_{ii}^1 ($i = 1, \ldots 10$) are zero (the distance from node A to node A is zero). The d_{ij} corresponding to a pair of nodes that are not directly connected are put equal to infinity (thus A is not directly connected to G, therefore $d_{1,7}^1 = \infty$). The rest of the matrix can be written by referring to the diagram (Figure 5.1) and writing the length of the link from node i to node j into the i, j space of the matrix. Next D^2 is obtained from D^1 by using the formula

$$d_{ij}^2 = \min_h (d_{ih}^1 + d_{hj}^1) \qquad i, j = 1, 2, \ldots 10$$

On examining D^2 it will be seen that it is not the same as D^1 therefore it is necessary to derive a new D matrix. We could obtain the matrix D^3 but it is quicker to obtain D^4 from D^2 by using

$$d_{ij}^4 = \min_h (d_{ih}^2 + d_{hj}^2) \qquad i, j = 1, 2, \ldots 10$$

The matrix D^4 so obtained has no infinite elements so we have obtained the lengths of a path between every pair of nodes. The lengths are the shortest possible for paths of four links or fewer. It might be that there is a shorter path, of more than four links, between some pairs of nodes. We therefore obtain D^8. This is the same as D^4, therefore all the shortest paths have four links or fewer, and D^4 is the final matrix. Some of the working follows:

D^1

	$j = 1$	2	3	4	5	6	7	8	9	10	
$i = 1$	0	15	∞	12	∞	∞	∞	∞	∞	∞	A
2	12	0	5	∞	7	∞	11	∞	∞	∞	B
3	9	6	0	∞	9	10	∞	∞	∞	∞	C
4	11	∞	∞	0	∞	12	∞	∞	13	∞	D
5	∞	5	7	∞	0	6	5	4	∞	∞	E
6	∞	∞	8	10	4	0	∞	5	6	∞	F
7	∞	8	∞	∞	3	∞	0	∞	∞	10	G
8	∞	∞	∞	∞	6	8	∞	0	4	8	H
9	∞	∞	∞	12	∞	8	∞	3	0	12	I
10	∞	∞	∞	∞	∞	∞	12	10	10	0	J
	A	B	C	D	E	F	G	H	I	J	

Example derivations of the elements of D^2 are given, then the full D^2:

$$d_{34}^2 = \min_h (d_{3h}^1 + d_{h4}^1)$$

$h =$		
1	$9 + 12 = 21$	
2	$6 + \infty = \infty$	
3	$0 + \infty = \infty$	
4	$\infty + 0 = \infty$	
5	$9 + \infty = \infty$	
6	$10 + 10 = 20 \leftarrow$	
7	$\infty + \infty = \infty$	
8	$\infty + \infty = \infty$	
9	$\infty + \infty = \infty$	
10	$\infty + \infty = \infty$	

Thus $\qquad d_{34}^2 = 20$

$$d_{82}^2 = \min_h (d_{8h}^1 + d_{h2}^1)$$

$h =$		
1	$\infty + 15 = \infty$	
2	$11 + 0 = 11 \leftarrow$	
3	$13 + 6 = 19$	
4	$16 + 26 = 42$	
5	$6 + 5 = 11 \leftarrow$	
6	$8 + 9 = 17$	
7	$11 + 8 = 19$	
8	$0 + 11 = 11 \leftarrow$	
9	$4 + \infty = \infty$	
10	$8 + 20 = 28$	

Thus $\qquad d_{82}^2 = 11$

D^2 $j = 1$ 2   3   4   5   6   7   8   9   10

$i =$	1	2	3	4	5	6	7	8	9	10	
1	0	15	20	12	∞	∞	26	∞	25	∞	A
2	12	0	5	24	7	13	11	11	∞	21	B
3	9	6	0	20	9	10	14	13	16	∞	C
4	11	26	20	0	16	12	∞	16	13	25	D
5	16	5	7	16	0	6	5	4	8	12	E
6	17	9	8	10	4	0	9	5	6	13	F
7	20	8	10	∞	3	9	0	7	20	10	G
8	∞	11	13	16	6	8	11	0	4	8	H
9	23	∞	16	12	9	8	24	3	0	11	I
10	∞	20	∞	22	15	18	12	10	10	0	J
	A	B	C	D	E	F	G	H	I	J	

Similarly we find D^4 and $D^8 (= D^4)$. The full D^4 is

D^4 $j = 1$ 2   3   4   5   6   7   8   9   10

$i =$	1	2	3	4	5	6	7	8	9	10	
1	0	15	∞	12	19	20	24	23	25	31	A
2	12	0	5	23	7	13	11	11	15	19	B
3	9	6	0	20	9	10	14	13	16	21	C
4	11	21	20	0	16	12	21	16	13	24	D
5	16	5	7	16	0	6	5	4	8	12	E
6	17	9	8	10	4	0	9	5	6	13	F
7	19	8	10	19	3	9	0	7	11	10	G
8	22	11	13	16	6	8	11	0	4	8	H
9	23	14	16	12	9	8	14	3	0	11	I
10	31	20	22	22	15	18	12	10	10	0	J
	A	B	C	D	E	F	G	H	I	J	

To find the path from A to J we note that the shortest distance of J from $A = d^4_{1,10} = 31$. Links leading into J are GJ, HJ and IJ. The shortest distance of G from $A = 24$ and the distance of G from $J = 10$ so that the distance from A to J via G is 34. We find the distance via H is 31 and via I 36. Thus the shortest path passes through H; by repeating this argument with H replacing J we find it passes also through E and, replacing H by E, it passes also through C.

The kth best route or k best routes (8), (9)

The k best routes problem is a generalization of the optimal route problem. For a distance network it would be to find the $(k - 1)$ shortest routes, between a particular pair or pairs of nodes, after the shortest (excluding routes with loops).

For $k = 2$ or 3 the shortest route methods can be used as follows. The second best route must differ from the shortest route in at least one link. One link of the shortest route is set equal to infinity. The shortest route between the pair of nodes concerned is then found. This is done with each link of the best route set equal to infinity in turn (i.e. one at a time). This process gives a number of routes which have at least one link different from the best. The shortest of these is the second best route. The third best route could be found in a similar way, one link in each of the best and second best routes being set equal to infinity and the best route of the resulting networks being found. If there are m links in the best route and n in the second best then the maximum number of routes that must be found to decide on the third best route will be $m \times n$. This method could, in principle, be extended beyond $k = 3$, but the number of shortest-route problems to be solved would soon become excessively large. Reference 8 gives references for some other methods, and a review of the problem is contained in reference 9.

The maximum capacity route (10)

The maximum capacity route problem can be stated thus: We are given a set of nodes, and links between some of the nodes. Each link has a non-negative capacity c_{ij} ($c_{ij} \neq c_{ji}$, in general), $c_{ij} = 0$ if i and j are not directly connected. It is required to find the route from node n to node m that allows the maximum flow to take place. (The capacity of a node is assumed to be infinite, i.e. $c_{ii} = \infty$.)

For any given route the capacity will be equal to that of the link whose capacity is the minimum among the links on that route.

The shortest route methods can be modified to cover the maximum capacity route problem. For example Minty's method would be changed to read:

Step 1. Label origin with capacity ∞. Go to Step 2.
Step 2. Look for links whose tails are labelled and whose heads are unlabelled. For each such link, find the minimum of the label and the link capacity. Tick the link for which this minimum is a maximum among those just found. Label the head of the link with this value. Return to the beginning of Step 2.

The matrix method would generate successive matrices by using:

$$c_{ij}^{m+h} = \max_{k} (\min (c_{ik}^{m}, c_{kj}^{h})) \qquad k = 1, 2, \ldots$$

Further details of these and other modifications will be found in reference 10.

The maximum flow problem (11)

This problem differs from the maximum capacity route problem in that we wish to determine the maximum flow possible between nodes m and n, say, making use of any of the several routes between them. More generally we might want to find the maximum flow possible between one set of nodes (the sources) and another set of nodes (the sinks). However this problem is the same as finding the maximum flow between two nodes as we can define a new node M connected by infinite capacity links to the sources and a new node N connected by infinite capacity links from the sinks: the problem is then to find the maximum flow between M and N.

Ford and Fulkerson (11) have developed methods for tackling this and other more complicated flow problems. For the maximum flow problem they give a labelling method. An initial flow pattern is set up in which the flow from node i to node j is f_{ij} ($\leqslant c_{ij}$): one might, for example, start with all $f_{ij} = 0$. Each node is given two labels, the first of the form $i+$ or $i-$, where i is the number of some other node, and the second the form e, where e represents a change of flow that one could consider making.

The process (given without proof) is:

Step 1. Set up the initial flow pattern.

Step 2. Label source $(-, \infty)$. (This labels the source but it is not yet scanned.) Go to Step 3.

Step 3. Select a labelled node which has not yet been scanned. Suppose it is node i and that it is labelled $(j\pm, e_i)$. Now consider all unlabelled nodes, of which node k is typical. If $f_{ik} < c_{ik}$ label node $k(i+, e_k)$ where $e_k = \min(e_i, c_{ik} - f_{ik})$. Consider the remaining unlabelled nodes, of which node l is typical. If $f_{li} > 0$ label node $l(i-, e_l)$ where $e_l = \min(e_i, f_{li})$. Node i is now scanned. Go to Step 4.

Step 4. Repeat Step 3 until either the sink is labelled and unscanned in which case go to Step 5; or until no more labels can be assigned yet the sink is unlabelled, in which case the optimal flow pattern has been reached.

Step 5. Suppose node n is the terminal node. Denote e_n by e. Set $r = n$. Go to Step 6.

Step 6. Change flows according to this rule. If node r is labelled $(q+, e_r)$ replace f_{rq} by $f_{rq} + e$. If it is labelled $(q-, e_r)$ replace f_{qr} by $f_{qr} - e$. Leave other flows unchanged. Set $r = q$. Go to Step 7.

Step 7. If node r is the source node, delete all labels and return to Step 2. If not, repeat Step 6.

The reader will find it instructive to work a small example of his own devising.

The longest route problem (12), (13)

In general the longest route between two nodes is unbounded because one can find a loop to circle indefinitely. If possible paths are restricted to avoid loops, then it is possible to find the longest route. Labelling methods can be easily adapted to do so, and an example is given below. One can similarly adapt the matrix method. The longest route problem lies at the heart of network planning which is an important application of networks and which we now discuss at some length.

Planning and scheduling with networks

In this section we are concerned with the use of networks (as models) in the development of methods for the planning, scheduling and controlling of large-scale projects. The network is used in all these methods to represent the sequence of activities and events of the project and the relationships that may exist between them. An event, which is a well defined point in time, is represented by a node of a network. An example of an event might be

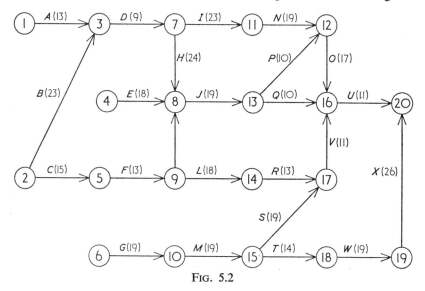

FIG. 5.2

"completion of Assembly 1" or "start of bench test". The links of the network represent the "activities" necessary to achieve the events. Each activity connects exactly two events; between any two events there should be not more than one activity. If there is more than one, then a dummy event can be inserted in the link representing one of the activities, to eliminate any possible ambiguity. The distances on the links are times to carry out the related activities. Dummy activities take no time. The links are all unidirected: one can move along them only in the direction of start to finish of the activity. All activities represented by links leaving an event can be started when that event has been reached but not before. An event has been reached when all activities represented by links leading to it have been completed and not before. There is at least one starting event which has no links leading to it and a unique terminating event, the end of the project, which has no links leading from it.

Typical applications include the planning of large scale development projects (weapons development, space travel and so on); the planning and control of constructional work; and the planning of cyclic operations so as to minimize the cycle length.

The basic ideas will be illustrated by means of an example. Consider a project of 24 activities and 20 events, related as shown in Figure 5.2. Event 20 is the "terminal event" and events 1, 4, 2 and 6, are assumed to occur at time zero (or now), and will be called "starting events". The numbers in brackets alongside the letters naming the activities are the directions of the activities, assumed to be fixed.

We are interested to know the shortest time in which the project can be completed. This is the longest of the routes starting from 1, 2, 4 and 6 to 20. We can determine the length of this using a labelling procedure which takes account of the uni-directional nature of the links. We label all starting events zero. The remaining events are labelled according to the following rule. At each stage we find an unlabelled event which has links joining it only from already labelled events. It is labelled with the maximum of the sums of the labels of the preceding events and the times of the linking activities.

In our example events 1, 2, 4 and 6 are labelled 0. Event 3 is labelled $\max (0 + 13, 0 + 23) = 23$; event 7 is labelled 32; event 5 is labelled 15; event 9 is labelled 28; event H is labelled $\max (32 + 24, 0 + 18, 28 + 14) = 56$; and so on. Eventually event 20 is labelled 113. The reader will readily convince himself that these labels represent the earliest times at which the events can be reached.

Unfortunately this labelling method has not told us which path is the longest. We can find this by working backwards from the terminal event and finding the longest time from it to each event. These times are subtracted from the label on the terminal event in the forward labelling. This backward labelling process can be summed up by saying we label the terminal event 113. The remaining events are labelled according to the following rule. At each stage we find an unlabelled event which has links leading from it only to labelled events. It is labelled with the minimum of the quantities formed by subtracting the times of the linking activities from the labels on the following events. Thus event 16 is labelled 102; event 12 is labelled 85; event 13 is labelled $\min (102 - 10, 85 - 10) = 75$; and so on. Again the reader will be able to convince himself that these are the latest times by which an event must be reached in order for the terminal point to be reached as quickly as possible.

The difference between the latest and earliest times for an event is called the slack for that event. It represents the amount by which an event might be delayed without delaying the completion of the project. The table overleaf shows the earliest, latest and slack times for the events in our example.

The path connecting the events which have zero slack is known as the critical path. The duration of the project is the duration of this critical path: the events on it must be reached at their earliest times if the project as a whole is to be completed at its earliest time. In our example the path joining events 2, 3, 7, 8, 13, 12, 16 and 20 is the critical path.

Table of earliest times (ET), latest times (LT) and slacks in example.

Event	ET	LT	Slack	Event	ET	LT	Slack
1	0	10	10	14	46	78	32
2	0	0	0	18	52	68	16
4	0	38	38	11	55	66	11
6	0	16	16	8	56	56	0
5	15	29	14	17	59	91	32
10	19	35	16	19	71	87	16
3	23	23	0	13	75	75	0
9	28	42	14	12	85	85	0
7	32	32	0	16	102	102	0
15	38	54	16	20	113	113	0

In fact, it is usually the activities—the individual jobs going to make up the project—which are the basic units in the project as opposed to the events: the events arise as a consequence of the completion of activities rather than, usually, having a significance of their own.

Consider an activity of duration T_{ij} which links event i to event j. Let the earliest times for the events be E_i and E_j, the latest times L_i and L_j. One can define the earliest and latest starting and finishing times for activities. The usual terminology is early start (E_i), early finish ($E_i + T_{ij}$), late finish (L_j) and late start ($L_j - T_{ij}$). These give the times by which, if the times for activities are adhered to, activity ij can start, can finish, must start and must finish respectively (the word must meaning in order for the project not to be delayed).

If the activity is on the critical path $E_i = L_i$, $E_j = L_j$ and $T_{ij} = L_j - L_i = L_j - E_i$. However if the activity is not on the critical path, $T_{ij} < L_j - E_i$. The difference $(L_j - E_i) - T_{ij}$ is referred to as the total float on activity ij. It represents the extent to which the start of activity ij can be delayed beyond E_i without delaying the completion of the project. In our example the total float on activity $M = L_{15} - E_{10} - 19 = 16$. Thus if the start of activity M were to be delayed by 16 times units (say weeks) the project would still be completed on time. These 16 weeks are the extent of our flexibility in scheduling the execution of activity M. (There may be many practical reasons to start activity M later than its earliest start time, or indeed as late as possible. Scarce resources might be involved in its execution and an activity which, if M were to start at its earliest start time, would necessarily be simultaneous with M may also require these scarce resources: such problems are discussed briefly below. Or M might simply cost a great deal of money to carry out, in which case we would prefer to defer the expense as long as is consistent with completing the project in the shortest possible time.)

If the start of activity M were to be delayed by 16 weeks, activities T, W and X would need to be started as soon as the events preceding them are reached to prevent a lengthening of the time taken to complete the project. Indeed 15–18–19–20 would become the joint critical path: the total float on an activity is, by definition, the difference between the length of the critical path and the length of the longest path which includes the activity. In that sense, the total float on an activity is more properly thought of as the total float on a path and represents the total delay in starting the activities going to make up the path which can be experienced without delaying the project.

A quantity more fundamentally related to the activity is $E_j - E_i - T_{ij}$ which is called the free float on activity ij. This represents the delay which could be tolerated in starting activity ij, without interfering with the schedule of earliest event times. For activity M, the free float is zero; for activity Q on the other hand it is 17. It is easy to see that free float must be zero unless node j has at least one other activity entering it. Free float as defined here is sometimes called early free float. The late free float on activity ij is $L_j - L_i - T_{ij}$: it represents the extent to which the start of activity T_{ij} can be delayed without interfering with the schedule of latest event times. Other types of float can be defined, although in practice total float is probably used most.

Variable Activity Durations. Hitherto we have assumed the durations of activities can be stated accurately. This is not usually the case: estimating the durations may be made difficult by the nature of the activities or because the job the activity represents is one that there is little experience of or because the estimator is an incurable optimist and so on. In this case the floats can be thought of as the lee-way in estimation, the extent by which our estimate can be optimistic for an activity without that activity causing a delay on the project as a whole. Not a great deal can be said in general about a network whose activities have durations which are random variables, even when their distributions are known (which they are usually not). The PERT method (14), (15) suggests a device for estimating distributions and a fairly crude method for taking account of variability. Objections, both theoretical and practical, have been levelled against it (16), (17), (18), (19). The basic problem, when the distributions are known, is that the critical path is uncertain: each of many paths through the network might be the critical path with a finite probability. What one usually does is to work with expected durations as if the durations were fixed at these values and then examine the situation by eye. The second and third critical paths can be found very readily. They are the paths with second and third lowest total float (the second can be got from the most critical by the deletion of one activity from it and so on, as with the second and third shortest routes). One can then, without too much difficulty, calculate the distribution of the maximum of the three times for the completion of these paths, bearing in mind that they are not independent. However if a great deal of variability is suspected simulation methods might be required.

Target Dates. In calculating the latest arrival times for events we assumed that the earliest arrival time for the terminal event was the latest time we would wish to get there. However in practice we might prefer to name some definite target time by which we would like the total project finished. Call this target time L. The terminal event is event t and its earliest arrival time E_t. If $E_t < L$ we can expect to beat the target date. For the typical event i, the latest arrival time becomes $L_i + L - E_t$ and slack is increased by $L - E_t$ at every event, including those on the critical path. Likewise the float on every path, including the critical path, is increased by $L - E_t$. Free floats, of course, remain unchanged.

If on the other hand $E_t > L$ negative slacks enter the scene. The project cannot be completed on time as presently scheduled and with the present planned activity times. Some paths, certainly the critical path and probably others, will have negative floats. (Paths other than the critical path which have negative floats are often referred to as sub-critical paths.) Free floats again remain unchanged.

Planning and Scheduling by Networks in Practice. Drawing a network can be more difficult than it appears. We shall not give a detailed discussion of the mechanics here (see for example references 20 and 21). However it is well to be clear that the approach assumes that activities leading to an event must be completed before those leaving it can begin: a common mistake is to overlook that one or more of the activities leaving an event can in fact start before all the activities entering it finish. In such cases use can be made of dummy activities. We also note that it is rare for there to be a unique network for a project, if only because an activity is not always a well-defined concept.

Things which cannot be incorporated into a network include so called tied jobs, where one job must be done a certain time after another, and non-concurrent jobs, where two jobs cannot for some physical reason be worked together. Things which can, however, be incorporated include the case where a job cannot be started until a fixed time after the completion of another and the case where some event must occur an exact time either after the start of the project or before the end of the project.

Identification of the critical path shows which activities should receive most managerial attention. Usually the durations of activities can be changed by a re-allocation of resources and there will often be scope to speed up the critical path by diverting resources from other paths, preferably those with high float, to it. Alternatively extra resources beyond these originally contemplated may be used; they would probably need to be if L, the target time, were less than E_t. If resources are shifted and consequently times changed the E's and L's must be calculated. The critical path might be changed; certainly the floats will be.

The fact that the durations of an activity are usually functions of the resources devoted to the activity introduces a further problem if the resource availabilities are limited. We have already briefly touched on this in mentioning the possibility of scheduling activities to start later than their earliest start times but within their total floats in order to avoid simultaneous calls on a scarce resource. No matter how well this device is exploited there will sometimes be occasions when constraints on resource availabilities cannot be satisfied without delaying the project. The implied problem of minimizing the time for the project subject to resource constraints is a difficult one. It is referred to variously as resource smoothing, resource allocation and resource scheduling. It can be formulated as an integer programming problem but for any moderately complex project the computer time required to solve the problem in this way is prohibitive. Usually heuristic methods are used. For a project with comparatively few activities and one or two scarce resources (say skilled men and bull-dozers) it might be enough to draw up (or have drawn up by a computer) a schedule of scarce resource use week by week and to re-phase the activities by eye. However manual methods are of little use in complex projects with many resources, and one usually uses a computer. More formal approaches are used in computer packages. Some allocate resources to activities in order of increasing total float. When an activity requires resources at a given time when all the resource has already been allocated its earliest start time is increased accordingly. Other packages work forward through time checking which activities are due to start and allocating the available resources to them in order of increasing total float. More complicated methods, combining both approaches in some cases, are also used.

Where the project being planned is one of many being planned to occur at the same time all of which draw on some of the same resources, resource smoothing is inevitably very difficult.

Scarce resources can usually be bought in at a price. Also a failure to meet L, the target date for the project, usually costs money (or earns it if the target date is beaten). When the effect of increasing the cost of carrying out an activity is to reduce, within limits, its duration linearly the total cost can be minimized using linear programming or network flow methods (22), (23), (24).

As well as being useful in planning a project networks are useful in controlling its progress. Clearly one will want to exercise strict control on the critical path activities. However delays to them inevitably occur on occasions. Delays also occur to other activities perhaps to the extent of making them critical. It will therefore be necessary from time to time to redraw the network or at least to recalculate earliest and latest start and finish times. Control will be diverted as necessary to the current critical path. There are many practical points concerned with control which we shall not discuss here. The reader will find interesting material in references 20 and 21.

The travelling salesman problem

What is the shortest path through a network which passes through all the nodes and returns to the starting node? This is the travelling salesman problem. The salesman must travel from home and make calls in each of a number of cities before returning home. What is his minimum distance route? In what follows we shall restrict our attention to the case where each node is passed once and once only, all nodes being assumed connected by links of distance d_{ij} as before ($d_{ij} = \infty$ if the link i to j does not exist). For the salesman it would probably be reasonable to treat the nodes as points on a plane map and the links as straight lines between the nodes. In that case $d_{ij} = d_{ji}$ and the theorems of Euclid's geometry hold. We shall deal generally however with the case in which the points cannot necessarily be drawn with distances to scale on a plane map and in which d_{ij} and d_{ji} are not necessarily equal. This allows the formulation to include some important problems which are not at first sight travelling salesmen problems, for example the problem of in what order to produce n items when the set up cost if item j follows item i is d_{ij} and the production cycle is to be repeated.

The travelling salesman problem can clearly be solved. If there are n nodes there are only $(n - 1)!$ closed paths which pass through each node once. One could calculate the length of all these paths to solve the problem. However $(n - 1)!$ is a very big number indeed for any reasonably big n ($10! = 3,628,800$) and computation times would be intolerable. One is interested therefore in methods for tackling the problem which find either the best route or a very good route with much less computation than would be implied by full enumeration of all routes.

It is possible to formulate the problem as one in integer programming but its solution using this approach would be very expensive in computer time. Dantzig, Fulkerson and Johnson (25), (26) have suggested an approach which amounts to an ingenious way of shortening the computation involved in a full integer programming approach. Likewise it is possible to develop a dynamic programming formulation (27), (28) but for a reasonably big program the method is expensive both of computing time and of computer storage space. There are other methods (see for example references 29 and 30) some of which are appropriate only in the Euclidean case. However it seems that the most promising approaches, computationally speaking, which guarantee finding the optimum are those based on the ideas of branch and bound and we go on to describe one such.

A Branch and Bound Approach. In a branch and bound approach the set of all possible routes which pass through each node only once is split into mutually exclusive subsets for each of which a lower bound on the length of the best possible route in that subset is computed. The process of splitting into subsets continues until a subset containing only one route is found. If the length of this route is lower than all the lower bounds on the other subsets it is the optimal route. If not all subsets whose lower bound is higher than the length of the discovered route can be rejected. The splitting process continues on the remaining subsets until a new subset is found which contains only one route and so on. The best route must eventually be found.

Little, Minty, Sweeney and Kanel (31) suggest an approach of this type. Subsets are formed by routes which include certain links but exclude others. Thus a typical subset might be: all routes in which the links i to j, k to l and m to n are included and links p to q and r to s are excluded. A new subset is formed at each iteration by a branching process exemplified by the splitting of the subset just defined: two new subsets, (i) that in which all routes in which the links i to j, k to l, m to n and t to u are included and links p to q and r to s are excluded and (ii) that in which all routes in which the links i to j, k to l and m to n are included and the links p to q, r to s and t to u are excluded. We have to decide how to branch (how to choose t and u, that is) and how to construct a lower bound for each subset so as to keep the search time reasonably low. We give the method of Little *et al.* for bounding although improvements have been suggested (see for example reference 32).

To take first the question of constructing a lower bound. Suppose we were dealing with a five city problem with the distance matrix at the top of page 121, so that, for example, the distance from city 1 to city 2 is 3, from city 5 to city 3 is 19 and so on. Now city 1 must be left for some other city so a distance

City	1	2	3	4	5
1	∞	3	2	9	5
2	6	∞	14	4	9
3	7	7	∞	5	10
4	3	3	3	∞	2
5	7	5	19	12	∞

of at least 2 must be travelled from city 1 to the next city. Likewise from city 2, at least a distance 4 is travelled and so on. If we subtract these row minima from the distances from each city it is clear that the problem will be unchanged except that $2 + 4 + 5 + 2 + 5 = 18$ must be added to the solution. The new distance matrix is:

$$
\begin{array}{ccccc}
\infty & 1 & 0 & 7 & 3 \\
2 & \infty & 10 & 0 & 3 \\
2 & 2 & \infty & 0 & 5 \\
1 & 1 & 1 & \infty & 0 \\
2 & 0 & 14 & 7 & \infty
\end{array}
$$

Now we can argue that a distance of at least 1 must be travelled from the city that precedes city 1 and so on. In a like manner, if we add a further $1 + 0 + 0 + 0 + 0 = 1$ to the answer, we have the original problem in the following matrix:

$$
\begin{array}{ccccc}
\infty & 1 & 0 & 7 & 3 \\
1 & \infty & 10 & 0 & 5 \\
1 & 2 & \infty & 0 & 5 \\
0 & 1 & 1 & \infty & 0 \\
2 & 0 & 14 & 7 & \infty
\end{array}
$$

$18 + 1 = 19$ is therefore a lower bound on the problem.

Suppose now however we are considering the subset of paths which link 1 to 2 to 3. We notice first that we must put the distance for travelling from 3 to 1 as infinity otherwise there is a risk of linking 3 to 1 which would give us a sub-cycle. Our problem now is to choose a link to 4, not from 1 or 2, a link to 5, not from 1 or 2, and a link to 1 not from 2 (a link to 1 from 3 has been inhibited). If we cross out the disallowed links in the distance matrix thus

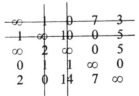

we see, by arguments exactly like those above, that we can increase the lower bound by $0 + 0 + 2 + 0 + 0 + 0 = 2$. So a lower bound for this subset is 21.

In branching we want to find a link whose presence is good and whose absence is bad. The good is for obvious reasons, the bad is so that a high lower bound can be put on a branch early leading to its early abandonment.

The matrix is kept in the form typified by the last one shown. We therefore see that a sensible choice for a link to include is one whose "distance" in the current matrix is zero. Imagine in our example we consider link 3 to 4. Now if one branch is to become all routes including 1 to 2 to 3 to 4 the other branch will be all routes including 1 to 2 to 3 but excluding 3 to 4. In any route of this second subset city 4 must be reached from somewhere other than 1, 2 or 3 and city 3 must lead to somewhere other than 1, 2 or 4. Therefore costs of reaching city 4 and leaving city 3 must be at least 7 and 5 respectively (the minima in the 4th column and 3rd row). In a like manner if we decide to branch on link 4 to 5 we have $0 + 5$, and on link 4 to 1 we have $0 + 2$. To ensure a high lower bound on the "excluding the new link" branch it is therefore best to choose link 3 to 4 to branch on.

In summary then we determine lower bounds by subtracting row and column minima to leave one zero in every row and column of the current matrix. The numbers subtracted are added to the current lower bound on that branch. A link with distance zero in the current matrix is chosen, that one for which the row minimum plus the column minimum (in both cases excluding the zero element identifying the link) is maximum. We branch on this link. The current matrix is revised as above, certain rows and columns being deleted and elements being set to infinity to prevent sub-cycles and to inhibit excluded routes. New bounds are determined. And so on.

Approximate Methods. Even the branch and bound method outlined above is quite a lengthy one. Attention has therefore been turned to the possibility of generating near optimum routes very quickly: one might be willing to forgo optimality in the interests of quick computation.

One such method has been suggested by Lin (33). Suppose we have an initial route typical links in which are i to j and k to l. If we break these two links we must replace them by i to l and j to k in order to retain a proper cycle. The decrease in distance achieved by this switch can be easily worked out. If it is positive the switch has paid off and we have a better route. We continue in this way, removing two links at each iteration and replacing them if distance is saved. When we have a route for which no savings can be made by breaking two links we have what Lin calls a 2-optimal tour. It is possible, in a similar way, to construct 3, 4, 5, . . . – optimal tours. In fact if we can find a 3-optimal tour there is some empirical evidence that we have found a route whose total distance is not far short of minimal (32).

Several other methods have been proposed which give at least good if not optimal routes (34, 35). Those which are designed to tackle the Euclidean problem usually make use of geometrical results. (An obvious one is that the route of minimum length does not cross itself.)

Vehicle scheduling

Suppose at each city the travelling salesman has to visit he must leave a quantity of leaflets, Q_1, at city 1 say, Q_2, Q_3 and so on. His starting node or base is city O. His complete tour takes him to n cities. What if his vehicle cannot hold more than C leaflets where $C < Q_1 + Q_2 + \ldots + Q_n$? Clearly he will need to return to base before his tour is complete unless he is allowed to buy a more capacious vehicle. His problem would now be to find a set of tours which, taken together, take him to every city but which each include a return to base and which each call for no more leaflets than his vehicle can hold. Moreover he would want the set of tours which minimizes his total distance travelled.

This problem is a simple example of vehicle scheduling. (The travelling salesman problem is, of course, an even simpler example; it is this problem with $C > Q_1 + Q_2 + \ldots + Q_n$. Part of the theoretical importance of the travelling salesman problem is that it is the simplest problem on which to try out methods of vehicle scheduling.) We note that it is exactly equivalent to the problem: We have many lorries of capacity C. How should we arrange deliveries of requirements $Q_1, Q_2, \ldots, Q_n$ at cities 1, 2, . . ., n to minimize distance travelled?

A more general problem is given by adding the complication that the lorries at our disposal have varying capacities $C_1, C_2, \ldots$ and so on with restricted numbers of vehicles of all but at least the smallest capacity. One could go on complicating the problem by introducing more bases, mixed product loads, compartmented vehicles, collection as well as delivery, specified delivery times and so on. An important further practical restriction would be on the distances and times spent by each vehicle on its route. Many computer programs have been written to accommodate some set or other of these various considerations. A deal of the work is based on a method proposed by Clarke and Wright (36) and we shall describe it briefly.

Suppose we have n cities requiring quantities $Q_1, Q_2, \ldots, Q_n$, the distances between cities are, as usual, d_{ij} ($=d_{ji}$) and m vehicles of capacities $C_1, C_2, \ldots, C_m$ are available. In what follows it is implicitly assumed that feasibility, in the sense of capacity and other restrictions, is always checked at each iteration, infeasible routes being ignored. We make a start by assuming that each vehicle visits one city and returns to base, which is city O. We now look to see if two cities can, with advantage, be linked into one route. A measure of the advantage to be gained by linking together cities i and j is

$$s_{ij} = d_{oi} + d_{oj} - d_{ij} = 2(d_{o1} + d_{oj}) - (d_{oi} + d_{ij} + d_{jo})$$

or, in words, the saving in distance travelled by linking cities i and j is the return distance when each was visited separately less the distance on the round trip when they are visited together. The two points with the highest saving are linked. As well as reducing the distance travelled this step saves a vehicle. We now turn to the two points with the next highest saving and so on until all links have been examined. The saving, in other words, is treated as a priority index for choosing links to establish. At each stage

$$s_{ij} = d_{oi} + d_{oj} - d_{ij}$$

is, in words, the saving from linking two routes whose last calls are at cities i and j: the last link of each route back to the base is saved at the expense of a new link between cities i and j.

The method does not guarantee minimal travelling distance but it is simple and quick and the sort of constraints met with in practice can be taken account of pretty readily, all important points when fresh schedules may be required every day. In some circumstances, however, it can lead to poor routes as it gives preference to circumferential routes over radial ones.

Other methods are based more directly on approaches to the travelling salesman problem (see reference 32 which also gives some interesting computational results) while others are based on more direct visual approaches (see reference 37, for example, which discusses and compares various methods including one ad hoc visual method, Clarke's and Wright's method and other methods which use various criteria for deciding on which cities to bring into which routes).

An even more general problem which has received much attention is that of depot location. Suppose there is some cheap method ("trunking") of moving large quantities from base (e.g. a factory) but the individual cities (customers) do not generally require large enough quantities to justify trunking direct to them. It might pay us to introduce new cities (depots) as staging posts between the base and the original cities: material will be trunked from base to new cities and transported from new cities to the original cities. How many new cities (depots) should we have and where? Which customers should be served from each depot? Moreover there might well be more than one base (factory) or we might want to decide where to site new factories. Again complications of many kinds can be imagined. We refer the interested reader to reference 38.

References

1. Pollack, M. and Wiebenson, W. Solutions to the Shortest-Route Problem—A Review. *Opns. Res.* **8.2** pp. 224–230 1960.
2. Dantzig, G. B. Discrete-Variable Extremum Problems. *Opns. Res.* **5.2** pp. 266–270 1951.
3. Dantzig, G. B. On the Shortest-Route Through a Network. *Management Science* **6.2** pp. 187–190 1960.
4. Moore, E. F. The Shortest Path Through a Maze. Proceedings of an International Symposium on the Theory of Switching, Part II, April 1957. *The Annals of the Computation Laboratory of Harvard University* **30** Harvard University Press 1959.
5. Shimbel, A. Structure in Communication Nets. Proceedings of the Symposium on Information Networks, Polytechnic Institute of Brooklyn; April 12–14 1954.
6. Bellman, R. On a Routing Problem. *Quart. Appl. Math* **16.1** 1958.
7. *Investigation of Model Techniques.* Second Annual Report July 1957–1958 Case Institute of Technology, Cleveland, Ohio, ASTIA Report No. AD 211968.
8. Pollack, M. The *k*th Best Route Through a Network. *Opns. Res* **9.4** pp. 578–580 1961.
9. Pollack, M. Solutions of the *k*th Best Route Through a Network—A Review. *J. Math. Analysis and Applications* **3** p. 547 1961.

10. Pollack, M. The Maximum Capacity (Route) Through a Network. *Opns. Res.* **8.5** pp. 733–736 1960.
11. Ford, L. R. and Fulkerson, D. R. *Flows in Network*. Princeton University Press 1962.
12. Peart, R. M., Randolph, P. H. and Bartlett, T. E. The Shortest-Route Problem *Opns. Res.* **8.6** pp. 866–868 1960.
13. Pollack, M. and Wiebenson, W. Comments on "The Shortest-Route Problem, by Peart, Randolph and Bartlett", *Opns. Res.* **9.3** pp. 411–412 1961.
14. Malcolm, D. G., Roseboom, J. H., Clark, C. E. and Fazar, W. Application of a Technique for Research and Development Program Evaluation. *Opns. Res.* **7.5** pp. 646–668 1959.
15. Pocock, J. W. PERT as an Analytical Aid for Program Planning—Its Payoff and Problems. *Opns. Res.* **10.6** pp. 893–903 1962.
16. Murray, J. E. *Considerations of PERT Assumptions*. Paper presented before 10th Anniversary Meeting of O.R.S.A., Washington D.C., May 1962.
17. Grubbs, F. E. Attempts to validate certain PERT Statistics or "Picking on PERT". *Opns. Res.* **10.6** pp. 912–915 1962.
18. Healy, T. L. Activity Subdivision and PERT Probability Statements. *Opns. Res.* **9.3** pp. 341–350 1961.
19. Roseboom, J. H. Comments on a Paper by Thomas Healy. *Opns. Res.* **9.6** pp. 909–910 1961.
20. Lockyer, K. G. *Introduction to Critical Path Analysis*. Pitman April 1967.
21. Battersby, A. *Network Analysis for Planning and Scheduling*. Macmillan April 1967.
22. Kelley, J. E. Jr. and Walker, M. R. *Critical-Path Planning and Scheduling*. Proceedings of the Eastern Joint Computer Conference pp. 160–173 Boston December 1959.
23. Kelley, J. E. Jr. Critical-Path Planning and Scheduling: Mathematical Basis. *Opns. Res.* **9.3** pp. 296–320 1961.
24. Fulkerson, D. R. A Network Flow Computation of Project Cost Curves. Paper P-1947 Rand Corporation March 1960.
25. Dantzig, G. B., Fulkerson, D. R. and Johnson, S. M. Solutions of a Large-Scale Travelling Salesman Problem. *Opns. Res.* **2.4** pp. 393–410 1954.
26. Dantzig, G. B., Fulkerson, D. R. and Johnson, S. M. On a Linear-Programming, Combinatorial Approach to the Travelling-Salesman Problem. *Opns. Res.* **7.1** pp. 58–66 1959.
27. Zubieta, R. H. G. *Solution of the Travelling Salesman Problem by Dynamic Programming on the Hypercube*. M.I.T. Interim Technical Report No. 18 May 1962.
28. Bellman, R. Dynamic Programming Treatment of the Travelling-Salesman Problem. *Journal of the Assoc. Com. Mach.* **9.1** pp. 61–63 1962.
29. Barachet, L. L. Graphic Solution of the Travelling Salesman Problem. *Opns. Res.* **5.6** pp. 841–845 1957.
30. Groes, G. A. A Method of Solving Travelling-Salesman Problems. *Opns. Res.* **6.6** pp. 791–812 1958.
31. Little, J. D. C., Munty, K. G., Sweeney, D. W. and Kanel, C. An Algorithm for the Travelling Salesman Problem. *Opns. Res.* **11** pp. 972–989 1963.
32. Christofides, N. and Eilon, S. An Algorithm for the Vechicle-Dispatching Problem. *ORQ* **20.3** pp. 309–318 Sept. 1969.
33. Lin, S. Computer Solutions of the Travelling Salesman Problem. *Bell Syst. Tech. J.* **44** 2245 1965.

34. Morton, G. and Land, A. H. A Contribution to the Travelling Salesman Problem. *J. R. Statist. Soc. B.* **17.**2 pp. 185–194 1955.
35. Nicholson, T. A. J. A Boundary Method for Planar Travelling Salesman Problems. *ORQ* **19.**4 pp. 445–452 1968.
36. Clarke, G. and Wright, J. W. Scheduling of Vehicles from a Central Depot to a Number of Delivery Points. *Opns. Res.* **11** p. 568 1963.
37. Gaskell, T. J. Bases for Vehicle Fleet Scheduling. *ORQ* **18.**3 pp. 218–295 1967.
38. Eilon, S., Watson-Gandy, C. D. T. and Christofides, N. *Distribution Management.* Griffin 1971.

Further reading

References 11, 20, 21, 32, 37 and 38 above.
Thornley, G. (Ed.) *Critical Path Analysis in Practice.* Tavistock Publications 1968.
Elmaghraby, S. E. The Theory of Networks and Management Science. Part 1 *Management Science (Theory Series)* **17.**1 pp. 1–34 1970, Part 2 *Management Science (Application Series)* **17.**2 pp. B54–B71 1970. (See also comments by Yen, J. Y. and rejoinder by Elmaghraby, S. E. *Management Science (Theory Series)* **18.**1 pp. 84–87 1971.)
Hu, T. C. Some Problems in Discrete Optimization. *Mathematical Programming* **1.**1 pp. 102–112 1971.

Examples for solution

1. Carry out the full working using Minty's method for the shortest route problem given in Fig. 5.1. Solve the same problem using D'Esopo's method.
2. Find the second shortest route from A to J for the problem given in Fig. 5.1 using the matrix method.

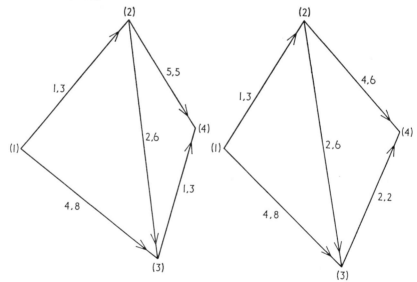

3. A contractor draws up two alternative networks (opposite) for a job. To each activity is attached two time estimates, and the probability of each of these is $\frac{1}{2}$.

The contractor has to pay a penalty of £kt^2, where t is the number of months taken to completion over 9 months. Which network represents the better plan?

4. Formulate the standard network planning problem as a linear programming problem, using the problem defined by Fig. 5.2. What is the significance of the slack values in the final tableau? And of the shadow prices?

5. In the problem defined by Fig. 5.2 each of activities A, B and C requires the use of a bull-dozer, only one of which is available, so that A, B and C can at best only be carried out in sequence, though in any order. How does this affect the completion time of the project?

Does your working give results consistent with allocating scarce resources according to total float?

How much time would be saved if two bull-dozers could be made available?

6. Solve the travelling salesman problem defined by the matrix on page 121.

7. Draw up a network for some reasonably complex project with which you are familiar in your everyday life, for example the time you spend between rising from your bed and leaving home or some project you plan in the house or garden. Does the network reveal any inefficiencies in your intuitive plans? If so, why are you not using the most efficient plan? Are there any morals to be drawn?

What was the most useful aspect of this exercise from your point of view? If possible, ask the same question of an engineer who has used networks to plan a complex project. In particular ask him about the relative usefulness of (a) drawing up the network, (b) determining the critical path, (c) any resource scheduling that was carried out, and (d) any up-dating of the network during the course of the project. Did he find it useful for exercising control?

8. A man regularly receives payments in two currencies A and B every Monday. He wishes to convert them to currency C by Friday at the latest. For various technical reasons the conversion rates vary throughout the week but in a predictable way. On Tuesday (day 2) 1 unit of A can be exchanged into $f(A, B, 2)$ units of B or $f(A, C, 2)$ units of C and so on. There is no interest differential associated with holding the money in any given currency and transactions of any kind and any number are allowed although exchange rates can be assumed not to vary within a day.

Formulate the man's problem in network terms.

6 Queues

Introduction

After he has selected the goods he wants, a shopper in a self service store must take them to a desk to be checked and paid for. He may be served immediately, or may have to wait for other customers to be served first. The customer would like always to have immediate service; the store manager would like to see the cashier busy most of the time. These requirements cannot both be met, as customers do not arrive regularly and some take longer to serve than others. If the cashier is usually busy, a queue will develop when customers arrive more frequently than usual or take longer than usual. If customers find that they often have to wait they may decide to shop elsewhere in future; if the queue gets too long it will begin to block the shop. For these reasons the manager might consider employing another cashier. He knows that it will double the cost of the checking service but what effect will it have on average waiting time or queue length? Will the extra cost be justified by avoiding loss of customers or by the extra shop space made available?

This is the kind of problem to be studied in this chapter. The basic features are that an input of some kind of unit is provided with a service by a service channel. The problem arises because of the irregularity in the rate of input or service or both, so that they cannot be matched exactly and the best compromise is sought. This queue situation can occur in a wide range of operations and its existence is not always obvious. One of the earliest examples to be studied was the automatic telephone exchange where the units are callers and the service channels are switches at the exchange; in this case if the channels are all busy, unsuccessful callers do not form a queue. In a factory a product may be processed by a number of machines in turn; if the processing time is not constant a queue problem arises, and the input to one service channel is the output from the previous one. Finished products may accumulate in the despatch bay and be sent away in batches by lorry; in this example, the service channel (lorry) serves several units simultaneously, a process referred to as bulk service. Similar problems arise in which the input is continuous and not a series of discrete units—for example in the storage of water in reservoirs (1)—but continuous inputs are not considered in this chapter.

Before a queuing problem can be analysed, information is needed about the input, the service and the behaviour of the units. The rate of arrival of units (or the intervals between arrivals) and the service time may be specified by frequency distributions. The arrival and service rates may be affected by the length of queue, or may change with time, and the service rate may depend on the type of unit being served. In many problems mathematical expressions can be found which give a good enough approximation to the actual distributions but sometimes the actual distributions, found by observation, must be used. The behaviour of the units is described by the queue discipline. When a queue forms, the units may be served in the order in which they arrive (as in the shop example) or in arbitrary order (as may happen with goods in a factory) or some types of unit may have priority. A unit is said to have pre-emptive priority if it not merely goes to the head of the queue but displaces any unit already being served when it arrives. Provided that the order of service is not related to service time, it does not affect the queue length or average waiting time but it does affect the time an individual unit has to wait. Other types of queue discipline are for units to leave a queue after waiting a certain time—they may be, for example, impatient customers or perishable materials—or for them not to join a queue which is greater than a certain length.

If the average rate of arrival is less than the average rate of service, and both are constant, the system will eventually settle down into a steady state which is independent of the initial state of the queue; the probability of finding a particular length of queue will then be the same at any time. (Note that the phrase steady state as applied to a queue does not refer to a state of unvarying behaviour of the queue. The size of the queue will fluctuate in the steady state but the statistical behaviour of the queue is steady. On average, the proportion of an hour in which the queue length has some specific value will be the same from hour to hour in the steady state. Likewise a customer can expect, on average, to have to wait the same length of time whenever he joins a queue which is in the steady state, although the waiting times of successive customers will vary.) If the rates are not constant, the system will not reach a steady state but it could remain stable. If the rate of arrival is not less than the rate of service the system is unstable and the probability of a long queue steadily increases; this happens even if the two rates are equal on average, because the time lost when the service channel is idle can never be made up. Imposing a limit on the maximum length of queue (so that further arrivals are not accepted) automatically ensures stability. Queuing situations which are unstable for a limited time are common in practice—rush hour traffic is an example.

The solution of a queuing problem consists in selecting the best compromise for the factors which can be controlled. In different problems different features of the system are important in measuring the effectiveness of the compromise. In the self service store example, average and maximum waiting time of a customer, or queue length may be important. The effectiveness of an automatic exchange is measured by the probability of obtaining a connection.

This chapter will be mainly concerned with estimating these and other measures of queuing situations from the known, or assumed, information on inputs and service by means of analytical models. There are limits on what problems can be solved analytically. Many problems must be solved by simulation experiments (see Chapter 8) or by a combination of both methods. To complete the solution of a problem it is necessary to examine the economics of the whole system and choose the optimum operating conditions. In practice this optimization (or at least approximate optimization) is often straightforward as the reasonable variation of the controlled factors is likely to be very limited; it is then only necessary to examine a few possible sets of conditions and to choose the best.

In general, mathematical solutions are most readily obtained for queues which have settled down to a steady state. Most of the analysis in this chapter will deal with this state. Steady state solutions are often useful in practical problems, but they should be used with caution; in some types of problem the operating conditions do not remain constant long enough for the situation to become steady.

Stock control is essentially a queuing problem (2) and in this case the optimizing process may be the more difficult part of the solution; this subject is not covered here but it is dealt with separately in the next chapter. One other problem should be mentioned as it looks like a queuing problem but is not included in the description above. The characteristic example is the arrival of taxis and potential customers at a taxi rank. Depending on the relative rates of arrival, either may form a queue. In this problem there are two inputs but no service channels in the sense used above; the situation is unstable unless the inputs adjust themselves to be exactly equal on average (see reference 3).

To summarize, a queue problem has the following basic components and there may be one or more of each:

(a) Input, specified by the type of unit and the time distribution of arrivals of units into the system.
(b) Queue (which may be of zero length). The queue discipline describes how the units leave the queue.
(c) Service channel, which serves the units and is specified by the distribution of service times.

To solve the problem, appropriate measures of the state of the system are calculated such as:

Average   (i) number in the system
           (ii) queue length
           (iii) waiting time

Probability of (i) n units in the system
           (ii) more than n units in the system
           (iii) waiting time of t to $t + dt$
           (iv) waiting time greater than t
           (v) service channels being idle

These measures are then used to decide the optimum operating conditions.

Throughout the chapter, we shall assume that inter-arrival times and service times are independent, both between themselves and between each other. There is practically no theory which deals with the case of statistical dependencies.

Solution by differential difference equations

The earliest method of analysis applied to queuing problems was the use of differential difference equations. The method depends on deriving the rate of change of the probability of a given state of the system. This is done by considering the probabilities of transitions (e.g. by the arrival of a unit or the completion of service) in an infinitesimal interval. In order that a problem can be solved explicitly by this method it is necessary that these probabilities should be fairly simple functions. This means in practice that the method is limited to a few types of input and service time distributions, although by skilful use of these a very wide range of distributions can be approximated.

The simplest queuing situation has an input of identical units, and un-limited queue served in order of arrival and a single service channel, the probabilities of an arrival and of a completion of service (of a unit already in the service channel) being constant, independent of time or of the state of the system. The constant probability of occurrence implies a Poisson distribution of the events and an exponential distribution of intervals between events. Thus, if the average rate of arrival of units is λ in unit time,

Probability of one arrival between time t and $t + dt$ is $\lambda\,dt$.

Probability of n arrivals in time t is $\dfrac{1}{n!}(\lambda t)^n\, e^{-\lambda t}$.

Probability of an interval between t and $t + dt$ before the next arrival is $\lambda\, e^{-\lambda t}\, dt$.

Probability of an interval greater than t is $e^{-\lambda t}$.

Average interval between arrivals is $\dfrac{1}{\lambda}$.

If the average service time is $\dfrac{1}{\mu}$, similar expressions with μ in place of λ apply to completions of service, provided that the service channel is busy; if the channel is unoccupied the probability of a completion of service is zero.

In this simple situation, the state of the system is completely described by the number of units in the system (including any being served). Let $P(n, t)$ be the probability of the system being in the state n at time t (i.e. that there are n units in the system). Consider the ways in which the state $n - 1$ may be reached at time $t + dt$; they can be tabulated as below.

Way		1	2	3	4
State at time t	No. in system	$n - 1$	$n - 1$	n	$n - 2$
	Probability	$P(n - 1, t)$	$P(n - 1, t)$	$P(n, t)$	$P(n - 2, t)$
Arrivals in dt	Number	0	1	0	1
	Probability	$1 - \lambda dt$	λdt	$1 - \lambda dt$	λdt
Completions of service in dt	Number	0	1	1	0
	Probability	$1 - \mu dt$	μdt	μdt	$1 - \mu dt$

There are, of course, a great many other ways in which state $n - 1$ can be reached at time dt. For example, it might be reached from state $n + 6$ at time t by there being 3 arrivals in dt and 10 completions of service. However, way 2 and all possible ways other than 1, 3 and 4 involve two or more events in the short time dt so that their probability is of the order of dt^2. The probability of the state $n - 1$ at $t + dt$ is the sum of the probabilities of the possible ways of reaching the state. If the terms in dt^2 are neglected it can be written:

$$P(n - 1, t + dt) = P(n - 1, t)(1 - \lambda \, dt - \mu \, dt) + P(n, t)\mu \, dt$$
$$+ P(n - 2, t)\lambda \, dt \qquad \text{for } n > 1$$

If $n = 1$ the state of $n - 2$ cannot occur and there is no possibility of a service finishing in the state $n - 1$ so the equation is slightly altered and becomes

$$P(o, t + dt) = P(o, t)(1 - \lambda \, dt) + P(1, t)\mu \, dt$$

When dt tends to zero, the fraction $[P(n - 1, t + dt) - P(n - 1, t)]/dt$ becomes the rate of change of $P(n - 1, t)$ and by dividing the above equations by dt we obtain:

$$d\frac{P(n - 1, t)}{dt} = -(\lambda + \mu)P(n - 1, t) + \mu P(n, t) + \lambda P(n - 2, t)$$

$$d\frac{P(o, t)}{dt} = -\lambda P(o, t) + \mu P(1, t)$$

These equations can be solved to give explicitly the probability of n in the system at any time. It can be shown that, provided μ is greater than λ, the system tends to a steady state. In this section, only this steady state will be considered; the rates of change of P are zero so that

$$\mu p(n) = (\lambda + \mu)p(n - 1) - \lambda p(n - 2) \qquad \text{for } n > 1$$

and

$$\mu p(1) = \lambda p(o)$$

where $p(n)$ is the steady state probability of n units in the system.

(The form of these equations exemplifies a general rule for writing down the steady state equations for a system in which the probabilities of changing from one state to another in a small time interval are constant. The probability of a state is multiplied by the probabilities of leaving it for other states and set equal to the sum of the products of the form: the probability of reaching it from another state times the probability of leaving that state.

In this case state $n - 1 (n > 1)$ can be left for states n and $n - 2$ with associated probabilities $\lambda \, dt$ and $\mu \, dt$. The dt's cancel in the final equation so we might as well work just with λ and μ, the rates of probability. State $n - 1$

can be reached from states n and $n - 2$ with associated rates μ and λ. Thus

$$(\lambda + \mu)p(n - 1) = \mu p(n) + \lambda p(n - 2)$$

which is the same as the equation above. This way of writing down the steady state equations is quite useful in more complicated analyses.)

From these equations we can infer that

$$\mu p(n) - \lambda p(n - 1) = \mu p(n - 1) - \lambda p(n - 1) = \ldots$$
$$= \mu p(1) - p(o) = 0$$

whence $\qquad p(n) = \rho p(n - 1) = \ldots = \rho^n p(o)$

where $\qquad \rho = \lambda/\mu < 1 \qquad$ (by assumption above).

The sum of the probabilities from $n = 0$ to ∞ must be 1 so that

$$1 = \sum_0^\infty p(n) = p(o)\sum_0^\infty \rho^n = \frac{p(o)}{(1 - \rho)}$$

Hence $p(o) = 1 - \rho$ and $p(n) = \rho^n(1 - \rho)$.

The average number of units in the system is

$$N = \sum_0^\infty np(n) = (1 - \rho)\sum_0^\infty n\rho^n = \frac{\rho}{(1 - \rho)}.$$

The probability that the service channel is idle is $p(o)$. The average utilization of the channel is $1 - p(o) = \rho$. This may be regarded as the proportion of time the channel is busy or the average number of units in the channel. The ratio of input rate to service rate, ρ, is often known as the traffic intensity, which in this case is equal to the utilization.

The average number of units in the queue (excluding any in the channel) is then $N - \rho = \rho^2/(1 - \rho) = Q$, say.

The probability that a queue exists is the probability that n exceeds 1, which is $1 - p(o) - p(1) = \rho^2$.

More generally, the probability that the number of units in the system exceeds n is

$$\sum_{n+1}^\infty p(n) = (1 - \rho)\sum_{n+1}^\infty \rho^r = \rho^{n+1}$$

The waiting time of a unit, from its arrival to the time it starts to be served, can be considered in two parts. There is a finite probability that the waiting time will be zero; this is the probability that there are no units already in the system, or $p(o) = 1 - \rho$. There is also the probability that the waiting time will be from t to $t + dt$; let this be $w(t)\, dt$. This waiting time occurs only if the last of the units already in the system finishes its service in the interval t to $t + dt$, all the others having been served during the period O to t. During this time the service channel is continuously busy so that the random completions of service give a Poisson distribution of completions in a given time. That is, the probability of $n - 1$ completions in the time t is

$$(\mu t)^{n-1} e^{-\mu t}/(n - 1)!$$

The probability of one completion from t to $t + dt$ is $\mu\, dt$. The probability of n units being in the system when one unit arrives is

$$p(n) = \rho^n(1 - \rho)$$

Thus the probability that this unit will have to wait a time t to $t + dt$ as a result of waiting for n previous units to be served is the product of these three probabilities (i.e. the joint probability of all three events occurring). Finally, the total probability of this waiting time arising in any way is the sum of all these products for all values of n from 1 to ∞.

$$w(t)\, dt = \sum_{n-1}^{\infty} \rho^n(1 - \rho)(\mu t)^{n-1}\, e^{-\mu t}\mu\, dt/(n - 1)!$$

$$= \mu\rho(1 - \rho)\, e^{-\mu t(1-\rho)}\, dt$$

or $\qquad w(t) = \rho(\mu - \lambda)\, e^{-t(\mu - \lambda)}$

as $\qquad \rho = \lambda/\mu$

The average waiting time of a unit is

$$W = Op(o) + \int_0^{\infty} tw(t)\, dt = \frac{\rho}{\mu(1 - \rho)} = \frac{N}{\mu} = \frac{Q}{\lambda}.$$

(The result $W = Q/\lambda$ is true for any queue with random arrivals, where the order of service does not depend on service time. This is made at least plausible by noting that the average customer has the average queue behind him when he starts to be served. Thus, he has waited on average long enough for an average queue length to arrive. But on average it would take Q/λ for Q customers to arrive.)

The probability of a waiting time greater than t is

$$w(>t) = \int_t^{\infty} w(x)\, dx = p\, e^{-t(\mu - \lambda)}$$

It should be noted that this last result includes the case where $t = 0$.

The total time spent by a unit in the system, including being served, can be obtained in a similar manner. In this case the probability of zero time is zero, and the probability $s(t)\, dt$ of a time from t to $t + dt$ is given in the same way as $w(t)\, dt$ except that there are now n completions in the interval O to t instead of $n - 1$. Following through the arithmetic it will be seen that

$$s(t) = (\mu - \lambda)\, e^{-t(\mu - \lambda)}$$

The average time spent within the system is

$$S = 1/(\mu - \lambda) = W + 1/\mu$$

and $s(>t) = e^{-t(\mu - \lambda)}$

All the probabilities and averages which have been derived so far refer to the whole of the time considered. Similar results referring only to the time when queue length or waiting time are greater than zero can be obtained by dividing by the probabilities of these conditions (ρ^2 or ρ respectively).

The results which have been derived can be used to examine the example mentioned in the introduction—that of a self service store with one cashier. In this case it is not unreasonable to assume random arrival and service times. (The average rate of arrival may depend on time of day, in which case the methods mentioned in the section on transient solutions would be needed.) Suppose that 9 customers arrive on the average every 5 minutes and the cashier can serve 10 in 5 minutes. That is,

$$\lambda = 1{\cdot}8, \qquad \mu = 2{\cdot}0, \qquad \rho = 0{\cdot}9 \qquad \text{(measuring time in minutes)}$$

The features which may be important to the manager are:

(a) The average number of customers waiting for service (which may decide whether a shopper comes into the store) which is

$$Q = \rho^2/(1 - \rho) = 0{\cdot}81/0{\cdot}1 = 8{\cdot}1$$

(b) The chance of having more people waiting than there is convenient room for—say 10 altogether—

$$p(>10) - \rho^{n+1} = 0{\cdot}9^{11} = 0{\cdot}31$$

(c) The chance of a customer having to wait long for service, say more than 2 minutes

$$w(>2) = \rho \, e^{-t(\mu - \lambda)} = 0{\cdot}9 \, e^{-2 \times 0{\cdot}2} = 0{\cdot}60$$

If service can be speeded up to 12 in 5 minutes by using a different cash register, the quantities then become

$$\lambda = 1{\cdot}8, \qquad \mu = 2{\cdot}4, \qquad \rho = 0{\cdot}75$$
$$Q = 0{\cdot}5625/0{\cdot}25 = 2{\cdot}25$$
$$p(>10) = 0{\cdot}75^{11} = 0{\cdot}042$$
$$w(>2) = 0{\cdot}75 \, e^{-1{\cdot}2} = 0{\cdot}23$$

It can be seen that this slight change in speed of service makes a great difference to the operation of the store.

Other applications of differential difference equations

The queue situations to which this method is applicable can be grouped in three classes according to the type of distributions of arrival intervals and service times.

(a) Exponential. The simplest case has been dealt with; other cases may have more complex queue discipline or the parameter λ or μ may be a function of time or of the number of units in the system.

(b) Erlang. Erlang distributions are derived by combining a number of identical exponential distributions. A constant rate can be considered as a special case of an Erlang distribution.

(c) Hyper exponential. The variance is greater than for an exponential distribution. These distributions appear to have very little practical application and are not further considered here.

In this section, special features of the method of solution for types (a) and (b) are discussed. The main results are included in the list at the end of the chapter.

As a useful case of class (a), consider the simple queue studied above but in which the parameters depend on the number of units in the system. The values of the parameters when there are n in the system can be written $\lambda(n)$ and $\mu(n)$. The steady state probabilities can be derived in the same way as before. It will be found that

$$p(n) = p(o) \frac{\lambda(n-1)\lambda(n-2)\ldots\lambda(1)\lambda(o)}{\mu(n)\mu(n-1)\ldots\mu(2)\mu(1)}$$

By a suitable choice of the functions $\lambda(n)$ and $\mu(n)$ several interesting situations can be derived as special cases of this model. We go on to examine some of these.

Exponential Distribution, Single Channel and Limited Queue Length. Suppose that the maximum number of units in the system is limited to L. Any units arriving when there are L already there do not join the queue. The situation is otherwise taken to be identical with that considered in the previous section. (In this case, as the number in the system is limited, a steady state is possible for any value of ρ and not only when the input rate is less than the service rate. However, if L is large and ρ is greater than one the steady state may be reached very slowly and in practice may not be achieved before the operation conditions change. In using the results it is necessary to check that the steady state is reached.)

Here we have

$$\begin{aligned}\lambda(n) &= \lambda \quad &\text{for} \quad & n < L \\ &= 0 \quad &\text{for} \quad & n \geqslant L \\ \mu(n) &= \mu \end{aligned}$$

Hence

$$\begin{aligned}p(n) &= \rho^n p(0) \quad & (n \leqslant L) \\ &= 0 \quad & (n > L)\end{aligned}$$
and $\quad p(0) = (1-\rho)/(1-\rho^{L+1})$

(if $\rho = 1$, $\sum_0^L \rho^n = L+1$ so that $p(0) = 1/(L+1)$).

The various measures of the state of the system can be obtained by calculations similar to those above. An important quantity in this case is the proportion of units lost to the system because they arrive when the system is full; this proportion is $p(L)$. Because some units are lost, the utilization of the service channel is no longer equal to ρ. It is

$$1 - p(0) = \rho(1-\rho^L)/(1-\rho^{L+1})$$

Exponential Distribution and Multiple Channels. It is again supposed that there is an input of identical units with mean rate λ but that there are c service channels in parallel, each with service rate μ. The units form a single queue and go to any channel which becomes free. In this case for a steady state to be possible λ must be less than $c\mu$. Here

$$\lambda(n) = \lambda$$
$$\text{and} \quad \mu(n) = n\mu \quad (n \leqslant c)$$
$$= c\mu \quad (n > c)$$

as the probability of a service finishing in the interval dt when n service channels are occupied is

$$1 - p \text{ (no service finishing)} = 1 - (1 - \mu\,dt)^n = n\mu\,dt$$

ignoring dt^2. This does assume that the service channels behave independently. Thus

$$p(n) = \rho^n p(0)/n! \quad \text{(for } 0 < n \leqslant c)$$
$$= c^{c-n}\rho^n p(0)/c! \quad \text{(for } n \geqslant c)$$
$$\text{where} \quad \rho = \lambda/\mu$$

With a multiple channel system there may again by an upper limit L to the number in the system, in which case $\lambda(n) = 0$ for $n \geqslant L$.

It will be seen that the expressions given above for $p(n)$ apply up to $n = L$ but with a different value of $p(o)$.

An important particular case is that where no queue is allowed; that is $L = c$. The steady state results are then considerably simplified and

$$p(n) = (\rho)^n/n! \sum_{r=0}^{c} \left(\frac{\rho}{r!}\right)^r \quad \text{(for } n \leqslant c \text{ and } c = L)$$

As for a single channel, an important quantity is the proportion of units lost to the system, which is $p(L)$, or $p(c)$ when no queue is allowed.

Example. The example of the self service store can now be completed by considering the effect of an additional cashier. Suppose as before that $\mu = 2\cdot0$ for each cashier and $\lambda = 1\cdot8$. Then $\rho = 0\cdot9$ and $c = 2$. The results needed are listed at the end of the chapter.

$$p(0) = 1/\left\{\sum_{i=0}^{c-1}\rho^i/i! + \rho^c/(c-\rho)(c-1)!\right\}$$
$$= 1/(1 + 0\cdot9 + 0\cdot9^2/1\cdot1 \times 1) = 0\cdot38$$

The probability of a customer having to wait at all is

$$p(>1) = c^{c-n}\rho^{n+1}p(0)/(c-\rho)c!$$
$$= 2^1 \times 0\cdot9^2 \times 0\cdot38/1\cdot1 \times 2 = 0\cdot28$$

The measures used previously can now be calculated.

The average number in the queue is

$$Q = \rho^{c+1}p(o)/(c-\rho)^2(c-1)!$$
$$= 0\cdot9^3 \times 0\cdot38/1\cdot1^2 \times 1 = 0\cdot23$$

The probability of having more than 10 customers in the system is

$$p(>10) = 2^{-8} \times 0.9^{11} \times 0.38/1.1 \times 2 = 0.00021$$

The probability of having to wait more than 2 minutes for service is

$$w(>2) = p(>1) e^{-\mu t(c - \rho)}$$
$$= 0.28 \times e^{2 \times 2 \times 1.1} = 0.0034$$

The introduction of an extra cashier thus reduces the queuing to a very low level.

It is of interest to notice what would happen if the number of customers now increased so as to bring the utilization of the cashiers back to the original level. In this case $\lambda = 3.6$, $\mu = 2.0$, $c = 2$ and the utilization is again 0.9. It will then be found that

$$Q = 7.7, \qquad p(>10) = 0.33, \qquad w(>2) = 0.38$$

which may be compared with the values (8.1, 0.31, 0.60) derived before for half the number of customers and one cashier. Although the number of customers is doubled the numbers waiting are about the same and the probability of a long wait is less. The system is thus not equivalent to the sum of two separate stores each like the original example.

These examples illustrate three features which are common to most queuing situations.

(a) Unless utilization of the service is fairly high (over $\frac{1}{2}$ say) the congestion is very slight.
(b) When the utilization approaches one a small change in it makes a large difference to the congestion.
(c) When service channels can be shared by one queue the congestion is much less than it would be for the same rates of input and service but with an independent queue for each service channel.

Machine Interference. In some industries, banks of machines are supervised by one operator. When a machine stops it has to wait for service if the operator is already busy. If an operator looks after too few machines the labour cost is high, and if the operator looks after too many machines the cost of lost output becomes appreciable. These costs have to be balanced so that the total cost per unit of production is minimized.

Such systems have analysed for random arrivals and negative exponential service. In the general case there are m units in the system, and c serves each with mean service rate μ. Each unit in the pool of potential customers has a probability $\lambda \, dt$ of joining the queue in the short interval dt. This means that the time spent in the pool between completing service and joining the queue again is exponentially distributed. Independence of arrivals and service is assumed. A steady state is always attained.

Here

$$\lambda(r) = (m - r)\lambda \qquad \text{for } 0 \leqslant r \leqslant m$$
$$= 0 \qquad\qquad \text{otherwise}$$

and

$$\mu(r) = r\mu \qquad \text{for } 0 \leqslant r \leqslant c$$

$$= c\mu \qquad \text{otherwise}$$

Thus

$$p(r) = \frac{m!}{(m-r)!r!}\left(\frac{\lambda}{\mu}\right)^r p(0) \qquad \text{for } r \leqslant c$$

$$= \frac{m!}{(m-r)!c!c^{r-c}}\left(\frac{\lambda}{\mu}\right)^r p(0) \qquad \text{for } c \leqslant r \leqslant m$$

$p(0)$ being found by the condition that

$$\sum_{0}^{m} p(r) = 1$$

As the maximum queue length is finite there is no limit to the ratio λ/μ.

As in other systems, it is better for two or more servers to work on the pool together as a team, rather than to split the pool into parts and to work independently.

The various measures of effectiveness of the system can be derived from the formula as before, though they are not of simple form. Naor (4) has given the solution in terms of tabulated Poisson functions and their cumulatives, and has discussed the solution in these terms. Cox (5) has given a table of the utilization of the service for a single service channel when the average time in the pool is at least eight times as long as the service time. It can be shown that queue length is independent of the form of the distribution of the input.

In his original paper Palm (6) gave a diagram showing the optimum number of machines to use in terms of the hourly cost of idle time, the hourly cost of labour, the arrival rate and the service rate for groups of machines tended by one operator. An extension of the model allows for a limited number of spare machines which are brought into the system to replace machines waiting or being served (7).

The assumptions of our theory are an idealization. With more machines to care for, travelling time between them increases, and so service takes longer. This becomes even more marked if the operators work as a team. It might well be that when much ground is to be covered, the increase in service time could outweigh the theoretical advantage of working as a team. This ought to be checked before machine interference formulae are applied, quite apart from the need to check that it is reasonable to use exponential service and running times.

The theory of machine interference is applicable to many situations: for example, the breakdown of machinery, the maintenace of a pool of equipment, the allotment of maintenance workers, and the number of shorthand writers attending a limited number of dictators. Machine interference situations are often referred to as closed queues although the words closed and cyclic (see below) are used interchangeably.

Exponential Distribution and Service in Series. It is supposed that each unit entering the system requires a number of services, which are carried out in succession (8). After receiving the first service at the first stage the unit joins a queue for the second service at the second stage and so on. At each stage there may be one or more service channels. The input for one stage is thus the output from the previous stage. With exponential distributions of input and service intervals, it can be shown that the output is also exponentially distributed so that each stage has an exponential input. In this case the state of the system is not completely described by the number of units present; it is necessary to specify the number at each stage (i.e. the number waiting for service or being served at that stage).

All the units pass through each stage so that for a steady state to be possible the average rate of input must not exceed the total rate of service at any stage. In the steady stage the average rate of input to each stage is the same and the stages can be considered separately. Suppose the rate of input is λ and at the jth stage there are c_j channels each with average service time $1/\mu_j$. Then, as in the previous section, the steady state probability of n_j units in the stage is

$$p(n_j) = v(n_j)p(o_j)$$

where

$$\begin{aligned}
v(n_j) &= \rho_j^{n_j}/n_j! & \text{for } n_j \leqslant c_j \\
&= c_j^{c_j-n_j}\rho_j^{n_j}/c_j! & \text{for } n_j \geqslant c_j
\end{aligned}$$

and $\quad \rho_j = \lambda/\mu_j$

The probability of the state of the whole system of k stages with n_j at the jth stage is the product of the probabilities for each stage and can be written

$$p(n_1, n_2, \ldots n_j \ldots n_k) = p(0)\prod_{j=1}^{k} v(n_j)$$

As before, $p(o)$ can be found by equating to unity the sum of the probabilities of all states and it is

$$p(o) = \prod_{j=1}^{k} \left\{1/ \sum_{n_j=0}^{\infty} v(n_j)\right\}$$

Erlang Distributions. The examples so far have been limited to those where the arrival interval and service time both have exponential distributions. With these distributions the probability of an arrival at any instant is quite independent of previous arrivals, and the probability of service being completed at any instant is quite independent of the time when service began. It is this property which allows simple transition equations to be written.

In practice the unrelated arrivals of customers might well be exponential, but the distribution of service times may be quite unlike the exponential. Transition equations cannot be written using such distributions because the probability of service being completed depends on when service began.

There are a number of ways of dealing with this. One way is to extend the use of the simple method by building up service time distributions from combinations of exponential distributions. This method is considered here.

We consider service to be in a number of exponential phases immediately following each other; all phases have to be completed before another unit can enter the service channel. The distribution of the whole service time is quite different from that of its components. When all k phases are identical, the service time has a chi-square distribution with $2k$ degrees of freedom. Because of the physical interpretation of chi-square, formulated by A. K. Erlang for just the reasons given above, the distributions are widely known as Erlang distributions. The family of Erlang distributions for $k = 1, 2, 3, \ldots$ is scaled so that the mean of the whole service time is the same for each. When $k \to \infty$, the service time is constant. Erlang also considered the cases when the phases are different from each other, and obtained much more general distributions. Indeed by suitable combination of exponential distributions it is possible to build up any distribution at all. However it might be complicated to do so and the resulting equations difficult to formulate correctly and to solve. The basic method is to represent the distribution in question by a number of routes along one of which the customer passes during service according to an assigned probability distribution; and each route is assembled from exponential phases.

The transition equations for systems with such distributions of service times can now be written, because the probability of passing from the jth to the $(j + 1)$th phase of the service is $\mu_j \, dt$, and it depends only on the presence of a unit in the jth stage.

For random arrivals and Erlang service time, a single-channel system is characterized by $p(n, j)$ which is the probability that there are n units waiting and the unit being served is in the jth phase of service. The equations for the steady state, with an arrival rate λ and a service rate $k\mu$ for each phase, and therefore μ for the whole system, are

$$
\begin{aligned}
\lambda p(o, o) &= && k\mu p(1, k) \\
(\lambda + k\mu)p(1, 1) &= \lambda p(o, o) &&+ k\mu p(2, k) \\
(\lambda + k\mu)p(n, 1) &= \lambda p(n - 1, 1) &&+ k\mu p(n + 1, k) && \text{for } n > 1 \\
(\lambda + k\mu)p(1, j) &= && k\mu p(1, j - 1) && \text{for } 1 < j \leqslant k \\
(\lambda + k\mu)p(n, j) &= \lambda p(n - 1, j) &&+ k\mu p(n, j - 1) && \text{for } n \, 1, \, 1 < j \leqslant k
\end{aligned}
$$

(We notice in passing that these steady state equations can also be written down without reference to the differential difference equation. In the case of the last equation for example, the state (n, j) can be left for the states $(n + 1, j)$ and $(n, j + 1)$ or, if $j = k$, $(n - 1, 1)$. Rates λ and $k\mu$ attach to these leavings. The state can be reached by leaving states $(n - 1, j)$ and $(n, j - 1)$ with associated rates λ and $k\mu$.)

In general, the solution of these equations requires the introduction of probability generating functions and numerical computation. For $k = 2$ it can be shown that

$$
p(n) = \sum_{i=0}^{n} \frac{(n + i + 1)!(1 - \rho)}{(2i + 1)!(n - i)!} \left(\frac{\rho}{2}\right)^{n+i} \qquad \text{where} \qquad \rho = \frac{\lambda}{\mu}
$$

but for larger values of k the probabilities have to be found numerically.

Average results can be expressed generally and the main ones are given in the list at the end of the chapter.

It is seen that the average queue length and average waiting time for negative exponential service ($k = 1$) are twice the queue length and waiting time for constant service ($k = \infty$).

A similar approach can be used to analyse systems with an Erlang arrival time distribution. Units are imagined to pass through k phases of an arrival channel before joining the queue. As soon as one unit is through the arrival channel, the next one is introduced.

The use of Erlang distributions does not necessarily imply that the phases of service and arrival have any physical reality, though that may be so.

Methods of solution of queuing problems with Erlang distributions are described in some detail by Morse (9). Tabulations of some of the more complicated examples have been published (10).

Other mathematical methods of solution

The previous sections have used the classical approach to the theory of queues, by the formation of differential difference equations for the distribution of queue size. In his book on queuing theory, Morse uses only this approach (9).

Other analytical techniques have been used to give both general and particular results. Some of the more important of these techniques are briefly described in this section.

Integral Equations. One approach leads to integral equations for the distributions of the waiting time. It is valid for general distributions of arrival and service time, but is not easily applicable to transient states of the system. It was first used by Lindley (11) for a single service channel. The analysis for such a queue is given here.

If W_n is the time the nth unit has to wait for service if it waits at all, and is minus the time the server has been idle if the nth unit does not have to wait, a_n is the interval between the arrival of the nth and $(n + 1)$th units, with distribution $a_n(t)\, dt$, and b_n is the service time of the nth unit, with distribution $b_n(t)\, dt$, then

$$W_{n+1} + a_n = W_n + b_n \qquad \text{for } W_n \geqslant 0$$
$$= b_n \qquad \text{for } W_n \leqslant 0$$

and on writing $U_n = b_n - a_n$,

$$W_{n+1} = W_n + U_n \qquad \text{for } W_n \geqslant 0$$
$$= U_n \qquad \text{for } W_n \leqslant 0$$

The distribution of W_{n+1} can be simply written down in terms of the distributions of W_n and U_n. If these are $W_n(t)\, dt$ and $U_n(t)\, dt$ respectively, then

$$W_{n+1}(t) = \int_0^\infty W_n(x) U_n(t - x)\, dx + U_n(t) \int_{-\infty}^0 W_n(x)\, dx$$

In writing this equation it is assumed that the time the nth unit waits is independent of the subsequent service time and of the time when the next customer arrives.

The service time and arrival interval distributions are known, so the distribution of U_n is known,

$$U_n(t) = \int_0^\infty a_n(x)b_n(t + x)\, dx$$

In the steady state the distributions of arrival, waiting, and service times are the same for each unit and we can write

$$W(t) = \int_0^\infty W(x)u(t - x)\, dx + u(t) \int_{-\infty}^0 W(x)\, dx$$

where

$$u(t) = \int_0^\infty a(x)b(t + x)\, dx$$

The integral equation for the waiting time distributions is soluble in terms of the distribution of u, which in turn is completely given by the known arrival time and service time distributions. Although the equation is soluble analytically for simple forms of $u(t)$, numerical computation would usually be required. The equation is of the Weiner-Hopf type, and also arises in the study of random walks and sequential tests of hypotheses.

With this technique Lindley studied queues with the following distributions:

(a) Regular input and Erlang service.
(b) Poisson input and general service.
(c) Erlang input and general service.

Smith (12) showed how to solve the integral equation for general distributions of service time and arrival interval. As one example of the method of solution he considered a service time that was a constant delay plus an Erlang delay and an arrival interval that was a constant delay plus an exponential delay.

Markov Chains. A sequence of events forms a Markov chain if the probability of each event can be expressed in terms of the previous event, irrespective of any information about earlier events. Hence a knowledge of any event makes all information about previous events irrelevant to the prediction of subsequent events.

In a similar way, a continous process is Markovian if a knowledge of any instantaneous state of the process makes all previous history irrelevant in predicting its future behaviour.

The instantaneous state of a queueing system may be described by the number of units in it. If the arrival and service distributions are exponential, this number of units is all that is needed to determine the probabilities of future instantaneous states, and the process is Markovian. For other distributions these probabilities depend also on the previous history, and the process is non-Markovian. However, the process can still be regarded as Markovian if the times since the previous arrival and the last completion of service are included in the description of the instantaneous state of the system.

If the queuing system is described in a Markovian way, it can be studied using the well-developed theory of Markov chains (13). There is, however, a further approach using Markov chains.

A queuing system with random arrivals is considered. If we know the queue size when a customer leaves, then previous information on queue size is of no predictive value. This is true about all instants when a customer leaves. This set of particular instants can then be thought of as a Markov chain embedded in the queuing process (14).

The analysis of embedded Markov chains has proved a fruitful approach to the analysis of queuing systems. It is used, for instance, by Bailey in the analysis of queuing for bulk service (see below).

Some quite general results can be obtained without carrying out the analysis necessary to give a complete description of the system. A good example of this type of ad hoc approach is D. G. Kendall's derivation of the average queue length and waiting time for a single queue with random arrivals and general service time distribution (3).

Let λ be the arrival rate, μ be the service rate, q be the size of queue a departing unit leaves behind it, q' be the size of queue the next unit leaves behind it, v be the service time of this second unit, r be the number of units arriving during the service time v (r is a random variable of mean value λv and variance $\lambda v + \lambda^2 var(v)$).

Then

$$q' = q - 1 + \delta + r$$

where $\delta = 1$ when $q = 0$ and $\delta = 0$ when $q \neq 0$.

For the steady state, we can equate expected values of both sides of the equation and the expected values of the squares of both sides.

As $\delta^2 = \delta$ and in the steady state, $E[q'] = E[q]$ and $E[q'^2] = E[q^2]$,

$$E[\delta] = 1 - E[r] = 1 - \frac{\lambda}{\mu} = 1 - \rho$$

and

$$E[2q(1 - r)] = E[(r - 1)^2] + E[\delta(2r - 1)]$$

Noting that r is independent of q and δ it follows that

$$E[q] = E[r] + \frac{E[r(r - 1)]}{2(1 - E[r])}$$

and hence

$$E[q] = \rho + \frac{\rho^2(1 + \mu^2 var(v))}{2(1 - \rho)}$$

From this expression for mean queue length at a departure, i.e. the mean number in the system, the mean waiting time can be obtained. If a departing unit has waiting and service times w and v and leaves q units behind, then q is the number of arrivals in time $w + v$, and so

$$E[q] = \lambda(E[w] + E[v])$$

whence

$$\frac{E[w]}{E[v]} = \frac{\rho}{2(1 - \rho)} (1 + \mu^2 var(v))$$

From this formula it is clear that, for a given arrival rate and service rate, waiting time will be a minimum when service time is constant. A similar result for the Erlang family of service times might have led us to expect this.

Special queue situations

The theory of queues has been extended to take in more and more features which appear in real life queuing situations, whether the queues be people, manufactured parts, repair jobs, or perishable goods. Some of these situations are dealt with briefly in this section.

Bulk Service and Bulk Arrival. Service of batches of units may take a number of different forms. One case is where the server waits for s units, and then serves them together, for example passengers on a coach tour. Another is where the server, when ready, takes the units waiting, though not more than s, and serves them together, for example passengers on public transport. (s may be a random variable, for example the number of unoccupied seats on the bus.)

In some instances the time spent waiting may be all that matters, the service time being irrelevant. The interval between successive services could then be regarded as being completely taken up by serving the previous batch, or to be the time when the service channel is ready for a new batch, the actual service time being shorter.

One case has been analysed by Bailey (15). Units arrive at random and are served in batches of not more than s, the server taking zero units if none is waiting. The distribution of intervals between service is chi-square with $2p$ degrees of freedom and mean p/a. The analysis uses embedded Markov chains and probability generating functions. There is no simple analytic solution, but a useful inequality for the average waiting time W, is

$$0 \leqslant W - \frac{p + s}{2a(s - m)} \leqslant \frac{p(s - 1)}{2am}$$

where m is the average number of arrivals per service interval. For example, if the arrival rate is nearly equal to the service rate, say $s = m + 1$, then the average waiting time, measured in service intervals is given by

$$\frac{m + 1}{2} + \tfrac{1}{2} \leqslant W \leqslant \frac{m + 1}{2} + 1 \qquad \text{for exponential service } (p = 1)$$

and

$$\tfrac{1}{2} \leqslant W \leqslant 1 \qquad \text{for regular service } (p = \infty)$$

In general, the greater the traffic intensity, m/s, the greater is the advantage of regular service over irregular service and the larger the batch size for a given traffic intensity, the greater is the advantage of regular service over irregular service.

The theory was developed to give a model of customers at a clinic, where requests for attention are effectively random and clinics are held each week or at irregular intervals. The theory of bulk service might also be applied to rubbish removal, bus and train services, bulk shipment of goods, train despatch from marshalling yards, lifts and so on.

Bulk arrivals have also been studied (16). Here the customers arrive in a group but are processed individually. Situations to which this theory might apply are railway marshalling yards, dealing with the morning's post and the provision of exits at a railway station.

Transient Solutions. Most of the previous analysis has been concerned with the steady state of queuing systems. For systems where this condition can occur, the steady state probability of a given state can be defined as the probability of finding the system in that state at a time sufficiently far in the future; that is, the steady state probability of the state n, $p(n)$, is the limit of the time dependent probability, $P(n, t)$, as $t \to \infty$. If such a system is known to be in the state k at a given instant, then immediately afterwards states near k are more likely than would otherwise be expected. The state probabilities tend gradually to the steady state probabilities. These changes in the probabilities are of interest in some problems, particularly after the occurrence of no units or a large number of units in the system, that is after idle or busy periods.

Transient probabilities are also of interest for systems which operate only for limited periods. In this case there is no need for a steady state to be possible. Indeed Bailey (17) gives an instance where it is quite suitable for an appointment system to have $\rho = 1$ because the period for which it operates is short enough for the waiting time of customers to remain small.

The transient solutions can be obtained by solving the time-dependent differential equations of the system. Morse (9) gives one way of doing this and Saaty (18) quotes transient solutions for a few types of system.

For systems having input or service rates which vary with time, all solutions can be regarded as transient. Random distributions with varying parameters have been solved for a single server queue; the results are rather complex (18). Another more common problem arises from the rush-hour type of situation; input, and perhaps also service rate increases for a limited period. This problem can be tackled by splitting the total period into intervals during which the rates can be taken as constant, and solving for each interval in turn. Cox (19) has used this method for a simplified analysis of a rush-hour. Usually, however, simulation methods are employed for such problems.

Queue Discipline. So far, in our queuing models, units have been served in the order in which they arrive. The queue discipline is thus first-come first-served. This is the discipline which normally comes to mind when we think of queues, but it is not the only one.

Units may be selected for service at random from those waiting. The average waiting time of units is the same as for first-come first-served queues. But because a unit may now be served out of turn and have to wait an excessively long time, there is a greater proportion of very long and very short waiting times, and the variance of the waiting time is greater than for first-come first-served queues. An example of random selection for service is the selection of trunk callers by the operator at a telephone exchange.

A further queue discipline is last-come first-served. The average waiting time is the same as for queues which are first-come first-served. But the variance of the waiting time is even greater than for random selection, and there is a correspondingly greater proportion of very long and very short waiting times. An example of last-come first-served discipline is the handling of goods which have to be stacked: foodstuffs in a warehouse or letters in an in-tray. It is not necessarily a bad policy for perishable goods if their survival time is short compared with the average waiting time, indeed it may be the best policy in some circumstances.

In short, for these three types of queue discipline the average waiting time is the same, but the variance of the waiting time, and the proportion of units waiting a long time, increase in the order first-come first-served, random, last-come first-served.

Queue discipline might be extremely important in handling of goods which deteriorate, the discipline which may be convenient to the stockroom being the one causing the greatest loss.

Priority. The units waiting for service may belong to two or more classes having an order of priority. The priority will be either priority of entry when the service is free, or pre-emptive priority (that is, priority to displace units being served if they are of lower priority).

The average waiting time of all the units remains unaltered if some of them are given priority (unless priority is related to the service time), but the average waiting time of the various classes is decreased or increased according to their order of priority. In the case of pre-emptive priorities, the behaviour of the class with first priority is as though there was no other type of unit in the system.

It may be that the high priority classes have a shorter average service time than those of lower priority. In this case the average number waiting for service and the average waiting times are reduced. Similarly, if priority is given to classes having longer average service time, the average number waiting for service and the average waiting time are increased. Having a shorter or longer service time may be an incidental characteristic of the classes selected for priority, or it may be the reason why they are given priority. In other cases, high priority might be given to customers whose time is very valuable.

Among priority systems which have been studied are:

Poisson arrival, *r* classes of priority, non pre-emptive service, general service times (20).

Poisson arrival, 2 classes of priority, pre-emptive service, exponential service times (21).

Poisson arrivals, a continuous number of priorities according to shortness of service, general service time (22).

Possible applications include a fitter giving priority to the repair of certain machinery, a traffic intersection where one stream of traffic has priority over others and a bank counter, where priority might be given to short transactions. In the last case it might be preferable to give the short transaction a separate server. Some supermarkets have a cashier reserved for customers who have bought few goods. Note that breakdown or generally unavailability of the server can be regarded as a class of customers enjoying pre-emptive priority.

Impatient Customers. Another feature of real life queues is the impatient customer who does not want to queue for too long. Two types of impatient customer have been studied:

the one whose decision to join is influenced by queue length,
the one who decides to leave the queue if the wait is too long.

When the decision to join the queue depends on the length of the queue, the arrival probability in the queue is effectively queue dependent—a situation described earlier. Another case studied is that of customers leaving after waiting for a time T in an exponential arrival and service system (23).

But here, as in the previous section, although some particular cases have been studied, there does not as yet appear to have been a systematic study of the loss of customers who are impatient.

The application of such a study are not only to human queuing systems where impatience is understood, but also to such queuing system as storing perishable goods, processing heated metal and communication of information, in each of which the unit loses its value if it waits too long.

Cyclic Queues. In closed systems, units may pass from one service facility to the next in continual circulation, either being served or waiting for service. At each state there may be a single server or a number of servers in parallel.

Koenigsberg (24) has analysed a cyclic system with m units in the system and k single-channel exponential service facilities of mean service rate μ_1, $\mu_2 \ldots u_k$. There are no arrival rates to consider, as the output of one stage is the input of the next stage. The equations governing the transition probabilities can be formulated as in previous examples. The probability of there being n_1 units waiting or being served at the first stage, n_2 at the second stage, and so on, is given by

$$p(n_1, n_2, \ldots n_k) = \frac{x_1^{n_1} x_2^{n_2} \ldots x_k^{n_k}}{Z_k^m}$$

where

$$x_i = \frac{\mu_1}{\mu_i}$$

and

$$Z_k^m = \sum_{\substack{\text{All partitions} \\ \text{of } m}} x_1^{n_1} x_2^{n_2} \cdots x_k^{n_k} = \sum_{\substack{i=1 \\ j=1 \\ j \ne i}}^{k} \frac{x_i^{m+k-1}}{k(x_i - x_j) \, \Pi}$$

If further

$$_iZ_{k-1}^m = \sum_{\substack{\text{All partitions} \\ \text{of } m \text{ excluding} \\ \text{the } i\text{th term}}} x_1^{n_1} x_2^{n_2} \cdots x_k^{n_k}$$

then the idle time of the ith stage D_i, can be written as

$$D_i = \frac{_iZ_{k-1}^m}{Z_k^m}$$

The throughput of the ith stage is $(1 - D_i)\mu_i$. As the throughput of all the stages must be equal, it follows that this expression has the same value for all values of i. It is of interest, too, that the throughput is independent of the order of the servers in this case.

The simplest particular case is that when all k servers have identical service times, μ. In this case

$$Z_k^m = \frac{(m + k - 1)!}{m!(k - 1)!}$$

$$Z_{k-1}^m = \frac{(m + k - 2)!}{m!(k - 2)!}$$

$$D_i = \frac{k - 1}{m + k - 1}$$

The rate of throughput is therefore $m/(m + k - 1)$. More difficult cases have been tackled. In the case where there is more than one server for each queue and no capacity limitations between queues it is usually the case that the time spent between queues influences the results only through its average and not the form of its distribution.

Obvious applications of the theory would be the movement of trucks on a closed loop or the movement of ferries between ports. Many industrial processes consist effectively of closed queues. Koenisberg's analysis was developed, for example, as a model of a particular type of mining operation.

Busy Period. So far we have discussed server utilization in terms only of the proportion of time the server is occupied. In some cases the length of time the server is kept continuously busy is of some importance. For example if the server is a machine a long spell of continuous serving might lead to the risk of breakdown or if the server is a man the standard of service he gives might deteriorate owing to fatigue. A period of continuous serving is called a busy period; the distribution of the lengths of busy periods has been studied for some simple queues (3).

Usefulness and limitations of queuing theory

Queuing theory has a number of limitations which prevent its usefulness as a means of solving a great many practical problems. Chief among these are the difficulty of studying transient solutions and the difficulty of modelling situations in which arrivals and service times exhibit any form of statistical dependence. In many cases the system being studied is always in a transient state and never has time to settle to a steady state behaviour. This may be because the parameters are changing through time or because the system returns again and again to the same initial conditions. Thus if one were studying the behaviour of a production process it would not be unusual to observe that rates of throughput on a particular piece of equipment varied throughout the shift nor would it be surprising if each day overtime were worked to clear up any backlog of queuing goods to get the next day off to a fresh start.

Other limitations are that many systems are more complex and the statistical distributions observed less simple than can easily be analysed. Many industrial processes are, for example, compounded of several interacting queues, some of which are cyclic, and whose interaction is strong enough to cast doubt on a simple analysis which treats each queue separately. These limitations are, in principle, less serious than the difficulties of transience and dependence since one can conceive of a sufficiently skilful analysis to take account of the most complex interactions and distributions, and even to some degree dependence. The resulting equations however, in addition to being difficult to formulate, would also be difficult to solve without recourse to heavy computing.

These various limitations of queuing theory have meant that simulation (see Chapter 8) has become very widely used as a means of studying queuing situations. It would, however, be wrong to dismiss queuing theory. In the first place there are plenty of situations of importance where the assumptions queuing theory makes and therefore the results of applying it are valid. Certainly if it can be used it is to be preferred to simulation as the cheaper and more accurate method.

In addition, and perhaps more importantly, queuing theory provides models which are good enough in a great many cases to give useful insight into the system under study and into how it might be improved. We have seen that queuing theory provides a number of general insights which apply to most systems: that the queue length increases rapidly when server utilization approaches 100% and that when variability is present 100% utilization is secured at the expense of infinite queues (or at least extensive overtime working); that waiting time can be reduced by pooling service, by reducing the variance of service time and by sensible priority systems just as much as by speeding up the service; and so on. These results can help us decide what type of change it is worth considering making even though simulation might be necessary to put a figure on the estimated effect of the change. Nor is the help queuing theory affords only qualitative: rough quantification using a simplified theoretical model can often cut the number of alternatives to be evaluated by simulation experiments and so reduce the frequently high computing cost associated with simulation.

Steady state formulae for queues

Most of the quantities likely to be of interest in queuing problems in the steady state are defined, and formulae for them are given, for the simple case; a selection of the more important results for other cases is given. For brevity, the word probability has been abbreviated to P. In all the formulae, $\rho = \lambda/\mu$. In making use of the formulae it should be remembered that the values given to the parameters assumed known will often in fact be estimates: when such is the case some care must obviously be exercised in the interpretation of the results and the value to be attached to them.

Contents List. Unless otherwise specified, the following conditions are satisfied:

(a) Unlimited input with Poisson distribution.
(b) Unlimited number in the system.
(c) Single queue served one unit at a time.
(d) Each unit requires service by only one channel (i.e. single stage service).

(i) With service in order of arrival.

Type (1) Single channel
     (2) Single channel, limited number in system
     (3) Multiple channels
     (4) Multiple channels, limited number in system
     (5) Multiple channels, multiple stages
     (6) Single channel, service rate proportional to number in system
     (7) Single channel, Erlang service
     (8) Single channel, general service

Exponential service } (1)–(6)

(ii) With priorities.

     (9) Single channel, general service
    (10) Single channel, exponential service
    (11) Single channel, exponential service, two classes, one with pre-emptive priority

Priorities in order of service time } (9)–(10)

Formulae
(1) Poisson input, unlimited queue length, single service channel with exponential service time distribution. Average rate of input λ and average rate of service μ. $\lambda < \mu$.

6

Traffic intensity $\rho = \lambda/\mu$

P of n units in the system $p(n) = \rho^n(1 - \rho)$

P of more than n units in the system $p(>n) = \rho^{n+1}$

Average number of units in the system $N = \rho/(1 - \rho)$

P of n units in the queue $q(n) = \rho^{n+1}(1 - \rho)$ (for $n > 0$)

    $q(0) = 1 - \rho^2$

P of more than n units in the queue $q(>n) = \rho^{n+2}$

Average number of units in the queue $Q = \rho^2/(1 - \rho)$

P of no waiting (up to start of service) $w(0) = 1 - \rho$

P of waiting from t to $t + dt$ $w(t)\, dt = \rho(\mu - \lambda)\, e^{-t(\mu-\lambda)}\, dt$

P of waiting longer than t $w(>t) = \rho\, e^{-t(\mu-\lambda)}$

Average waiting time   *in queue* $W = \rho/(\mu - \lambda)$

P of time from t to $t + dt$ spent in the system $s(t)\, dt = (\mu - \lambda)\, e^{-t(\mu-\lambda)}\, dt$

P of more than time t spent in the system $s(>t) = e^{-t(\mu-\lambda)}$

Average time spent in the system $S = 1/(\mu - \lambda)$

P that a queue exists $p(>1) = \rho^2$

P that a unit needs to wait for service $p(>0) = \rho$

Utilization of the service channel $u = \rho$

The formulae for $q(n)$, $q(>n)$ and Q, if divided by ρ^2 apply to the time during which a queue exists; those for $w(t)$, $w(>t)$ and W if divided by ρ refer to the units which need to wait.

(2) Number in the system limited to L but otherwise as type (1) with no restriction on λ and μ.

$$p(0) = (1 - \rho)/(1 - \rho^{L+1})$$
$$p(n) = \rho^n p(0) \qquad \text{(for } n \leqslant L)$$
$$u = 1 - p(0)$$
$$N = \frac{\rho - (L + 1)\rho^{L+1} + L\rho^{L+2}}{(1 - \rho)(1 - \rho^{L+1})}$$
$$Q = N + p(0) - 1$$

(3) Poisson input, unlimited single queue, c service channels in parallel, each with exponential service time distribution. Average rate of input λ and average rate of service by each channel μ. $\lambda < c\mu$.

$$u = \rho/c$$
$$p(0) = \left\{ \sum_{i=0}^{c-1} \rho^i/i! + \rho^c/(c - \rho)(c - 1)! \right\}^{-1}$$
$$p(n) = \rho^n p(0)/n! \qquad \text{(for } n \leqslant c)$$
$$ = c^{c-n}\rho^n p(0)/c! \qquad \text{(for } n \geqslant c)$$
$$p(>n) = c^{c-n}\rho^{n+1}p(0)/(c - \rho)c! \qquad \text{(for } b \geqslant c - 1)$$
$$N = \rho^{c+1}p(0)/(c - \rho)^2(c - 1)! + \rho$$
$$Q = N - \rho$$
$$w(>t) = p(>c - 1)\, e^{-\mu t(c-\rho)}$$
$$W = Q/\lambda$$
$$S = W + 1/\mu = N/\lambda$$

(4) Number in the system limited to L, no restriction on λ or μ, and otherwise as type (3).

$$p(o) = 1 \Big/ \Big\{ \sum_{i=0}^{c-1} \rho^i/i! + \rho^c[1 - (\rho/c)^{L-c+1}]/(c - \rho)(c - 1)! \Big\}$$

$$p(n) = \rho^n p(0)/n! \qquad \text{(for } n \leqslant c)$$
$$= c^{c-n}\rho^n p(0)/c! \qquad \text{(for } L \geqslant n \geqslant c)$$

In the particular case where $c = L$ (no queue allowed),

$$p(n) = \rho^n/n! \sum_{i=0}^{c} \rho^i/i! \qquad \text{(for } n \leqslant c \text{ and } c = L)$$

(5) Poisson input of average rate λ, k stages of service in series with c_j channels at the jth stage each exponential service time distribution of mean rate μ_j.

$\lambda < c_j\mu_j$ for all j, $\rho_j = \lambda/\mu_j$

P of $n_1, n_2, \ldots n_j \ldots$ units at stages $1, 2, \ldots j \ldots$ is

$$p(n_1, n_2 \ldots n_j \ldots n_k) = p(0) \prod_{j=1}^{k} v(n_j)$$

where

$$v(n_j) = r_j^{n_j}/n_j! \qquad \text{(for } n_j \leqslant c_j)$$
$$= c_j^{c_j - n_j}\rho_j^{n_j}/c_j! \qquad \text{(for } n_j \geqslant c_j)$$

and

$$p(0) = \prod_{j=1}^{k} \Big(1 \Big/ \sum_{nj=0}^{\infty} v(n_j) \Big)$$

Where $c_j = 1$ for all j (one channel at each stage) the results for type (1) apply to each stage (putting μ_j for μ).

(6) Poisson input of average rate λ, unlimited queue, single service channel, with probability $n\mu \, dt$ of service finishing in the interval t to $t + dt$.

$$p(n) = \rho^n e^{-\rho}/n! \qquad \rho_0 = e^{-\rho}$$
$$N = \rho$$
$$Q = \rho - 1 + e^{-\rho}$$
$$W = Q/\lambda$$
$$S = 1/\mu$$

(7) Poisson input of average rate λ, unlimited single queue, single service channel, with Erlang service time distribution of mean rate μ, $\lambda < \mu$. P of service time from t to $t + dt$ is

$$\mu(t) \, dt = (\mu k)^k e^{-\mu k t} t^{k-1} \, dt/(k - 1)!$$
$$u = \rho$$
$$p(0) = 1 - \rho$$
$$N = Q + \rho$$
$$Q = (k + 1)\rho^2/2k(1 - \rho)$$
$$W = Q/\lambda$$
$$S = N/\lambda$$

When $k \to \infty$ the service time is constant at $1/\mu$ so that
$$Q = \rho^2/2(1 - \rho)$$

(8) Poisson input of average rate λ, unlimited single queue, one service channel with a general service time distribution of mean $1/\mu$ and coefficient of variation v, $\lambda < \mu$.

$$p(0) = 1 - \rho$$
$$N = Q + \rho$$
$$Q = \rho^2(1 + v^2)/2(1 - \rho)$$
$$W = Q/\lambda$$
$$S = N/\lambda$$

(9) Poisson input of average rate λ, unlimited single queue, single service channel. Units in the queue are served in order of increasing service time (which is known accurately in advance). General distribution of service time, with probability $F(t)$ of a time less than t. Average waiting time of a unit with service time t is

$$W_t = W_0/\left[1 - \lambda \int_0^t t' \, dF(t')\right]^2 \quad \text{if } t \leqslant t_o$$

$$N = W_o \int_0^{t_o} \left\{ dF(t)/\left[1 - \lambda \int_0^t t' \, dF(t')\right]^2 \right\}$$

where units with service time greater than t_o never reach the service channel, t_o being given by

$$\lambda \int_0^{t_o} t \, dF(t) = 1$$

and where

$$2W_o = \lambda \int_0^{t_o} t^2 \, dF(t)$$
$(W_t = \infty$ if $t > t_o$ and $N = \infty$ if $t_o < \infty)$.

(10) As for (9) but exponential service of mean rate μ.

$$W_t = W_o/\{1 - \rho[1 - e^{-bt}(1 + \mu t)]\}^2 \quad \text{if } t \leqslant t_o$$

$$N = \lambda\rho \int_0^\infty e^{-\mu t} \, dt/\{1 - \rho[1 - e^{-\mu t}(1 + \mu t)]\}^2 \quad \text{if } t_o < \infty$$

where

$$\rho[1 - e^{-\mu t_o}(1 + \mu t_o)] = 1$$

and

$$W_o = \lambda\rho \qquad\qquad\qquad \text{if } t_o = \infty$$
$$= (1 - \lambda t_o \, e^{-\mu t_o})/\mu \qquad \text{if } t_o < \infty$$

(11) Two Poisson inputs, 1 and 2, of rates λ_1 and λ_2.
Unlimited single queue, single service channel. Units 1 have pre-emptive priority over units 2. Exponential service of rates μ_1 and μ_2.
The results for units 1 are exactly as for queues type (1) (with λ_1 for λ and μ_1 for μ).
For units 2, the average number in the system is

$$N_2 = \rho_2[1 + \mu_1\rho_1/(1 - \rho_1)\mu_2]/(1 - \rho_1 - \rho_2)$$

References

1. Moran, P. A. P. *The Theory of Storage*. Methuen & Co. Ltd 1959.
2. Karush, W. A Queueing Model for an Inventory Problem. *Opns. Res.* **5.5** pp. 693–703 1957.
3. Kendall, D. G. Some Problems in the Theory of Queues. *J.R. Statist. Soc. B* **13.2** pp. 151–173 1951.
4. Naor, P. On Machine Interference. *J.R. Statist. Soc. B* **18.2** pp. 280–287 1956. *Some Problems of Machine Interference*. Proceedings of the First International Conference on Operational Research. John Wright & Sons Ltd 1957.
5. Cox, D. R. A Table for Predicting the Production from a Group of Machines Under the Care of One Operative. *J.R. Statist. Soc. B* **16.2** pp. 285–287 1954.
6. Palm, D. C. The Assignment of Workers in Servicing Automatic Machines. *J. Industrial Engrg.* **9.1** pp. 28–42 1958.
7. Toft, F. J. and Boothroyd, H. A Queueing Model for Spare Coal Faces. *Opns. Res. Quart.* **10.4** pp. 245–251 1959.
8. Jackson, R. R. P. Random Queueing Processes with Phase-type Service. *J.R. Statist. Soc. B* **18.1** pp. 129–132 1956. Queueing Systems With Phase Type Service. *Opns. Res. Quart.* **5.4** pp. 109–120 1954.
9. Morse, P. M. *Queues, Inventories and Maintenance*. John Wiley & Sons Inc. 1958.
10. Peck, L. G. and Hazelwood, R. N. *Finite Queueing Tables*. John Wiley & Sons Inc. 1958.
11. Lindley, D. V. The Theory of Queues with a Single Server. *Proc. Camb. Phil. Soc.* **48** pp. 277–289 1952.
12. Smith, W. L. On the Distribution of Queueing Times. *Proc. Camb. Phil. Soc.* **49** pp. 449–461 1953.
13. Meisling, T. Discrete-time Queueing Theory. *Opns. Res.* **6.1** pp. 96–105 1958.
14. Kendall, D. G. Stochastic Processes Occurring in the Theory of Queues and Their Analysis by the Method of the Imbedded Markov Chain. *Ann. Math. Stat.* **24** pp. 338–354 1953.
15. Bailey, N. T. J. On Queueing Processes with Bulk Service. *J.R. Statist. Soc. B* **16.1** pp. 80–87 1954.
16. Cox, D. R. and Smith, W. L. *Queues*. Methuen & Co. Ltd. 1961.
17. Bailey, N. T. J. A Note on Equalizing the Mean Waiting Times of Successive Customers in a Finite Queue. *J.R. Statist. Soc. B* **17.2** pp. 262–263 1955.
18. Saaty, T. L. Resumé of Useful Formulae in Queueing Theory. *Opns. Res.* **5.2** pp. 161–200 1957.
19. Cox, D. R. The Statistical Analysis of Congestion. *J.R. Statist. Soc. A* **118.3** pp. 324–335 1955.

20. Cobham, A. Priority Assignment in Waiting Line Problems. *Opns. Res.* **2.1** pp. 70–76 1954 and (correction) **3.4** p. 547 1955.
21. Stephen, F. F. Two Queues Under Pre-Emptive Priority With Poisson Arrival and Service Rates. *Opns. Res.* **6.3** pp. 399–418 1958.
22. Phipps, T. E. Machine Repair as a Priority Waiting Line Problem. *Opns. Res.* **4.1** pp. 76–85 1956.
23. Barrer, D. Y. Queueing with Impatient Customers and Indifferent Clerks. *Opns. Res.* **5.5** pp. 644–649 1957; Queueing with Impatient Customers and Ordered Service. *Opns. Res.* **5.5** pp. 650–656 1957.
24. Koenigsberg, E. Cyclic Queues. *Opns. Res. Quart.* **9.1** pp. 22–35 1958.

Further reading

References 9, 16, 18 and 19 above.
Benson, F. and Gregory, G. Closed Queueing Systems: a Generalisation of the Machine Interference Model. *J.R. Statist. Soc. B* **23.2** pp. 385–393 1961.
Saaty, T. *Elements of Queueing Theory.* McGraw-Hill 1961.
Lee, A. M. *Applied Queueing Theory.* Macmillan 1966.
Jackson, R. R. P. and Adelson, R. M. A Critical Survey of Queueing Theory. Part 1. *ORQ* **13.1** Part 2 *ORQ* **13.4** 1962.

Examples for solution

1. A queue has a Poisson input of mean rate λ and the probability of a service finishing in the interval t to $t + dt$ is $n\mu dt$, where there are n units in the system. Initially there are no units in the system; find the expected number at time t, from the differential difference equations.

2. A colliery working one shift per day uses a large number of locomotives which break down at random intervals; on average one fails per 8 hour shift. The fitter carries out a standard maintenance schedule on each faulty loco. Each of the five main parts of this schedule take on average $\frac{1}{2}$ hour but the time varies widely. How much time will the fitter have for the other tasks (which are interrupted to deal with locos) and what is the average time a loco is out of service?

3. Examine graphically for the simple queue with one server, Poisson arrivals and exponential service time how the following vary with λ/μ:

    (i) the average waiting time,
    (ii) the proportion of waiting times exceeding double the average,
    (iii) the proportion of time there are 5 or more customers queuing.

What inferences do you draw?
Likewise examine how the average waiting time in this same queue, but with a general service time varies with the mean and variance of the service time. Draw contours of equal waiting time on a graph whose axes are the mean and variance of service time and comment.

4. In a busy bank the 10 counter clerks each handle any type of business and each has his own queue. The manager realizes that customers who want only to cash cheques are frustrated to find themselves behind someone paying in large quantities of cash. He thinks it would be worth reorganizing his counter assistants to reduce waiting time and he is sure this can be achieved only through different queue disciplines as he does not believe that large reductions in service time are possible even if the clerks specialize.

Make use of the formulae given in the chapter to help him decide what to do.

5. A fleet of N ships is plying between two ports, loading at one and unloading at the other. The time between ports has an Erlang distribution made up of n exponentially distributed stages each with mean $1/n\lambda$. Loading times are exponentially distributed with mean $1/\mu_1$ and unloading times are exponentially distributed with mean $1/\mu_2$. There is capacity at either port to handle only one ship at a time.

Show that the average numbers of ships waiting to be, and being, loaded and unloaded is independent of n.

6. Consider a variety of queuing situations from your every-day life—e.g. buying a train ticket, going to the barber, waiting for a bus, making a telephone call, buying goods in a small general store. How many of them can be modelled in a comparatively simple way? Are arrivals and service times independent? Is queue discipline affected by the customers and/or the servers being human beings?

Try to predict some of the measures of performance of some such systems by modelling them, making what simplifying assumptions are necessary and using observed values of the parameters. Make more detailed observation to check the assumptions and the predictive accuracies of your models. Are you left with a higher or lower opinion of the usefulness of queuing theory?

7 Stock control

Introduction

In a few industries it is the practice for goods to be supplied daily to meet each day's requirements, and for virtually no stocks to be held. In most industries, however, demand and supply are not matched so closely; stocks are held and, even so, temporary shortages are sometimes experienced. For example, raw materials are held against uncertain shipments, work in progress is held to avoid the flow of work in one department being interrupted by variations in production in another, finished goods are held against the risk of lost sales, and spare parts are held to avoid costly production stoppages.

The theory of stock control, or inventory control as it is perhaps more widely known, is applicable to all these types of stockholding. Its aim is to find the optimum balance between costs of throughput, shortages, stock-holding and administration.

The earliest developments of stock control theory were in the years just before and after the 1914–18 war, when several economic lot-size formulae were developed: formulae which specify the lot size that minimize the combined costs of buying material for stock and of paying interest on money tied up in stock. There were few further developments until the first probabilistic studies of stock control with shortages in the mid-1940's (1). In 1951–52 came a series of foundational papers, notably those of Dvoretzky, Kiefer and Wolfowitz (2), which considered the best form and structure of optimum stock control policy—previous work had been limited to finding the optimum setting for whatever particular type of control policy had been selected. In the rest of the 1950's there were many papers at all levels of sophistication. In addition to the mathematical treatment of particular stock control activities there have been broad studies of the whole support system for manufacturing equipment, including spares buying, overhaul schedules, repair standards, standby equipment, and the design of equipment for reliable operation and quick maintenance (3). Much current research in stock control is reported in such journals as *Operations Research, Operational Research Quarterly, Management Science* and *Naval Research Logistics Quarterly*.

This chapter is a brief introduction to stock control theory. For simplicity, the discussion is mainly in terms of stock flowing into an industry. With suitable changes the discussion also applies to stocks flowing out of an industry, the most important difference being that the aim would then be to increase income rather than to reduce expenditure.

The first part of the chapter is an extended discussion of the nature of stock control costs and of some of the economic problems of managing a stock control system: reference to the main theoretical ideas are given and gaps in theory pointed out. The middle part of the chapter describes some simple models of stock control, with indications of their application and significance. The final part of the chapter is a brief survey of recent developments in theory and practice, with comments on their likely significance for the future.

Before leaving this introductory section, however, it would be well to mention one very important point.

Generally speaking stock control theory is concerned with optimizing the operation of a stores system about which certain decisions have already been taken. Typical of such decisions are that the material in question should be held in stock, that the stocks will be held in specified places and that the stocks will be held in a certain form (e.g. unprocessed, ready for immediate assembly, and so on). Usually also a decision is supposed to have been taken about the quantity and type of information that will be kept as a routine.

It cannot be too much emphasized that these decisions are almost certain, in most cases, to be more important in influencing profits or costs than the more detailed stock control rules with which most theory deals. They are particularly important in complex stores systems where stocking is possible at many sites in many forms and in which some central control and transfer of material between stores is possible in principle.

Often these decisions can be taken without recourse to sophisticated mathematical methods. A clear head might be needed in taking the right economic view but generally once the right questions are posed their solution is comparatively easy, although in some cases a good deal of data processing (for example in comparing policies of greater and lesser centralization) might be necessary.

We shall comment on these decisions as they arise in our general discussion.

The nature of stock control costs and stock control systems

There are four main costs associated with a stock control system:

  the value of stock throughput,
  the cost of shortages,
  the cost of stockholding, and
  the cost of operating the system.

In this part of the chapter the four costs are in turn defined, discussed and related to the costs which have already been discussed. There is then a brief description of the operating rules with which O.R. studies have been mainly concerned and of the estimation and measurement that is needed in order to find operating rules which are optional. Finally there is a discussion of systems of several stores whose operation is interdependent.

Value of Stock Throughput. The value of stock throughput in, say, a year is the total value of material received by a stores system in the year. Apart from alterations in the level of stockholding and from the loss or scrapping of stock, it is equal to the total value of material issued by the stores system in a year.

It is sometimes thought that the value of stock throughput is quite outside the sphere of control of a stock control system—that it is completely determined by needs which arise outside the system. If that view is taken, then stock control, however good it is in itself, can offer scope only for quite small savings compared with savings possible in the major cash flows of an industry. It may well be that a reduction of 20% in the combined costs of shortages, stockholding and operation of the stores system would only effect a saving equivalent to a 1% reduction in the value of stock throughput.

Control of the value of stock throughput is in fact one of the most important responsibilities of a stock control system. The value of throughput can be reduced both by price reductions, which are discussed later and which are generally recognized to be a responsibility of the purchasing part of a stock control system, and by reductions in the volume of throughput, which are usually considered to be the responsibility of user departments but which can be made by purchasing material of higher quality. The control of throughput has had much less attention from O.R. workers than might be expected from this brief outline of its importance.

Cost of Shortages. The cost of a shortage is the extra cost of getting material in a hurry, over and above the normal costs of providing the material, together with all the extra consequential losses due to delays or lost sales, over and above what would have been incurred even if the material had been in stock. For example, if a brake rod of a winding engine fractures and a replacement is not in stock, the shortage cost is the cost of special delivery together with the cost of lost winding time but excluding the cost of the time which would in any case have been needed to do the repair if the brake rod had been in stock.

The concept of a shortage cost is simple but the estimation of shortage costs is not, because the consequences of shortages are so varied and far-reaching. The estimation of some shortage costs is a matter of patiently following through the consequences; this can be done as part of an O.R. study but would almost certainly be too difficult for a stock controller to do as a routine. Other shortage costs defy measurement, for example, the long term effects of failing to supply a customer. Where possible, shortage costs ought to be estimated sufficiently closely to give an idea of the economic level of shortages at which a stock control system should be aimed. Where that is impossible the usual practice for O.R. workers is either to aim at a control system which improves other aspects of a control system while keeping shortages at or below their previous level, or to make senior management responsible for deciding the general shortage level to be tolerated. This handing back of responsibility is at its simplest a request to choose between 90% or 95% service but sometimes takes the form of asking management to choose the most desirable point on a curve of the sort shown in Figure 7.1. Once the O.R. worker has managed to construct such a curve, senior management can decide the point at which to strike the balance between the measureable costs of the system and the intangible effects of the quality of service provided.

The discussion so far has covered the value of stock throughput and the cost of shortages. Except where sales are lost, the annual value of throughput is not usually permanently affected by shortages; throughput is only temporarily held up and is compensatingly higher after a shortage. It is, however, sometimes thought that an increased incidence of shortages of spare parts leads to higher stock throughput by encouraging unofficial hoards, some of

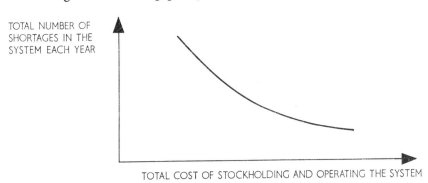

FIG. 7.1. The balancing of shortages against known system costs.

whose locations may be forgotten. Against this opinion is the view that a higher incidence of shortages of spares leads to lower stock throughput, because material is less likely to be thrown away before the end of its useful life.

Cost of Stockholding. The cost of stockholding is the cost of storage space plus the cost of tied-up capital. It is sometimes taken to include also the cost of deterioration and the losses due to writing off stock which is no longer wanted; for simplicity the discussion here will exclude these.

In studying any stock control problem it is not the total cost of stockholding which is needed but the marginal cost of stockholding over the range of changes being considered. For example, if the changes being considered are limited increases in order quantities only, then the costs to be considered are the extra cost of storage space (probably no extra cost if the space already allocated to that type of item is not exceeded) and the extra cost of tied-up capital.

For convenience, the marginal costs are often taken to be the same for a whole range of different types of store. Sometimes the simplification is taken even further: the cost of storage space is taken to be proportional to the value of material, rather than the volume, so that all stockholding costs can be considered to be a straight percentage of the value of material in stock.

The cost of storage space is reasonably straightforward. The cost of tied-up capital is a simple enough concept but is not easily applied; it is sometimes taken to be the prevailing interest rate, and sometimes taken to be the return on capital investment in the organization. There is no simple rule. If in the long run the only effect of a stock reduction is that less money is borrowed, then the prevailing interest rate should be used. But if sooner or later a stock reduction will lead to profitable investment which would not otherwise have been made, then the cost of stockholding should include a term to represent the profitability of this investment. This rule is probably adequate for most stock control studies.

Stockholding may be used to reduce the value of stock throughput not by reducing the volume of throughput but by reducing the price. Discounts are often available if goods are bought in sufficiently large quantities. Theoretically even quite small discounts are worth taking—for example, it could be worth buying an extra two months' stock in order to get a 1% discount—but in practice such theoretical results have to be applied carefully in order to avoid stockholding being suddenly increased by such an amount as to require a major change in the amount and distribution of capital in an organization. There are also fluctuations in market prices, particularly for raw materials and stockholding may be used to profit from these fluctuations; this important use of stocks is only occasionally treated in stock control theory (4).

Stockholding affects shortages directly: the more the stockholding, the fewer the shortages. One of the main contributions of stock control theory has been the development of a statistical understanding of methods of guarding against shortages caused by fluctuations of demand in the lead-time, i.e. the period between making a decision to buy material and receiving it from the supplier, including the time for processing documents before the order goes to the supplier.

Costs of Operating the System. The operating cost of a stores system covers the work of ordering and receiving material, keeping records, transporting stocks within an organization, issuing stocks to users, reviewing stocks to discover obsolete material and errors in records, and introducing improved methods of working. For the purposes of this chapter it excludes the cost of shortages and the cost of stockholding.

Although the value of the various activities is difficult to determine, their costs are not; most of them can be discovered or deduced from operating records or from special activity surveys. The most important point to remember is that in any application what is needed is not the total cost of an activity but the marginal cost of the activity over the range of changes being considered.

It is through the deployment of operating effort that other costs are largely affected. If operating effort is spent on searching the market for favourable prices and in obtaining competitive quotations for material, the value of throughput can be reduced. If operating effort is spent on hastening and progressing orders, the cost of shortages can be reduced. And if operating effort is spent on frequent ordering and extensive transport within the organization, stockholding can be reduced.

No O.R. study of the optimal deployment of operating effort over these various activities has been reported; the balance between the activities is in practice settled by management within an allowed expenditure. Detailed O.R. studies of stock control have concentrated on the optimal control of some particular activity. For example, ordering has been very extensively studied to find rules for when and how much to order in such a way that the combined costs of stockholding, shortages and operating are as low as possible; advanced mathematical theory was needed in this field because simple models could barely compete with existing intuitive controls. In contrast to the ordering activity with its many theoretical models, other stock control activities have received much less attention; for example, the activity of hastening outstanding orders (5).

A general point about the cost of operating the system is that it will be higher the more individual attention is given to items in the system. For very important items, for example those with a high throughput and those for which a shortage is catastrophic, individual attention may be desirable. Less important items might be classified so that within each classification items are controlled by the same general rules. Thus one might have two classifications of run of the mill items, the first including all items whose shortage would have little or no effect and the second those whose shortage might interfere with production. These classifications are further sub-classified according to price, demand and so on. For each of the resulting final classifications blanket policy decisions are taken including decisions about the degree of control. For cheap unimportant items very crude control rules indeed might be best; high throughput items with expensive shortage costs might justify individual treatment to the extent that demand for the item is the subject of a special study and that the shortage cost is estimated with some care.

The Organizing of Stock Movements. Within any stores system one must decide when and how much of each type of material is ordered, transferred, or issued. This leads to the question: what are the decisions, for each type of material, which will minimize the total costs of throughput, shortages, stock-holding and operating? For convenience, we shall discuss only material being brought into a store (re-provisioning); similar considerations apply to material being issued.

Within any particular stores system, the methods and frequencies of re-provisioning have to be decided. Basically, there are two main types of re-provisioning: re-provisioning each item when its stock has dropped to some predetermined level, and re-provisioning all items of a particular kind on some scheduled date. In most practical cases the distinction is blurred; it is often a matter of individual preference whether provisioning is considered to be of one type or the other.

In the first type of re-provisioning, an order is placed for item i when the amounts on hand and on order are equal to or below the level s_i, called the re-order level; the quantity ordered is sufficient to raise the amounts on hand and on order to the level of S_i. This is a (s, S) policy; it is usually called a re-order level policy. It has been subjected to extensive mathematical analysis. It is common to find published exploratory analysis confined to re-provisioning with zero lead-time.

In the second type of re-provisioning, an order is placed for a whole group of items every t units of time; for item i the quantity ordered is sufficient to raise the amounts on hand and on order to the level S_i. This is a (t, S) policy, and is usually called a cyclical review policy. It has not been extensively analysed, though it is almost certainly the most common method used for replenishing stocks.

The concentration of O.R. analysts on the uncommon type of re-provisioning is not altogether whimsical; (s, S) re-provisioning is better than (t, S)

re-provisioning in many circumstances. Specifically, if the throughput, holding, shortage and operating costs associated with each item are independent of the throughput, holding, shortage and operating costs of all other items, then (s, S) re-provisioning is preferable; in this case the stores system is said to be separable. If, however, a stores system is non-separable, (s, S) re-provisioning is not always the better method; for example, if the batching of orders for a wide range of items leads to a discount on the total value of the order, then (t, S) re-provisioning may be better than (s, S) re-provisioning (6).

In practice, a more advanced type of re-provisioning may be preferable to either of these elementary types. A more general type of re-provisioning is to review stocks every t units of time, and to order item i if the amounts on hand and on order are equal to or below the level s_i. This may be described as a (t, s, S) policy. More advanced systems are possible: for example, when demand is very variable over the period to be covered, it would be advantageous to have emergency action levels in addition to (t, s, S) re-provisioning. An example of a complex system in use in the Coal Board is a cyclical review system with two supplementary action levels; the higher level is for the placing of supplementary orders and the lower level for emergency action. The need for complex systems like these is only just beginning to be recognized. Their satisfactory mathematical analysis appears to be beyond the scope of methods currently available.

Basic Problems of Choosing Re-provisioning Policies. Many O.R. studies have been concerned in some way or other with the problem of choosing re-provisioning policies: whether (s, S), (t, S), or (t, s, S) policies are to be used in the stores system and within that decision, what values of t are to be used for various groups of items and what particular values of s and S are to be used for each individual item.

The basic research problem posed is:

(a) In what ways can available information, for example on usage and costs, be used to make a re-provisioning decision.

(b) What is the effect of a re-provisioning decision in terms of its physical effects (for example, numbers of shortages, transactions, or items in stock).

(c) How are the physical effects translated into cost effects.

Satisfactory answers to each of these parts of the problem have to be found and tested. If the answers fit together sufficiently well to explain what is currently happening, then an apparently satisfactory model has been produced; there is a good discussion of the development up to this point in Chapter 4 of Hanssmann's book (4). The next step, often mathematical and the main topic of the middle part of this chapter, is

(d) To manipulate the model to discover ways in which the available information can be used to give lower total costs.

The final step is to test these conclusions, which to meet the operational requirements of the stores system must completely specify the procedures by which available information is to be used for each decision.

Most published papers seem to fall into two main streams of development, neither of which fully cover the four main parts of the research problem described in the previous paragraph. The first main stream assumes that available information is perfect and that there is an exactly specified understanding of the probabilistic, physical and cost effects of decisions; this stream of development concentrates on mathematical studies of optimizing total system costs. The second main stream is concerned mainly with the fact that available information is not perfect and concentrates on studies of forecasting and estimation; for example, Brown (7) has extensively studied the use of exponential smoothing for predicting demand (see below).

Single and Multi-level Stores Systems. The ideas discussed in the previous section have been taken furthest for single stores operating in isolation from other stores. In many large organizations there are stores holding the same material at different administrative levels. For example, spares for mining equipment are held by manufacturers at their factories and in depots in different parts of the country and similar spares are held by the National Coal Board in central stores serving between ten and forty collieries and in colliery stores. In such cases there are problems of deciding which items should be centrally stocked and how often items held centrally should be distributed to the subsidiary stores. There is also the larger question of where to locate subsidiary and central stores. Some of the advantages of centralized holding are the possibilities of lower stock-holding, more discount buying, and less deterioration. On the other hand, centralized holding may lead to poorer availability, higher transport costs, and the double handling of material.

Some studies of multi-level stores systems have been reported (4) but there is little comprehensive theory as yet. A practical two-level system has been designed and introduced for coalface machinery spares in the Coal Board; the system works satisfactorily although the theory is by no means exact (8). Clark and Scarf (9) have produced a satisfactory theory of optimal control rules in a system of the very simplified form

$$[\ ] \rightarrow [\ ] \rightarrow [\ ] \rightarrow [\ ]^{---}$$

The arrows show the flow of stocks down to the lowest level, at which all demands originate. They conjecture that it is likely that the theory will also be satisfactory for a system of the general form

with demands arising at any level of the system. In both the simple and more general form, the theory of the system assumes that the probability distribution of demands is known.

In practice, the probability distribution of demands is not known. From time to time parameters, such as the average demand, are re-estimated and new control policies are determined. This may have serious repercussions in a multi-level system. If the demand at the lowest level happens to be a little higher than usual, the next order to the next highest level will not only cover the extra usage but also a further amount to increase safety stocks. The fluctuation in demand at the lowest level is therefore magnified at the next level. In a system with several levels of storage, a small fluctuation in usage at the lowest level can become several years boom and slump for the manufacturer. This has been demonstrated and discussed by Forrester in a large-scale simulation of the operation of a manufacturing system with a factory, factory store, wholesale store, and retail store (10). Although this type of instability has been demonstrated, no theoretical or practical control system has been designed which embraces the robustness needed to cope with uncertain estimates and the optimal cost characteristics associated with the balancing of the different costs discussed earlier in this chapter.

Single and Multi-level Information. One way of avoiding the worst effects of demand fluctuations in a multi-level stores system is to have at some central point complete information on stocks and usage at all the stores in the system. For example, a large computer installation is being brought into use by the Air Force; it will eventually maintain records of stocks and issues at all Air Force bases throughout the world. It will thus be possible to exercise control in two important ways: firstly, alterations in the demand rate for a particular item can be followed quickly without either the time lag or the serious fluctuations in stock which occur when information is channelled up through stores at different levels, and secondly, shortages in one part of the system can quickly be met by transferring material from another part of the system. For the system to be effective, information on issues will be flown in almost every day, presumably on flights which would be made for other purposes. It would be possible to centralize not only the information on stocks, but also to centralize the decision taking, so that re-provisioning action for all parts of the system is taken centrally rather than at each store in the system.

In contrast to this type of highly developed central control, most systems of multi-level storage do not have central information available on the state of the entire system. This disadvantage is sometimes partly overcome in practice by stocking most material at central stores and very little at subsidiary stores. The central stores in effect provide both central stocks and central information, though these two functions are often not clearly distinguished.

Some simple models and their application

The models in this section illustrate the mathematical approach to stock control without introducing heavy mathematical analysis. Models such as these have been widely used to give general management some appreciation of O.R. thinking. Their usefulness in this chapter lies in their simple demonstration of the structure of optimal policies and the nature of optimal decisions.

The discussion of each model is by no means exhaustive; in particular, there is no discussion of the more complicated analyses which are available for the situations which the models represent.

Model 1 Discounts. Price reductions may sometimes be obtained by buying larger quantities of goods than would ordinarily be bought. Whether such discounts are worth the increased stockholding can be checked easily and quickly. The discount is worth taking if

$$\frac{\text{(Discount in \%)}}{\text{(Extra month's supply bought to get discount)}} > \frac{100h}{24}$$

where h is the fractional cost of stockholding per year. This rule can easily be derived by comparing the increased stockholding cost with the saving in value of annual stock throughput. In practice the rule will often indicate that discounts are worth taking; for example, if the cost of stockholding is 12% of initial cost per year, a 5% discount would appear to be worth taking if it could be had without buying more than another 10 months' supply.

In practice the risk of obsolescence or of long-term price changes would also need to be considered before large amounts of stock are bought.

Model 2 Optimum Order Quantities. If the stock of an item just before each order is delivered is B, its order quantity is Q, and its price is P, then the average number of that item in stock is

$$B + \frac{Q}{2}$$

and the annual cost of stockholding is

$$hP\left(B + \frac{Q}{2}\right)$$

where h has the same meaning as in Model 1. If the ordering cost is S and the annual demand is D and the demand is regular then the annual cost of ordering is

$$\frac{SD}{Q}$$

The way in which stocks vary with time and the way in which costs depend on Q are shown in Figures 7.2 and 7.3.

The total cost of ordering and stockholding has its minimum value

$$hPB + \sqrt{2SDhP}$$

when Q takes on the value Q^* which is equal to

$$\sqrt{\frac{2SD}{hP}}$$

As the total cost is not very sensitive to errors when Q is near Q^*, there is no virtue in being over-precise. For example, if Q is $0{\cdot}8\ Q^*$ or $1{\cdot}25Q^*$, then the total cost is increased by less than $2\frac{1}{2}\%$.

Two general conclusions can be drawn from the formula for Q^*: that the value of stock ordered should be proportional to the square root of the value of annual usage, and that the amount of stock ordered measured in terms of years' supply ordered should be proportional to the inverse of the square root

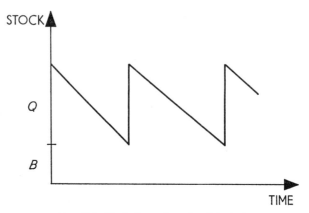

Fig. 7.2. Variation of stock with time.

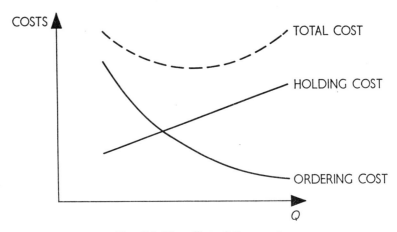

Fig. 7.3. The effect of Q on cost.

of the value of annual usage. This means that order quantities should vary over a much wider range than is perhaps instinctive. For example, using costs applicable to the National Coal Board, an item with a usage of more than £1,000 per year should be ordered in quantities of less than a month's supply, and an item with a usage less than £1 per year should be ordered in quantities of at least three years' supply.

Model 3 A Simple Model with Shortages. Figure 7.4 shows the simple deterministic model which is being considered. If the stock of an item just after each order comes in is A, its order quantity is $Q(>A)$, its price is P, and its shortage cost is R per unit time per item short, then its annual stockholding cost is

$$\frac{hPA^2}{2Q}$$

its annual shortage cost is

$$\frac{R(Q-A)^2}{2Q}$$

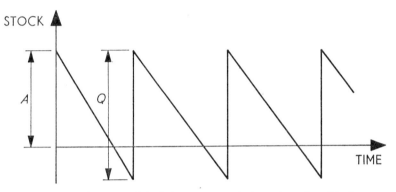

FIG. 7.4. Simple model of shortages: variation of stocks with time.

and its annual ordering cost is

$$\frac{SD}{Q}$$

From this it follows that the optimum value of Q is

$$\sqrt{\frac{2SD}{hP}}\sqrt{\frac{R+hP}{R}}$$

the optimum value of A is

$$\sqrt{\frac{2SD}{hP}}\sqrt{\frac{R}{R+hP}}$$

and the minimum total cost is

$$\sqrt{2SDhP}\sqrt{\frac{R}{R+hP}}$$

Two points should be noticed about these expressions. The order quantity is greater than the optimum order quantity of Model 2 as is general whenever shortage costs are considered, but the total annual cost is less.

Model 4. Suppose a new plant is to be ordered and we have the option to buy a particular spare part with the plant. When the plant is written off so will be any stock of the part. If the part is needed during the life of the plant and the part is not in stock it must be bought at a price of P, the same as its initial purchase price, but a shortage cost R is incurred. Records for similar parts on similar plants suggest that there is a probability *prob(r)* that the part will be required r times during the life of the plant.

How many of the parts should be bought to minimize expected cost?

Suppose the life of the plant is short enough for holding costs to be ignored (it is not too difficult to take account of holding costs but we shall not do so). The total expected cost if x units of the spare are bought is

$$Px + (P + R)\sum_{r=x}^{\infty}(r - x)prob(r)$$

This is least when $x = X$ defined by

$$\sum_{X+1}^{\infty} prob(r) \leqslant \frac{P}{R + P} < \sum_{X}^{\infty} prob(r)$$

This is a particular form of a more general result which occurs very widely and is informative in indicating whether a system is optimally balanced: that for minimum cost

$$(\text{probability of shortage}) \sim \frac{\text{cost of buying}}{\text{cost of shortage (including cost of buying)}}$$

The formula indicates a very wide range of shortage probabilities.

Model 5 Simple Buffer Stocks. It is sometimes more useful and acceptable to set the buffer stock level, that is the average level of stock just before goods are received, to give a specified probability of run-out in the lead-time, rather than to attempt to minimize total costs. Some guide to a suitable probability could be had from the formula of Model 4 or preferably from a similar formula more appropriate for general use (12):

$$\frac{(\text{holding cost per unit per year})}{(\text{holding cost per unit per year}) + (\text{run-out cost per unit})(\text{orders per year})}$$

For a lead-time L years, an average annual demand D, and a standard deviation of demand in a year σ, the chance that usage in the lead-time will exceed

$$LD + K\sigma\sqrt{L}$$

can be calculated on the assumption that the probability distribution of demand is a Normal distribution. In this expression $K\sigma\sqrt{L}$ is the buffer stock and LD is the average usage in the lead-time. For example, there would be a 1% chance that usage in the lead-time will exceed

$$LD + 2\cdot33\sigma\sqrt{L}$$

We therefore know that if we use that quantity as the re-order level there will be a 99% chance of stocks lasting until the new stock is received. In studies of the usage of engineering spares in the Coal Board, the Normal distribution has been found to be satisfactory for spares used at the rate of more than 12 to 15 a year; for such spares σ is about $0.25D$.

For low usage spares a Poisson distribution is more appropriate; in this case σ is $\sqrt{D}$. For making approximate calculations, the same values of K can be used as for the Normal distribution: for example, there is approximately a 1% chance that usage in the lead-time will exceed

$$LD + 2.33\sqrt{LD}$$

Model 6 Central Stores. The elementary ideas of the previous model can be used to decide whether it is worthwhile to hold the buffer stock of an item in a central store rather than to hold independent buffer stocks at each subsidiary store.

For an item which is to be given a particular level of protection at each of the stores independently, there would be a stock reserve of $K\sigma L$ at each of n subsidiary stores each having a demand rate D; the total reserve would be $nK\sigma\sqrt{L}$. For the same level of protection at the central store the stock reserve would need to be $K\sigma\sqrt{nL}$. The stockholding could therefore be reduced by

$$K\sigma\sqrt{nL}(\sqrt{n} - 1)$$

that is, by $(\sqrt{n} - 1)$ times the necessary central reserve.

This saving is gained at the expense of some increase in transport cost, because the item is received at the central store and distributed rather than being received at each subsidiary store direct from the supplier. If the cost of distribution is C per item, it follows that centralizing is worthwhile if

$$CnD < hPK\sigma\sqrt{nL}(\sqrt{n} - 1)$$

This means that for a given group of stores the centralizing of a particular item depends on the expression $P\sqrt{L} . \sigma/D$. The decisions taken are illustrated in Figures 7.5 and 7.6.

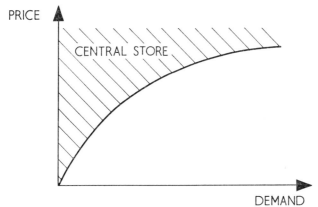

FIG. 7.5. Centralizing for items with Poisson demand.

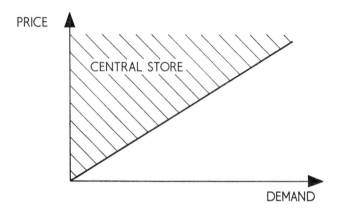

FIG. 7.6. Centralizing for items with normal demand.

In practice, many more factors would have to be taken into account before making a decision on the value of centralization in a particular organization.

Model 7 Cyclical Review. In cyclical review, stocks are re-provisioned at intervals of T. As a first approximation, the optimal interval between reviews can be derived from the simple analysis of Model 2:

$$\sqrt{\frac{2S}{hPD}}$$

though no account of fluctuations in demand is taken.

If account of fluctuations is taken, the period during which the buffer stock must guard against fluctuations in demand is longer than just the lead-time L; it is in fact the period $L + T$, so the buffer stock has to be

$$K\sigma\sqrt{L + T}$$

The average stock is therefore

$$K\sigma\sqrt{L + T} + \frac{DT}{2}$$

As the number of orders is $1/T$ per year, the total cost each year is

$$\frac{S}{T} + hP\left[K\sigma\sqrt{L + T} + \frac{DT}{2}\right]$$

which is minimized when the interval between reviews is

$$\sqrt{\frac{2S}{hPD}}\Bigg/\sqrt{1 + \frac{K\sigma}{D\sqrt{L + T}}}$$

which means that when buffer stocks and shortages are considered the interval between reviews should be less than in the simple case when they are not considered. In fact it should be reduced by a factor

$$\sqrt{1 + \frac{\text{Buffer stock}}{\text{Expected usage in period covered by buffer}}}$$

This is in interesting contrast to the result of Model 3, which indicated that in a re-order level system the consideration of shortages leads to the interval between consecutive orders being increased rather than decreased.

Model 8 A Re-order Level System. The final example is a more detailed model of the re-order level system. The expressions for stockholding and shortages are only approximate, but hold when the chance of shortages is not very great.

An item with price P and average annual demand D is ordered in amounts Q each time the amount on hand and the amount on order falls to M. The average lead-time is L. The cost of each order placed is S, and if there is a shortage during the lead-time it costs R to meet that shortage and to avoid any further shortage before the end of the lead-time. The probability that there is a demand X in the lead-time is $p(X)$, which covers both variation in demand and variation in the lead-time.

The buffer stock is approximately

$$M - LD$$

so the average annual stockholding cost is approximately

$$hP\left(\frac{Q}{2} + M - LD\right)$$

The probability that a shortage occurs during the lead-time is approximately

$$\sum_{M+1}^{\infty} p(X)$$

so the average annual cost of ordering and shortages is approximately

$$\left(S + R\sum_{M+1}^{\infty} p(X)\right)\frac{D}{Q}$$

Using differentiation for Q and differencing for M, it follows that the total average annual cost is minimized if

$$Q \simeq \sqrt{\frac{2D(S + R\sum_{M+1}^{\infty} p(X))}{hP}} \quad \text{and} \quad p(M+1) \leqslant \frac{hPQ}{RD} \leqslant p(M)$$

For example: the average consumption of an article is 7 per week following the Poisson distribution, the lead-time is 14 days, its price is 50p, stock-holding cost 25% per year of the value of stock, ordering costs 30p, and the shortage cost is £1. Then

$$Q \simeq \sqrt{[1,752 + 5,840 \sum_{M+1}^{\infty} p(X)]} \quad \text{and} \quad p(M+1) = \frac{Q}{2,920}$$

These equations can be used iteratively to find the best values of M and Q, 21 and 44, giving a total cost of £6·353 per year. If the ordinary square root formula of Model 2 had been used for Q, then the values of M and Q would have been 21 and 42, giving a total cost of £6·358.

Production scheduling

We have hitherto assumed that the items being controlled have behaviours independent of one another. This is often the case for materials bought into a firm, although many raw materials have uses which depend on the use of some other material and consequently demands are not always statistically independent.

Likewise reprovisioning decisions cannot always be judged independent of one another. To someone buying in material from outside the dependence might manifest itself by a complicated price discount structure. The supplier will be willing to give discounts if the buyer can be persuaded to place orders which reduce the supplier's cost of meeting them, for example by enabling him to schedule his manufacturing more expediently. In the case where the supplier and stockist are one and the same (as is the case if we are considering the stock of finished goods held by a factory to meet demand from whole-salers, for example) the problem becomes one of scheduling production rather more than one of stock control. Putting it another way, the problem remains a stock control problem but the pattern of orders placed on the manufacturing capacity seriously influences the cost of stock throughput.

The problem of designing systems which optimize in such circumstances is unsolved except in trivial, and probably unrealistic, cases. We shall content ourselves with a few general remarks on the problem.

It is usually difficult to assign costs to the effect of different ordering policies on production even if one can predict the effects. The difficulties are often circumvented by attaching value to smooth production and to an absence of deviations from productions schedules. This accords well with commonsense. If production is planned some weeks ahead one can probably carry it out at least cost and the smoother production is planned to be the better, overtime and fluctuating labour forces being unnecessary. Equally deviations from the plan are, if at short notice, likely to cost something even if the immediate effect is not obvious.

For these reasons preference is often given to cyclic review over a re-order level system. Cyclic review generates orders for material at times which can be predetermined in the interests of production planning. The times can be set to avoid the worst effects of competition between materials for a common manufacturing facility and to take advantage of similarities in demand patterns so that if two materials with related demands run out they run out together. The cycle for any particular material may be a sub-cycle of the total cycle. Thus we may have a 24 week cycle overall but some materials are on a 12 week cycle, others on a 6 week cycle, others on 4 and others 3. In this way the production plan can be built up to take advantage of the desirability of long cycles for some material and short for other. Additionally we may decide to manufacture a material only if its stock is below a certain level.

In a way this device aims to get the best of both cyclic reviews and a re-order level system. The straight re-order level system, optimum if items are independent one of another, generates a more or less haphazard output of orders which are difficult to plan for. Fluctuating lead times often result. However it is necessary in any system to have some sort of provision for inserting emergency orders, whether they upset production plans or not.

Forecasting

The problem of forecasting demand is an important one. The accuracy with which demand can be forecast has, it goes without saying, an important bearing on the cost of a stock control system.

In the case of important items forecasts of demand will usually be made taking account of many factors which might influence demand and which are themselves more easily forecast. For many items, however, the amount of effort required to make individual forecasts will not be justified by results. In such cases forecasts built up from past demand may be used. The most common method used is exponential smoothing which will be described below. Exponential smoothing was suggested by Brown (7).

It is a simple method of forecasting future results, taking account of any trend and seasonal patterns in the past results. It requires storage of only a little amount of data and is well suited for use as a routine forecasting procedure on a computer. Other methods, similar in general principle but slightly more complex, have been suggested. Examples are Brown's least squares forecasting method (11) and the Box-Jenkins method (12).

Before discussing exponential smoothing it may be worth pointing out that one ought, in theory, to choose that combination of forecasting policy and stock control policy which as a combination minimizes costs. This is difficult if not impossible to do except by simulation.

That the forecasting policy and the stock control policy interact can be readily seen. The re-order level in a re-order level system, for example, depends on the probabilities ascribed to demands in the lead time which depend on the forecasting method employed. Moreover the behaviour of the system will be influenced by uncertainty in forecasting demand. In Model 8 above it was assumed not that one could forecast demand but rather that one knew D, the underlying average demand. If one were instead estimating D by forecasting based on observed data but using the results of Model 8 to set levels it is clear that stocks and shortages would be different from the values given even ignoring approximations in the mathematics. If, to be precise, one forecast D by the demand in some previous time period, stocks would be higher than Model 8 predicts and shortages lower. This is because when demand is high by chance stocks are put up unnecessarily and vice versa, but stocks cannot be run down with the same facility as they are built up.

We go on to describe exponential smoothing introducing first some notation. We shall work in time units of one month just for ease of exposition. The notation to be used is:

x_t Sales figure for the tth month.

y_t De-seasonalized sales figure for the tth month (equal to the actual result when there are no seasonal effects).

s_t Estimate of the seasonal factor for the tth month, and the same month in following years, made in the tth month.

$\hat{x}_{t,T}$ Estimate made in the tth month of the sales figure for the $(t + T)$th month.

$\hat{y}_{t,T}$ Estimate made in the tth month of the sales figure for the $(t + T)$th month before any allowance for seasonal effects is made.

(We define the notation in terms of demand. The same forecasting method could, however, be used for forecasting other things like lead time. We shall also assume that seasonal effects are multiplicative: that is the demand in say June is made up of a deseasonalized demand multiplied by some number which is the same every June. Additive seasonal effects can be dealt with by simple modifications to what follows.)

The exponential smoothing model described here assumes that a linear trend as well as multiplicative seasonal factors, is appropriate. A description of other combinations of trend and seasonal effects is given in reference 7, which also explains the theoretical background of this method more fully.

The method involves smoothing the results (to eliminate misleading exceptional results) by taking a weighted average of all past results, attaching more weight to recent results and less to older ones. This is done by calculating the value of a smoothing function, u_t, in the tth month from the expression:

$$u_t = py_t + (1 - p)u_{t-1}$$

where p is a weighting coefficient within the range 0 to 1, and y_t (calculated as x_t/s_{t-12}) is the de-seasonalized current sales figure.

Expanding this expression for u_t gives:

$$u_t = py_t + p(1 - p)y_{t-1} + p(1 - p)^2 y_{t-2} + \ldots$$

It is seen that the weight attached to each result is reduced by a proportion $(1 - p)$ for each month of the age of the result, the exact weight being dependent upon the chosen value of p. A small value of the weighting coefficient p means that even results from many months ago have some effect on the value of u_t. On the other hand, a relatively large value of p causes more emphasis to be put on recent results with the resultant liability that u_t may be affected unduly by chance fluctuations in the results. The value of p to give the best forecasts for any particular set of results must be chosen by trials with various values.

If there is no trend nor seasonal pattern in the data then u_t is the best estimate of all future results. If there is a trend present then it may be estimated by an expression similar to that for the smoothing function:

$$b_t = q(u_t - u_{t-1}) + (1 - q)b_{t-1}$$

where q is another weighting coefficient within the range 0 to 1.

The expression for b_t may also be expanded showing that it too is a weighted function of the past results. It is simply calculated each month as the weighted sum of two figures—a current estimate of the trend and last month's weighted estimate of the trend. Once more the best value to take for q must be determined in each case by trials with past data.

Like other moving averages the smoothing function, u_t, lags behind the true results whenever there is any trend present. To overcome this in exponential smoothing a bias correction factor is introduced whereby the estimate of the current average level, $\hat{y}_{t,0}$, is taken not as u_t but as

$$u_t + b_t(1 - p)/p$$

Having obtained a valid estimate of this current point any forecasts of the future may be made by adding to it the appropriate number of times the estimated monthly trend and then making any necessary allowance for seasonal effects.

Seasonal effects may be dealt with as follows. An estimate of the seasonal effect for one month in a particular year is given by the ratio of the actual month's result to the estimated average sales level that month, $\hat{y}_{t,0}$. An estimate of the seasonal factor for that month in any year may then be obtained from the typical exponential smoothing form of equation in which a weighted average is taken of the most recent estimate and the previous value of the factor, thus:

$$s_t = r \frac{x_t}{\hat{y}_{t,0}} + (1 - r)s_{t-12}$$

where r is another weighting coefficient, within the range 0 to 1, to be determined by trial.

In summary, to produce a forecast by the exponential smoothing method, the following steps are taken. (It is assumed that the best set of values for p, q, r has already been found):

(i) The seasonal effect is removed from the last available result, x_t, by dividing by the most recent estimate of the seasonal factor, s_{t-12}, to give y_t.

(ii) The smoothed demand, u_t, is calculated.

(iii) The trend, b_t, is calculated.

(iv) The bias correction factor is calculated and added to the value of u_t to give a true estimate of the current average sales level, $\hat{y}_{t,0}$.

(v) The forecast of sales T months ahead without seasonal allowance, $\hat{y}_{t,T}$, is made:

$$\hat{y}_{t,T} = \hat{y}_{t,0} + T \cdot b_t.$$

(vi) The completed forecast is made by allowing for the seasonal effects:

$$\hat{x}_{t,T} = \hat{y}_{t,T} \cdot s_{t-12+T}$$

(vii) The estimate of the current seasonal factor, s_{t-12}, is revised to give s_t.

(viii) The most recent estimates of u_t, b_t and s_t, s_{t-1} . . . s_{t-11} are recorded for future use.

As has already been mentioned, the only way of selecting the best set of weighting coefficients for making forecasts on a particular series of results is to perform several trial run-throughs on past data and compare the resultant forecast errors. Generally the criterion used for selecting the best set is the mean squared error, the set of coefficients being taken which gives the minimum value.

If only values of the coefficients rising in steps of 0·1 are to be considered when choosing the best set, to test all combinations of the three coefficients would require 9^3, or 729, trial runs. Even on a computer this is a lot of work. However, it may be shown that the set of coefficients (p, q, r) gives exactly the same forecasts as (q, p, r). From this result it has been argued, not rigorously but with the backing of many practical results, that the best set of coefficients will have $p = q$. On this understanding the number of trial runs required will be cut considerably.

Apart from choosing the set of weighting coefficients to be used, the other problem in setting up a forecasting system based on exponential smoothing is to choose suitable initial values for u_t, b_t, and the seasonal factors. Provided that a long series of past results is available then the choice is not very important as the effect of the starting values on the current values of the various factors will be negligible. In such a case suitable values are:

$$u_0 = x_0$$
$$b_0 = 0$$
$$s_0, s_{-1}, \ldots, s_{-11} = 1$$

If there are not many past results available these initial values may have to be chosen more carefully. One method which is often used is to fit a trend line by eye or approximate regression techniques to the first part of the series of results and then use the estimates so obtained as starting values before working through the whole series of results.

Brown (11) suggests that the values of the weighting coefficients may be arbitrarily increased at times when important changes are expected in the situation affecting the sales of any particular item. The idea behind this is to try to pick up information on the effects of the change as soon as possible. Once the change period is over the coefficients may take their normal values once more.

The great difficulty with this procedure is in knowing just when to alter the values of the coefficients. All too often the first evidence received of a change in the basic situation is a drastic swing in the results. Nevertheless, if sufficiently accurate advance warning can be obtained, by watching results in a lead series for instance, then the changed coefficients should give better forecasts during the period of change.

More generally, the comparison of forecast errors with standards to check that the forecasting system is performing satisfactorily, may be desirable. This amounts to a statistical test of whether the average error is significantly different from zero. Brown (11), Trigg (13), (14) and others have devised methods of performing this test sequentially each time a new observation becomes available. Trigg (13) applies the exponential smoothing technique to the series of forecast errors $\hat{x}_{n-1,1} - x_n$ and absolute values of forecast errors $|\hat{x}_{n-1,1} - x_n|$ and computes the statistic

$$\frac{\text{smoothed error}}{\text{smoothed absolute error}}$$

He derives a distribution for this statistic and shows how to set quality control limits. When the tracking signal, as it is called, trips a limit, control action can be taken such as decreasing the forecasting time constant, resetting the forecast to the present level, or even trying a new model. Thus the tracking signal shows when action must be taken, but does not indicate what the action should be.

If a series is fairly stable then the value of p used in exponential smoothing should be close to zero in order to reduce the variance of forecast errors; at the same time the tracking signal is likely to be nearly zero. On the other hand, if the series to be forecast is unstable, then a value of p close to one is desirable so that its vagaries can be rapidly followed; in this case, the tracking signal is likely to approach plus or minus one. In a second paper, Trigg and Leach (14) use this idea to suggest using a value of p equal to the absolute value of the tracking signal. This scheme has the virtue of constantly making minor adjustments to the predictor automatically, which ought greatly to reduce the number of occasions when the user must himself intervene. Trigg's experience of using the system confirms this.

Brown (11) has designed a method of changing the predictor weights in the light of every new observation. At each stage, Brown calculates those predictor weights which minimize the discounted squares of *backward* prediction errors, i.e.

$$\sum_{j=0}^{\infty} \lambda^j (\hat{x}_{n-j-1,1} - x_{n-j})^2 \text{ for some } \lambda, 0 < \lambda < 1$$

The resulting optimal weights are then used to calculate $\hat{x}_{n,k}$. Methods like this which revise the weights at each stage are known as adaptive forecasting systems, and are feasible only on a large computer. Brown shows how to do the computations for a wide range of underlying models and develops time-saving updating procedures.

Recent developments in theory and practice

The models described earlier in the chapter are obviously simplified representations of the situations they purport to describe and there is a continuing output of papers on more advanced models and applications. The purpose of this final part of the chapter is not to review all of the advanced theory but to survey four main lines of development which appear likely to be important in future. The topics covered are the development of exact and widely applicable mathematical descriptions of stock control systems, the manipulation of models to minimize total cost within other restrictions, the monitoring of stores systems which have adopted "optimal" control rules, and the control of stocks by computer.

Development of Exact Mathematical Descriptions of Stores Systems. Several of the simple models described earlier in the chapter suffered from the drawback that the stochastic nature of stock control was introduced almost as an afterthought into what were basically deterministic models; indeed, the stochastic nature was brought in only where a deterministic estimate would give a gross caricature of the essential nature of the process. Thus $M - LD$ was used in Model 8 to indicate the buffer stock, but $LD - M$ was not used to indicate the severity of shortages.

One field of endeavour has therefore been the development of precise probabilistic descriptions of simple stock control systems with stationary characteristics. In analysing such systems, the duality of queuing systems and stock control systems has proved useful. The demands or orders in a stock control system can be regarded as customers of a queuing system; for example, the orders in a stock control system with random demands, fixed order quantities, Q, and variable lead-time can be regarded as a queuing system with Erlang E_Q arrivals, general service time, with an infinite number of service channels. But whether or not a stock control system is regarded as a queue, there is a serious drawback to stationary probability analysis in that its methods cannot be usefully extended to the non-stationary state.

For this reason, dynamic programming formulations have been widely used in stock control theory. In the earliest use of dynamic programming (2), however, there was a different and stronger reason for using it: that it provided a means of discovering optimal policies without assuming a particular form of optimal policy. Indeed it provided a means of discovering the optimal forms of the optimal policy. Thus, if the probability distributions of demand are known and various cost functions are convex, then under fairly general conditions the optimal form of the optimal policy is an (s, S) policy. A good deal of later work has concentrated on using dynamic programming not as a means of investigating a dynamic situation but as a means of discovering the appropriate form of the optimal policy for particular stationary situations; a good example is the paper by Beckman (15).

The problem of varying demands has, however, been tackled by Karlin (16), who produced a theory which will cope both with the situation of known but varying demand distributions and with the situation of progressively learning about an unknown but constant demand distribution belonging to some known but fairly general family of demand distributions.

The use of dynamic programming is, however, limited in practice if not in theory by the fact that it either has to deal with a simplified situation or its generates an enormous amount of computation. Apart from the fact that it is always a discrete time analysis, the basic simplicity is to arrange for the state of the system to be completely specified at any instant by one, and only one, variable. For example, the stock in hand completely specifies a discrete time system in which material ordered at one time point is received at or before the next time point. For a more complicated example, if shortages are "back-logged"—met out of ordinary stock when it is finally delivered—if the lead-time is constant, and if attention is focused on all time points later than one lead-time into the future, then the stock in hand plus the stock on order completely specifies the system. If the dynamic programming formulation can in some way be limited to one variable, there is a good chance that the amount of computation will be practicable and there is even a chance that an analytic solution might be devised.

It may, however, not be possible to capture the essentials of the situation in one variable. For example, the stock on hand and the outstanding orders must be separately listed. If the lead-time is variable. For another example, even with constant lead-time the stock on hand and the outstanding orders must be separately listed if orders are not backlogged or if the possibility of hastening action is considered. If the dynamic programming formulation cannot be limited to one variable, then there is a risk that computation will grow quite beyond practical limits if a single-variable dynamic programme has 100 computations at each stage, a three-variable dynamic programme would have of the order of 10^6 computations at each stage, with serious extension of computing time and an even more serious problem of storage. The chance of finding an analytic solution will also be reduced. If an analytic solution can be found, there will still be important problems of computation and presentation for implementation.

Dynamic programming formulations will therefore not be a high-road to the successful practical solution of the more complicated problems of stock control. At present the alternatives are not particularly promising. Mills (17) has suggested a method of setting up approximate stock control equations and solving them; there is no indication of how good an approximation his approach is, or indeed whether it is valid at all in all practical situations. Apart from this suggestion, the only other alternative is simulation, which would, like dynamic programming, require immense quantities of computation. (That is to use simulation as a means of finding optimum policies. As a means of exploring the behaviour of a theoretically derived stock control policy simulation has much to recommend it. In complex situations there may be so many idealizations in the model building that simulation before implementation is at least desirable and arguably essential.)

Adjusting Optimal Systems to Meet Restrictions. Whatever the degree of complexity of a model, it will usually at some stage in an O.R. study lead to recommendations for re-provisioning rules, which may then prove not to be wholly acceptable.

Objections should be carefully listened to, as they may indicate a weakness in the mathematical model of the system. If the objections show that the model is in some way inadequate, then the system should be amended even if only a rough and approximate amendment is possible. But if, on careful hearing, the objections only amount to the complaint that earlier and cruder rules are being violated, then the value of the optimal rules should be demonstrated and their use recommended. Workers in the N.C.B., for example, have rejected the suggestion that order quantities should all be about three months' supply (an earlier rule), but have accepted the suggestion that order quantities should not be more than two or three years' supply (as a way of allowing for obsolescence risks not dealt with in the theoretical model).

In the case where the form of the rules themselves is acceptable but the optimal total cost of, say, stockholding is not, the rules may have to be redesigned, so that the restriction on stockholding is met, while still giving an optimum balance between the other costs of the system. The way to do this is to introduce a subsidiary parameter, λ, which plays a role similar to that of a Lagrange multiplier but without any requirement for mathematical continuity. That means replacing the optimal rules found by minimizing.

(Throughput value) + (Short. cost) + (Stock. cost) + (Operat. cost)

with the rules found by minimizing

(Throughput value) + (Short. cost)
$$+ (1 + \lambda)(\text{Stock. cost}) + (\text{Operat. cost})$$

where the value of λ is adjusted by trial and error until the stockholding cost is just within the required restriction. When several restrictions are to be met simultaneously, more complicated expressions of the same type are applicable; for instance, there might be restrictions on parts of the total cost within particular departments or during particular time periods. This sort of approach may be thought of as replacing the measured values of the cost parameters by notional values and then using the notional values as "dial-settings" for the stores system. Although this idea of changing the cost parameters has been introduced as a means of meeting restrictions, it can equally well be used either for analysis of the senstivity of the system to cost estimates or as a means of varying the behaviour of a stores system in response to changes in the general economic climate or of market conditions.

The form of the expressions in the preceding paragraph leads to the general conclusion that optimal rules retain their form under all types of aggregate cost constraint. For example, if an optimal system does not include any rule limiting safety stocks to, say, one month's supply, then no rule of this form should be introduced in an attempt to keep stockholding down.

Monitoring the Use of Optimal Rules. If the study of a model leads to its application in a stores system, there is then the problem of knowing whether it is being used and the problem of whether its total effect is within reasonable distance of that predicted. The first of these is perhaps mainly an audit problem, while the second requires an understanding of how the effects of controls on individual items are aggregated to produce the total response of the system.

The performance of individual control policies has been studied as a problem in servo-theory transfer functions by Brown (7), and as a problem in the probability theory of variances and covariances by Geisler (18).

The performance of total stock control systems has been interestingly treated by Brown (7). His analysis invokes the lognormal distribution as the distribution of the values of the parameters controlling a process: for example, the distribution of price or of average demand in a large sample. Hanssmann has used a similar idea (4). Wagner (19) has considered the whole question of the systematic control of stock, the usefulness of a variety of indices of performance, and problems of economically devising such indices. Many of the topics are given an extensive mathematical treatment. In practice, however, it is likely to be some time before accounting methods will be replaced by other methods of overall control, since many parts of the stores system are still inadequately studied—for example, the control of new material, the efficient layout of stores, the quality of human judgments which must, for the present, be fed into a stores system until more is known of how they can be replaced.

The Control of Stocks by Computer. Quite apart from the use of computers to carry out the lengthy calculations which can result from stock control theory, computers are being increasingly used to control stocks. In this brief section, no attempt will be made to do more than give an outline of present practice in controlling stocks by computer.

The first point to note is that computers are being used in a variety of industries in this country to keep records of stocks and stock movements, and to initiate re-provisioning of both process stocks and engineering spares. The basic problems of feasibility have therefore been tackled and overcome. In most of the systems stock control is done in discrete data processing runs at daily or weekly intervals, though a few use random access storage and up-date the computer records as the information arises. Some of the systems are limited to stock recording, others provide a variety of output including order, invoices, and shortage reports, and others include stock control as part of a much wider pattern of production control by computer.

The fact that these systems exist means that problems of errors in information, errors in data preparation, and errors in computer functioning must have been met and at least partially solved. Some of the errors are detected by human scrutiny of input, some are detected by programmed checks in the computer, some are detected by human scrutiny of output, and some no doubt go undetected.

Problems of estimation and control have usually been solved in a simple way. Exponential smoothing is widely used for up-dating estimates of demand and estimates of the variability of demand. If any attempt is made to use cost-optimal control rules, the control levels are usually fed in as data rather than being computed by the machine.

References

1. Pitt, H. R. A Theorem on Random Functions with Applications to a Theory of Provisioning. *J. London Math. Soc.* **21** pp. 16–22 1946.

2. Dvoretzky, A., Kiefer, J. and Wolfowitz, J. The Inventory Problem. *Econometrica* **20**.3 187–222 1952 and **20**.3 pp. 450–466 1952.
3. Bovaird, R. L., Goldman, A. S. and Slattery, T. B. Concepts in Operational Support Research. *Management Science* **8**.2 pp. 113–137 1962.
4. Hanssmann, F. *Operations Research in Production and Inventory Control*. John Wiley & Sons Inc. 1961.
5. Barankin, E. W. A Delivery-Lag Inventory Model with an Emergency Provision (The Single-Period Case). *Nav. Res. Logist. Quart.* **8**.3 pp. 285–311 1961.
6. Naddor, E. A Comparison of (t, Z) and (z, Z) Policies. *Opns. Res.* **10**.3 pp. 401–403 1962.
7. Brown, R. G. *Statistical Forecasting for Inventory Control*. McGraw-Hill Inc. 1959.
8. Boothroyd, H. and Tomlinson, R. C. The Stock Control of Engineering Spares. *Opns. Res. Quart.* **14**.3 pp. 317–332 1963.
9. Clark, A. J. and Scarf, H. Optimal Policies for a Multi-Echelon Inventory Problem. *Management Science* **6**.4 pp. 475–490 1960.
10. Forrester, J. W. Industrial Dynamics. *Harvard Business Review* **36**.4 pp. 37–66 1958.
11. Brown, R. G. *The Smoothing, Prediction and Forecasting of Discrete Time-Series*. Prentice Hall 1962.
12. Box, G. E. and Jenkins, G. M. Some Statistical Aspects of Adaptive Optimisation and Control. *J.R. Statist. Soc.* Series B **24**.2 1962.
13. Trigg, D. W. Monitoring a Forecasting System. *O.R.Q.* **15**.3 1964.
14. Trigg, D. W. and Leach, A. G. Exponential Smoothing with an Adaptive Response Rate. *O.R.Q.* **18**.1 March 1967.
15. Beckmann, M. An Inventory Model for Arbitrary Interval and Quantity Distributions of Demand. *Management Science* **8**.1 pp. 35–57 1961.
16. Karlin, S. Dynamic Inventory Policy with Varying Stochastic Demands. *Management Science* **6**.3 pp. 231–258 1960.
17. Mills, H. D. Inventory Valuations—An Analytic Technique. *Management Science* **8**.1 pp. 58–68 1961.
18. Geisler, M. A. Statistical Properties of Selected Inventory Models. *Nav. Res. Logist. Quart.* **9**.1 pp. 137–156 1962.
19. Wagner, H. M. *Statistical Management of Inventory Systems*. John Wiley & Sons Inc. 1962.

Further reading

References 4, 7 and 11 above.

Whitin, T. M. *The Theory of Inventory Management*. Princeton University Press 1953.

Arrow, K. J., Karlin, S. and Scarf, H. *Studies in the Mathematical Theory of Inventory and Production*. Stanford University Press 1958.

Magee, J. F. *Production Planning and Inventory Control*. McGraw-Hill Inc. 1958.

Lampkin, W. A Review of Inventory Control Theory. *Production Engineer* **46**.2 pp. 57–66 1966.

Eilon, S. and Lampkin, W. *Inventory Control Abstracts*. Oliver and Boyd 1968.

Forrester, J. W. Industrial Dynamics—After the First Decade. *Management Science (Theory Series)* **14.7** pp. 398–415 1968 and A Response to Ansoff and Slevin. *Management Science (Theory Series)* **14.9** pp. 601–618 1968.

Ansoff, H. I. and Slevin, D. P. An Appreciation of Industrial Dynamics. *Management Science (Theory Series)* **14.7** pp. 383–397 1968 and Comments on Professor Forrester's "Industrial Dynamics—After the First Decade". *Management Science (Theory Series)* **14.9** p. 600.

Box, G. E. P. and Jenkins, G. M. Some Recent Advances in Forecasting and Control. Part 1. *Appl. Statist.* **17.2** pp. 91–109 1968.

Examples for solution

1. Construct a suitable model for purchasing decisions about a raw material where quantity discounts are available and where there is a risk of the material becoming obsolete before it is all used. What is the relative importance of the price discount and the risk of obsolescence? What are the main weaknesses of your model? Would the weaknesses invalidate your results? What further work would you need to do before you could hand over your theory for every day use in a firm?

2. If the risk of shortages is considered, Model 3 indicates that the optimum order quantity should be increased, but Model 7 indicates that the optimum period between orders should be decreased. Can both conclusions be correct? If not, which conclusion is correct? Or is neither?

3. In Model 2, the optimum order quantity is given as

$$\sqrt{\frac{2SD}{hP}}$$

If D is not known exactly but a distribution of D is known, should the optimum order quantity be

$$\sqrt{\frac{2S}{hP}}\,\sqrt{E(D)} \quad \text{or} \quad \sqrt{\frac{2S}{hP}}\,E(\sqrt{D})?$$

Or should it be different from both these?

4. How good is the stock control in a situation familiar to you? Is enough money being wasted to make the situation worthy of much study? If so, what aspects of it would you study first? Would the theoretical content of this chapter be of any use to you at all?

See also example 4 of Chapter 3 and example 4 of Chapter 8.

8 Replacement

Introduction

Most equipment needs to be replaced sooner or later. The replacement should be made when the new equipment offers more economical or efficient service than the old. This might happen, for example, because

the old equipment has failed and does not work at all,

the old equipment has deteriorated and works badly or requires expensive maintenance,

a better design of equipment has been developed,

the old equipment is expected to fail shortly.

The problem is to decide the best policy to adopt with regard to replacement and some aspects of this problem have been studied extensively. Since the behaviour of equipment is not deterministic this study involves probability and has led to the development of the branch of probability theory known as renewal theory. In most of this chapter, however, a simpler, approximate, approach will be adopted by using average values instead of probability distributions. We will also assume independence in the deterioration of different pieces of equipment. An indication of the methods and scope of renewal theory is given in the last section.

The general approach to replacement problems can be considered in two stages. First it is necessary to decide on a measure of the utility or effect of any policy which might be adopted. Possible types of policy and measures to use are discussed in the first section of the chapter. Secondly the value of the measure must be determined for different policies so that the optimum can be selected. Examples of methods for doing this are given later. For convenience they are divided into examples of equipment which is replaced because it deteriorates gradually and of equipment which is replaced because it fails suddenly, although in practice some items of equipment may belong to both these categories. Some examples are based on ones given in references 1 and 2. Many of the models which have been developed for replacement problems are summarized by Dean (3).

Policies and measures of their effect

The need for replacement arises in many different situations so that different types of decision may have to be taken. For example:

(a) Where a large amount of similar equipment is in use a simple rule is needed for deciding as a routine when to replace.

(b) Expensive equipment can be considered individually to decide whether to replace now or if not when to reconsider the question.

(c) It may be necessary to decide whether to wait for equipment to fail, which might cause some loss, or to replace earlier at the expense of a higher cost for equipment.

(d) It is necessary to decide whether to replace by the same or a different type of equipment.

The ultimate objective is usually to enable the organization concerned to maximize its profit. As in other operational research problems it is often convenient to use more limited criteria to compare alternative policies and to measure the extent to which they achieve the objective. Two criteria of particular use in considering replacement are outlined here. Some of the difficulties in evaluating policies are discussed in references 4, 5 and 6.

(i) Average total annual cost. If the replacement policy is not expected to affect the revenue it is sufficient to consider the average cost. The expenditure on replacement plus the running costs are averaged over the length of time between replacement. This approach is often used for deciding how long to keep motor vehicles or other equipment whose running costs may be expected to increase with age. If the interval between replacements is more than 3 or 4 years, the effect of the timing of the expenditure may become important so that criterion (ii) should be used.

(ii) Present value. Because money can be invested and produce a return, any delay in receiving (or spending) a given sum reduces its effective value. The present value (its calculation is described later) summarizes in a single figure the value of all payments and receipts in a period, taking into account when they occur. It is particularly useful when several types of equipment are involved and they may be replaced at different times so that costs and revenue are not constant. The same principles can be used to calculate an average percentage return on capital corresponding to (i) when the extra costs and revenue are not constant; the percentage is such that the present value is exactly equal to the capital invested. In this case the average percentage return calculated for each alternative policy is used as the decision criterion.

It is worth remarking that various tax allowances and the like can have an important bearing on replacement policy. Costs used should be true costs net of tax allowances. We also note that a replacement policy costs something to administer: there might be a premium on policies which are simple to operate.

Replacement of equipment which deteriorates

When equipment deteriorates gradually, running costs increase or revenue drops with age and it may become economical to replace it. A simplified numerical example is given first, in which the effect of the time value of money is ignored and the average total annual cost is used as a criterion. The example also illustrates the question of replacement by different equipment. This approach is then generalized and finally the use of present value is described.

Example 1 Minimum Average Annual Cost. Suppose a firm is considering when to replace its snoggle-casting machine whose cost price is £12,200 but whose scrap value is only £200 as the firm has a monopoly of this type of work. The maintenance costs are, from experience, expected to be:

Year	Maintenance cost (£)
1	200
2	500
3	800
4	1,200
5	1,800
6	2,500
7	3,200
8	4,000

Other running costs and the value of the output are expected to be constant. The costs required may now be tabulated:

Year	Maintenance cost	Total cost to date (less scrap value)	Average annual cost to date
	£	£	£
1	200	12,200	12,200
2	500	12,700	6,350
3	800	13,500	4,500
4	1,200	14,700	3,675
5	1,800	16,500	3,300
6	2,500	19,000	3,167
7	3,200	22,200	3,171
8	4,000	26,200	3,275

The last line is superfluous, since the machine should be replaced during the seventh year, but it is of interest to note the comparative flatness of the curve of average cost against time near the minimum. The absolute minimum average annual cost will be less than £3,167, probably about £3,160.

The firm now receives an offer from another firm to sell them a somewhat shoddy snoggle-casting machine for only £7,500. The engineer inspects the machine and reports that it is likely to cost them about £400 in spares costs in the first year and that these costs are likely to rise by about £500 per annum. The scrap value of the second machine is reckoned to be negligible, and their present machine has done five years service. Should the firm replace with the second machine or not?

We first work out the minimum average annual cost of the new machine, just as before:

Year	Maintenance cost	Total cost to date	Average annual cost to date
	£	£	£
1	400	7,900	7,900
2	900	8,800	4,400
3	1,400	10,200	3,400
4	1,900	12,100	3,025
5	2,400	14,500	2,900
6	2,900	17,400	2,900

The minimum average cost comes somewhere in the sixth year and is probably about £2,870. Hence this machine is more economical than the previous machine and it should be installed. However, it should not be introduced straight away. The maintenance cost of the old machine does not reach £2,870 a year until half-way through the seventh year, and it is then that the new machine should be installed.

General Model—Minimizing Average Cost. A simple general model can easily be constructed for a situation in which we wish to minimize the average annual cost of equipment whose maintenance costs are given as a function increasing with time, whose scrap value is constant and which is to be replaced with a like machine. The model given here is due to Clapham (see reference 3).

If the maintenance costs decrease or remain constant with time, the best policy is never to replace the equipment; unfortunately this desirable state of affairs is rarely met with in practice. If the maintenance costs fluctuate with time, equipment should only be replaced when the maintenance costs are increasing, but a slightly more complicated analysis is required.

Let C = capital cost of equipment,
S = scrap value of equipment,
n = number of years equipment is to be in use,
T = average annual total cost,
$f(t)$ = rate of expenditure on maintenance.

We want to find the value of n that minimizes T. Now the cost incurred in every period of n years

$$= C + \int_0^n f(t)\, dt - S$$

Hence average annual cost is given by:

$$T = \frac{C - S}{n} + \frac{1}{n} \int_0^n f(t)\, dt$$

Differentiating with respect to n, we obtain

$$\frac{dT}{dn} = -\frac{C - S}{n^2} - \frac{1}{n^2} \int_0^n f(t)\, dt + \frac{1}{n} f(n)$$

Hence for $dT/dn = o$

$$f(n) = \frac{C - S}{n} + \frac{1}{n} \int_0^n f(t)\, dt = T$$

It can be shown that this solution, $T = f(n)$, is a minimum for T, provided that $f(t)$ is non-decreasing and $f(o) = 0$. Hence, in this type of example equipment should be replaced when the average cost to date becomes equal to the current maintenance cost.

Using this result we can decide when to replace equipment provided we have an explicit expression for the maintenance costs. In the above example the yearly maintenance costs were given and it was not necessary to use this result as we could more simply replace when the average annual cost reaches a minimum. The table confirms that this occurs when the average annual cost becomes equal to the current maintenance cost.

It would not be hard to refine the previous model so as to allow for a variable scrap value, but it is simpler to include the change in the scrap value as an extra maintenance cost, called depreciation. Thus a car-owner, in calculating what it costs him to run his car, would allow so much for maintenance and so much for depreciation.

Present Value. A more difficult adjustment to make before we can claim to represent a real situation is one which allows us to take account of changes in the value of money. There are several possibilities which we might have to take into account. A manufacturer may have a certain amount of capital to spend or he may have to borrow. He might be allowed to borrow only a limited amount of money, and have to decide how to lay it out on various items. He may also have to take into account the prevailing tax laws. However, for illustrative purposes we shall first consider a simple case.

We shall suppose that the present value of £1 to be spent a year hence is £v. It is less than £1 because we could invest the £v and get a return which would bring the total to £1 in a year; inflation would also decrease the present value. We can put

$$v = 1/(1 + i)$$

where i is the highest interest rate we can get by investment (as a proportion, not percentage; it also includes, if appropriate, the rate of inflation although care must be taken not to double count inflation). For simplicity, i is taken to be constant. v is called the discount factor.

If R_n is the running cost of a machine in the nth year of its life, then the total value $P(r)$, of all expenditure on the machine, if we replace it after r years is given by

$$P(r) = C + R_1 + vR_2 + v^2R_3 + \ldots + v^{r-1}R_r$$

Suppose this is to be paid off in fixed annual payments X, so that after r years we will have paid off the total cost of the machine, then the present worth of r of these payments is

$$X + vX + v^2X + \ldots + v^{r-1}X = X(1 - v^r)/(1 - v)$$

(In a sense X can be regarded as the average annual cost).
This must equal $P(r)$, hence

$$X = \left(\frac{1-v}{1-v^r}\right) P(r)$$

We wish to find the replacement period r that minimizes X, and it can be shown that the required period r is that which gives:

$$\frac{1-v^{r-1}}{1-v} R_r - P(r-1) \leqslant 0 \leqslant \frac{1-v^r}{1-v} R_{r+1} - P(r)$$

(This approach is for the discrete case. Had we wanted directly to adapt the continuous model above we could have used e^{-at} as the present value of £1 spent at time t where $e_1^{-a} = v$.)

Example 2 Use of Present Value. For a numerical example let $v = 0.9$, $C = £3,000$ and the R's be as given in the table.

In the table we work out successively v^{r-1}, $v^{r-1}R_r$, $P(r)$ and $(1-v^r)R_{r+1}/(1-v)$. When the entries in the last two columns become the same it is time to replace the machine.

Year r	R_r	v^{r-1}	$V^{r-1}R_r$	$P(r)$	$\left(\dfrac{1-v^r}{1-v}\right)R_{r+1}$
1	500	1	500	3,500	600
2	600	0·9	540	4,048	1,520
3	800	0·81	648	4,688	2,710
4	1,000	0·729	729	5,417	4,471
5	1,300	0·6561	853	6,270	6,552
6	1,600				
7	2,000				

By year 5 the entry in the last column has passed that in the fifth. Hence the optimum replacement interval is just under five years, and the discounted cost about £6,000.

The extension of this approach to consider the offer of a new machine, as in example 1, is easy and is left to the reader.

Comments on Examples 1 and 2. It is perhaps timely to remind the reader of a particular assumption of the many we have made in examples 1 and 2. We have implicitly assumed that a machine has to be installed to do a job which has to be done forever. We have been concerned with doing the job as cheaply as possible, not with whether the job should be done at all. Putting this another way, we have not looked at the machine as a capital investment. Were we to do so, we should want to look at the profit deriving from the use of the machine, compared with other alternatives including doing nothing, and not merely at costs. However, there is not much difference in the arithmetic despite the difference in criterion.

Other Extensions. There are other deficiencies in the simple models described above. One of the more important is the assumption that future costs are predictable. In practice they will be random variables and a probabilistic approach is necessary. The same goes for the assumption that the historical costs for the machine due to be replaced are appropriate estimates of the costs of the machine by which it is to be replaced. However if one is happy to have a blanket policy for say a fleet of lorries, average costs can be used and treated as fixed. Eilon *et al.* (7) describe an interesting case study.

Another difficulty is that maintenance costs do not always follow a smooth path through time. Often they are incurred in discrete lumps as it may be installing a new gearbox or reconditioning the bodywork of a lorry. In such cases a replacement policy of the type: decide before undertaking a major repair whether to undertake it or to scrap the equipment, might be best. Drinkwater and Hastings describe such an approach (8).

Replacement of items which fail expensively

We now consider what is the best policy for replacing items of a large collection which do not deteriorate gradually but are liable to fail without prior warning, such as light bulbs. A related problem is the staffing problem where leaving represents failure. If failure involves no extra expense the best policy is always to wait for failure before replacing.

Example 3 Light Bulb Problems. For instance, suppose we have a large number of light bulbs, all of which we must keep in working order. If a bulb fails in service, it costs £1 to replace; but if we replace all the bulbs in the same operation we can do it for only £0·35 a bulb. (The £1 might include an allowance for costs incurred as a consequence of the bulb failing.) If the proportion of bulbs failing in successive time intervals is known, it is then possible to decide on the best replacement policy, under certain simplifying assumptions. The bulbs are indistinguishable so we cannot, for example, replace individual bulbs at a given age.

The given distribution of bulb lives is as follows:

Proportion failing during first week   = 0·09
Proportion failing during second week = 0·16
Proportion failing during third week   = 0·24
Proportion failing during fourth week = 0·36
Proportion failing during fifth week   = 0·12
Proportion failing during sixth week   = 0·03

If we assume:

(a) that all bulbs failing during a week do so just before the end of the week and that group replacements can only be made at the end of a week,

(b) that the actual percentage of failures during a week for a sub-population of bulbs with the same age is the same as the expected percentage of failures during the week for that sub-population,

we can then calculate the cost per bulb per week of replacing all bulbs after one week, two weeks, etc.

We need also to know what will be the cost per bulb per week if we do not use group replacement at all. This is equal to the cost of replacing a bulb divided by the average life of a bulb.

In this example, the average life equals:

$$1 \times 0.09 + 2 \times 0.16 + 3 \times 0.24 + 4 \times 0.36$$
$$+ 5 \times 0.12 + 6 \times 0.03 = 3.35 \text{ weeks}$$

hence the cost per bulb per week if no group replacement is used is $1/3.35$ = £0·30.

We may now tabulate the cost per bulb per week for various group replacement policies:

Replace after week	Proportion failed in week	Total proportion of failures to date	Total cost of replacing this week (£)	Average cost of replacing this week (in £ per week)
1	0·09	0·09	0·35 + 0·09	0·440
2	$0.16 + (0.09)^2 = 0.17$	0·26	0·35 + 0·26	0·305
3	$0.24 + 2 \times (0.09 \times 0.16)$ $+ (0.09)^3 = 0.27$	0·53	0·35 + 0·53	0·293
4	$0.36 + 2 \times (0.09 \times 0.24)$ $+ (0.16)^2 + 3 \times (0.09)^2$ $\times 0.16 + (0.09)^4 = 0.43$	0·96	0·35 + 0·96	0·327

The minimum cost per bulb per week is obtained by replacing all bulbs after three weeks, with an average cost of £0·293 per bulb per week.

It is not too difficult to generalize this model using algebraic symbols and this is left as an exercise for the reader. Nor is it too difficult to allow different cost models, for example one could cost the replacement of bulbs that have failed at £0·35 plus so much per day since they failed (that is assuming that they are not replaced until the end of the week but that their being in a failed condition incurs cost at a fixed rate through time—this would be the cost of down-time if they were machines).

A practical objection to the policy implied in the model is that it involves replacing bulbs which have been in use for only a short time. Thus at the end of the third week some bulbs will be replaced which were installed at the end of the second week. Such bulbs could be marked when put in and not be replaced until the sixth week. Woodman (9) has examined such policies.

Other generalizations can be made. Suppose instead of light bulbs we were considering the components of vehicles. We might have a group replacement policy for say gearboxes and clutches. A gearbox fails in service and has to be replaced. While we have the gearbox out we could replace the clutch more cheaply than if we waited for the due time. Should we do so? More complicated situations can easily be imagined.

To find optimum replacement policies in such circumstances can be quite difficult. It may not be easy to guess even the structure of the optimum policy and dynamic programming methods might be necessary. However optimum policies will often be so complicated that the cost of administering them means they are not truly optimal. A good example of a fairly complicated situation is reference (3) of Chapter 3.

Another extension, which is developing a literature of its own, is into the problem of how system (as opposed to engineering) design can be exploited to reduce the consequence of failure of a particular component. If, for example, the £1 cost of a light bulb failing in service could be saved by having a spare light bulb available at every point through which the current is switched as soon as the original bulb fails, it might pay us to consider installing such spares. Redundance theory (10) deals with this kind of problem. It has applications in computer design, space technology, etc.

Example 4 Staffing Problems. Another form of problem is the staffing problem. An example is given here. A research team is planned to rise to a strength of 50 chemists and then to remain at that level. The wastage of recruits depends on their length of service and is as follows:

Year:	1	2	3	4	5	6	7	8	9	10
Total percent who have left up to the end of the period:	5	36	56	63	68	73	79	87	97	100

What is the recruitment per year necessary to maintain this strength? There are eight senior posts for which length of service is the main criterion. What is the average length of service at which a new entrant can expect to be promoted to one of these posts?

Suppose the intake is 100 per year then when equilibrium is reached the distribution of length of service of the team will be as follows:

Years	Number of chemists
0	100
1	95
2	64
3	44
4	37
5	32
6	27
7	21
8	13
9	3
10	0
	Total 436

i.e. an intake of 100 per year gives a total strength of 436. To maintain a strength of 50 requires recruitment of

$$50 \times 100/436 = 11 \cdot 5 \text{ per year}$$

We have assumed that all those who completed x years service but left before $x + 1$ years service actually left immediately before completing $x + 1$

years. If we assume that they left immediately after completing x years service the total becomes 336 and the required intake is

$$50 \times 100/336 = 14.9$$

In practice, chemists may leave at any time in the year and 13 is a reasonable answer.

This problem can also be analysed in two other ways. It can be done by the light bulb approach or by calculating the average length of service of all chemists. This is approximately 4 years, which corresponds to 25% wastage and therefore 25% recruitment per year. The above method does, however, offer advantage when the second stage of the problem is tackled.

With 50 chemists in the team the distribution of the completed length of service of the chemists will be:

Years	Number of chemists
0	12
1	11
2	7
3	5
4	4
5	4
6	3
7	2
8	2
9	0
10	0

i.e. chemists can expect to be promoted to the senior posts after completing 5 and before completing 6 years of service.

Again it is not too difficult to generalize this model. In fact it is based on a fundamental result of renewal theory (see below). Note, however, that the model assumes that people joining at different times have the same statistical pattern of leaving. Whether this is a valid assumption, and whether the pattern can be estimated reliably, are cautionary questions.

Distribution of lives

In all but the last example we have assumed that all items considered behave in the same way, which is the average of what is observed. In many cases this simplification gives sufficiently accurate results but for some problems it is important to consider the distribution of behaviour. Renewal theory deals only with the second class of examples discussed above, where items fail suddenly and can be regarded as having definite lives. The types of probability distributions of lives which have been observed to occur can be classed according to the kind of variation with age of the conditional probability of failure, $\phi(t)$. This is the probability that an item which has survived to a given time, t, will fail in the next instant.

If failure depends entirely on some external mechanism such as loss or serious misuse, $\phi(t)$ is constant, independent of the age of the item. A constant $\phi(t)$ can also arise for other reasons. It leads to a negative exponential distribution of life.

Most types of equipment become more liable to fail as they age; that is, $\phi(t)$ increases with t. This leads to a life distribution with a single peak; for example, the life may be approximately represented by a normal distribution. If some of the new items are faulty, $\phi(t)$ may at first decrease as the faulty items are eliminated then increases as the remainder age. This leads to a life distribution with two peaks.

Staff usually show the opposite effect; after a short time in a job, they are less likely to leave the longer they stay. Thus $\phi(t)$ rises quickly to a maximum then drops. This gives a life distribution with a flatter tail than the exponential and it is often closely fitted by a log-normal distribution.

Renewal theory

Difficulties can arise in analysing the effect of successive replacements of equipment, when the life of each replacement is a random variable. This analysis gave rise to renewal theory which now has applications and interest outside the field of replacement. The theory as it is relevant to replacement is described clearly by Cox (11). Some basic ideas are outlined here, followed by an example of the application of the theory.

Renewal Process. Suppose only one item is in use at any time and that it is replaced as soon as it fails. Let the life of the ith item be x_i $(i = 1, 2, . . .)$ and suppose x_i are identically and independently distributed random variables with a probability density function $f(x)$ which is zero for negative x. If the first item starts at time $t = 0$ then the $n + 1$th item will start at

$$t = S_n = x_1 + x_2 + . . . + x_n$$

The process thus described is called an ordinary renewal process. The theory studies various random variables associated with the process such as the time for n renewals, S_n (the first item is not counted as a renewal), and the number of renewals up to time t, N_t. Probably the most important quantity studied is the expected number of renewals up to time t, $H(t) = EN_t$, which is known as the renewal function.

Renewal Equation. The renewal equation is an integral equation for the renewal function and it can be used as the basis for much of renewal theory.

Let $P_n(t)$ be the probability that $N_t = n$. Then $P_{n+1}(t)$ can be derived by supposing that the first renewal is at time z (i.e. $x_1 = z$) and that n renewals occur from z to t. As the x_i are independent the probability of n renewals in z to t is $P_n(t - z)$. Thus, as z can take all values from 0 to t,

$$P_{n+1}(t) = \int_0^t P_n(t - z)f(z)\,dz$$

The expected number of renewals up to time t is therefore

$$H(t) = 0P_0(t) + \sum_0^\infty (1 + n)P_{n+1}(t)$$

$$= \sum_0^\infty \int_0^t (1 + n)P_n(t - z)f(z)\,dz$$

But

$$\sum_0^\infty P_n(t) = 1$$

and

$$\sum_0^\infty nP_n(t - z) = H(t - z)$$

so that, putting

$$F(t) = \int_0^t f(z)\,dz$$

$$H(t) = F(t) + \int_0^t H(t - z)f(z)\,dz$$

This equation is known as the renewal equation. For suitable forms of $f(x)$ explicit solutions are possible by using Laplace transforms; where a full solution is not possible it is possible to obtain asymptotic results.

Forward Recurrence Time. If we start to observe a renewal process at a random point in time, the time to the next renewal is called the forward recurrence time. Let us denote it by y. What is the distribution of y?

In a general way one can see that our starting point is more likely to fall into a long life than a short one. In fact the probability that we shall fall into a life of length x is proportional to $xf(x)$, say $kxf(x)$. Given that we have fallen into a life of length x the conditional distribution of the time up to the next renewal is uniform in the range 0 to x, that is the conditional probability density function is $1/x$ in the range 0 to x and 0 elsewhere. Thus the unconditional probability density function of y is

$$\int_y^\infty kxf(x)\,\frac{dx}{x} = k(1 - F(y))$$

where

$$F(y) = p(x \leqslant y)$$

k must be chosen so that

$$\int_0^\infty k(1 - F(y))\,dy = 1$$

and this implies $k = 1/Ex$ where Ex is the average value of x. It will be found that

$$Ey = \frac{1}{2}\left[Ex + \frac{Vx}{Ex}\right]$$

where Vx is the variance of x.

This result is important to bear in mind when looking at such problems as the staffing problem discussed above. If we look at the distribution of lengths of service of the members of the team at any one point in time it is not $f(x)$, so to speak, but $(1 - F(y))/Ex$. The distribution of the backward recurrence time, the time since the last renewal, is the same as for the forward recurrence time. Thus in a team of 50 chemists the number with between 4 and 5 years of completed service is

$$\frac{1 - 0 \cdot 68}{4 \cdot 36} \times 50$$

and not, as might be rashly thought $(0 \cdot 68 - 0 \cdot 63) \times 50$.

Example 5 Application of Renewal Theory. The following example (12) illustrates the renewal theory approach to a problem similar to the light bulbs example above.

A quantity, n, of new items are put into store and it is assumed that:

(a) The items while in storage become more likely to fail.
(b) The times taken for each item to fail are independent, identically distributed, random variables with cumulative distribution function $F(x)$.

As the items fail they are replaced with new ones. After an interval t_o all n items are replaced.

Suppose the cost of replacing an item before t_o is b while the cost of replacing all at one time is a per item.

Let $N(t_o)$ denote the number of replacements up to t_o. We wish to find t_o so as to minimize the expected average cost per year of keeping a stock of n good items.

The average cost up to time t_o is:

$$C(t_o) = \frac{(a + bN(t_o))}{t_o}$$

Taking expectations,

$$EC(t_o) = \frac{(a + bEN(t_o))}{t_o}$$

we define

$$nH(t_o) = EN(t_o)$$

as the expected number of replacements. Averaging over all the items so as to find the expected number of replacements for each item we get:

$$EH(t_o) = H(t_o)$$

as the failure times are identically distributed.

Now $H(t_o)$ satisfies the renewal equation

$$H(t_o) = F(t_o) + \int_0^{t_o} H(t_o - t) \, dF(t)$$

If we assume that $F(t)$ is a gamma distribution with parameters $\alpha = 1$, $\beta = 1/u$

$$F(t) = \int_0^t u^2 x \, e^{-ux} \, dx$$

then it can be shown with difficulty that

$$H(t_o) = \tfrac{1}{2}[ut_o - e^{-ut_o} \sinh (ut_o)]$$

Hence

$$EC(t_o) = \frac{a}{t_o} + \frac{bn}{2} \left[u - \frac{e^{-ut_o}}{t_o} \sinh (ut_o) \right]$$

The unique value of t_o which minimizes $EC(t_o)$ satisfies the equation

$$(1 + 2ut_o) = \left(1 - \frac{4a}{bn}\right) e^{2ut_o}$$

provided $a < bn/4$. Otherwise, the expected cost is minimized by the policy of replacing items only as they fail.

References

1. Churchman, C. W., Ackoff, R. L. and Arnoff, E. L. *Introduction to Operations Research*. John Wiley & Sons Inc. 1957.
2. Yaspan, A. J., Sasieni, M. W. and Friedman, L. *Operations Research; Methods and Problems*. John Wiley & Sons Inc. 1959.
3. Ackoff, R. L. (Ed.) *Progress in Operations Research* Vol. 1. John Wiley & Sons Inc. 1961. See chapter on Replacement by Dean, B. V.
4. Preinreich, G. A. The Economic Life of Industrial Equipment. *Econometrica* **8.12** pp. 12–44 1940.
5. Morrett, A. J. and Bourock, G. *Business Economics and Statistics*. Hutchinson & Co. Ltd 1962.
6. Olmer, F. J. A New Approach to the Determination of Replacement Costs. *Management Science* **6.1** pp. 111–122 1959.
7. Eilon, S., King, J. R. and Hutchinson, D. E. A Study in Equipment Replacement. *Opl. Res. Qtrly* **17.1** 1966.
8. Drinkwater, R. W. and Hastings, N. A. J. An Economic Replacement Model. *Opl. Res. Qtrly* **18.2** 1967.
9. Woodman, R. C. Replacement Rules for Single and Multi-Component Equipment. *Appl. Statist.* **18.1** pp. 31–40 1969.
10. Barlow, R. E. and Proschan, F. *Mathematical Theory of Reliability*. John Wiley & Sons Inc. 1965.

11. Cox, D. R. *Renewal Theory*. Methuen & Co. Ltd 1963.
12. Klein, M. and Rosenberg, L. Deterioration of Inventory and Equipment. *Nav. Logist. Res. Quart*. **7.1** pp. 49–62 1960.

Further reading

References 9, 10 and 11 above.
Hastings, N. A. J. The Repair Limit Replacement Method. *Opl. Res. Qtrly* **20.3** pp. 337–349 1969.
Radner, R. and Zorgenson, D. W. *Studies in Applied Probability and Management Science*. Arrow, K. J., Karlin, S. and Scarf, H. (Ed.) Stanford University Press 1962.
Jardine, A. K. S. (Ed.) *Operational Research in Maintenance*. Manchester University Press 1970.

Examples for solution

1. The following are the costs of running a particular car to date and the forecast into the future. Assuming that the car will be replaced by a similar car (similar in all respects including price and value) when is the best time to replace it and what will be the average yearly running cost?

Year	Resale value at end of year	Petrol and tax during year	All other running costs during year
	£	£	£
0	700		
1	625	90	10
2	575	90	30
3	550	90	50
4	500	90	70
5	450	90	90
6	400	90	110
7	350	90	130
8	300	90	150

2. The owner of the above car is offered a car of a different make with the following costs. Should he change to using this and if so when?

Year	Resale value at end of year	Petrol and tax during year	All other running costs during year
	£	£	£
0	500		
1	400	70	10
2	325	70	20
3	250	70	30
4	175	70	50
5	100	70	75
6	25	70	120
7	Nil	70	200

3. The following mortality rates have been found for a certain type of coal cutter motor.

	10 weeks	20 weeks	30 weeks	40 weeks	50 weeks
Total % failure to end of 10 weeks period	5	15	35	65	100

If the motors are replaced over the weekend the total cost is £200. If they fail during the week the total cost is £1,000 per failure. Is it best to replace the motors before failure and if so when? (Work in periods of 10 weeks.)

4. A colliery recruits boys at 16 and trains them for face work immediately. At $16\frac{1}{2}$ they do $\frac{3}{4}$ stint and at 18 they do a full stint. Assuming the following probabilities of leaving the colliery and no recruitment from other collieries, what rate of recruitment for face training is necessary to keep a face manpower doing 100 stints. Assume that those who leave do so at $16\frac{1}{2}$ or at the whole years.

Ages	Probability of leaving
16 to $16\frac{1}{2}$	0·10
$16\frac{1}{2}$ to 17	0·05
17 to 18	0·10
18 to 19	0·01
19 to 20	0·01
20 to 25	0·05 (i.e. 0·01 per year)
25 to 30	0·05
30 to 35	0·05
35 to 40	0·05
40 to 45	0·10
45 to 50	0·20
50 to 55	0·20
55 to 60	0·03

5. A machine is made up of two sub-machines A and B. The performance of A, given adequate routine maintenance, does not deteriorate except in the very long run. However A is subject to a good deal of buffeting and now and again is damaged beyond repair. Such damage occurs randomly, on average twice a year. B on the other hand has a performance which deteriorates through time although it practically never breaks down. Because B's performance deteriorates the rate of output of the machine is $f(t)$ where t is the time in years since B was last overhauled and f is decreasing.

If A is replaced when damaged it costs C_1, an overhaul of B costs C_2, and to overhaul B when A is replaced costs C_3 ($<C_2$). What policy should be adopted about overhauling B? (The costs include associated downtime.)

6. What are the equipment replacement rules in your organization? Are they sensible? Do practical considerations prevent use of theoretical replacement models?

9 Simulation

Introduction

There are many problems met with in O.R. which are not amenable to solution by existing analytical techniques such as linear programming, dynamic programming, queuing theory and so on. Such problems occur in all sorts of problem fields—transport systems, economic systems, inventory systems, job scheduling and so on.

The difficulties usually arise because of the complexity of the system being considered. The system may contain a multiplicity of different component parts, the relationships between which may be complex, and may have various random elements. Such characteristics, indeed, are typical of industrial and economic systems.

To use the standard analytical tools, it is often necessary to make quite broad assumptions and simplifications. This in itself is not, of course, necessarily a bad thing, if the parts of the system omitted from the model are genuinely unimportant, if the approximations made do not substantially affect the results, then this approach is efficient, and focuses attention on the important parts of the system.

Frequently, however, it is not possible to make the assumptions necessary to allow formulation of the problem in a way suitable for solution by analytic techniques. Yet the components of the system may be clearly identifiable, and the relationships between them, and the random processes associated with them may be more or less understood. For instance, suppose the problem is to improve the efficiency of a port. Ships arrive at intervals spaced according to a certain distribution. They must then wait for a suitable tide to enter the port. Each then requires a vacant berth in order to load or unload cargo, and a tug to maneouvre it to the berth. Loading and/or unloading takes a time which is random with a certain distribution, which may vary according to the type of cargo. Suppose ships have to queue what is considered an excessive time in order to use the port; how is this to be reduced? In such a system, we may easily be able to understand each small operation separately, and to analyse it (for instance by queuing theory), but the working of the whole is beyond the capabilities of existing techniques, without drastic and unjustifiable simplification.

In such a case, it is frequently possible to tackle the problem by means of simulation.

Simulation involves the setting up of an analogue of the system under study, in which all relevant components are defined, and the way in which they change through time and affect each other are exactly specified. This analogue is then set in motion, and its behaviour observed. It is allowed to run for a set time, and the values taken by variables in the analogue compared to the values taken by the corresponding variables in the real system. If the correspondence is close, then the analogue may be considered to be a good representation of reality. The analogue may then be modified to represent a proposed change of policy, and re-run. The effects of the change of policy on the analogue can be measured, and parallel effects in the real system predicted. In other words, we estimate the outcome of different policies by conducting experiments on the analogue. (It would be possible, alternatively to experiment on the system itself. Simulation has two advantages over this procedure; it is cheaper, and it is possible to conduct closely controlled experiments. Frequently, of course, experiments on the real system may be just impossible. For instance, building factories of three different sizes on the same site.)

In the broadest sense of the word simulation, the analogue may be of one of many different kinds.

(a) The analogue may be a scale model, for example a model aircraft in a wind tunnel or a model railway.

(b) The analogue may be physical, but in a different physical system. Coloured water in tubes has been used to simulate the flow of coal in a mine. More common is the use of electrical circuits. Such a model has been used to simulate ventilation flows in a mine.

(c) At a higher level of abstraction, one can formulate the working of the system as a set of mathematical equations and logical relationships.

It is possible that these are directly soluble, but in general the procedure will be to calculate each change in each part of the system separately. The calculations will usually proceed sequentially, each calculation depending in some way upon the results of previous calculations. Such a procedure is known as digital simulation.

Clearly such calculations can be repetitive, tedious, and time consuming, and are prime candidates for computerization. It is with computerized digital simulations that the bulk of this chapter will be concerned. However, it is worth noting that digital simulations can be performed by hand, and in some cases it is convenient to do so to gain a preliminary understanding of the working of the system.

(d) The word simulation is also sometimes applied to certain kinds of iterative calculating procedure, often involving sampling from distributions, which do not explicitly involve the passage of time. This kind of procedure can be used to solve mathematical problems such as complex integrations or sets of differential equations. Such methods are often known as Monte Carlo methods, although this term has sometimes been used to cover the whole field of simulation, particularly in the earlier years of the technique.

The basic method of digital simulation is this. The main components of the system are first identified. To fix our ideas, suppose the study is of a post office with several counter assistants. The main components will be assistants and customers. We then define each of the operations that may take place in the system.

First, a customer arrives in the system. We must specify how this is to occur. We may, for instance, specify that customers arrive according to a Poisson distribution with some given mean. Alternatively we might list arrival times and treat them as data: but this would be avoided if the arrival pattern could be adequately modelled statistically and arrival times generated by sampling on the model—the latter is simply quicker. He joins a queue for one of the assistants. Typically we may suppose that he joins the shortest queue, and, in the event of there being more than one of equal length, the one with the best looking female assistant, or the one nearest the door, or some other such more or less arbitrary rule. The queue then proceeds according to a "first in, first out" discipline, the service time of each customer being sampled from, say, a normal distribution with mean and variance which may depend on the assistant. Once served, the customer leaves the system.

To simulate the system, we start by sampling an arrival time for the first customer. We send him to the assistant prescribed by our arbitrary rule, where he is served immediately. We determine his service time by sampling from the appropriate distribution, and make a note of the time at which his service will be completed. We then sample the next arrival time, and so on. At each stage, we must take care to admit each customer at the appropriate time, remove a customer from the system and up date the queue as each service is completed, and so on. We also calculate as the simulation proceeds, statistics such as average waiting time, average queue length, and so on.

This simple example has all the main characteristics of simulations: some sort of mechanism is needed for time advance to proceed to the next relevant event (arrival of customer, finishing service), previously defined rules are used on each occasion to regulate the changes in the system, and sampling from distributions plays an important part.

Simulation has been used in a great variety of fields. They include economic analysis, transport systems, military conflicts, machine shop scheduling, maintenance operations, many kinds of queuing situation, chemical plants and many others.

Economic models are conveniently handled by means of simulation because, frequently, many of the relationships are stochastic and lagged in time, which makes them very difficult to analyse by analytical methods.

Machine shop studies usually involve queues of orders. Raw materials, held in stock, are processed through various machines to meet these orders. Intermediate queues build up at each machine. Inventory levels fluctuate. No technique exists to solve this kind of problem analytically. A large proportion of simulation studies, in fact, involve interlocking queues processed by different types of server. Queuing theory is, unfortunately, unable to solve any but the simplest kinds of situation and recourse has to be had to simulation.

Transport systems can frequently be formulated in this manner. An example is the coal transport system in a mine, where bunkers are "queues", belts or locomotives are "servers". Ports, telephone exchanges, and computers can all be viewed similarly.

The pros and cons of simulation

Simulation has the merit of being, superficially at least, easily understandable by management. They can see, in the computer print-out, an analogue of the real system progressing in a manner very similar to the systems with which they are familiar, and this makes the results easy to accept.

In fact, management are often invited to take part in simulation experiments. This is frequently the case where an important link in the system is a management decision-making process which is not fully understood. The simulation proceeds until such a decision is required, the management is presented with all relevant information, and asked to make the decision. This is fed back to the simulation, which resumes, and so on. This kind of simulation is often known as a "management game", particularly when two or more people are involved in a competitive or collaborative situation.

The roles are sometimes altered when the system itself is understood and the aim is to train the manager. Taking part in such a game can be a very efficient means of demonstrating to a manager the effects of his decisions, and of getting him to improve them.

Another advantage of simulation is that, in constructing the model, the process of specifying precisely the interactions of various parts of the system can in itself give some insight into the way it works. Furthermore, after running the simulation, it is possible to examine the records of the run in detail and identify bottlenecks and other causes of trouble. This facility allows the experimenter to suggest improvements that might not have been considered had he not been able to inspect the internal workings of the system.

The principal disadvantage of simulation is that it may be a rather costly way of getting an answer.

The system needs to be modelled and much observation may be necessary. The other aspect of modelling is writing the computer program. This can be a lengthy business. Simulation programs, like most computer programs, have a habit of growing spontaneously (some would say exponentially) both in size and complexity. Development costs of a reasonably complex model can be expected to be in the thousands of pounds. It is worth giving consideration to using one of the simulation languages that have been developed. These take a little time to master, but the effort can save a considerable amount of programming time. The penalties are some loss in flexibility—quite a small loss in the case of the best languages—and some loss in efficiency of execution.

To obtain a single estimate of the statistic under study may require many simulation runs with the consequent expense of computer time. The cost of a single estimate might be anything up to £500. This contrasts with queuing theory, where a single calculation yields the answer (provided the theory exists to deal with the problem). To obtain further estimates when the input parameters are changed, the simulation has to be run again many times, whereas with queuing theory each new estimate can be calculated at once. Moreover, simulation is non-optimizing. It will only yield estimates of the effects of a given operating policy. The onus is on the user of the simulation to propose and test better policies. This contrasts with analytic models which, within the confines of the model as formulated, will find the optimum policy from the whole class of possible policies by mathematical maximization. Clearly some skill is called for in deciding what policies to simulate and in designing the experiment generally.

Recently it has been proposed that simulation could be combined with hill-climbing techniques to seek an optimum automatically. The idea is that system parameters can be altered according to some hill-climbing routine, and the simulation repeated, as often as necessary to achieve an optimum with respect to those parameters. Essentially, this is just what the O.R. man does when he examines the output and suggests changes. However, in this case the man has an advantage over the machine in that he may propose organizational changes, which involve changes in the model, that are not easily expressible as changes in system parameters. For instance, in the post office example, he may suggest that all counter assistants deal with all types of transaction, rather than have specialist counters, or that the post office employ only young attractive female assistants.

Hill-climbing techniques are a simple case of a more general possibility, namely that one might be able to build a crude theoretical model of the system under study which relates the output to the input. This might be helpful in the selection of policies worth simulating, initially by starting to simulate policies at or near the optimum of the theoretical model, but later in the process by using the simulation results to better the theoretical model (for instance, by improving the estimates of the parameters in it) so that a new theoretical optimum can be found. Cycling between the simulation and the theory goes on.

Opponents of simulation point to a further weakness in the simulation approach. It is claimed, with some justification, that the use of simulation can lead to slackness in the formulation of the model, precisely because it is possible to include awkward and detailed characteristics. This could lead to insufficient critical examination of what is relevant and what is not, and to a poor understanding of the structure of the system as a whole. This is really a criticism of the way the technique is used rather than of the technique itself, but it is true that there is a temptation to apply simulation indiscriminately because it appears, superficially, easy to apply in circumstances where other techniques cannot be used straightforwardly.

The techniques of simulation are largely concerned to reduce its disadvantages, that is to reduce the costs of using it. We shall discuss two broad classes of technique: those concerned with structuring simulation programs to ease their writing and those concerned with the design of simulation experiments. We shall also discuss methods for sampling from distributions and some aspects of validating simulation models.

Structure of simulation programs

The terminology in this field has not been effectively standardized, but the terms used here seem to be the most common.

A simulation views the system it is simulating, as a collection of component parts, or *entities*. Each entity has certain attributes, which may be numerical, or logical, and which may be fixed for the duration of the simulation, or variable.

In the post office example, customers and servers are entities. One of the attributes of a customer is the time required to serve him, and another is the number of the queue he is in. A third attribute is his position in the queue.

Similarly in a port simulation, the entities would be ships, tugs and berths. Ships would have the following attributes:

Capacity   —fixed, numerical — *quantitive*.
Type of cargo   —fixed, logical — *qualitative*
Location (at sea, in port, berthed)—variable, logical
Amount of cargo on board   —variable, numerical

Tugs would be either busy or idle, and similarly with berths. It may be useful also to have an entity called TIDE, which has the attribute of being IN or OUT.

One special kind of attribute is a clock. The current value of the clock of an entity at any time, is the time at which something significant next happens to it. Entities which have a clock are called active, those without are passive. There is often some choice as to which entities are to be designated passive, and which active. For instance, one might designate ships as active entities, and follow the simulation through from the point of view of the ships, or designate the berths active, and follow the simulation from that point of view.

A convenient way of holding much of the information about entities is to define sets. The sets relate to groups or classes of entities—e.g. the class of ships in the port simulation—and any member of the class may belong to the set at any given moment. For instance the sets defined on the class of ships could be the set ATSEA, the set INPORT, and the set BERTHED. As the simulation proceeds, each ship is transferred from one set to another. There may be some redundancy in the way the state of the system is stored when a simulation uses sets; for instance, each ship will have attributes which indicate whether or not it is a member of the set ATSEA, INPORT, etc.; and, also, there may be stored separately a list of the ships currently in the set ATSEA. This redundancy is essentially a cross-reference, and makes the information required at various points in the simulation easy to obtain.

The state of the world changes from time to time, as attributes alter. Simulation regards these changes as occurring at discrete points in time. Such changes are governed by certain rules, and occur at times determined by the previous course of the simulation.

misleading:

A set of rules governing a particular kind of change is called an activity. For instance, the activity FINISH SERVICE in the post office example might consist of the following set of rules:

"when an end of service is due,   *Changes in states.*
remove the customer from the system,
note his total waiting time,
free the server".   *Cause an event to occur*

The activity START SERVICE might be:

"if server is free
and if there is one or more person in his queue,
engage the server,
note when this service will end".

What goes into each individual activity is to some extent arbitrary. For instance, the two examples just given might be consolidated into a single activity, with a little modification.

An actual occurrence of an activity during the simulation at a particular point in time, together with any consequent occurrences of other activities (e.g. the examples above), is called an event. Thus an event might involve several activities (e.g. customer arrives, joins queue of zero length, starts service). (We might call an event which is an occurrence of a single activity a "simple event", and one which involves more than one related activities a "compound event"; this is not, however, standard terminology.)

Thus, to illustrate the terms:

FINISHING SERVICE is an activity
STARTING SERVICE is an activity

Assistant A finishes serving customer X at time 65·7 *is a simple event; and Assistant A finishes serving customer X, and starts serving customer Y, at time* 65·7 *is a compound event.*

Note that, in simulations, each change occurs instantaneously at a discrete point in time. This may seem something of a disadvantage in theory where simulating a continuous process—e.g. loading of a ship, or travel of a machine along a coal face. In practice, however, it is rarely a serious disadvantage, since we only need to know the state of the process at critical points—e.g. when the ship is full, or the machine reaches the end of the face.

We really want the computer (which we shall assume we are using) to do no more than to follow the development, through time, of the system and to record certain aspects of its behaviour. Putting this another way we should like the computer to keep an up-to-date log of the state of the system. The state of the system changes only at events and the changes which take place at an event are specified by the activity or activities which occur then.

It follows therefore that we need the means of answering two questions, firstly when does the next event occur and secondly what activities then take place. The first question is comparatively easily answered. For each of the active entities, those which have clocks associated with them, we know the time when something significant is going to happen to it. The smallest of these times is the time of the next event. The process of searching through these times to find the smallest is called the time scan and is an integral part of any simulation program. (A small but important point is that there may be two or more equally smallest times and we must be careful to recognize this possibility by treating them as occurring simultaneously as opposed to treating them as occurring in some order with a very small time between them (see below).)

The decision of which activity or activities then take place can be approached *activity based* in a number of ways, although there are basically two. In the first place we might list all possible activities associating with each a set of necessary and sufficient conditions for it to occur. If these conditions are satisfied the activity is performed. Secondly we might take advantage of the fact that we know *event based* which entity is associated with the next event. We can thus, from our knowledge of the current state of the system, infer at least one activity which occurs at the event. The activities which might occur as a consequence of this activity occurring are also known and named beforehand. Whether these activities can occur is checked and those of them that can are allowed to do so. The differences between the two approaches, called respectively the activity based approach and the event based approach, are not all that easy to understand. Discussion around an example might help.

Example Problem. The example used here will be that of loading/unloading facilities at a warehouse for goods which are transported by lorry. There are two types of lorry which are exclusive: those which deliver incoming goods and those which collect outgoing goods.

The warehouse has 5 loading/unloading platforms, each of which may be used for either purpose. Incoming goods are of many types, but are always fairly small items that can be handled either manually or by fork-lift truck (of which each platform has at least one). Outgoing goods on the other hand, are quite bulky, being fully assembled machines, and require a crane. There is only one crane which can serve any platform.

The statistical distributions of loading times, unloading times, times between arrivals of lorries to load and times between arrivals of lorries to unload are all known and we have means of sampling from them.

There is one further complication. Access to the bay from the main road is restricted. It is down a narrow lane, which allows only one lorry at a time, in one direction. The lane takes 4 minutes to travel. Once out of the lane, lorries are immediately in the loading bay, so that if all loading platforms are occupied, congestion is caused; consequently, if all platforms *are* occupied, newly arrived lorries must wait in a queue at the outer end of the lane. Remotely operated traffic lights at the outer end of the lane are red if a lorry is coming out along the lane or if there are five or more lorries within the bays and the lane; otherwise it is green. Traffic lights at the inner end of the lane are red if a lorry is coming in along the lane and green otherwise.

Describing the System. We wish to simulate this system with the present physical facilities to see, perhaps, how it will respond to increases in the volume of traffic. To do so we shall have to have some means of keeping a record of the current positions of all lorries, platforms, lights and cranes. The simulation will proceed by updating these records at appropriate moments, making at each stage, of course, all the appropriate checks.

It is clear that not all entities need to have clocks. For instance, although it may be convenient to have clocks for lorries, platforms and crane, it would be possible to manage with clocks for lorries only. Alternatively, it would be possible to manage with clocks for platforms, crane and only those lorries currently in the lane. We shall give lorries clocks: they will be our active entities. Note that at times even the active entities can have no specific time attached to them. For instance, while entities are idle (platforms vacant) or queuing (lorries waiting to enter lane), there is no specific time in the future that something is going to happen to them. While they are in such a state their clocks will have no specific values. Such entities, therefore, will sometimes appear in the table, and sometimes not. This is a book-keeping matter that exercises the ingenuity of simulation language compiler-writers. When an entity is in the table, i.e. its clock has a definite value, it is variously called engaged or committed, otherwise it is free.

In order to describe the system it will be convenient to number the lorries and to record the type of each lorry (loading or unloading), the location of each lorry and the state of the crane (B for busy or I for idle). It will be convenient to define sets of lorries, call them WORLD, QIN, LIN, PLAT, QCRANE, QOUT and LOUT. The location of a lorry is defined by which set it currently belongs to. It is in one of WORLD (the outside world), QIN (queuing to enter the lane to come in), LIN (in the lane coming in), PLAT (at a platform) or LOUT (in the lane coming out). Lorries in PLAT might also belong to the sets QCRANE (waiting for a crane) or QOUT (waiting to enter the lane to come out). We shall record which set each lorry is in and which lorries are in QIN, QCRANE and QOUT. We shall also record the number of lorries in the lane or at platforms, NLILP.

We must now identify what activities there are in this system. The easiest way of doing this is to consider each type of entity in turn and trace its passage through the system. Let us, in this case, start with a lorry.

First of all, it will *arrive* at the outer end of the lane; *if there is a queue, it will join it*. It will travel down the lane, and at the other end immediately *occupy a platform*. If it is an unloading lorry, it will *start unloading*; otherwise it will wait until it can *engage the crane, and then start loading*. Next it will *finish loading or unloading* and if necessary wait for the lane to become free. Then it will *start out along the lane*, and 4 minutes later *leave the system*.

For each of the above activities, we will now specify exactly the conditions under which it takes place. Notice that we take care to specify these conditions completely; if they are satisfied for an activity, then that activity can certainly take place, regardless of what is going on elsewhere, or of the previous history of the system. In other words, in each case they are necessary and sufficient conditions.

Following the conditions, we will specify what actions need to be executed. Again, we will be quite explicit and precise; we will specify the actions to be taken in terms of the variables listed above. The activities are as follows.

LORRY ARRIVAL

 Conditions: Time-cell of lorry L = *PRESENT TIME*
   Lorry L in WORLD

 Actions: Put L on tail of QIN
   Remove L from WORLD
   Remove L from time scan
   Sample arrival time of next lorry of same type, number lorry
   L + 2, put in WORLD, and set up corresponding time-cell.

(Note: we have put every lorry as it arrives into QIN; if there is no need for it to wait, it will automatically be brought out of QIN by the next activity. Numbering the next lorry L + 2 keeps even numbers for one type of lorry, odd for the other.)

ENTER LANE

 Conditions: At least 1 lorry in QIN
   NLILP < 5
   No lorry in LOUT

 Actions: Take first lorry L from QIN
   Put lorry in LIN

   Set time-cell of L to PRESENT TIME +4

   Increase NLILP by 1.

(Note: take first lorry L for QIN implies reducing the number of lorries in QIN by 1.)

ARRIVE AT PLATFORM

 Conditions: Time-cell of lorry L = *present time*
   Lorry L in LIN

 Actions: Take lorry L from LIN
   Put in PLAT
   If lorry is to load, join QCRANE and remove from time scan
   If lorry is to unload, sample unloading time u, and set time-
     cell to *PRESENT TIME* + u.

(Note: in this case we have rolled into one the activities *OCCUPY PLAT-FORM* and *START UNLOADING*, making a slightly more complex activity.)

ENGAGE CRANE

 Conditions: At least one lorry in QCRANE
   Crane is I

 Actions: Take 1st lorry L from QCRANE
   Set crane to B
   Sample loading time v and set time cell to *PRESENT TIME* + v.

FINISH LOADING/UNLOADING

Conditions: Time-cell of lorry L = *PRESENT TIME*
L in PLAT

Actions: Take L from PLAT
Put L on tail of QOUT
Remove L from time-scan
If lorry is to load, set crane to I.

(Note: again, for simplicity, we have put every lorry into QOUT.)

ENTER LANE (OUTWARDS)

Conditions: At least one lorry in QOUT
No lorry in LIN

Actions: Take all lorries from QOUT and put into LOUT
Set all their time-cells = *PRESENT TIME* + 4

LEAVE SYSTEM

Conditions: Time-cell of lorry L = *PRESENT TIME*
L in LOUT

Actions: Take L from LOUT
Put L into WORLD
Remove L from time-scan
Decrease NLILP by 1.

These activities do not ask the computer to record any measures of the system. If we wanted to record the time spent waiting by each lorry at the outer end of the lane, just as an example, we should need to add to the activity *ENTER LANE* an instruction increase total waiting time by the number of lorries in QIN times the last time advance.

Nor have we included instructions to stop the program or to print. The reader might care to devise some. Initial conditions would also need specifying. The easiest would be to start with all sets empty except WORLD which contains one lorry of each type, numbered 1 and 2.

We have also referred to current time as present. We can program the computer to record the value of a variable *PRESENT TIME*, namely the time attached to the event to which we have just advanced. Alternatively we can always call the present zero by incorporating instructions in the time scan to reduce all times by the time of the next event when we advance to it.

After we have done this for the passage of the lorry through the system, we do it again for all other types of entity. In this case, we see that this adds nothing, since all types of change in the system have already been dealt with.

 Activity-Based Simulation. There remains only the problem of devising a system for applying these rules. There are, as we have already said, basically two types of approach to this problem, the activity-based approach and event-based approach.

The activity-based approach uses the list of activities as it stands. The computer, at each event, goes through the complete list of activities, trying each one in turn and for each lorry in the time-scan where relevant.

Having gone through the complete list, we now come to the problem of dealing with conditional activities. For instance, if in going through the list once we have succeeded in executing only the activity LEAVE SYSTEM for one of the lorries, we must have some means of checking whether we can now admit another lorry from QIN, since the conditions for activity ENTER LANE, which did not hold when we first looked at them, may now hold as a consequence of executing LEAVE SYSTEM.

The easiest way of doing this is simply to check through the whole list again. This is, in fact, what a purely activity-based simulation would do. If any activity is executed on this second run-through, we must go through the list yet again, until we run completely through the list without succeeding with any activity.

Conversely several activities may be executable at an event unconditionally on each other (because of the simultaneous occurrence of two or more events, for example) and one might prefer to execute them in a specific order. One might wish to do this because the execution of one such activity might inhibit the execution of a second whereas the second would give more advantage in the real system. If the desired order for execution is unchanging the activities are, of course, listed in that order. But if the preferred order depends on the state of things, quite subtle programming may be necessary.

Event-Based Simulation. The activity-based approach, in its most straightforward form as described above, is clearly inefficient in many respects. Very often many activities will be attempted when they are completely irrelevant. With fairly simple modifications, the efficiency of this approach can be greatly improved, as will be discussed later.

In this section, however, we will discuss the opposite type of approach, the event-based. With this approach, the structural unit of the simulation is not a set of rules (or section of program) relating to an activity, but a set of rules relating to the whole complex of activities that might be executed at a single compound event. That is, instead of making sure that conditional activities are executed by attempting all activities again and again, specific instructions are included which direct the computer directly to the relevant ones.

The first step, as always, is the time scan. In this approach, however, we make a note of which lorry has the earliest clock. The simulation then branches according to the current location of this lorry (which we shall call *L*).

Since we have already established that lorry *L*'s time-cell is the present time, and its location, we can without further testing proceed to executive the appropriate actions—e.g. if lorry *L* is in WORLD, we executive the Actions part of *LORRY ARRIVAL* without bothering with the Conditions. Thereafter, however, we must make specific provision for any conditional activities that this might have made possible. The only relevant one here is that lorry *L* might be able to enter the lane immediately so we attempt this (this time, of course, testing the conditions).

If L fails to enter at this attempt, under what circumstances will it be able to enter later? There is only one kind of activity which might lead to it being able to enter; another lorry leaving the system. Consequently, after any lorry leaves the system, we must test to see how many of the lorries in QIN we can admit.

Thus in each section of the simulation we have the following sequence:

(a) Execute 1st activity.
(b) Attempt all conditional activities that might have been made possible (consequences of 1st activity).

Note that, in this simulation, the event-based version branches immediately after the time-scan according to the current location of the lorry. In other simulations, this branching may be governed simply by the identity of the entity concerned (a different branch for ships, tugs, berths, etc.), or by some other attribute of the entity. The point is that the simulation branches directly to the relevant activities, without attempting a lot of irrelevant ones.

A point which is sometimes of importance arises because of the possibility, remarked on earlier, that two events might occur simultaneously. The difficulty this causes is that some of the activities conditional on the first activity may not be possible, but are made possible by the execution of the second activity (i.e. the one associated with the second simultaneous event) or the activities conditional on it and made possible by it. One must be on one's guard against this possibility but it is not too difficult to take account of, for example by methods analogous to the repeated checking of the activity list in an activity-based simulation. Conversely, as with an activity-based simulation, we might want to treat simultaneous events in a specific order, changing or unchanging as the case may be. Again, as for an activity-based system, some care may be needed to implement a changing order.

Discussion of Activity vs. Event-Based. The relative advantages and disadvantages of the two approaches should be fairly clear from the above discussion. The activity-based approach is simpler to set out and program for a computer; the penalty is inefficiency in execution. The event-based approach can get very complicated to program, particularly with more complex systems than this one. Execution is of course much more efficient.

In practice, the pure activity-based approach as outlined above is seldom used. The efficiency of execution can usually be improved greatly by adding additional routing instructions which direct the simulation around obviously irrelevant activities. For example, if activity *LORRY ARRIVAL* succeeds, then there is no point in trying *ARRIVE AT PLATFORM* for that particular lorry, and a little manoeuvring can avoid this. Conversely, programming of the event-based type of simulation can be simplified by various strategems.

Three Phase Structure. Such modifications usually tend to bring the simulation closer to some kind of three-phase structure. This structure makes a distinction between bound activities (those brought about only by the passage of time) and conditional activities.

The sequence in this three phase structure is:

(a) Time Scan (T-phase).
(b) Execute any relevant bound activity (B-phase).
(c) Attempt all conditional activities in turn (repeat if necessary) (C-phase).

This structure retains the simplicity of programming of the activity-based approach, since consequences do not have to be explicitly programmed to follow every activity, but achieves some increase in efficiency by arranging that only relevant B-activities are attempted.

Simulation languages

Mention has already been made of computer simulation languages. We shall discuss why these languages are useful, the modelling concepts underlying their construction, the sorts of facilities they provide, and the ease with which they are implemented. Aspects of some languages are described in a little more detail, to illustrate different approaches to simulation languages. However, our discussion is expository and is not intended as a comparative review. The interested reader is referred to references 1, 2 and 3 where he will also find source references unless otherwise indicated. In practice the user of a simulation language will almost certainly find his choice of language limited by availability on the computer he is using. He will also find that most computer manufacturers provide clear and readable manuals for the simulation languages they offer.

There are two main reasons why simulation languages are useful.

The first is that, in the process of constructing a simulation, there are certain kinds of task that crop up again and again. In the simulation languages, specific routines can be built in which make it unnecessary to program these tasks in detail, and this saves much routine work and reduces the possibility of errors.

The second is that there are, as discussed earlier, certain common features in the structure of simulations. By providing a framework corresponding to a basic type of structure, the language makes it relatively easy to formulate and debug a simulation.

Recurring Tasks

(a) *Random number generation*. A facility to generate pseudo-random numbers is, of course, required constantly. Furthermore, it is usually necessary not only to have a single stream of random numbers, but several parallel streams (the reason for this lies in achieving variance reduction (see below)). The facility to do this is supplied in most simulation languages, although surprisingly the streams are limited to quite a small number in some languages.

(b) *Sampling*. Samples of various quantities from random distributions are also constantly required in simulations. These distributions may either be of some common analytic form (e.g. normal, binomial, negative exponential, Poisson, etc.) or may be special to the particular problem, probably specified as histograms. Most languages include the facility to sample easily from either the standard distributions or from histograms.

(c) *Set handling*. Simulations usually involve much moving of entities from queue to queue, or simply from place to place. Consequently, some means is needed of specifying where each entity is at each moment of time, and of changing this location in the simulation. Likewise, the entities may change from category to category, e.g. BUSY to IDLE or WAITING REPAIR. Furthermore, some means is needed of handling queues. The simulator should be able to specify easily that the head member of any queue (or the tail member, or any other) be removed, and added to the tail of another queue.

These set-handling and queue-handling facilities exist in most languages, although their power varies widely.

(d) *Testing*. In a simulation of any complexity, there is a constant need to check what states various parts of the system are in. For example, in a port simulation, questions that may frequently need to be answered could include: is there a berth free?; is there a ship in QIN?; are there more than 5 ships in QBERTH?; is there a ship in a berth whose cargo is more than 10,000 tons of type 3?—and so on.

Furthermore, there is frequently a need to locate entities with certain properties—e.g. "take the first ship in QBERTH with more than 10,000 tons of grain on board. If there is no such ship, take the first ship with grain on board. If there is no such ship, take the first ship in QBERTH" —etc.

This kind of locating and testing facility is usually provided in the simulation languages, although again the power of the facility provided varies widely from language to language.

(e) *Collection and tabulation of results*. A simulation without output is not much use. The most useful kind of output is not usually a single figure, but a series of tables, histograms, etc. A good simulation language provides facilities for easy compilation and printing of tables and histograms.

(f) *Time scanning and time advancing*. This is one facility that is always needed. It is necessary to be able to set up "time-cells" connected with various entities, to scan them for the least, and to advance simulation time to that point.

Some languages do this automatically, without the programmer having to arrange for it at all. Others require the programmer to specify time-cells, and only the scanning itself is done automatically.

Common Structural Features. There are certain structural features which can be built into a simulation language to some extent. For instance, some languages are oriented towards an activity-based type of simulation, others towards an event-based type, and others towards a three-phase type. The organization of the language eases the formulation of the simulation in terms of its own particular structure.

Some languages go further in aiding formulation. As explained below, the programmer does not even have to organize his simulation into activities, etc., for these languages—he only has to specify, in flow diagram form, the flow of material, machines, etc., through the system.

The discipline imposed by the structure of the languages can have both advantages and disadvantages. The main advantage is that the programmer is forced to specify the simulation in such a way that omissions and logical errors are difficult to make; the disadvantages lie in the restrictions imposed on the programmer by the implicit structure. As might be expected, the languages that go furthest towards formalizing formulation of problems are also the least flexible.

Frequently it is not obvious from the users point of view whether a simulation language is organized internally on an activity basis, an events basis, or any other particular basis. The form of the instructions that the programmer himself writes is not always directly indicative of the internal organization.

This is especially true of the flow-diagram languages. The statement-description languages on the other hand, usually reveal their structure more clearly. The two types are discussed in turn below.

Statement-Description Languages. The most widely-used statement-description languages are probably CSL, SIMSCRIPT, SIMON and SIMULA. There are various versions of each. There are many other languages with more limited implementation, for example ESP and GSP.

In these languages, the programmer writes a simulation in statements, in the same way as writing a FORTRAN or ALGOL program. The way the activities were written out on page 211, though not written in any specific simulation language, illustrates the type of statement one uses. Indeed, most languages are based originally on one of the two general-purpose languages; SIMON actually consists of FORTRAN or ALGOL sub-routines. CSL is FORTRAN-based, and includes FORTRAN as a sub-set. SIMULA is ALGOL-based, and includes ALGOL as a sub-set. SIMSCRIPT was originally based on FORTRAN, but in later versions has become more independent of it. All provide the six facilities described above.

The languages differ in their underlying structure. CSL is fundamentally activity-based; SIMSCRIPT event-based; SIMON is three-phased; and SIMULA calls itself process-based—this is a combination of event-based and activity-based, with a bias towards the former.

To give some idea of the structural facilities available let us consider CSL in a little more detail. It is fundamentally an activity-based language. Each activity is written as a distinct section of program, in the usual form with tests preceding actions. Even if an activity were a bound activity, its onset determined simply by the passage of time, it would still have to be written as a conditional activity, with the first and only test being that the appropriate time-cell had a value equal to the current time. However CSL deviates from the purely activity-based structure in two respects.

The first is that there is only one pass through the activity set after each time-scan, unless a RECYCLE statement is encountered. Thus, if a simple activity is such that it can have no repercussions elsewhere in the system, it will not include a RECYCLE statement. On the other hand, if there is an activity (such as the tide coming in) which may cause a number of other activities to be made possible, then a RECYCLE statement would be included in the actions part of that activity.

The second is related to the first. It is that the activities need not all be attempted on each pass; the programmer can include provision to jump to various different activities, depending upon the outcomes of particular tests. This means that the program can be routed to avoid attempting irrelevant activities.

Used skilfully, this facility can allow the programmer to structure his simulation very efficiently from an execution point of view. Indeed, he can make the simulation more event-based than activity-based if he so wishes. However, he can equally, if he wishes, ignore all such subtleties, and make the programming very simple, by writing it as a pure activity-based simulation.

SIMSCRIPT and SIMULA, as mentioned above, are each based on different types of structure. Each is a language that in power is equal to or greater than CSL. However SIMON is rather different. It is not, in fact, a separate "language" at all; it is simply a collection of sub-routines written either in FORTRAN or in ALGOL. The user writes his simulation in one of these two general purpose languages, making frequent use of the sub-routines. Each sub-routine has to be called as needed, and there are restrictions imposed by the general purpose language itself on the form of the statements. This means that the language can be slightly awkward to use until its intricacies have been mastered, and the power of some of the facilities is restricted. On the other hand, the fact that it is programmed in each of the two principal general purpose languages means that SIMON is virtually universally available. GASP and FORSIM are FORTRAN packages similar in principle to SIMON.

Flow Diagram Languages. Two example flow diagram languages are GPSS3 and HOCUS (4).

Apart from the basic similarity of being flow-diagram languages, these two languages differ completely in conception. HOCUS aims at simplicity and ease of use by non-experts; GPSS3 requires much more of the user in terms of programming aptitude. HOCUS is relatively inefficient in execution; it is based on a very simple three-phase structure, but in such a way that there is inevitably a large proportion of conditional activities. GPSS3 has a very sophisticated internal structure, which is again basically three-phased but organized in such a way that only relevant conditional activities are attempted. This leads to great efficiency in execution. Again, HOCUS is written in basic FORTRAN, and is, therefore, in principle, universally available. GPSS3 requires a special compiler, which has so far been written only for a limited range of computers.

The basic concept in GPSS3 is that of an entity, or "transaction", flowing through the system. The passage of the entity through the system is specified by the programmer, using a special kind of flow diagram. The elements of the flow diagram are drawn from a set of standard types of element, each of which represents one step in the progress of the transaction. These steps are very simple ones, such as "engage facility", "enter Q", "leave Q", "advance time", and so on. There are a large number of standard types of element (about 40).

There are thus three steps in drawing up a GPSS3 simulation. The first is to compile a flow diagram of the system, describing each stage in words. The second is to translate this into a GPSS3 type of flow diagram, using the standard GPSS3 symbols. The final step is to translate the GPSS3 flow diagram on to cards for feeding into the computer, which is a purely mechanical step.

It is clear that there is a great deal of modelling power embodied in the GPSS3 system. The price to be paid for this is a certain loss of flexibility. Because of the straight line flow structure of GPSS3, it is difficult to incorporate complex testing procedures in a simulation. In particular, it is difficult to allow for simultaneous conditions to be tested—such as testing *both* for the tide to be in *and* for a berth to be free, at the same time, before entering the port.

The learning of a new symbolism in order to use GPSS3, the difficulty of incorporating complex logic, and the terse nature of the final program (there is no scope for using mnemonics), are to be weighed against its advantages in efficiency of execution, and its power in aiding formulation by means of the flow diagram approach. In many ways, it can be said to be a lower-level language than the statement description languages; its advantages and disadvantages compared with them are similar to the advantages and disadvantages of assembler languages as compared with high-level languages. Which approach is preferable is largely a matter of personal taste.

In contrast to GPSS3, HOCUS has only two types of element in it; the queue and the "activity". This simplicity is deliberate; the language was developed with the aim of reaching a wide spectrum of users, including design engineers, work study engineers, etc., as well as O.R. specialists. It is designed for simulating relatively small systems, the emphasis being on ease of formulation.

Each entity is conceived of as travelling in a closed loop, alternatively through "activities" and queues. (What HOCUS calls an "activity" is, in fact, a process which lasts for a definite time; what we have called an activity is an instantaneous change in the system. HOCUS is actually organized internally as a three-phase simulation; the start of each process is a conditional activity (in our sense) and the end of the process is a bound activity (in our sense).) It is surprising how many systems can be formulated in these simple terms with relatively little manipulation, although there are some constraints on the complexity of the logic that can be incorporated, since the programmer must stick to the standard formats for applying logical tests.

For each "activity", or process, the simulator has to specify the conditions which must prevail for it to start, the length of time it takes, and so on. Each queue simply has a maximum size and a discipline specified. The language is designed in such a way that hand simulations, using counters, can easily be performed; this is a great aid to debugging. In the original version it could be used conversationally on a small computer, which also speeds up debugging.

By and large, simulation languages are not as widely used as they might be. The reasons are probably, firstly, that most languages are fairly narrowly implemented, and secondly, that there is a barrier to be overcome in learning any language in the first place. It always *seems* quicker to use the general purpose language with which the user is usually already familiar.

This attitude is understandable, but probably misguided. The effort expended in learning the language can repay handsomely in reduced debugging. The task of debugging a complex simulation is a formidable one, and is frequently grossly under-estimated. The discipline imposed by a good language, and its facilities for performing routine tasks, can reduce the number of errors tremendously.

One other drawback is the inefficiency, in general, in running time when using a simulation language. On the whole, however, it seems likely that this cost is less than the cost of the time saved on debugging, except in special circumstances (for example when the program is to be used many times and program efficiency dominates). The best policy is probably: use a simulation language, and design your runs carefully.

Statistical aspects of simulation

Nearly all simulations contain random elements (e.g. arrival times, service times). Consequently the output of these simulations will not be exact answers, but series of randomly distributed figures. In fact, when talking of the theory of simulation, very often the aspect that is uppermost in people's minds is the statistical aspect. (However, simulations can be and are used which are completely deterministic. The aim in these cases would be to study the working of large and complex systems under various operating conditions.)

A number of statistical problems crop up, some of which are peculiar to simulation. First of all, there is the problem of generating the appropriate random variables, sampled from the appropriate distributions, within the simulation. Then there is the problem of deciding whether the simulation accurately represents the real situation. Finally, there is the problem of deciding how long to simulate, which parameters to vary and so on.

Random numbers

We shall show presently that a sample from any distribution can be obtained by a transformation from the uniform distribution. We shall, therefore, initially concentrate on the problem of generating values for the uniform distribution, and later show how the various transformations to other distributions are obtained. The uniform distribution is the one for which each value in a given range (say 0 to 1) is equally likely.

Thus we need some means of sampling real values that are equally probable in the range (0, 1). To do this it is sufficient to obtain integer numbers that are equally probable in a range $(0, N)$ since, by dividing by N, we can normalize these random numbers to the range (0, 1). Numbers distributed uniformly in the range (0, 1) are called random numbers.

Methods of Obtaining Random Numbers. Strictly speaking random numbers can be obtained only from random processes, since the word "random" implies that the numbers obtained are unpredictable. Various mechanical, electrical and electronic devices have been built in the past to produce such numbers and their inventors have gone to tremendous pains to ensure the unpredictability of the results. Tocher (5) gives a number of examples, including a description of the ERNIE generator used to pick premium bond numbers. However, there are a number of disadvantages associated with the use of these generators:

(i) Nature tends to be systematic.
(ii) The equipment tends to be cumbersome and difficult to maintain.
(iii) It is impossible to repeat a simulation using the same set of "random" numbers.

The last point is a very important one. In practice a highly desirable feature of simulation models is that one should be able to repeat the simulation process changing only one exogenous variable and keeping everything else constant. This requires the ability to generate exactly the same sequence of random numbers over and over again. At first sight this might seem to defeat the whole purpose of using random numbers, but it will be shown that the properties one is really interested in can still be retained, even though the "random" numbers used may be predictable.

The main requirements of the sequence of numbers produced are that they should be:

(i) Statistically independent.
(ii) Uniformly distributed.
(iii) Reproducible.
(iv) Non-repeating for any specified length.
(v) Capable of being generated at high speed.
(vi) Needing a minimum amount of core storage.

We could store a table of random numbers on disc or tape and use these as required, but it is quicker and more convenient to generate numbers by a recurrence relationship. Because the numbers generated by a procedure of this sort are not, strictly speaking, random they are commonly referred to as "pseudo-random" numbers. They clearly satisfy (v) and (vi) above, and we will discuss the extent to which the remaining four requirements are satisfied by various possible recurrence formulae.

The type of recurrence relationship most commonly used was first suggested by Lehmer (6). It takes the general form:

$$n_{i+1} = [an_i + c](mod\ m)$$

where "*mod m*" in the above expression means that we divide $(an_i + c)$ by m and take the remainder as the value of n_{i+1}, e.g. 15(*mod* 10) is 5; 20(*mod* 9) is 2; etc.

Eventually such sequences will repeat, but we can use number theory to show what values of a, c and m should be taken to maximize the length of cycle and satisfy requirements (ii) and (iii) above. In practice c is often put equal to zero so that

$$n_{i+1} = an_i\ mod\ m$$

Such a relationship defines a multiplicative congruential generator. The theory shows that to maximize the length of cycle, using this form of generator, it is important that *a be chosen relatively prime to m* (i.e. the highest common factor of a and m is 1). Otherwise the period will be shortened and the common factor repeated in all terms.

When programming a multiplicative generator on a computer which works in binary arithmetic it is usual to take m as 2^b where b is the word length used. Taking b as the word length of the machine has the advantage that the "*mod m*" process is achieved automatically, since only the bottom b bits are retained, higher bits being lost. It can be shown that with $m = 2^b$ for $b > 2$, the maximum attainable period is 2^{b-2}; it can also be shown that a should be chosen according to the formula

$$a = 8t \pm 3$$

where t is any positive integer; and that choosing a value of a near to $\sqrt{m}$ minimizes first order serial correlation.

The following summary shows how values of a and n_1 (the initial value in the sequence) should be chosen to ensure that the cycle length is a maximum and how to use them to generate a sequence of pseudo-random numbers:

(1) Choose any odd number as a starting value n_1.
(2) Choose an integer $a = 8t \pm 3$, where t is any positive integer for a constant multiplier. Choose a close to $2^{b/2}$.
(3) Compute an_1 using fixed point integer arithmetic. This product will consist of $2b$ bits, from which the high-order b bits are discarded and the low-order b bits represent n_2. (The integer multiplication instruction in FORTRAN automatically discards the high-order b bits.)
(4) Calculate $r_2 = n_2/2^b$ to obtain a uniformly distributed variable defined on the unit interval.
(5) Each successive random number r_{i+1} is obtained from the low-order bits of the product an_i when it is divided by 2^b.

Tests for Random Numbers. Kendall and Babbington Smith (7, 8) have proposed certain tests which can be made on a sequence of random numbers to investigate the extent to which the sequence is uniformly distributed and the numbers are statistically independent.

A straightforward test is the frequency test. This is used to check that the numbers are uniformly distributed. One simply counts how many of a stream of random numbers fall into various ranges and using, say, the χ^2 test one compares observed and expected frequencies.

The frequency test merely tests the probability of occurrence of each number but does not exclude the possibility of serial correlation between the numbers in successive positions.

Thus, the sequence 0·1, 0·2, 0·3, 0·4, 0·5, 0·6, 0·7, 0·8, 0·9. 0·0, 0·1, . . . will satisfy the frequency test but is clearly not a random sequence. Serial tests have been devised which test the correlation between successive numbers. One might, for example, examine successive non-overlapping pairs of a stream of random numbers and count how many define points falling into various sub-divisions of the unit square. (If overlapping pairs are used, as Kendall and Babbington Smith suggested, some care is necessary (9).)

The resulting numbers can then be tested as before. This serial test tests only first order correlation (i.e. the correlation between one number and the next). The principle used to test first order correlation could be extended to groups of three digits or more, but as the number of digits considered increases so the range of values tested increases, and the expected number in each cell drops, reducing the effectiveness of the test.

To overcome this difficulty, the poker test was suggested. This involves testing groups of five numbers and comparing actual and expected values (using a χ^2 test) for all numbers in different ranges, one pair from the same range, two pairs, three from the same range, four from the same range and all five from the same range.

The gap test deals with the length of gaps between successive numbers in a given range. If we denote the gap length by k (when two consecutive numbers in the range occur, $k = 0$), then the probability of obtaining a gap of length k is $p^k(1 - p)$ where $(1 - p)$ is the probability that an arbitrary number lies in the defined range. For a given sequence we can again compare actual and expected values using the χ^2 test.

Various other tests are possible (see for example reference 10) but in practice one is usually only concerned that the numbers should pass certain tests relevant to the application.

There is a good deal of evidence that multiplicative congruential relationships generate numbers which pass most of the general tests which have been proposed. However in any specific application there is much to be said for the user devising his own statistical tests if certain combinations of the random numbers or certain types of correlation which are not tested by the standard tests are likely to influence the results.

Sampling from distributions

We now go on to consider what transformations of random numbers are needed to obtain random samples from the commonly used distributions, and the problem of sampling from observed data that does not conform to any of these distributions. We recall that a continuous distribution is defined by

$$f(x)\, dx = p(x < X \leqslant x + dx)$$

where X is the random variable in question and we shall define

$$F(x) = p(X \leqslant x) = \int_{-\infty}^{x} f(y)\, dy$$

f is called the probability density function (p.d.f.), F the probability function or the cumulative density function (c.d.f.). If X is a random variable which can take only a number of defined values $a_1, a_2, a_3, \ldots$ its distribution is defined by

$$p(X = a_i) = f(a_i)$$

and the c.d.f. is $\Sigma f(a_i)$ where the summation extends over all a_i for which $a_i \leqslant x$.

Several methods for transforming random numbers to give an independent sample from a general distribution are available. (We shall restrict our attention to independent samples: extension of the methods described to cover the generation of dependent samples is not too difficult.) We begin by discussing an elementary technique.

Consider the following discrete probability distribution:

x	0	1	2	3	4	5	6	7	8	9	10	11
$f(x)$	0·02	0·06	0·08	0·10	0·16	0·20	0·14	0·10	0·06	0·04	0·02	0·02

It would be possible to set up a hand-simulation experiment to sample values from this distribution by marking a number of discs (in the manner described below) and choosing discs at random.

No. of discs	1	3	4	5	8	10	7	5	3	2	1	1
Mark	0	1	2	3	4	5	6	7	8	9	10	11

The selection of these discs could be made by shuffling them and picking one out of a top hat. Another approach, however, would be to number the discs sequentially from 1 to 50 and sample a random number uniformly distributed over the range 1–50 using a random number generator. The value for x is obtained by referring to the appropriate disc.

Having reached this stage it becomes obvious that all we need to store are the serial numbers defining the end-points for each value of x:

Range	1	2–4	5–8	9–13	14–21	22–31	32–38	39–43	44–46	47–48	49	50
Value	0	1	2	3	4	5	6	7	8	9	10	11

This procedure could now be programmed for a computer quite simply. In practice it is much more efficient, in terms of computation speeds, programming and storage requirements, to approximate to a theoretical distribution and use one of the techniques described below, but in some cases (e.g. where it is not possible to obtain a good fit using a standard distribution) the histogram technique may still be useful.

There are three basic methods for sampling from the standard probability distributions

the inverse transformation method,
the rejection method, and
the composition method.

Each of these will now be discussed in more detail.

The Inverse Transformation Method. To generate random variates from some particular distribution with p.d.f. $f(x)$ we first obtain the c.d.f. $F(x)$, which is defined over the range 0–1. We can then generate uniform variates r (also defined over the range 0–1) and since x is uniquely determined by $r = F(x)$ we can obtain x by the inverse transformation $x = F^{-1}(r)$.

It is intuitively obvious that this will give the required distribution, but the following argument puts the point mathematically:

$$\text{Prob } (X \leqslant x) = F(x)$$

By definition,

$$\text{Prob } (r \leqslant F(x)) = F(x)$$

Therefore

$$\text{Prob } (F^{-1}(r) \leqslant x) = F(x) = \text{Prob } (X \leqslant x)$$

since F is non-decreasing. Hence $F^{-1}(r)$ has the same distribution as X.

For some distributions it is possible to obtain $F^{-1}(r)$ analytically but in many cases this is not possible, and it is necessary to use an approximation. Quite a good approximation for most distribution is given by

$$x = A + Br + Cr^2 + a(1 - r)^2 \log r + br^2 \log (1 - r)$$

for suitable choices of A, B, C, a and b. This is known as the Russell approximation to the c.d.f. and is discussed by Tocher (5).

The Rejection Method. This requires $f(x)$ to be bounded, and x to have a finite range $a \leqslant x \leqslant b$. The steps in the procedure are as follows (it is left to the reader to satisfy himself that the procedure is a valid one):

(i) Choose c so that $f(x) \leqslant c$ for $a \leqslant x \leqslant b$.
(ii) Define x as a linear function of r, $x = a + (b - a)r$.
(iii) Generate pairs of random numbers (r_1, r_2).
(iv) If $cr_2 \leqslant f(a + (b - a)r_1)$ accept the pair and use $x = a + (b - a)r_1$ as the random variate.

The expected number of trials before a pair is found is equal to $c(b - a)$, so that for some p.d.f.'s the method is fairly inefficient.

The Composition Method. This technique, also known as "the method of mixtures", involves representing the desired distribution as a mixture of several distributions, i.e.

$$f(x) = \sum_i p_i g_i(x) \qquad 0 \leqslant p_i \leqslant 1 \qquad \sum_i p_i = 1$$

In other words, the observation has come from distribution $g_i(x)$ with probability p_i. A random variable is used to select the distribution from which to sample for a particular value of x, and a variate then sampled from that distribution.

Sampling from some Specific Distributions. We now consider how these methods just described can be used to obtain random variables from some standard probability distributions, more by way of example than in an attempt to cover the field fully.

The exponential distribution is often required. It arises as the distribution of the time between successive events when events are occurring through time independently of each other and with a constant probability of occurrence in each small time interval. For this distribution

$$F(x) = 1 - e^{-Ax}$$

$1/A$ being the mean, and the inverse transformation method is comparatively straightforward. We find x for which

$$F(x) = r$$

and this is

$$-\frac{1}{A} \log (1 - r)$$

or, since $1 - r$ is uniformly distributed in $(0, 1)$, we might as well take

$$x = -\frac{1}{A} \log r$$

A good many distributions can be built up by combining exponential distributions (see page 141). Simple addition and the method of mixtures can be used to generate samples from almost any distribution although one must clearly be careful to avoid excessive computation.

The normal distribution is one of the most commonly used statistical distributions. The central limit theorem states that the distribution of the sum of N independently distributed random variates with means m_i and variances v_i as N becomes large approaches asymptotically the normal distribution with mean

$$m = \sum_i^N m_i$$

and variance

$$V = \sum_1^n V_i$$

Thus any measurement which represents the effects of a number of independent additive causes will tend to be normally distributed, regardless of the underlying distribution of the measurements of individual causes.

Several methods for sampling from the normal distribution are available. The simplest takes advantage of the central limit theorem and merely involves adding groups of uniform variates.

Suppose we take groups of k uniformly distributed random variates r_1, $r_2 \ldots r_k$. The mean and variance of the r's are $\frac{1}{2}$ and $\frac{1}{12}$ respectively. From the central limit theorem, groups of k variates will thus tend to be distributed normally with mean $k/2$ and variance $k/12$.

Taking $k = 12$ for convenience

$$y = r_1 + r_2 + \ldots + r_{12} - 6$$

will thus be distributed approximately normally with mean 0 and variance 1 and a random variate from the normal distribution with mean m and variance V can be obtained from y by making the transformation

$$x = m + Vy$$

Note that normal variates obtained in this way will be truncated at $m \pm 6V$, though in most applications this will not be a cause for concern.

The binomial distribution gives the probability that an event occurs x times out of n trials when trials are independent and the probability of occurrence, say p, is the same at each trial. It finds application in sampling experiments where sampling takes place with replacement and sampled elements have only two kinds of attributes.

For large n a normal approximation can be used. However, a simple method based on the rejection procedure will be more efficient in many cases. This involves generating n random numbers in the range (0, 1) and counting the number for which $r \leqslant p$.

When we have large n and small p, the probability of x successes in n trials is given by the Poisson distribution with the single parameter $m = np$. An example of a variable that might be expected to have the Poisson distribution is the number of aircraft arriving at an airport in a fixed time period.

Poisson variates can be generated by summing exponentially distributed variables and counting the number that need to be generated before their sum exceeds the required mean m.

Thus if t_i are exponential variates with unit mean, x is given by

$$\sum_{i=0}^{x} t_i \leqslant \lambda \leqslant \sum_{i=0}^{x+1} t_i \qquad (x = 0, 1, 2, \ldots)$$

and we can use the technique previously described for generating exponential variates.

References 2 and 5 discuss more fully sampling from most of the distributions in common use. Reference 2 gives FORTRAN sub-routines for carrying out the sampling.

Design of simulation experiments

One can represent a simulation process schematically in the following way:

$$\text{FACTORS} \underset{\longrightarrow}{\overset{\longrightarrow}{\longrightarrow}} \boxed{\begin{array}{c} \text{SIMULATION} \\ \text{MODEL} \end{array}} \overset{\longrightarrow}{\underset{\longrightarrow}{\longrightarrow}} \text{RESPONSES}$$

The factors and responses are sometimes termed input variables and output variables, or independent and dependent variables, or exogenous and endogenous variables. The problem is to estimate the effect on the response variables of different levels of the factors. This is done by running the simulation model a number of times, varying the factor levels and recording the effect this has on the response variables. The results are then analysed and conclusions drawn. The response variables are usually random variables, with a mean and variance which can be estimated from the results, and one wants to obtain unbiassed estimates of the means of the response variables with minimum variance for a given expenditure on computer time. The purpose of studying experimental design then is to learn how to get good value for money from the computer. We shall be concerned mainly with those aspects of experimental design which are peculiar to simulation experiments. However the general principles of experimental design should not be overlooked as far as they are relevant (see for example reference 11).

Starting Conditions. One of the problems in trying to design simulation experiments is that starting conditions can influence the simulation results. In some cases this may not be important because the system under study may always start from the same conditions in each real life run. The post office starts each day with no queues. However if one is simulating a system which is continuous (this includes the case where the system stops overnight but starts where it left off) there is a problem. It may take some time for the simulation to overcome the artificiality introduced by the abrupt beginning of the operation. Possible solutions are to exclude data from some initial period from consideration, or to choose starting conditions that make the excluded interval as short as possible.

A pilot run can be carried out to decide what period to exclude. Many queuing simulations start with no queue and all servers idle, which is probably an untypical situation. The process of converging to an equilibrium position could be accelerated by choosing more reasonable starting conditions (that is conditions which have non-zero probabilities) which would allow a reduction in the "warming up" time of the simulation.

A problem arises in choosing starting conditions when comparing two or more alternative systems. Suppose we know enough about each system to be able to construct reasonable starting conditions, then the investigator has three choices:

   (i) Test each system starting "empty and idle".
  (ii) Test each system using a common set of starting conditions that is essentially a compromise between the two different sets of starting conditions.
 (iii) Test each with its own reasonable starting conditions.

(ii) is preferable to (iii) since in general one should compare alternatives under as close to identical conditions as possible.

Variance Reduction Techniques. Various techniques exist which will substantially reduce the computer time needed to achieve a given level of confidence in the results. These techniques, known as variance reduction techniques, are discussed below.

(i) *Repetition of random number streams.* A large proportion of simulations involve comparisons of a sequence of alternatives, so that the investigator is concerned with relative rather than absolute results. If these were field experiments rather than simulated experiments one would aim to compare alternatives under closely identical conditions. For example, in experiments on crops the investigator would use alternative seeds or fertilizers close together, in order to minimize the effect of variation in soil conditions. In a simulation experiment the corresponding "experimental medium" is a sequence of exogenous events which describe the activities of the outside world to the model. For example, this synthetically generated sequence can be customer orders, equipment failures or aeroplane arrivals. The sequence is a function of a sequence of pseudo-random numbers, or it can be drawn from actual operations. In either case, the investigator can reproduce and re-use the identical sequence of events for different runs of the model. This procedure will allow a much smaller sample size to be used to produce equivalent results than generating and using separate and independent sequences for each run.

If there is more than one sequence (arrivals, service times, server breakdowns and so on) one must, generally speaking, use a different random number sequence for each to guarantee reproduction of the same conditions: otherwise there is a risk that the random numbers will refer to different sequences under different policies, as the order of events might be changed.

To put the point formally, consider the following example. Two policies X and Y, are to be compared. Policy X leads to results denoted by the random variable x, and policy Y leads to results denoted by the random variable y. We want to obtain an estimate of the mean of the random variable $z = x - y$, to decide which policy is better.

(a) With completely random sampling

$$Var(z) = Var(x) + Var(y)$$

(b) With correlated sampling, $z^1 = x - y$ will have the same mean as z but a smaller variance, given by:

$$Var(z^1) = Var(x) + Var(y) - 2Cov(x, y)$$

Thus if $Cov(x, y)$ can be made large and positive the variance of z^1 will be considerably less than that of z. This can be achieved by using a common stream of pseudo-random numbers.

(ii) *Control variables.* A number of variance reduction techniques are built round the use of control variables of one sort or another. Suppose we wish to estimate the distribution of a random variable X, or its mean. (X might be the total customer waiting time in a queuing system.) If x is an observed value of X, x is just a function of the values assumed by the random variables, say $r_1, r_2, \ldots, r_n$, in the run leading to the observation. Let Y be some other function of the random variables, whose observed value is y when the random variables take the values $r_1, r_2, \ldots, r_n$. (Y might be the average value of the random variables, or the average time between arrivals.) One would generally expect X and Y to be correlated.

Now suppose we know *a priori* some property of Y, for example its mean or its distribution in repeated sampling. We can take advantage of this knowledge in a number of ways to improve our estimates about X. To take a simple example, suppose we simulate the operation of a post office for 100 days and note that the average waiting times for customers on each of the days were $x_1, x_2, \ldots, x_{100}$. Assume we also noted the number of customers arriving day by day: $y_1, y_2, \ldots, y_{100}$. If by chance y_n were higher than average we would expect x_n to be higher than average and if y_n were lower we would expect a lower x_n. In other words X and Y are positively correlated. Moreover we know from records or we predict that on average 800 customers per day will arrive at the post office. We could estimate EX, the average waiting time, by

$$\bar{x} = (x_1 + x_2 + \ldots + x_{100})/100$$

The variance of this estimator is $V(X)/100$, $V(X)$ being the variance of X, assuming the days have been simulated independently. Suppose instead we estimated EX by

$$Z = \bar{x} - \bar{y} + 800$$

where

$$\bar{y} = (y_1 + y_2 + \ldots + y_{100})/100$$

This estimator is unbiased as

$$Ez = EX - EY + 800 = EX$$

and its variance is

$$\{V(X) + V(Y) - 2\, Cov\,(X,\, Y)\}/100$$

where $Cov\,(X,\, Y)$ is the covariance of X and Y, which we believe to be positive. If X and Y are so strongly correlated that $2\, Cov\,(X,\, Y) > V(Y)$, the variance of the second estimator is lower than that of the first and it is to be preferred.

We might be able to get an even lower variance by using an estimator of the form $\bar{x} - a(\bar{y} - 800)$ where a is estimated from the observations by, say, least squares. We must be careful here to avoid introducing bias however: one should estimate one a from half the data to apply to the other half and another a from the second half to apply to the first. Thus, splitting the 100 days into two sets of 50 in the above example, we choose a_1 to minimize

$$\sum_{i=1}^{50}(x_i - a_1(y_i - 800) - \bar{x}_1)^2$$

where

$$\bar{x}_1 = (x_1 + x_2 + \ldots + x_{50})/50$$

so that

$$a_1 = \sum_{i=1}^{50} (x_i - \bar{x}_1)(y_i - 800) \bigg/ \sum_{i=1}^{50} (y_i - 800)^2$$

Similarly

$$a_2 = \sum_{i=51}^{100} (x_i - \bar{x}_2)(y_i - 800) \bigg/ \sum_{i=51}^{100} (y_i - 800)^2$$

where

$$\bar{x}_2 = (x_{51} + x_{52} + \ldots + x_{100})/50$$

We then use

$$\sum_{i=1}^{50} (x_i - a_2(y_i - 800)) + \sum_{i=51}^{100} (x_i - a_1(y_i - 800))$$

as our estimate of EX. Tocher (5) gives the theory of this method and also describes a superior method suggested by Tukey (12), which involves splitting the data into more than two parts for the analysis.

If the distribution of Y is known there are other possibilities. One such has been suggested by Fieller and Hartley (13) and is also discussed by Tocher (5).

Divide the range of the two statistics x and y into intervals and denote by n_{ij} the number in a sample of N falling into the ith x-category and the jth y-category. The unknown probability associated with this cell is denoted by p_{ij}. The marginal frequencies and probabilities are given by:

$$n_{.j} = \sum_i n_{ij}$$

$$p_{.j} = \sum_i p_{ij}$$

(this is the distribution of y which we know),

$$n_{i.} = \sum_j n_{ij}$$

$$p_{i.} = \sum_j p_{ij}$$

(this is the distribution of x which we require),

$$N = \sum_i n_{i.} = \sum_j n_{.j}$$

and

$$\sum_i p_{i.} = \sum_j p_{.j} = 1$$

The conditional probability of a sample falling in the cell (i, j) given that it falls in the jth column is $p_{ij}/p_{.j}$ which is estimated by $n_{ij}/n_{.j}$ (for $n_{.j} > 0$).

Now

$$p_{i.} = \sum_j p_{ij} = \sum_j p_{.j} p_{ij}/p_{.j}$$

so an estimate of $p_{i.}$ is provided by

$$\overset{*}{p}_i = \sum_j p_{.j} u_{ij}$$

where

$$u_{ij} = \frac{n_{ij}}{n_{.j}} \text{ if } n_{.j} > 0 \text{ and } u_{ij} = \frac{n_{i.}}{N} \text{ if } n_{.j} = 0$$

This leads to a slight bias in $\overset{*}{p}_i$ which is approximately equal to

$$\sum_j \exp(-Np_{.j})$$

and can be made negligible if the sample size N and the cell boundaries are chosen so that $Np_{.j}$ are fairly large. This can be ensured before the experiment since the $p_{.j}$ are known.

The variance of $\overset{*}{p}_i$ consists of four terms. The first is the usual binomial variance of the unadjusted estimate p_i; the second can be ignored for large N; the third is of the same order as the bias, and the fourth, representing the main variance reduction, is of the form

$$-\sum_j (p_{ij} - p_{i.}p_{.j})^2 / Np_{.j}$$

which is zero if

$$p_{ij} = p_{i.}p_{.j}$$

that is if x and y are independent. At the other extreme of complete dependence

$$var(\overset{*}{p}_i) = 0$$

Between these two extremes a significant reduction in variance can be achieved if x and y are highly correlated.

Yet another possibility is so to generate random numbers as to take a sample which is stratified with respect to the control variable Y. If we split the range of Y into n intervals which are such that $V(X|Y$ lies in the ith interval) $= V_i$, sampling theory shows that we should choose to take

$$\frac{100 p_i \sqrt{V_i}}{\sum_1^n p_i \sqrt{V_i}} \%$$

of our samples to give values of Y lying in the ith interval and to estimate EX by $\Sigma p_i \sqrt{V_i} \Sigma S_i / \sqrt{V_i}$ where $p_i = p(Y$ lies in the ith interval) and $S_i =$ sum of X's for which Y is in the ith interval. In other words we should give greater sampling weight to those intervals of Y within which there is a higher variance of X. More generally if there is reason to suppose V_i is less than $V(X)$ for all i, but the V_i are not known, we should sample representatively with $100 p_i \%$ of our sample giving Y's in the ith interval.

What these ideas amount to in practice is to doctor the random numbers so as to generate samples from the joint probability density function of the random variables conditional upon Y lying in a given interval. In general this is too difficult to do. However it is possible in some simple cases. In the post office example it might be that customers arrive at random at the same rate throughout the day. We believe that the variance of waiting time is quadruple on those days for which Y, the number of customers, is over 800 than on those days when Y is below, so we would like to make twice as many runs to give above average Y's as given below. Now Y is approximately normally distributed, being a Poisson variate with high mean, and we can sample values of Y giving double weighting to values above average. An arrival pattern can now be generated corresponding to each fixed Y because the conditional arrival pattern given Y is given by inserting Y points at random during the day.

Direct stratification is rarely as simple as this, but there are two other possible ways of indirectly stratifying the sample. The first of these is by a technique known as splitting (13). Here we use as our control variable some quantity which manifests its value early in the simulation run. As soon as the value is manifested we stop simulating and decide whether to continue to the end of the run which we do with a probability dependening on the value of the control variable. An example might be the case where we are simulating a system where there is a rush hour phenomenon. On say 15% of days this leads to very long waiting times with high variability; on the other 85% of days the rush hour is handled with only moderate waiting times. The bad 15% are characterized by the fact that the queue in question happens by chance to be above a certain number at the start of the rush hour. If we denote the queue size at the start of the rush hour by Y it might pay us to run the simulation until the start of the rush hour to establish the value of Y for that run and then to let the run continue to the end if Y exceeds some critical figure but to let only say 10% of runs continue if Y is below the critical figure, the decision being taken by generating a random number in the range 0 to 1 and continuing if its value is less than 0·1. We shall need to give 10 times the weight to runs in which Y is below the critical value as to those in which it is above in estimating the average value of X, the variable of interest.

A somewhat similar idea, often called Russian roulette (13), is appropriate if the calculation of y, an observation of the control variable is much easier than the calculation of x. In this case we generate the random numbers, and calculate only y. We then decide whether or not to regenerate the random numbers to calculate x according to the value of y. In the post office example we would calculate the number of arrivals in a whole day and, if this were in excess of 800, then go through the random numbers again to calculate x; if the number of arrivals were less than 800 we would toss a coin to decide whether to calculate x.

Finally in this discussion of control variables we note that sometimes one chooses starting conditions by sampling them from a distribution. If we believe that the starting conditions correlate with the variable of interest we can use them as a control variable. Stratification is trivially easy in this case.

(iii) *Antithetic variables.* In the control variable method we sought a second estimate with a known expected value and a strong positive correlation with the variable of interest. The use of antithetic variables (14) requires an estimator with the same expected value as the variable of interest but negatively correlated with it. Such an estimator could be obtained by running the simulation again and arranging for a low value in the first run to be replaced by a high value on the second run and vice versa. A method which can be used is to enter the sampling routine on the ith occasion with the random number $(1 - p_i)$ instead of p_i. Thus the run is repeated with the same initial conditions and random number generators associated with each sampling process giving the sequence $(1 - p_1)$, $(1 - p_2)$, $(1 - p_3)$, . . . in place of the sequence p_1, p_2, p_3 . . . .

Denote the two estimators by X and Y. Then $\frac{1}{2}(X + Y)$ will be an unbiased estimator of EX, and its variance will be:

$$var\left(\tfrac{1}{2}(X + Y)\right) = \tfrac{1}{4} var(X) + \tfrac{1}{4} var(Y) + \tfrac{1}{2} cov(X, Y)$$

The use of antithetic variables will generally ensure that $cov(X, Y)$ is negative thus reducing the variance compared with independent estimators. More subtle antithetic methods can be readily developed.

(iv) *Estimation when simulating a continuous process* (15). We have hitherto tended to discuss the situation where one is simulating a process which has a single measure attached to it. For example, we might have been thinking of estimating the total customer waiting time per day in a post office. Suppose instead we had wanted to estimate the average length of queue over the day. Two methods for doing this suggest themselves.

The values of the state variables can be recorded at equidistant time intervals during the course of the simulation—time slicing; or the values of the state variables (which only change when an event occurs) can be recorded at every event. Clearly some information is lost be the time slicing method.

Consider time slicing. If N observations x_1, x_2, x_3 . . . x_N of a state variable X are taken at times t, $2t$, $3t$, . . ., Nt, an unbiased estimate of EX is given by

$$m_1 = \sum_{i=1}^{N} \frac{tx_i}{Nt} = \frac{1}{N} \sum_{i=1}^{N} x_i$$

The variance of this estimate of the mean may be reduced by increasing the number of observations from N to kN where $k = 2, 3$ . . . .

This can be done in three ways: we can extend the run length from $Nt = T$ to kT, or we can carry out k replications, or we can reduce the sampling interval from t to t/k.

It is not self-evident which of these is better (they are not the same since the variance of m depends on the correlation present in the series of x's). It can be shown that, where the covariance function of x, $R(a)$, is positive and non-increasing for $a \geqslant 0$, the greatest reduction in the variance of the estimated mean is generally achieved by replication, and the next greatest by extension of the simulation run. An exception to this general result must be mentioned however and that is that if one has to run for a long time in each replication to remove the effect of the initial conditions, extension of the run might be preferable.

Event sequencing, which is the name given to the second method of estimation, takes the following form. If the state variable takes on values x_1, x_2, . . . changing at times t_1, t_2, . . . an unbiased estimate of the mean is given by:

$$m_2 = \frac{1}{T} \sum_{i=1}^{n} x_i(t_i - t_{i-1})$$

The variance of m_2 can be reduced either by increasing the length of the run or by replication. As before, it can be shown that it is generally better to replicate than increase the run length, with the same proviso.

Verification of simulation models (16), (17)

Any simulation model should be validated. The problem is: how can we be sure (and convince others) that the model we have built is a sufficiently good representation of the real-life system to allow conclusions to be drawn (and actions to be taken) on the strength of the results? The process of verification involves three stages:

(a) Testing the structure of the model.
(b) Testing the input data.
(c) Testing the complete model.

We are not, of course, concerned with making a test that will lead us to accept the model as a true representation of what really happens or to reject it completely and start all over again. We want to ensure that the model we are going to use is sufficiently good for the use to which it is going to be put. No model will ever be completely realistic, and we have to decide what order of error can be tolerated, bearing in mind the effects of errors on the action that will be recommended on the basis of the results.

Verifying the Structural Relationships. The process of building up a simulation model involves formulating a set of relationships between the variables included in the model. One needs to test, therefore both that sufficient variables have been included and that the relationships that have been assumed are correct.

There are two approaches to the problem of deciding how much detail to incorporate. One is to start with a model that contains every possible variable, and then simplify down to the point where any further simplification will cause too much error in the results. The other is to start with a very simple model and build in more and more detail until the results become sufficiently accurate. The second approach seems to have a clear advantage over the first, since there is no effort wasted in collecting data and formulating relationships that are not going to be used in the final model. The structural relationships will usually have been formulated after discussion with the people on the job, and one really has to assume that they are correct. If the errors in the results seem to indicate that the structure of the model is faulty, then one must go back to the people directly concerned and discuss the problem with them, to try to discover where the model is going wrong.

Verification of the Input Data. In the case where input data is provided by reading historical records, then no verification is needed. However, if some form of sampling is used—either from histograms constructed from observed data or from theoretical frequency distributions whose parameters have been estimated from the data, then it is desirable to check:

(i) If a theoretical distribution is assumed, that the observed data actually corresponds to the distribution.

(ii) For autocorrelation. If this effect is present, its effect on the results should be investigated to see whether it is worth incorporating into the model.

(iii) For correlation between different types of input data. Two or more input variables may in practice be correlated. If this correlation has an important effect on the results, it should be included.

One can sometimes allay doubts on these points by running the simulation with input data generated by a variety of statistical assumptions. In some cases one finds the precise assumptions chosen do not critically affect the results.

Verification of the Complete Model. This involves testing the model's ability to predict the behaviour of the system under study. In order to test the degree to which data generated by computer simulation models conform to observed data, two alternatives are available—historical verification and verification by forecasting. Whichever method is used, one is then faced with the problem of testing the "goodness of fit" of a simulated series of observations with the observed series. The characteristics one might want to test are usually a consequence of what one wants to use the simulation for and little more can be said than that some sort of testing should be done. It should be noted that the statistical test will usually be that the simulated and the observed series come from the same population and not a test of whether the simulated series is from a population defined by the observed series. Note too that one will often need to have recourse to distribution free tests.

References

1. Tocher, K. D. Review of Simulation Languages. *Opl. Res. Qly* **16.2** pp. 189–218 1965.
2. Naylor, T. H., Balinlly, J. L., Burdick, D. S. and Chu, K. *Computer Simulation Techniques*. John Wiley & Sons New York 1966.
3. Hollingdale, S. H. (Ed.) *Digital Simulation in Operational Research*. English Universities Press London 1967.

4. P–E Consulting Group, Egham, Surrey. *HOCUS. A New Approach to Simulation.*
5. Tocher, K. D. *The Art of Simulation.* English Universities Press London 1963.
6. Lehmer, D. H. Description of "Random Number Generation on the BRL high-speed computing machines". *Math. Rev.* **15** p. 559 1951.
7. Kendall, M. G. and Babington Smith, B. Randomness and random sampling numbers. *J. Roy. Statist. Soc.* **101** pp. 147–166 1938.
8. Kendall, M. G. and Babington Smith, B. Second paper on random sampling numbers. *J. Roy. Statist. Soc. Suppl.* **6** pp. 51–61 1939.
9. Good, I. J. The Serial Test for Sampling Numbers and other tests for randomness. *Proc. Camb. Phil. Soc.* **49.2** pp. 276–284 1953.
10. Gruenberger, F. and Mark, A. M. The d^2 Test of Random Digits. *Math. Tables Other Aids. Comp.* **5** 1951.
11. Hunter, J. S. and Naylor, T. H. Experimental Designs for Computer Simulation Experiments. *Management Science (Theory Series)* **16.7** pp. 422–434 1970.
12. Tukey, J. W. *On the distribution of the fractional part of a statistical variable.* Mathematical Abstracts, Academy of Sciences, U.S.S.R. Moscow. 1934.
13. Curtiss, J. H. *et al.* "Monte Carlo Method". *National Bureau of Standards Applied Mathematics Series* **12** 1951.
14. Hammersley, J. M. and Morton, K. W. A New Monte Carlo Technique: Anithetic Variates. *Proc. Camb. Phil. Soc.* **52.3** pp. 449–475 1956.
15. Gafarian, A. V. and Anckev, C. J. Mean Value Estimation from Digital Computer Simulation. *Opns. Res.* **14.1** pp. 25–44 1966.
16. Naylor, T. H. and Finger, J. M. Verification of Computer Simulation Models. *Management Science (Application Series)* **14.2** pp. B92–B106 1967.
17. Naylor, T. H., Wertz, K. and Wonnacott, T. *Some Methods of Analysing Data Generated by Computer Simulation Experience.* Communications of the A.C.M. 1967.

Further reading

References 1, 2, 3 and 5 above.
Laski, J. G. On Time Structure in (Monte Carlo) Simulations. *Opl. Res. Qly* **16.3** pp. 329–340 1965 and the subsequent correspondence in *Opl. Res. Qly* **17.1** 1966.
Hammersley, J. M. and Handscomb, D. C. *Monte Carlo Methods.* Methuen & Co. Ltd 1964.
Gordon, G. *System Simulation.* Prentice Hall, Inc. 1969.
Elton, M. and Rosenhead, J. Microsimulation of Markets. *Opl. Res. Quart.* **22.2** pp. 117–144 1971.

Examples for solution

1. If you have suitable facilities to allow you to do so, program and execute the lorry example on page 211. Use a simulation language if one is available.

2. Consider a simple queue with one server, and random arrivals and exponential service time. What are the activities in this system? For each, specify the tests to be carried out before the activity can be started.

Sketch out two flow diagrams for programs to simulate this system, one activities based, the other events based. Include provision for sampling from the relevant distributions and for stopping the sum after a sample of 100 waiting times have been collected.

This program is to be used to estimate average waiting time. List and discuss possible variance reduction devices that you might use.

3. Take 50 random numbers* in the range 0 to 1 and use them to estimate as accurately as you can the expected value of the largest of a random sample of 5 numbers distributed uniformly in 0 to 1.

4. Simulate the life history of an item in a single store. Assume that demand for the item is Poisson with mean 5 per time unit, but that this is not known to the man operating the store who assumes that demand in the next time unit will be Poisson with mean equal to the demand in the previous time unit. Try a variety of stock control policies each with a lead time of one time unit. Compare the results you get with the theoretical predictions and comment on your findings.

Choosing what you consider to be the best stock control policy for the item, simulate the operation of this policy against different forecasting methods. Comment on your results.

Carry out simulations using the best two or three forecasting methods, but allowing mean demand to jump from 5 to 10 per time unit some way through the simulation. Again comment.

5. List the recurrent decisions and some recent one-off decisions in your organization where simulation might help or might have helped but is not or was not used. Why was it not used?

Bearing in mind the pros and cons of simulation, what types of decision would you recommend it should be used for in the future?

Who should carry out the simulation exercises? Should they be carried out by teams and, if so, who should be in the teams?

6. "The difficulty of modelling human behaviour and especially the process of making value judgements mean that simulation is useless except for modelling inanimate systems." Discuss.

Is this criticism any more or less valid of simulation than of any other model building technique?

7. Tocher (1) draws the distinction between machine based and materials based simulation languages. In a machine based language the active entities are in the simulation all the time (usually being physically fixed objects). In a materials based language the active entities move in and out of the system. The lorry example (page 211) has the structure of a materials based language. If the example had been cast in the structure of a machine based language what would have been the active entities? Would the same sets have been necessary? Consider the activity *ENGAGE CRANE.* Would it be suitable as written on page 211 without revision?

Is Tocher's distinction a useful one?

8. How could the lorry example (page 211) be given a three phase structure? How does this structure differ from the event-based structure described on page 213?

---

* Most sets of statistical tables include a table of random numbers. See for example Lindley, D. V. and Miller, J. C. P. *Cambridge Elementary Statistical Tables.* Cambridge University Press 1953.

Solutions to examples

Chapter 2

1. Following the standard method the final table is:

		E 13	F 19	G 25	H 21	I 36	Total
A	7	23	27	500 32	30	450 43	950
B	−5	15	15	20	300 16	35	300
C	0	14	1,000 19	25	350 21	37	1,350
D	22	250 35	44	200 47	45	60	450
Total		250	1,000	700	650	450	

Solution A sends 500 to G, 450 to J
B sends 300 to H
C sends 1,000 to F, 350 to H
D sends 250 to E, 200 to G

(Care must be taken as this is a degenerate problem. In the final solution a "small quantity" is being transported from B to G.)

2. The solution can readily be derived from the solution to example 1 and is

Solution A sends 700 to G, 450 to J
B sends 650 to H
C sends 1,000 to F
D sends 250 to E

3. Let x_1, x_2, x_3, x_4 and x_5 be tonnages of G, M, H, S and W produced respectively. Suppose $x_6/10$, $x_7/10$, $x_8/10$, $x_9/10$ are the tonnages of TL, UM, YF, BM not used respectively. Then

$$
\begin{aligned}
x_1 + x_2 + 2x_3 + 2x_4 + 3x_5 + x_6 &= 1{,}300 \\
2x_1 + x_2 + 3x_3 + 3x_4 + 2x_5 + x_7 &= 2{,}500 \\
4x_1 + 4x_2 + 2x_3 + x_4 + 4x_5 + x_8 &= 2{,}400 \\
3x_1 + 4x_2 + 3x_3 + 3x_4 + x_5 + x_9 &= 2{,}950
\end{aligned}
$$

Profit $= 120x_1 + 110x_2 + 60x_3 + 90x_4 + 135x_5$

and this is to be maximized subject to be above constraints and with all the variables non-negative.

The first basic feasible solution is easily found using an all slack basis. The optimum solution is to make 500 tonnes of Godite and 400 tonnes of Sterite. The reduced costs are 0, 10, $\frac{360}{7}$, 0, $\frac{375}{7}$, $\frac{240}{7}$, 0, $\frac{150}{7}$ and 0. The shadow prices are therefore $\frac{240}{7}$, 0, $\frac{150}{7}$, 0. Profit is 96,000p.

4. Let there be x_1 litres of d in A
$\qquad x_2$ litres of e in A
$\qquad x_3$ litres of f in A
$\qquad y_1$ litres of d in B
$\qquad y_2$ litres of e in B
$\qquad y_3$ litres of f in B
$\qquad z_1$ litres of d in C
$\qquad z_2$ litres of e in C
$\qquad z_3$ litres of f in C

Then

$$\frac{x_1}{x_1 + x_2 + x_3} \geqslant \tfrac{1}{2} \quad \text{i.e.} \quad -x_1 + x_2 + x_3 \leqslant 0$$

$$\frac{x_2}{x_1 + x_2 + x_3} \leqslant \tfrac{1}{4} \quad \text{i.e.} \quad -x_1 + 3x_2 - x_3 \leqslant 0$$

$$\frac{y_1}{y_1 + y_2 + y_3} \geqslant \tfrac{1}{4} \quad \text{i.e.} \quad -3y_1 + y_2 + y_3 \leqslant 0$$

$$\frac{y_2}{y_1 + y_2 + y_3} \leqslant \tfrac{1}{2} \quad \text{i.e.} \quad -y_1 + y_2 - y_3 \leqslant 0$$

Also

$$x_1 + y_1 + z_1 \leqslant 500{,}000$$
$$x_2 + y_2 + z_2 \leqslant 500{,}000$$
$$x_3 + y_3 + z_3 \leqslant 300{,}000$$
$$\text{Profit} = -1{\cdot}5x_1 + 2{\cdot}5x_2 + 1{\cdot}5x_3 - 3{\cdot}0y_1 + 1{\cdot}0y_2 - 4{\cdot}0z_1 - 1{\cdot}0z_3$$

The best policy is to make 1,000,000 litres of A

$\qquad\qquad$ containing 500,000 litres of d
$\qquad\qquad\qquad\qquad$ 250,000 litres of e
$\qquad\qquad\qquad\qquad$ 250,000 litres of f

giving a profit of 250,000p. The shadow prices are 1·75, 0·25, 1, 0, 0·5, 0 and 0 and the reduced costs of the non-basic x, y, z's are 0·5, 1, 4·5 and 1.

5. We consider all combinations of the required widths which do not exceed 205 cm wide and whose scrap width is less than 55 cm

80 cm	70 cm	55 cm	Scrap width (cm)	Length cut (m)
1	1	1	0	x_1
1	0	2	15	x_2
0	2	1	10	x_3
0	1	2	25	x_4
2	0	0	45	x_5
0	0	3	40	x_6

with these combinations the production of,

$$80 \text{ cm wide strip} = x_1 + x_2 \qquad\qquad + 2x_5 \geqslant 700$$
$$70 \text{ cm wide strip} = x_1 \qquad\qquad + 2x_3 + x_4 \geqslant 1,000$$
$$55 \text{ cm wide strip} = x_1 + 2x_2 + x_3 + 2x_4 + 3x_6 \geqslant 700$$

$$\text{The scrap} = 15x_2 + 10x_3 + 25x_4 + 45x_5 + 40x_6 + 80x_7 + 70x_8 + 55x_9$$

where x_7, x_8 and x_9 are the slack variables of the three constraints.

Minimizing the scrap is equivalent to minimizing the total length of roll used up. The computation is easier if the function for total length of roll used is minimized rather than the scrap and

$$\text{Length of roll used} = x_1 + x_2 + x_3 + x_4 + x_5 + x_6$$

There are two alternative solutions to the problem:

$$x_1 = 700 \text{ m} \qquad\qquad x_1 = 400 \text{ m}$$
$$x_3 = 150 \text{ m} \qquad\qquad x_3 = 300 \text{ m}$$
$$x_2, x_4, x_5, x_6 = 0 \qquad\qquad x_5 = 150 \text{ m}$$
$$x_2, x_4, x_6 = 0$$

The scrap $= 270\frac{5}{6}$ m². In the first case the shadow prices are $\frac{1}{2}$, 1 and 0 and the reduced costs are 0, $\frac{1}{2}$, 0, $\frac{1}{2}$, 2 and 1; in the second case the shadow prices are $\frac{1}{2}$, $\frac{1}{2}$ and 0 and the reduced costs of x_2, x_4 and x_6 are $\frac{1}{2}$, $\frac{1}{2}$ and 0.

6. The following conditions can be inferred:

(a) No new napkin is bought unless it is used immediately.

(b) No napkins will be sent for fast laundry service if they are not to be used for 4 days.

(c) All dirty napkins are sent to the laundry at the end of the day when they are used, i.e. there is no stock of dirty napkins.

(d) Napkins used on the last day of the week are not available for the final stock.

The problem can be set up in transportation form. The day's requirements, the final store, and a spare column are the destinations; the number of used napkins on each day, the initial store, and the number bought are the origins.

The cells in the table indicate the amount sent to the laundry on the ith day for use on the jth day. It is therefore obvious that:

(i) if $i + 2$ is greater than j, the cell represents an "impossible route",

(ii) if $i + 2$ or $i + 3$ is equal to j, the napkins are sent for fast laundry service,

(iii) if $i + 3$ is less than j, the napkins are sent for slow laundry service.

In order to ensure that sufficient napkins are available for purchase, a very high number (200) is given to the capacity of this origin, the spare column (which has zero costs) requires the same number (200).

The numerical solution is below. The costs are in units of 5p.

Destination		Day 1	Day 2	Day 3	Day 4	Day 5	Day 6	Day 7	Final store	Spare	Total
Origin		0	0	0	0	−1	−1	−1	−1	−3	
Initial store	0	25 / 0	10 / 0	0	15 / 0	0	0	0	0	0	50
Day 1	2			2	10 / 2	15 / 1	1	1	1	0	25
Day 2	2				5 / 2	2	20 / 1	1	1	0	25
Day 3	2					2	2	25 / 1	5 / 1	0	30
Day 4	2						2	2	30 / 1	0	30
Day 5	3							2	2	15 / 0	15
Day 6	3								15 / 2	5 / 0	20
Day 7	3									25 / 0	25
Bought	3	3	15 / 3	30 / 3	3	3	3	3	3	155 / 0	200
Total		25	25	30	30	15	20	25	50	200	420

The solution, which is not unique, indicates that 15 napkins are bought on the second day and 30 on the third day, the remainder being laundered as follows:

Day	Slow	Fast	Bought
1	15	10	—
2	20	5	15
3	30	—	30
4	30	—	—
5	—	—	—
6	—	15*	—
7	—	—	—

Cost = 290 × 5p.

7. Artificial road and rail depots are introduced at the collieries and washeries. It is assumed that it is necessary to send from each colliery to one of its depots and to receive at each washery from its depots. If we introduce the following symbols:

$$c_{ij} = \text{road costs},$$
$$d_{ij} = \text{rail costs},$$
$$b_i = \text{colliery capacity},$$
$$b_{i1} = \text{colliery road capacity},$$
$$a_{1j} = \text{washery road capacity},$$
$$a_j = \text{washery requirement},$$
$$b_{i2} = \text{colliery rail capacity},$$
$$a_{2j} = \text{washery rail capacity},$$

---

* May be sent to fast service on either 5th or 6th days.

The problem can be written

	Washery 1	Washery 2	Road depots				Rail depots				Total
			Col A	Col B	Wash 1	Wash 2	Col A	Col B	Wash 1	Wash 2	
Colliery A			0				0				b_1
Colliery B				0				0			b_2
Road depot — Col A			0		c_{11}	c_{12}					b_{11}
Road depot — Col B				0	c_{21}	c_{22}					b_{21}
Road depot — Wash 1	0				0						a_{11}
Road depot — Wash 2		0				0					a_{12}
Rail depot — Col A							0		d_{11}	d_{12}	b_{12}
Rail depot — Col B								0	d_{21}	d_{22}	b_{22}
Rail depot — Wash 1	0								0		a_{21}
Rail depot — Wash 2		0								0	a_{22}
Total	a_1	a_2	b_{11}	b_{21}	a_{11}	a_{12}	b_{12}	b_{22}	a_{21}	a_{22}	

The cells without a cost are impossible routes.

For computation the table (including the answer) is:

		Washery 1	Washery 2	Road depots				Rail depots				Total
				Col A	Col B	Wash 1	Wash 2	Col A	Col B	Wash 1	Wash 2	
		7	8	0	2	5	8	0	2	7	8	
Colliery A	0			1,100 0				1,300 0				2,400
Colliery B	−2				600 0				900 0			1,500
Road depot — Col A	−2			0		0·4	1,100 0·6					1,100
Road depot — Col B	−2				100 0	600 0·3	0·7					700
Road depot — Wash 1	−7	600 0				0						600
Road depot — Wash 2	−8		1,100 0				900 0					2,000
Rail depot — Col A	0							700 0		300 0·7	1,000 0·8	2,000
Rail depot — Col B	−2								100 0	0·8	900 0·6	1,000
Rail depot — Wash 1	−7	300 0								200 0		500
Rail depot — Wash 2	−8		1,900 0								100 0	2,000
Total		900	3,000	1,100	700	600	2,000	2,000	1,000	500	2,000	

Hence the answer may be written:

Road

	Wash 1	Wash 2
Col A	0·4	1,100 0·6
Col B	600 0·3	0·7

Rail

	Wash 1	Wash 2
Col A	300 0·7	1,000 0·8
Col B	0·8	900 0·6

Total received: Wash 1—900; Wash 2—3,000.

Cost = £2,390.

8. Question 3. The shadow prices represent the increase in profits from unit increases in the tonnages of each coal available.

Question 4. For the first four constraints the shadow prices do not have a very clear cut meaning. They represent the gain in profit from allowing the specifications to be broken by 1 litre in the total quantities made, which are not determined *a priori*. Thus the shadow price on the first constraint is 1·75. This tells us that if we make 1,000,000 litres of A using only 499,999 gallons of crude d our profit will be increased by 1·75p.

For other constraints the shadow prices represent the gain in profit from unit increases in capacity.

Question 5. The shadow prices represent the reduction in length of roll used if an order is cut by 1 metre.

Question 4. Suppose the capacities were $500 + D$, $500 + E$ and $300 + F$. The optimum policy for small D, E and F would be

$$x_1 = 500 + D$$
$$x_2 = 250 + \tfrac{1}{2}D$$
$$x_3 = 250 + \tfrac{1}{2}D$$
$$S_6 = 250 - \tfrac{1}{2}D + E$$
$$S_7 = \quad 50 + F$$

S_6 and S_7 being the slacks on the 6th and 7th constraints. Thus feasibility (and the optimum policy) remain as long as $F \geqslant -50$ and both $D \geqslant -500$ and $D - E \geqslant 500$.

Let the price of crude d be denoted by $9·5 + p$. Following the usual procedure for parametic programming we find that the reduced costs in the final tableau are unchanged except for that of S_5, the slack in the 5th constraint, whose reduced cost is $0·5 - p$. Profit is $250,000 - 50,000p$. Thus until $p = 5$ there is no change in policy. When $p = 5+$, S_5 enters the basis to replace x_1. It will be found that the new optimal solution is: make nothing. Thus if the price of crude d increases beyond 10 we are best off out of business.

9. One can simply replace x, the variable not constrained to be non-negative, by $x_1 - x_2$ both x_1 and x_2 being $\geqslant 0$. See page 93 for example use of this device.

10. It is clear that it is profitable to meet all demand and since total profit is £ $(7 \times$ total demand $-$ transport costs $-$ new fixed costs) we want to minimize transport costs. Also there is no point in expanding capacity at A' and B' unless present capacity is fully used. One assumption is needed, namely that transport costs from any new plant at C would be 3 to A, 3 to B and 0 to C.

Let the flow from A' to A be x_{AA} and so on. Let extra plant installed at A', B' and C be $100u$, $100v$ and $100w$ units respectively where u, v and w are integers. Then

Transport costs $= 2x_{AB} + 3x_{AC} + 2x_{BA} + 3x_{BC}$ — fixed costs
$$+ 3x_{CA} + 3x_{CB} - 100u - 100v - 300w$$

The availability constraints are:

$$x_{AA} + x_{AB} + x_{AC} \leqslant 1{,}000 + 100u$$
$$x_{BA} + x_{BB} + x_{BC} \leqslant 2{,}000 + 100v$$
$$x_{CA} + x_{CB} + x_{CC} \leqslant 100w$$

The requirement constraints are

$$x_{AA} + x_{BA} + x_{CA} \geqslant 550$$
$$x_{AB} + x_{BB} + x_{CB} \geqslant 1{,}650$$
$$x_{AC} + x_{BC} + x_{CC} \geqslant 1{,}100$$

11. No. The optimal solution will include only two y's (in the notation of page 44) in the basis. This is because there can be no advantage in including more. A graph should make the point clear enough.

12. Introduce t, u, v and w as slack variables.

$x + y + z \geqslant 1$ can be written as $-x - y - z + t = -1$;
$3x - 4y + z \leqslant 0$ as $3x - 4y + z + u = 0$ and
$6x + 2y - 7z = 1$ as $6x + 2y - 7z + v = 1$ *and*
$-6x - 2y + 7z + w = 1$.

Following the rules for constructing the dual we therefore have, as the dual problem

max $a - c - d$ for non-negative a, b, c, d, e, f, g, subject to

$$a - 3b - 6c + 6d + e = 6$$
$$a + 4b - 2c + 2d + f = 3$$
$$a - b + 7c - 7d + g = 7$$

Chapter 3

1. If $f_i(W) =$ the maximum value of a cargo containing packages of kinds $1, 2, \ldots, i$, where W, the weight of a cargo, varies from 0 to 100, then

$$f_1(W) = 38 \left[\frac{W}{29} \right]$$

$$f_2(W) = \max_{0 \leqslant n \leqslant \left[\frac{W}{22} \right]} (27n + f_1(W - 22n))$$

$$f_3(W) = \max_{0 \leqslant n \leqslant \left[\frac{W}{16} \right]} (19n + f_2(W - 16n))$$

In $f_3(W)$, for example, n is the number of packages of the third kind included in the cargo and $(W - 16n)$ is the maximum weight left to be filled with the first and second kinds.

The problem has $f_3(100)$ for its solution, which is computed by first finding f_1 and f_2 for $0 \leqslant w \leqslant 100$.

f_1 is quite simply given by

$$f_1(W) = \begin{matrix} 0, & 0 \leqslant W < 29 \\ 38, & 29 \leqslant W < 58 \\ 76, & 58 \leqslant W < 87 \\ 114, & 87 \leqslant W \leqslant 100 \end{matrix}$$

f_2 will differ from f_1 only where putting $n = 0$ in the expression $27n + f_1(W - 22n)$ does not give the maximum value. This occurs when

$$\begin{matrix} 22 \leqslant W < 29 & (n = 1, f_2 = 27) \\ 44 \leqslant W < 51 & (n = 2, f_2 = 54) \\ 51 \leqslant W < 58 & (n = 1, f_2 = 65) \\ 66 \leqslant W < 73 & (n = 3, f_2 = 81) \\ 73 \leqslant W < 80 & (n = 2, f_2 = 92) \\ 80 \leqslant W < 87 & (n = 1, f_2 = 103) \\ 95 \leqslant W < 100 & (n = 3, f_2 = 119) \end{matrix}$$

The solution for any value of $W \leqslant 100$ and any number of packages $\leqslant 3$ is given in the following table.

	n_1	f_1	n_2	f_2	n_3	f_3
$0 \leqslant W < 16$	0	0	0	0	0	0
$16 \leqslant W < 22$	0	0	0	0	1	19
$22 \leqslant W < 29$	0	0	1	27	0	27
$29 \leqslant W < 38$	1	38	0	38	0	38
$38 \leqslant W < 44$	0	0	1	27	1	46
$44 \leqslant W < 45$	0	0	2	54	0	54
$45 \leqslant W < 51$	1	38	0	38	1	57
$51 \leqslant W < 58$	1	38	1	65	0	65
$58 \leqslant W < 66$	2	76	0	76	0	76
$66 \leqslant W < 67$	0	0	3	81	0	81
$67 \leqslant W < 73$	1	38	1	65	1	84
$73 \leqslant W < 74$	1	38	2	92	0	92
$74 \leqslant W < 80$	2	76	0	76	1	95
$80 \leqslant W < 87$	2	76	1	103	0	103
$87 \leqslant W < 95$	3	114	0	114	0	114
$95 \leqslant W < 96$	1	38	3	119	0	119
$96 \leqslant W < 99$	2	76	1	103	1	122
$99 \leqslant W < 100$	1	38	1	65	3	122

The solution, $f_3(100) = 122$, results from either of two policies:

$$(2 \times 29) + (1 \times 22) + (1 \times 16) = 96 \text{ tonnes,}$$
$$(2 \times 38) + (1 \times 29) + (1 \times 19) = \pounds 122,$$

or

$$(1 \times 29) + (1 \times 22) + (3 \times 16) = 99 \text{ tonnes,}$$
$$(1 \times 38) + (1 \times 29) + (3 \times 19) = \pounds 122.$$

2. Define

$H_i =$ maximum number of weighings required to determine the odd sack among i sacks, using an optimal policy, with the direction of bias known.

Then if we put s sacks on each side of the balance, having chosen s optimally, we have

$$H_i = \min_s [\max (H_{i-2s}, H_s)], + 1$$

since we shall know in which of the three groups, $i - 2s$, s, and s, the odd sack lies. The solution is given by $s = [i/3] = $ nearest integer to $i/3$: since H_{i-2s} increases as H_s decreases with s, and vice versa, the minimum of $[\max (H_{i-2s}, H_s)]$ occurs when H_{i-2s} and H_s are as nearly equal as possible.

We can thus obtain the value of H_i for any value of i by using the above equation and the following weighing policy for m, a multiple of 3.

(1) If $H_i = H_m = 1 + H_{m/3}$, put $m/3$ aside and weigh $m/3$ against $m/3$.
(2) If $H_i = H_{m+1} = 1 + H_{m/3+1}$, put $m/3 + 1$ aside and weigh $m/3$ against $m/3$.
(3) If $H_i = H_{m+2} = 1 + H_{m/3+1}$, put $m/3$ aside and weigh $m/3 + 1$ against $m/3 + 1$.

Thus

$$H_{32} = 1 + \max (H_{10}, H_{11}) = 2 + \max (H_3, H_4) = 3 + \max (H_2, H_1) = 4$$

where $s = [\frac{32}{3}] = 11$, $[\frac{11}{3}] = 4$, $[\frac{4}{3}] = 1$.

To determine the maximum number of sacks that can be handled by a given number of weighings, define $n_r = $ maximum number of sacks from which the odd sack can be separated in r weighings.

Now n_r must be divisible by 3 (i.e. $s = n_r/3$) because, if this is not the case, H_{n_r-2s} and H_s will not be equal, and the same minimum of $[\max (H_{n_r-2s}, H_s)]$ will be achieved if the smaller of the two quantities is increased to equal the larger, such that $n_r - 2s = s$, and $s = n_r/3$. Since

$$s = n_r/3$$
$$\therefore \qquad s = n_{r-1}$$
$$\therefore \qquad 3n_{r-1} = n_r$$
$$\therefore \qquad n_r = 3^r$$

An alternative proof is as follows: From (1) above, putting $H_m = H_{3r}$,

$$H_{3r} = 1 + H_{3r-1} = 2 + H_{3r-2} = \ldots = r - 1 + H_3 = r$$

From (2),

$$H_{3r+1} = 1 + H_{3r-1+1}$$
$$= 2 + H_{3r-2+1} = \ldots = r - 1 + H_{3+1} = r + H_2 = r + 1$$

From (3),

$$H_{3r+2} = 1 + H_{3r-1+1}$$
$$= 2 + H_{3r-2+1} = \ldots = r - 1 + H_{3+1} = r + H_2 = r + 1$$

$$\therefore \qquad H_i = r$$

where $3^r \geqslant i > 3^{r-1}$. And in particular, for $r = 5$, $n_r = 243$.

3.

$$f_i(a, b) = \max \begin{pmatrix} f_{i-1}(a-1, b) + X_{ai} \\ f_{i-1}(a, b-1) + X_{bi} \\ f_{i-1}(a, b) + X_{hi} \end{pmatrix}$$

$$f_0(a, b) = 0$$
$$f_1(0, 0) = 200$$
$$f_1(1, 0) = \max \begin{pmatrix} f_0(0, 0) + X_{a1} \\ f_0(1, 0) + X_{h1} \end{pmatrix} = \begin{matrix} 250 \\ 200 \end{matrix}$$

9

Similarly, $f_1(0, 1) = 260$; $f_1(1, 1) = 260$; $f_1(0, 2) = 260$; $f_1(1, 2) = 260$.

$$f_2(0, 0) = f_1(0, 0) + X_{h2} = 420$$

$$f_2(1, 0) = \max \begin{pmatrix} f_1(0, 0) + X_{a2} \\ f_1(1, 0) + X_{h2} \end{pmatrix} \begin{matrix} = 460 \\ = 470 \end{matrix}$$

Similarly $f_2(0, 1) = 490$

$$f_2(1, 1) = \max \begin{pmatrix} f_1(0, 1) + X_{a2} \\ f_1(1, 0) + X_{b2} \\ f_1(1, 1) + X_{h2} \end{pmatrix} \begin{matrix} = 520 \\ = 540 \\ = 480 \end{matrix}$$

Similarly $f_2(0, 2) = 550$; $f_2(1, 2) = 550$.
    Proceeding in this manner we find

$$f_3(1, 1) = f_2(0, 1) + X_{a3} = f_2(1, 0) + X_{b3} = 730,$$

and

$$f_4(1, 2) = f_3(1, 1) + X_{b4} = 1060,$$

giving the following solutions:

	Face			
	1	2	3	4
Solution (1)	H	B	A	B
Solution (2)	A	H	B	B

N.B. In this problem there are 39 possible combinations of outputs and a total of 24 equations. If there were two machines of type A and five faces there would be 45 equations and 186 possible output combinations. Thus the dynamic programming approach becomes rapidly more efficient as the problem increases in size.

4. Let $f_i(x) =$ expected total cost for an i-interval period, starting with an initial level x, and using an optimal ordering policy. Then

$$f_1(x) = \min_{y \geqslant x} [k(y - x) + \sum_{y+1}^{\infty} c(s - y)p(s)]$$

and we have

$$f_i(x) = \min_{y \geqslant x} [k(y - x) + \sum_{y+1}^{\infty} c(s - y)p(s) + f_{i-1}(0) \sum_{y+1}^{\infty} p(s) + \sum_0^y f_{i-1}(y - s)p(s)]$$

by enumerating the cases corresponding to an excess of demand over supply and being able to fulfil the demand. Similar equations can be derived for more complicated models.

5. Suppose we are just about to buy our first lorry. We propose to follow an optimal policy and let us suppose the expected total future discounted cost of doing so is C. If we replace this first lorry after time T and there after use an optimal policy the expected total future discounted cost will be

$$P + \int_0^T Q\, e^{2at} 2a\, e^{-at}\, dt + e^{-aT} C$$

(the purchase price)   (the discounted running costs)   (costs from the first replacement onwards)

It follows that

$$C = E \min_{T} \left[P + \int_0^T 2aQ \, e^{at} \, dt + e^{-aT} C \right]$$

Differentiation shows us that the optimal value of T is given by

$$C = E[2aQ \, e^{aT} - e^{-a\hat{T}} C] = 2aEQ \, e^{a\hat{T}} - e^{-aT} C$$

so that the optimal value of T is

$$\hat{T} = \frac{1}{2a} \log \left[\frac{C}{2Q} \right]$$

Substituting this in the equation defining C gives

$$C = E[P + 2Q \, e^{a\hat{T}} - 2Q + e^{-a\hat{T}} C]$$

$$C = E \left[P + 2Q \sqrt{\frac{C}{2Q}} - 2Q + e \sqrt{\frac{2Q}{C}} C \right]$$

$$C - 2E\sqrt{2Q}\sqrt{C} - (P - 2EQ) = 0$$

$$\sqrt{C} = E\sqrt{2Q} \pm \sqrt{(E\sqrt{2Q})^2 + P - 2EQ}$$

$$C = 2(E\sqrt{2Q})^2 + P - 2EQ \pm 2E\sqrt{2Q}\sqrt{(E\sqrt{2Q})^2 + P - 2EQ}$$

It is clear that the $+$ sign is the relevant one. If $Q = 2$ with probability $\frac{1}{2}$ and 8 otherwise, then $E\sqrt{2Q} = \frac{1}{2}(2 + 4) = 3$ and $EQ = 5$. Substitution gives $C = 100$.

Assuming all lorries equal amounts to using an average Q throughout we then have

$$C = \min_{T} \left[P + \int_0^T 2a \, EQ \, e^{at} \, dt + e^{-aT} C \right]$$

and we find that $C = 60 + 20\sqrt{5} \doteqdot 105$.

6. Consider the general l.p. problem in this form:
   Maximize

$$c_1 x_1 + c_2 x_2 + \ldots + c_n x_n$$

for non-negative

$$x_1, x_2, \ldots, x_n$$

subject to the m constraints

$$a_{11} x_1 + a_{12} x_2 + \ldots + a_{1n} x_n \leqslant b_1 \text{ up to}$$
$$a_{m1} x_1 + a_{m2} x_2 + \ldots + a_{mn} x_n \leqslant b_m$$

Let

$$P_r(d_1, d_2, \ldots, d_m)$$

be the maximum value of

$$c_1 x_1 + c_2 x_2 + \ldots c_r x_r$$

for non-negative

$$x_1, x_2, \ldots, x_r$$

subject to the m constraints

$$a_{11}x_1 + a_{12}x_2 + \ldots + a_{1r}x_r \leqslant d_1 \text{ up to}$$
$$a_{m1}x_1 + a_{m2}x_2 + \ldots + a_{mr}x_r \leqslant d_m$$

Then

$$P_r(d_1, d_2, \ldots, d_m)$$
$$= \max_{x_r \geqslant 0} [P_{r-1}(d_1 - a_{1r}x_r, d_2 - a_{2r}x_r, \ldots, d_m - a_{mr}x_r) + c_r x_r]$$

This recurrence relation gives the solution which is

$$P_n(b_1, b_2, \ldots, b_m)$$

(This treatment is not very rigorous as it pays no attention to the possibility of inconsistency in some of the sub-problems, but the computational steps should be clear.)

In the example given

$$P_1(d_1, d_2) = \max 6x \quad \text{for} \quad x \geqslant 0, 2x \leqslant d_1, x \leqslant d_2$$
$$= \min [3d_1, 6d_2]$$

if $d_1, d_2 \geqslant 0$, otherwise equations are inconsistent

$$P_2(d_1, d_2) = \max_{y \geqslant 0} [\min (3d_1 - 9y, 6d_2 - 42y) + 2y]$$

$$= \max \left[\min (3d_1, 6d_2), 2 \min \left(\frac{d_1}{3}, \frac{1}{7} d_2 \right) \right]$$

$$P_3(d_1, d_2) = \max_{z \geqslant 0} \left[\max \left(\min (3d_1 - 3z, 6d_2 - 12z), \right. \right.$$
$$\left. \left. 2 \min \left(\frac{d_1 - z}{3}, \frac{d_2 - 2z}{7} \right) \right) + 3z \right]$$

for $z \geqslant 0$, $z \leqslant d_1$, $z \leqslant d_2$.

It will be found that

$$P_3(10, 18) = \max [30, 27] = 30$$

(because either $z = 0$ or its highest allowable value).

Check: In the standard notation the problem is maximize U for non-negative x, y, z, v, w subject to

$$U - 6x - 2y - 3z = 0$$
$$2x + 3y + z + v = 10$$
$$x + 7y + 2z + w = 18$$

v and w being slack variables.

The final tableau is

$$U + 7y + 3v = 30$$
$$x + \tfrac{3}{2}y + \tfrac{1}{2}z + \tfrac{1}{2}v = 5$$
$$\tfrac{11}{2}y + \tfrac{3}{2}z - \tfrac{1}{2}v + w = 13$$

7. The general functional equation is

$$f_i(x) = \max_{0 \leqslant y \leqslant x} [\sqrt{y} + f_{i-1}(a(x-y))]$$

and

$$f_0(x) = \sqrt{x}$$

We thus have

$$f_1(x) = \max_{0 \leqslant y \leqslant x} [\sqrt{y} + \sqrt{a(x-y)}]$$

and we choose

$$y_1 = \frac{x}{1+a}$$

to give

$$f_1(x) = \sqrt{1 + a}\sqrt{x}$$

Similarly

$$f_2(x) = \max_{0 \leqslant y \leqslant x} [\sqrt{y} + \sqrt{1 + a}\sqrt{a(x-y)}]$$

and we choose

$$y_2 = \frac{x}{1 + a + a^2}$$

to give

$$f_2(x) = \sqrt{1 + a + a^2}\sqrt{x}$$

We find that

$$f_N(x) = \sqrt{1 + a + a^2 + \ldots + a^N}\sqrt{x}$$

However this implies

$$y_N = \frac{x}{1 + a + a^2 + \ldots + a^N}$$

and, for large N, this is negligibly small. We find that the optimum policy in planning over many years is to sell little or no wheat but to keep ploughing it all back. When infinity comes one has a bumper crop, but that may be too late to pay the bills. This policy is not very sensible and points to two deficiencies in the model. In the first place we almost certainly should discount and this we go on to do. We note also that the model does not assume diminishing returns from increased sowing of seed, clearly a false assumption if only because land is limited.

If we discount the revised equation is

$$f_i(x) = \max_{0 \leqslant y \leqslant x} [\sqrt{y} + \alpha f_{i-1}(a(x-y))]$$

and we find that

$$y_1 = \frac{x}{1 + a\alpha^2} \quad \text{and} \quad y_n = \frac{x}{1 + a\alpha^2 + a^2\alpha^4 + \ldots + a^N\alpha^{2N}}$$

Thus if $\alpha^2 a < 1$ we adopt what appears to be a more sensible policy of selling a proportion $1 + a\alpha^2$ of the crop each year in planning for a long period ahead. However it is by no means certain that $\alpha^2 a < 1$ for reasonable values of a and α. In this case we still plough back the lot and the second questionable assumption would need modifying.

If A is a random variable the farmer must decide his attitude to risk. If he is willing to work on expected values we replace any function of a by its expected value and the above formulae are modified accordingly. (Note that we do not simply replace a by $Ea = Aq$ everywhere it occurs but rather, for example, $\sqrt{a}$ by $E\sqrt{a} = q\sqrt{A}$). However the farmer might prefer to take a more conservative attitude to risk and deliberately sell more than the calculations based on expected values would suggest.

Chapter 4

1. For an individual rational behaviour is that which maximizes his personal utility: in other words, behaviour that is consistent with the adopted objectives.

An organization usually has stated objectives. These objectives may not be entirely compatible with the personal objectives of the members of the organization, and some of these members will be in a position to influence the actions of the organization. A company usually has several stated objectives and these may be incompatible.

2. Using Bayes' theorem: for some given θ_0,

$$pr(\theta = \theta_0/\text{zero demand is observed})$$

$$= Kpr(\text{zero demand is observed}/\theta = \theta_0)pr(\theta = \theta_0)$$

(where K is a constant), the posterior distribution of θ is

$$pr\left(\frac{\theta = \theta_0}{x}\right) = K e^{-\theta_0} \lambda e^{-\lambda\theta_0}$$

For this to be a distribution, we see that

$$K = \frac{\lambda + 1}{\lambda}.$$

For $\theta = \theta_0$, the utility of d_1 is

$$c_1\theta^{k_1}pr\left(\frac{\theta = \theta_0}{x}\right)$$

and similarly, the utility of d_2 is

$$c_2\theta^{k_2}pr\left(\frac{\theta = \theta_0}{x}\right).$$

Over all possible values of θ, the utility of d_1

$$= \int_0^\infty c_1 \theta^{k_1} (\lambda + 1) \, e^{-(\lambda+1)\theta} \, d\theta$$

with a similar expression for d_2.
  The transformation

$$u = (\lambda + 1)\theta$$

enables us to identify this integral with the standard definition of a gamma function.
Thus the utility of d_1

$$= c_1 (\lambda + 1)^{-k_1} \Gamma(k_1 + 1)$$

and the utility of d_2

$$= c_2 (\lambda + 1)^{-k_2} \Gamma(k_2 + 1)$$

To see when d_1 is to be preferred to d_2 we calculate the ratio:

$$\frac{\text{utility } d_1}{\text{utility } d_2} = \frac{c_1}{c_2} (\lambda + 1)^{k_2 - k_1} \frac{\Gamma(k_1 + 1)}{\Gamma(k_2 + 1)}$$

which, for the values given, reduces to $1/(\lambda + 1)$ which is always less than one (λ is necessarily positive).

3. For the shipper, utility after shipment is

without insurance, $U_1 = \tfrac{9}{10} \log \{100 + 10\} + \tfrac{1}{10} \log \{100\}$

with insurance, $U_2 = \log \{100 + 10 - a\}$

where a is the premium and all figures are thousands of pounds.
  For insurance to be worthwhile for the shipper,

$$U_2 > U_1$$

and this leads to $a < 1 \cdot 04$.
  For the insurer, utility after shipment is

if insurance is not effected, $V_1 = \log \{50,000\}$

and

if insurance is effected, $V_2 = \tfrac{9}{10} \log \{S + a\} + \tfrac{1}{10} \log \{S + a - 10\}$

where $S = 50,000$.
  For insuring to be worthwhile,

$$V_2 > V_1$$

which implies that $a > 1$.
  A premium lying between £1,000 and £1,040, say £1,020, would therefore be fair in that both insurer and insured would have increased their utilities with such a premium.

5. (a) The gain matrix for A is:

B

Guesses

		1	3	6	Row Minima
	1	−1	1	1	−1
A Draws	3	3	−3	3	−3
	6	6	6	−6	−6
Col. Maxima		6	6	3	

There is no saddle point or dominance. The game is solved in the usual way and it is found to have a value of $+\frac{2}{3}$ to A. The answers are

(i) The game is unfair to B,
(ii) $A(6, 2, 1)$; $B(3, 7, 8)$,
(iii) $\frac{2}{3}$ units.

(b) The gain matrix for A is now:

B

Guesses

		1	3	6
	1	−2	4	7
A Draws	3	4	−6	9
	6	7	9	−12

Again there is no saddle point or dominance and we proceed in the usual way to find that

(i) The game is unfair to B. The value to A is $\frac{7}{3}$.
(ii) $A(15, 11, 10)$ $B(15, 11, 10)$.

(c) The gain matrix for A is now:

B

		1	3	6
	1	$-n$	4	7
A	3	4	$-3n$	9
	6	7	9	$-6n$

We find that for the game to be fair we must have $n = 1 + \sqrt{15}$.

6. The gain matrix for A is:

		B			
		11	12	21	22
	11	0	2	−3	0
A	12	−2	0	0	3
	21	3	0	0	−4
	22	0	−3	4	0

where ij means hold i and guess j.

It will be found that any of the following four solutions holds, each with a value 0:

$A(0, 3, 2, 0)$, $B(0, 3, 2, 0)$
$A(0, 4, 3, 0)$, $B(0, 3, 2, 0)$
$A(0, 3, 2, 0)$, $B(0, 4, 3, 0)$
$A(0, 4, 3, 0)$, $B(0, 4, 3, 0)$

7. Represent nature's strategy by $N(x_1, x_2, x_3, x_4, x_5)$; here the value of each x indicates the proportion of the strata driven through if nature does its worst consistent with the restrictions given above. In this problem, since all the gains are negative the value of the game will be negative. Hence we do not need to put

$$V = V_1 - V_2.$$

The restrictions on the strata may be written:

$x_1 \leqslant 0\cdot1$
$x_2 \leqslant 0\cdot2$
$x_3 \leqslant 0\cdot2$
$x_4 \leqslant 0\cdot6$

The additional restriction is:

$$x_1 + x_2 + x_3 + x_4 + x_5 = 1$$

Solving the game in the usual way we find the strategy for the colliery is

$M(0, \frac{5}{9}, \frac{4}{9}, 0)$.

The value of the game is 36·8/9.

The cost of powder per metre should not exceed 36·8/9 units. This upper limit can be assured by using powders 2 and 3 only and for every 9 units of cost used to purchase powder, 5 units should be used to buy powder 2, and 4 units should be used to buy powder 3.

If any other powder is bought the maximum possible cost will be greater. If only powder 2 is bought the cost may increase due to relatively less of type B strata being found and more of types C, D and E. If only powder 3 is bought the cost will again be liable to increase if, by mischance, we meet more of types E or A strata. Of course, if nature is in the event very favourable towards us we shall have spent more than we need have done: this is in the nature of the theory of games approach.

The shadow prices on the constraints are 0, 0, $\frac{5}{9}$ and $\frac{3}{9}$ and they represent the change in the value of the game for unit change in the restrictions.

For example, if the restriction on strata D were that it could not be more than 70% of the total (instead of 60%) the value of the game would become (36·8/9 + 0·3/9) since the restriction would have been relaxed by $\frac{1}{10}$ of a unit.

8. We can draw up a decision tree for this problem but some preliminary thought can save a good deal of work. Specifically we note the following:
  (i) selling by auction gets an expected 110 units and is preferable to private sale if there is time;
  (ii) there is no point in putting the land into the agent's hands at 110 or 120 units, it might as well be solved by auction now;
  (iii) there is no point in auctioning the land until the end of the fourth month as one might as well take the chance of getting 130 or 140 units for it now.

There are thus only four alternative strategies: put up for sale through the agent at 140 or 130 and in each case either sell by auction after month 4 or sell privately after month 6. These strategies are easily costed out. Thus if we put the land up for sale at 140 for the full 6 months our expected return is $130 \times 0.7 + 100 \times 0.3$. We find that this is in fact the best policy.

9. Assume profits and utilities are the same thing.

Without a survey the expected profit is 5·6; with the first survey 6·6; and with the second 7·1 (because with the first survey, for example, the loss of 10 if no oil is there is avoided). Thus the first survey is worth 1 unit and the second 1·5 units. 1·5 units is the value of perfect information.

The assumption about utilities might not be justified. The loss of 10 units might bankrupt a small company.

Chapter 5

---

1. The full workings are summarized in these tables. The ticked links give the shortest route tree.

Minty's Method

(1) Stage no.	(2) Link deleted at end of stage no.	(3) Additional links considered	(4) Sum of label and length	(5) Link ticked	(6) Node labelled	(7) Value of node
1	3 1 2	AB AC AD	0 + 15 = 15 0 + 10 = 10 0 + 12 = 12	AC	C	10
2	3 4 5	CB CE CF	10 + 6 = 16 10 + 9 = 19 10 + 10 = 20	AD	D	12
3	5 8	DF DI	12 + 12 = 24 12 + 13 = 25	AB	B	15
4	4 7	BE BG	15 + 7 = 22 15 + 11 = 26	CE	E	19
5	7 6 5	EG EH EF	19 + 5 = 24 19 + 4 = 23 19 + 6 = 25	CF	F	20
6	6 8	FH FI	20 + 5 = 25 20 + 6 = 26	EH	H	23
7	8	HJ HI	23 + 8 = 31 23 + 4 = 27	EG	G	24
8		GJ	24 + 10 = 34	DI	I	25
9		IJ	25 + 12 = 37	HJ	J	31

Terminal node (J) labelled—end.

D'Esopo's Method

(1) Control register no.	(2) Index node	(3) Index node label	(4) Connected nodes	(5) Index no. of connected node	(6) Sum of index node label plus length	(7) Labels at end of cycle	(8) Ticked links at end of cycle
1	A	0	B C D	2 3 4	$0 + 15 = 15*$ $0 + 10 = 10*$ $0 + 12 = 12*$	$A0$ $D12$ $B15$ $C10$	AB AC AD
2	B	15	A C E	1 3 5	$15 + 0 = 15$ $15 + 5 = 20$ $15 + 7 = 22*$	$A0$ $D12$ $B15$ $E22$ $C10$	AB BE AC AD
3	C	10	A B E F	1 2 5 6	$10 + 9 = 19$ $10 + 6 = 16$ $10 + 9 = 19\dagger$ $10 + 10 = 20*$	$A0$ $F20$ $B15$ $C10$ $D12$ $E19$	AB AC AD CE CF
4	D	12	A F I	1 6 7	$12 + 11 = 23$ $12 + 12 = 24$ $12 + 13 = 25*$	$A0$ $D12$ $I25$ $B15$ $E19$ $C10$ $F20$	AB CE AC CF AD DI
5	E	19	B C G F H	2 3 8 6 9	$19 + 5 = 24$ $19 + 7 = 26$ $19 + 5 = 24*$ $19 + 6 = 25$ $19 + 4 = 23*$	$A0$ $F20$ $B15$ $G24$ $C10$ $H23$ $D12$ $I25$ $E19$	AB DI AC EG AD EH CE CF
6	F	20	C D E H I	3 4 5 9 7	$20 + 8 = 28$ $20 + 10 = 30$ $20 + 4 = 24$ $20 + 5 = 25$ $20 + 6 = 26$	$A0$ $F20$ $B15$ $G24$ $C10$ $H23$ $D12$ $I25$ $E19$	AB DI AC EG AD EH CE CF
7	I	25	D F H J	4 6 9 10	$25 + 12 = 37$ $25 + 8 = 33$ $25 + 3 = 28$ $25 + 12 = 37*$	$A0$ $E19$ $I25$ $B15$ $F20$ $J37$ $C10$ $G24$ $D12$ $H23$	AB CF IJ AC DI AD EG CE EH
8	G	24	B E J	2 5 10	$24 + 8 = 32$ $24 + 3 = 27$ $24 + 10 = 34\ddagger$	$A0$ $E19$ $I25$ $B15$ $F20$ $J34$ $C10$ $G24$ $D12$ $H23$	AB CF GJ AC DI AD EG CE EH
9	H	23	E F I J	5 6 7 10	$23 + 6 = 29$ $23 + 8 = 31$ $23 + 4 = 27$ $23 + 8 = 31\ddagger$	$A0$ $F20$ $B15$ $G24$ $C10$ $H23$ $D12$ $I25$ $E19$ $J31$	AB DI AC EG AD EH CE HJ CF
10	J	31	G H I	8 9 7	$31 + 12 = 43$ $31 + 10 = 41$ $31 + 10 = 41$	As above	
11	End						

* New labels.   † Re-label E, tick CE and delete tick on BE.   ‡ Re-label J.

2. The shortest route uses links AC, CE, EH and HJ. We replace the lengths of each of these by ∞ in turn and find the four new shortest route matrices. The one of these which has the shortest route from A to J gives us the answer, which is $ACFHJ$ of length 34. (It would actually be quicker to use a labelling method in this case but the matrix method is suggested for the sake of practice.)

3. One can calculate the probability of completion for every possible completion time for each network. These are:

For the first network

Completion time	Probability	Penalty
6	6·25%	
7	6·25%	
8	18·75%	
9	18·75%	
10	18·75%	£k
11	18·75%	£$4k$
12	12·50%	£$9k$
	100·00%	

Exp. Penalty £$0·206k$

Prob. of completion $\leqslant 9$ is 50%.

For the second network

Completion time	Probability	Penalty
6	6·25%	
7	12·50%	
9	18·75%	
10	37·50%	£k
11	25·00%	£$4k$
	100·00%	

Exp. Penalty £$0·137k$

Prob. of completion $\leqslant 9$ is 37·5%.

If expected penalty cost is the only consideration then we choose the second network. If there are additional costs—such as wages—then the probability of completion in $\leqslant 9$ enters the problem.

4. Let x_i be the time at which event i is reached. The problem is: minimize x_{20} for non-negative $x_1, x_2, \ldots, x_{20}$ subject to

$$x_3 - x_1 \geqslant 13$$
$$x_3 - x_2 \geqslant 23 \text{ etc.}$$

(another constraint is for example, $x_{13} - x_8 \geqslant 19$).

The values of the slacks in the final tableau are the slacks on the corresponding events. The shadow prices are zero for non-negative slacks. Thus constraints which have non-zero shadow prices lie on the critical path and these shadow prices will all be 1 as they represent the reduction in project time per unit of reduction, at the margin, in the time of an activity on the critical path.

5. For this simple case we can enumerate the six possible ways of scheduling the single bull-dozers use. Thus the ordering ABC would mean the new earliest time for event 3 would be 36 and for event 5 it would be 51. The slack on 3 is 0 and on 5 it is 14. This means the shortest time to complete the project would become

$$\max (113 + 36 - 0, 113 + 51 - 14) = 149$$

Evaluating other possible orderings in a similar way we find that ABC or BAC is best.

The total floats on A, B and C are 10, 0 and 14. Thus working by total float would suggest an ordering BAC which is consistent with the result above.

If two bull-dozers are available we need to consider which two activities to put them on first. If we choose A and B event 3 can be started at 23 and event 5 at time 28, being 13 (the time when the bull-dozer on A becomes free) plus 15 (the time taken to carry out C). Since the late time for event 5 is 29 no time at all is lost. Thus the extra bull-dozer saves any delay.

6. Using the branch and bound approach outlined in the chapter we find the best route is 134521 and is 20 long. The full working is rather lengthy but the following shows the branching route followed. (The lower bounds are given in brackets. Only those starred need actually have been calculated. The others are given to help the reader check that he understands the method, and he is advised to verify them.)

All possible routes (19)*							
Routes including 3 to 4 (20)*				Routes excluding 3 to 4 (20)*			
Inc. 2 to 1 (20)*		Exc. 2 to 1 (29)		Inc. 2 to 4 (20)		Exc. 2 to 4 (28)	
Inc. 5 to 2 (20)*	Exc. 5 to 2 (35)			Inc. 5 to 2 (20)	Exc. 5 to 2 (23)		
Inc. 1 to 3 and 4 to 5 (20)*				Inc. 1 to 3 (24)	Exc. 1 to 3 (24)		

8. There can never be any point in exchanging only part of the holding in any given currency. We can therefore represent the man's problem for currency A in the following way. Let node $C.4$, for example, represent having the money which was originally

in currency A in currency C on day 4. The distance from, for example, B.3 to C.4 is $\log f(B, C, 4)$; that from B.3 to B.4 is zero; and there is no link from B.2 to B.4 or to C.4; and so on. The problem is then simply one of finding the longest route from A.1 to C.5, all links being uni-directional.

The problem for currency B can be similarly formulated.

Chapter 6

1. The average number in the system at time t is given by:

$$N(t) = \sum_0^\infty nP(n, t)$$

so that

$$\frac{dN(t)}{dt} = \sum_0^\infty n\frac{dP(n, t)}{dt} = \sum_1^\infty n\frac{dP(n, t)}{dt} \tag{1}$$

$[dP(n, t)]/dt$ can be found as in the text, putting $n\mu$ for μ, and is

$$-(\lambda + n\mu)P(n, t) + (n + 1)\mu P(n + 1, t) + \lambda P(n - 1, t) \qquad \text{for } n > 0$$

and

$$\frac{dP(0, t)}{dt} = -\lambda P(0, t) + \mu P(1, t)$$

Substituting those values in equation (1),

$$\frac{dN(t)}{dt} = -\sum_1^\infty n(\lambda + n\mu)P(n, t) + \sum_1^\infty n(n + 1)\mu P(n + 1, t) + \sum_1^\infty n\lambda P(n - 1, t)$$

$$= -\sum_1^\infty n(\lambda + n\mu)P(n, t) + \sum_2^\infty (n - 1)n\mu P(n, t) + \sum_0^\infty (n + 1)\lambda P(n, t)$$

$$= \sum_0^\infty P(n, t)(-n(\lambda + n\mu) + (n - 1)n\mu + (n + 1)\lambda)$$

(as the extra terms added to the first two sums are all zero)

$$= \sum_0^\infty P(n, t)(\lambda - n\mu)$$

$$= \lambda - \mu N(t) \qquad \text{as} \qquad \sum_\infty^0 P(n, t) = 1$$

To solve this differential equation, multiply by $e^{\mu t}$ giving

$$\frac{d}{dt}[e^{\mu t}N(t)] = \lambda e^{\mu t}$$

$$e^{\mu t}N(t) = \frac{\lambda e^{\mu t}}{\mu} - \frac{\lambda}{\mu} \qquad \text{as } N(0) = 0$$

$$N(t) = \frac{\lambda}{\mu}(1 - e^{-\mu t})$$

2. As there is a large number of locomotives, the input rate of $\frac{1}{8}$ per hour may be assumed independent of the number out of use.

The distribution of maintenance time on each part of the schedule is not given. As it varies widely, the simplest assumption is an exponential distribution; this gives an Erlang distribution of the total service time with mean rate $\frac{2}{5}$ per hour.

As the average input is 1 per shift and the average time per locomotive is $2\frac{1}{2}$ hours the fitter will have, on average, $5\frac{1}{2}$ hours per shift for other work. (Alternatively, using the formula, the proportion of idle time is $p(0) = 1 - \rho = \frac{11}{16}$.)

From the formulae for single channel Erlang service, the average time out of service (average time in the system) is

$$S = ((k + 1)\rho^2/2k(1 - \rho) + \rho)/\lambda$$

where $k = 5$, (the number of maintenance stages) $\rho = \frac{1}{8} \div \frac{2}{5} = \frac{5}{16}$, $\lambda = \frac{1}{8}$. Thus

$$S = (\tfrac{15}{176} + \tfrac{5}{16}) \times 8$$
$$= \tfrac{70}{22}$$
$$= 3 \cdot 18 \text{ hours.}$$

(If it is assumed that, in spite of the five part schedule, the total maintenance time is exponentially distributed, the time out of service is

$$S = 1/(\mu - \lambda) = \tfrac{40}{11} = 3 \cdot 64 \text{ hours}$$

At the other extreme, if the service time is taken to be constant, from the formula for $k = \infty$

$$S = [\rho^2/2(1 - \rho) + \rho]/\lambda = \tfrac{135}{44} = 3 \cdot 07 \text{ hours.})$$

3. Most inferences can be summed up by saying how critical the effect of small changes in λ/μ (i.e. the server utilization) is on the behaviour of the queue when λ/μ is reasonably big. In any system where congestion is a worry it pays to look first at the high congestion points.

One comment of possible practical significance in the case of general service times is that reducing the variability in service times reduces waiting time just as reducing the average does. Less obvious is that reducing the variability even at the expense of increasing the average within limits can pay off. Note also that reducing the average pays off only if in doing so the variability is not too greatly increased.

4. There are a number of changes the manager might consider making. For example he might:

    (a) organize a common queue which all customers join and the head of which goes to the next clerk who falls free;
    (b) have one or more clerks doing nothing but cash cheques;
    (c) give priority, either with 10 separate queues or with a common queue, to those wishing to cash cheques;
    (d) try to schedule in some way or other the paying in of large cash sums.

There are many other possibilities.

The formulae can be used to give rough guidance about the relative merits of doing these things for different ratios of cheque cashers and other types of customer, and for the different service times (which need measuring).

There are a number of important practical points, some of which limit the inferences which can be drawn without more data collection, physical experimentation or both. For example in system (a) the average service time will almost certainly be increased by the time spent going from the head of the queue to the counter. In system (b) one would expect not only the average service time of cheque cashers to be lower than the general average but also the variance. Systems (c) and (b) might both be unacceptable to some customers, although some sort of financial incentive aimed to achieve them might be more acceptable.

A more general practical problem is that arrival densities are likely to vary throughout the day. One would probably find that the "best" solution varied with the time of day and some time-tabling of systems would be needed.

It might be desirable, having used the theoretical results to get a rough assessment of the best solution, to simulate its operation, but this is a case where it might be cheaper and more effective to try out the solution in practice.

The use of queuing theory exemplified here is one of its main values.

5. Let

$$p(N_1, N_2; M_1, M_2, \ldots, M_n; Q_1, Q_2, \ldots, Q_n)$$

= prob (N_1 ships at loading port; N_2 ships at unloading port; $M_1, M_2, \ldots, M_n$ ships in each stage of the trip from loading to unloading port; $Q_1, Q_2, \ldots, Q_n$ in each stage of the return trip),

where

$$N_1 + N_2 + M_1 + M_2 + \ldots + M_n + Q_1 + Q_2 + \ldots + Q_n = N$$

Also let $p = 0$ if any of $N_1, N_2, M_1, M_2, \ldots, M_n, Q_1, Q_2, \ldots, Q_n$ is negative. The general steady state equation is then

$$p(N_1, N_2; M_1, M_2, \ldots, M_n; Q_1, Q_2, \ldots, Q_n)(\mu_1 + \mu_2 + n\lambda(N - N_1 - N_2))$$
$$= p(N_1 + 1, N_2; M_1 - 1, M_2, \ldots, M_n; Q_1, Q_2, \ldots, Q_n)\mu_1$$
$$+ \sum_{i=1}^{A-1} p(N_1, N_2; M_1, M_2, \ldots, M_i + 1, M_{i+1} - 1, \ldots, M_n;$$
$$Q_1, Q_2, \ldots, Q_n)n\lambda(M_i + 1)$$
$$+ p(N_1, N_2 - 1; M_1, M_2, \ldots, M_n + 1; Q_1, Q_2, \ldots, Q_n)n\lambda(M_n + 1)$$
$$+ p(N_1, N_2 + 1; M_1, M_2, \ldots, M_n; Q_1 - 1, Q_2, \ldots, Q_n)\mu_2$$
$$+ \sum_{i=1}^{n-1} p(N_1, N_2; M_1, M_2, \ldots, M_n; Q_1, Q_2, \ldots, Q_i + 1,$$
$$Q_{i+1} - 1, \ldots, Q_n)n\lambda(Q_i + 1)$$
$$+ p(N_1 - 1, N_2; M_1, M_2, \ldots, M_n; Q_1, Q_2, \ldots, Q_n + 1)n\lambda(Q_n + 1)$$

and there are other equations to cover the case when either or both of N_1 and N_2 is zero.

The form of the equations lead one to suggest a solution of the form

$$p\alpha \frac{a^{N_1} b^{N_2} C^{\Sigma M_i} d^{\Sigma Q_i}}{\Pi M_i! \ \ \Pi Q_i!}$$

By substitution we find that if we choose $a = b = n\lambda$, $c = \mu_1$ and $d = \mu_2$ we have a solution.

The probability that

$$N_1 + N_2 = N_3 (\leqslant N)$$

is now the sum of p over all N's, M's and Q's which are such that

$$N_1 + N_2 = N_3$$

and

$$N_1 + N_2 = N - (M_1 + M_2 = \ldots + M_n) - (Q_1 + Q_2 + \ldots + Q_n)$$

This is proportional to

$$(n\lambda)^{N_3} \sum_{\substack{\text{All possible} \\ M\text{'s and } Q\text{'s}}} \Pi \frac{\mu_1^{M_i}}{M_i!} \Pi \frac{\mu_2^{Q_i}}{Q_i!}$$

$$= (n\lambda)^{N_3} \sum_{\Sigma M + \Sigma Q = N - N_3} \frac{(n\mu_1)^{\Sigma M} (n\mu_2)^{\Sigma Q}}{(\Sigma M)! \, (\Sigma M)!}$$

$$= (n\mu_1 + n\mu_2)^N \left(\frac{\lambda}{\mu_1 + \mu_2}\right)^{N_3}$$

The constant of proportionality has now to be chosen to make the sum of these probabilities equal to one and is in fact

$$\frac{1 - \lambda/(\mu_1 + \mu_2)}{1 - (\lambda/(\mu_1 + \mu_2))^{N+1}} \frac{1}{(n\mu_1 + n\mu_2)^N}$$

Thus

$$p(N_1 + N_2 = N_3) = \frac{1 - \rho}{1 - \rho^{N+1}} \rho^{N_3}$$

where

$$\rho = \frac{\lambda}{\mu_1 + \mu_2}$$

and since this independent of n so is $E(N_1 + N_2)$.

Chapter 7

1. One simple model is as follows. The demand for an item is D a year, its price is P, and it is normally bought in amounts of T years' supply at a time. The annual cost of throughput, stockholding and ordering is therefore

$$DP + hP(B + DT/2) + S/T$$

where h is the holding cost as defined in Model 2 in the chapter, B is the buffer stock, and S is the ordering cost.

If an extra t years' supply was bought, a fraction b of the price would be deducted as discount, so the annual cost of throughput, stockholding, and ordering would be

$$DP(1 - b) + hP(1 - b)[B + D(T + t)/2] + S/(T + t)$$

A proportion f of the extra stock bought, Dt, might become obsolete during the year and be used or sold off at a fraction k of the original price—the loss would be

$P(1 - b - k)fDt$ in the period between one order and the next,
$P(1 - b - k)fDt/(T + t)$ per unit time.

It would be worth taking the discount only if the cost of throughput, stock-holding, ordering and possible obsolescence were less than the costs that would otherwise be incurred. This leads to the rule that it is worth buying $T + t$ years' stock to get a fractional discount b, rather than buying T years' stock at full price, if

$$b > \frac{[1 - (2S/hPDT(T + t))](ht/2) + (1 - k)ft/(T + t)}{1 + ft/(T + t) + h[B/D + (T + t)/2]}$$

The first term in [ ] in the numerator is an indication of the extent to which it is worth buying the larger quantity purely for the reduction in ordering cost; in fact a slight variation in the formulation of Model 2 would lead to an equation in which the term in [ ] is set equal to zero.

The simplest way of examining the inequality for b is to simplify the RHS by approximations which are known to increase it: thus, for example, if

$$b > ht/2 + ft/(T + t)$$

then the more complicated inequality is certainly true (all the variables are essentially positive).

The effect of obsolescence is to push up the discount which must be offered to make its acceptance worthwhile. In the simplified inequality above, the first term might be from 0·01 for low holding cost and little extra stock to 0·25 for high holding cost and two years extra stock, while the second term might be from 0·01 for low obsolescence risk and little extra cost to 0·50 for high obsolescence risk and much extra stock compared with what would otherwise be bought. The decision would usually be dominated by obsolescence cost rather than storage cost.

The conceptual weaknesses in this particular model are that it does not take account of

(a) the variability of demand;
(b) the uncertainty of the time of obsolescence;
(c) the possibility that some or all of the obsolescence can be avoided because there is some sort of warning of its imminence.

The first two of these probably mean that the full formula is too low an assessment of the risk associated with buying the extra quantity, whilst the third means that the full formula is too high. A simplified version of the formula like that above is perhaps to be preferred because it errs on the side of not taking discounts.

Before the full formulae can be used, and probably before a simplified formula can be used, some simplification of presentation is necessary. If possible the parameters should be estimated for clearly defined categories of material and then "built" into tables or formulae. For the remaining parameters the results need to be presented in such a way that the operator can soon get an instinctive feel of the way in which his estimates affect the outcome. Finally, the procedure would need to be tested, firstly to see whether it could be used and understood and secondly to see whether the total effect on throughput, stocks and obsolescence was beneficial.

2. The question pointed out that Model 3 and Model 7 appear to lead to contradictory conclusions. If $Q = TD$ is substituted in Model 3 and the optimum value of T is found it is then clear that the models do in fact lead to contradictory conclusions about whether the interval between orders should be increased or decreased.

There are two clear differences between the models: firstly Model 3 is deterministic and Model 7 makes some attempt to cover fluctuations, and secondly Model 3 considers shortage costs and Model 7 takes a fixed probability of shortage per order—in Model 7, the minimization is with respect to T, but as T is decreased the number of shortages per year is increased even though the number of shortages per order is unaltered.

It seems therefore that the conclusion is sensitive to the structure of the model and to the type of restriction within which any adjustment is being allowed. Rather than follow this through directly, it is perhaps preferable to consider what effects might be expected in an actual re-order level system or in an actual cyclical review system, and to ask whether it is possible to predict the form of the effect of taking shortages into account.

Firstly, consider a re-order level system. The full cost expression for annual cost is

$$C = \text{(Stockholding cost)} + \text{(Ordering cost)} + \text{(Shortage cost)}$$

and for an increase in the order quantity, Q, we have

$$\frac{\Delta C}{\Delta Q} = \frac{\Delta(\text{Stock})}{\Delta Q} + \frac{\Delta(\text{Order})}{\Delta Q} + \frac{\Delta(\text{Short})}{\Delta Q}$$

The terms are

$+$ve $-$ve $-$ve

In the simplest case, Q is regarded solely as a means for balancing storage costs and ordering costs, the second term being what pushes Q up. The effect of the third term is to push Q up more strongly. The introduction of a consideration of the risk of shortage therefore causes the order quantity to be increased.

Secondly, consider a cyclical review system. The full cost expression is unchanged, and for an increase in the review period, T, we have

$$\frac{\Delta C}{\Delta T} = \frac{\Delta(\text{Stock})}{\Delta T} + \frac{\Delta(\text{Order})}{\Delta T} + \frac{\Delta(\text{Short})}{\Delta T}$$

The terms are

$+$ve in the simplest model	$-$ve	unknown because the fre-
$-$ve in a full model		quency of orders is de-
		creased but the intensity of
		shortages per order is in-
		creased

If the third term is sufficiently positive to be larger than the switch from $+$ to $-$ in the first term, the consideration of shortages would lead to an increase in T; otherwise the consideration of shortages leads to a decrease in T. In general this means that the introduction of the consideration of shortages might cause T to be increased or decreased.

3. The simplest generalization of Model 2 is to take the expression for annual cost

$$hP(B + Q/2) + SD/Q$$

and to realize that we wish to minimize the total expected cost. If D is variable, we therefore wish to minimize

$$hP(B + Q/2) + SE(D)/Q$$

which leads to the first of the suggested expressions.

Chapter 8

1. We may obtain the minimum average yearly running cost by tabulating as follows:

Sell after year	Depreciation	Petrol and tax	Other running costs	Total cost	Average annual cost
1	75	90	10	175	175
2	125	180	40	345	172·5
3	150	270	90	510	170
4	200	360	160	720	180

(costs in £)

Since the total running cost per year of the car increases after year 3 the average annual cost will now continue to rise. Hence it is best to replace the car at the end of the third year, when the average yearly running cost will be £170.

(Note: Since increases in the third column are constant, it could, strictly, be omitted; it is, however, required to answer the second question.)

2. We find first the minimum average yearly running cost of the new car as above.

Sell after year	Depreciation	Petrol and tax	Other running costs	Total cost	Average annual cost
1	100	70	10	180	180
2	175	140	30	345	172·5
3	250	210	60	520	173·3

(costs in £)

The total running cost per year of the car is increasing, and so we can infer that the minimum average yearly cost is £172·50. Hence it is better not to replace the original car by the new one.

3. If motors are replaced only on failure the average cost per motor per week = £1,000/average motor-life. Now

average motor-life

$$= (0·05)10 + (0·10)20 + (0·20)30 + (0·30)40 + (0·35)50 \text{ weeks}$$
$$= 38 \text{ weeks}$$

Hence

average cost per motor per week = $£\dfrac{1,000}{38} = £26·3$ approx.

If motors are replaced after 10 weeks,

average cost per motor = $(0·05)£1,000 + £200 = £250$

giving an average cost per week of £25.

If motors are replaced after 20 weeks,

average cost per motor $= (0 \cdot 15)£1,000 + (0 \cdot 05)^2 £1,000 + £200$
$$= £352 \cdot 5$$

∴   Average cost per week $= £17 \cdot 625$.

If motors are replaced after 30 weeks,

average cost per motor

$$= (0 \cdot 35)£1,000 + 2(0 \cdot 15)(0 \cdot 05)£1,000 + (0 \cdot 05)^3 £1,000 + £200$$
$$= £565$$

∴   Average cost per week $= £18 \cdot 8$.

Hence motors should be replaced every 20 weeks.

4. Suppose intake of trainees $= 100$ per half year.
   When the system is stable, the colliery age-distribution will be as follows:

Age	Number employed	Stints worked
16 –16½	100	
16½–17	90 ⎫	$260 \times \frac{3}{4}$
17 –18	170 ⎭	
18 –19	150	150
19 –20	148 – 2 3 ‹ 2	2,794
	(2 less each year till 41)	
41 –42	102	470
	(4 less each year till 46)	
46 –47	78	420
	(8 less each year till 56)	
56 –57	4⅘	12
	(⅘ less each year till 61)	

Hence

total number of stints worked $= 260 \times \frac{3}{4} + 3,846$
$$= 4,041 \text{ stints}$$

Therefore, to keep 100 stints going we required an intake of

$$100 \times \frac{100}{4,041} = 2 \cdot 47 \text{ per } \tfrac{1}{2} \text{ year}$$

or say, 5 recruits per year.

5. Whatever we do the average annual cost associated with replacing A will be $2C_1$.
   If we treat B independently of A, and if output is valued at V, we would overhaul B every T years where T minimizes

$$g(T) = \frac{C_2}{T} - \frac{V}{T} \int_0^T f(t) \, dt,$$

which is when

$$VTf(T) = C_2 + V \int_0^T f(t) \, dt$$

The value of T which satisfies this equation would minimize annual cost.

An alternative policy is to overhaul B when A fails. In this case the average annual cost for B is

$$2C_3 - 2V \int_0^\infty \left[\int_0^x f(t)\,dt \right] e^{-\frac{1}{4}x} \tfrac{1}{2} dx$$

A third policy is to overhaul B when either it is T_1 years since it was last overhauled or when A breaks down and it is at least T_2 ($<T_1$) years since B was last overhauled. In this case the average annual cost for B is more complicated but it can be derived thus.

Consider a time at which we overhaul B. Let the future average annual cost be h. Because A breaks down at random h is independent of whether this overhaul was as a consequence of A breaking down or not. In fact the whole future is independent of this. Assume we are estimating costs for N years ahead. Then if N is large

Nh	$=$	$E_T j$	$+$	$E_T(N - T)h$
the total expected cost over the N years		the expected cost up to and including the next overhaul of B		the subsequent expected costs, T being the time up to the next overhaul of B

Now

$$j = C - V \int_0^T f(t)\,dt \qquad (C \text{ is } C_2 \text{ or } C_3)$$

$$p(T < T_2) = 0$$

$$p(t < T \leqslant t + dt) = e^{-\frac{1}{4}t}\tfrac{1}{2}\,dt / (1 - e^{-\frac{1}{4}T_2}) \qquad \text{if} \qquad T_2 < t < T_1$$

$$p(T = T_1) = (1 - e^{-\frac{1}{4}T_1})/(1 - e^{-\frac{1}{4}T_2})$$

thus

$$E_T j = \int_{T_2}^{T_1} \left[C_3 - V \int_0^T f(t)\,dt \right] e^{-\frac{1}{4}t}\tfrac{1}{2}\,dt / (1 - e^{-\frac{1}{4}T_2})$$
$$+ C_2(1 - e^{-\frac{1}{4}T_1})/(1 - e^{-\frac{1}{4}T_2})$$

and

$$E_T(N - T)h = Nh - hET$$

which can be found without to much difficulty. Eventually we find

$$h = E_T j / ET.$$

Which of these policies is the best is simply a matter of feeding in the appropriate numerical values and working the costs out.

We have not exhausted all possible policies, although we have included the sensible ones.

Chapter 9

2. The activities are:

(i) arrival of a customer;
(ii) a customer joining the queue;

(iii) a customer starting service;
(iv) a customer completing service.

The tests are as follows (assuming three sets of customers, ARR those who have arrived but have not yet joined the queue, Q those queuing and S those being served);

(i) Is time cell of next arrival $=$ now?
(ii) Is there a customer in ARR?
Is there a customer in S?
(iii) Is S empty?
Is there at least one customer in Q?
(iv) Is time cell of next departure $=$ now?

In the activities based approach we shall keep two time cells, TA the time of the next arrival, and TD, the time of the next departure. The time scan consists of scanning these two cells to find the smaller of the two. It is convenient to advance time so that "now" is time zero and we can do this by subtracting the smaller (in general the smallest) time from the other (in general the others). Thus an activities based simulation might have this structure:

Initial conditions
$a =$ number of customers in ARR $= 0$
$b =$ number of customers in Q $= 0$
$c =$ number of customers in S $= 0$
$R =$ first random number
$TA = -d \log R$ ($d =$ average time between arrivals)
$TD = \infty$
$n =$ number of customers served $= 0$
$w =$ total waiting time to date $= 0$

Program to be cycled: each cycle to last until a clear cycle of the activities has been made (i.e. until no activity can be performed).
Find smaller of TA and TD $=$ T, say

$$TA = TA - T$$
$$TD = TD - T$$
$$W = W + bT$$

Activity (i)
If $TA = 0$ then $a = a + 1$.
Read new R and set $TA = -d \log R$.

Activity (ii)
If $a = 1$ and $c = 1$ then $b = b + 1$ and $a = a - 1$.

Activity (iii)
If $c = 0$ and $b \geqslant 1$ then $c = c + 1$ and $b = b - 1$.
Read new R and set $TD = -e \log R$ (e being the average service time).

Activity (iv)
If $TD = 0$ then $c = c - 1$, $TD = \infty$, $n = n + 1$.
If $n = 100$ then stop and print $w/100$.

In this case an events based simulation is easily constructed. One simply notes which of TA and TD is the smaller at the time scan stage and branches the program to go to activities (i), (ii) and (iii) if TA is the smaller and straight to activity (iv) if TD is.

A great many variance reduction devices are possible in this case. Some examples, all of which ignore the fact that we can solve the problem theoretically, are:

(i) We could run the program in blocks of four to take advantage of antithetic variables. If two random number streams are kept going, R for arrivals and P for service times, we could run first with R and P, then with $1 - R$ and P, then with $1 - R$ and $1 - P$, and then with R and $1 - P$, where $1 - R$ is the random number stream each member of which is $1 - $ the corresponding number of R.

(ii) We could use some short runs of the program to generate a sample of starting conditions on which to base further runs.

(iii) We could use the time up to the 100th arrival, which would have an approximately normal distribution, as a control variable and likewise the total of the 100 service times.

3. Suppose a typical set of 5 numbers is X_1, X_2, X_3, X_4 and X_5 with an average of S. The straightforward estimate is the average over the 10 samples of 5 of

$$\max (X_1, X_2, \ldots, X_5)$$

An antithetic estimate is obtained by taking the average of

$$\max (1 - X_1, 1 - X_2, \ldots, 1 - X_5) = 1 - \min (X_1, X_2, \ldots, X_5)$$

S is a possible control variable and $ES = 0.5$. Thus

$$\tfrac{1}{10}\Sigma \max (X_1, X_2, \ldots, X_5) - \tfrac{1}{10}\Sigma S + 0.5$$

is an unbiased estimator and, since S is obviously positively correlated with

$$\max (X_1, X_2, \ldots, X_5)$$

it has a lower variance than the uncontrolled estimator. Also S is symmetrically distributed about 0.5 so, if n samples have $S < 0.5$ and $10 - n$ have $S > 0.5$,

$$\frac{1}{2n} \sum_{\substack{\text{Over samples} \\ \text{with } S < 0.5}} \max (X_1, X_2, \ldots, X_5) + 2(10 - n) \sum_{\text{Other samples}}$$
$$\max (X_1, X_2, \ldots, X_5)$$

while being a slightly biased estimator, probably has a lower variance than the uncontrolled one.

With such a small sample, splitting and Russian roulette are of no value. If we were to think of using them we might decide to reject, say, half the samples for which S has an extreme value (< 0.25 or > 0.75 say) and accept all the others.

The reader is urged to do the arithmetic and to try out other variance reduction ideas. If he has access to a computer he can, of course, work with much bigger samples than 50 and the results will be more interesting.

For comparative purposes, the theoretical results are:

$$EX = E \max (X_1, X_2, \ldots, X_5) = 0.833$$
$$VX = 0.020$$

So, the variance of the straightforward estimator is $0.020/n$, n being the number of sets of 5. In this case $n = 10$.

4. As an exercise in simulation, this is comparatively straightforward and the results are more interesting than the methodology. However it should be noticed that the advancing of time from event to event in this simulation is best done by advancing the simulation in fixed steps of one time unit at a time.

The results will serve to reveal some of the shortcomings of conventional stock control theory which often assumes that the underlying distribution of demand is known. In fact (see page 175) one can expect to get higher stocks and fewer shortages than the theory predicts. If the underlying distribution of demand is unchanging with time, the best way to forecast future demand is to average all previous demand; but, when the distribution of demand is liable to change suddenly, forecasting methods which give greater weight to more recent results are better.

7. The active entities would have been LANE, PLAT 1, PLAT 2, . . ., PLAT 5, CRANE, NEXT LORRY 1, NEXT LORRY 2. It is necessary to have active entities NEXT LORRY 1 and 2 so that lorry arrivals can be logged.

All sets but WORLD are necessary.

The activity ENGAGE CRANE is still required. (The reader will find it instructive to "program" the activities, on the lines of page 211, for the newly based simulation.) However in ENGAGE crane we can delete L from the third line and we must replace L by CRANE in the fifth line.

8. Activities *LORRY ARRIVAL, ARRIVE AT PLATFORM, FINISH LOAD-ING/UNLOADING, LEAVE SYSTEM* could all be programmed as bound activities. Thus, considering *LEAVE SYSTEM* as an example, one could attach to the time-cells of all lorries entering LOUT the letters LS. If the lowest time-cell has LS attached to it we execute *LEAVE SYSTEM*: if not we do not attempt it.

The point is that from the moment a lorry joins LOUT, which it does when *ENTER LANE (OUTWARDS)* is performed on it, nothing can prevent the conditions for *LEAVE SYSTEM* from being satisfied in precisely four minutes time.

The other activities, the so-called conditional activities (viz. *ENTER LANE, ENGAGE CRANE, ENTER LANE (OUTWARDS)*) are all cycled at each event.

In this case it is only the fact that *all* conditional activities are attempted at every event which distinguishes the three-phase structure from the events-based structure. This is because all events correspond to a bound activity. However, in a more complex situation this would not be the case. If, for example, the lorries were subject to random breakdowns when in LOUT we could not make *LEAVE SYSTEM* a bound activity as we would not know that it was bound to be the next thing to occur to a lorry in LOUT.

This could apparently be got round by increasing the time-cell of the relevant lorry by the duration of the breakdown, but it is not difficult to imagine a fairly complex range of activities that might be triggered by the breakdown and which would destroy this possibility. For example all broken down lorries might have to reverse to the warehouse with a whole string of effects depending on other lorries.

Index